THE HOPE
of
ISRAEL

THE HOPE
of
ISRAEL

THE RESURRECTION OF CHRIST
IN THE ACTS OF THE APOSTLES

BRANDON D. CROWE

Baker Academic
a division of Baker Publishing Group
Grand Rapids, Michigan

© 2020 by Brandon D. Crowe

Published by Baker Academic
a division of Baker Publishing Group
PO Box 6287, Grand Rapids, MI 49516-6287
www.bakeracademic.com

Printed in the United States of America

Library of Congress Cataloging-in-Publication Data
Names: Crowe, Brandon D., author.
Title: The hope of Israel : the resurrection of Christ in the Acts of the Apostles / Brandon D. Crowe.
Description: Grand Rapids, MI : Baker Academic, a division of Baker Publishing Group, [2020] | Includes bibliographical references and indexes.
Identifiers: LCCN 2019027595 | ISBN 9780801099472 (paperback)
Subjects: LCSH: Jesus Christ—Resurrection—Biblical teaching. | Bible. Acts—Criticism, interpretation, etc.
Classification: LCC BS2625.6.R47 C76 2020 | DDC 226.6/06—dc23
LC record available at https://lccn.loc.gov/2019027595

ISBN 978-1-5409-6268-3 (casebound)

Unless otherwise indicated, all Scripture quotations are the author's translation.

20 21 22 23 24 25 26   7 6 5 4 3 2 1

For Ethan

מַשְׂכִּיל לְאֵיתָן הָאֶזְרָחִי
חַסְדֵי יְהוָה עוֹלָם אָשִׁירָה לְדֹר וָדֹר אוֹדִיעַ אֱמוּנָתְךָ בְּפִי

A maskil of Ethan the Ezrahite.
I will sing of the steadfast love of the LORD forever;
with my mouth I will make known your faithfulness
to generation upon generation.
Psalm 89:1

Contents

Preface

We never caught the stranger's name. A friend and I—two college students—had just finished an impromptu conversation at a bookstore with two other patrons when the stranger approached us. He had overheard our conversation (about Christianity and another religion), and he proceeded to offer his perspective. The stranger cut to what he saw as the heart of the issue, which was the singularity of the resurrection of Jesus. This, he argued, was the crux of what made Christianity distinctive.

I have often thought back upon that encounter. And as I have studied and taught the New Testament and early Christianity in the years that followed, I continue to be impressed with the insightfulness of the stranger's succinct observation. The resurrection makes all the difference.

The focus of this volume is the resurrection of Christ, specifically in the New Testament book of Acts. I will give sustained attention in part 1 to the apostolic exposition of the resurrection in Acts, which is substantial. I will then synthesize and tease out these insights in part 2, in order to consider the wide-ranging implications of the place of the resurrection in Acts. The present study can easily be read as a stand-alone volume, yet it also serves well as a follow-up to my recent study of the Gospels, *The Last Adam: A Theology of the Obedient Life of Jesus in the Gospels* (Baker Academic, 2017). In that volume I argued for a pervasive Adam Christology in the Gospels, concomitant with the wide-ranging obedience of Jesus. In the Gospels the resurrection is the vindication of Jesus's obedience. In the present volume I focus more on the message about Christ in Acts, specifically in relation to his resurrection. The obedient life of Jesus is the presupposition for Jesus's resurrection, and the emphasis on the resurrection in Acts is the corollary to the perfect obedience of his life in the Gospels. Moreover, the resurrection proves to be a major artery that connects many features of Luke's second volume.

As with any project this size, I have many people to thank. First, I would like to thank the board of trustees, faculty, administration, and staff of Westminster Theological Seminary for providing the support and resources necessary to complete a project with so many moving parts. I would also like to thank the board of trustees for granting a professional advancement leave in 2019, which allowed me to finalize the manuscript.

Second, thanks to all who offered feedback on portions of the manuscript and/or served as conversation partners, especially Greg Beale, William Edgar, Richard Gaffin, Mark Giacobbe, Charles Hill, Josh Leim, Vern Poythress, Lane Tipton, Chad Van Dixhoorn, and Carlton Wynne. I have also benefited from the exegetical labors of many students at Westminster Theological Seminary—especially in the courses on the Gospels and PhD/ThM seminars on Acts. In many cases my own thinking has been sharpened and sparked by their observations and our discussions. Pip Mohr assisted with indexing.

Third, I am immensely grateful to all those who have contributed to the ever-expansive field of Luke and Acts scholarship. The notes throughout manifest my indebtedness to the diligent labors of many. My desire is to add some new angles to an already fruitful conversation.

Fourth, thanks to Bryan Dyer and the entire professional team at Baker Academic. It has again been a pleasure to work with such a capable ensemble.

Finally, thanks to my family for their persistent love and encouragement, including my parents, parents-in-law, and especially my wife, Cheryl, and our children. I dedicate this volume to my son Ethan, whose name derives from the author of Psalm 89. This psalm expresses hope in the promised king of the Davidic covenant who will reign forever, which is realized through the resurrection of Jesus (cf. Acts 2:30–31). More than that, Psalm 89 extols the covenantal love of God that is to be made known from generation to generation. I thus write on a topic with keen awareness of its importance for the next generation.

Abbreviations

2 Tim.	2 Timothy	James	James	2 John	2 John
Titus	Titus	1 Pet.	1 Peter	3 John	3 John
Philem.	Philemon	2 Pet.	2 Peter	Jude	Jude
Heb.	Hebrews	1 John	1 John	Rev.	Revelation

Textual

ℵ	Codex Sinaiticus	E	Codex Laudianus
A	Codex Alexandrinus	Ψ	Codex Athous Laurae
B	Codex Vaticanus	latt	all Latin witnesses
C	Codex Ephraemi Rescriptus	𝔐	Majority text
D	Codex Bezae	𝔓	Papyrus

Bible Versions and Modern Editions

CSB	Christian Standard Bible	NASB	New American Standard Bible
ECM	*Editio Critica Maior*	NET	New English Translation
ESV	English Standard Version	NIV	New International Version
KJV	King James Version	NRSV	New Revised Standard Version
LXX	Septuagint		
MT	Masoretic Text	OG	Old Greek
NA²⁷	*Novum Testamentum Graece*, Nestle-Aland, 27th ed.	SBLGNT	SBL Greek New Testament
		Theod.	Theodotion
NA²⁸	*Novum Testamentum Graece*, Nestle-Aland, 28th ed.	THGNT	Tyndale House Greek New Testament

Apocrypha and LXX

| 1 Macc. | 1 Maccabees | Sir. | Sirach |
| 2 Macc. | 2 Maccabees | Wis. | Wisdom of Solomon |

Dead Sea Scrolls and Related Literature

1QH^a	Thanksgiving Hymns	4Q521	Messianic Apocalypse
4Q174	Florilegium, or Midrash on Eschatology	4QFlor	Florilegium, or Midrash on Eschatology
4Q385	*Pseudo-Ezekiel^a*	4QMMT	*Miqṣat Maʿăśê ha-Torah*
4Q386	*Pseudo-Ezekiel^b*	CD	Damascus Document
4Q388	*Pseudo-Ezekiel^d*		

Old Testament Pseudepigrapha

2 Bar.	2 Baruch	4 Macc.	4 Maccabees
1 En.	1 Enoch	Pss. Sol.	Psalms of Solomon
4 Ezra	4 Ezra	Sib. Or.	Sibylline Oracles
L.A.B.	Liber antiquitatum biblicarum	T. Ab.	Testament of Abraham
		T. Benj.	Testament of Benjamin
Liv. Pro.	Lives of the Prophets	T. Jud.	Testament of Judah

Mishnah and Talmud Tractates

b.	Babylonian Talmud	*Sanh.*	*Sanhedrin*
m.	Mishnah		

Targumic Texts

Tg. Ps.-J.   *Targum Pseudo-Jonathan*

Other Rabbinic Works

Lev. Rab.	*Leviticus Rabbah*	*Pirqe R. El.*	*Pirqe Rabbi Eleazar*
Mek. R. Ishmael	*Mekilta de Rabbi Ishmael*		

Apostolic Fathers

1 Clem.	*1 Clement*	Ign., *Phld.*	Ignatius, *To the Philadelphians*
2 Clem.	*2 Clement*		
Barn.	*Epistle of Barnabas*	Ign., *Pol.*	Ignatius, *To Polycarp*
Diogn.	*Epistle to Diognetus*	Ign., *Rom.*	Ignatius, *To the Romans*
Herm.	*Shepherd of Hermas*	Ign., *Smyrn.*	Ignatius, *To the Smyrnaeans*
Ign., *Eph.*	Ignatius, *To the Ephesians*	Ign., *Trall.*	Ignatius, *To the Trallians*
Ign., *Magn.*	Ignatius, *To the Magnesians*	Pol., *Phil.*	Polycarp, *To the Philippians*

New Testament Pseudepigrapha

Acts Thom.	Acts of Thomas	Gos. Jud.	Gospel of Judas
Ep. Apost.	*Epistula apostolorum*	Gos. Thom.	Gospel of Thomas

Other Greek and Latin Works

Amphilochius of Iconium

Iambi   *Iambi ad Seleucum*

Athanasius of Alexandria

C. Ar.	*Orationes contra Arianos*
Ep. fest.	*Epistulae festalis*
Inc.	*De incarnatione*

Athenagoras

Res.   *De resurrectione*

Augustine

Enarrat. Ps. Enarrationes in Psalmos

John Calvin

Inst.   *Institutio christianae religionis*

Cyril of Jerusalem

Cat.   *Catecheses*

Epictetus

Diatr.   *Diatribai (Discourses)*

Epiphanius of Salamis

Pan.   *Panarion*

Eusebius of Caesarea

Hist. eccl.   *Historia ecclesiastica*

Gregory Nazianzen

Carm.   *Carmina theologica*

Hippolytus

Haer.	Refutatio omnio haeresium
Noet.	Contra haeresin Noeti

Irenaeus

Epid.	Epideixis tou apostolikou kērygmatos (Demonstration of the Apostolic Preaching)
Haer.	Adversus haereses (Against Heresies)

Jerome

Epist.	Epistulae

Josephus

Ag. Ap.	Against Apion
Ant.	Jewish Antiquities
J.W.	Jewish War

Justin

1 Apol.	First Apology
Dial.	Dialogus cum Tryphone

Origen of Alexandria

Cels.	Contra Celsum
Hom. Jos.	Homiliae in Josuam
Princ.	De principiis

Philo

Contempl. Life	On the Contemplative Life

Suetonius

Jul.	Divus Julius

Tertullian

Marc.	Adversus Marcionem
Praescr.	De praescriptione haereticorum
Res.	De resurrectione carnis
Virg.	De virginibus velandis

Francis Turretin

Inst.	Institutio theologiae elencticae

Modern Works

AB	Anchor Bible
ABRL	Anchor Bible Reference Library
AGJU	Arbeiten zur Geschichte des antiken Judentums und des Urchristentums
AJEC	Ancient Judaism and Early Christianity
AnBib	Analecta Biblica
ANF	*The Ante-Nicene Fathers.* Edited by Alexander Roberts and James Donaldson. 1885–87. 10 vols. Repr., Peabody, MA: Hendrickson, 1994
ANRW	*Aufstieg und Niedergang der römischen Welt.* Part 2, *Principat.* Edited by H. Temporini and W. Haase. Berlin: de Gruyter, 1972–
BBR	*Bulletin of Biblical Research*
BBRSup	Bulletin of Biblical Research Supplement Series
BDAG	Bauer, W., F. W. Danker, W. F. Arndt, and F. W. Gingrich. *Greek-English Lexicon of the New Testament and Other Early Christian Literature.* 3rd ed. Chicago: University of Chicago Press, 2000
BDF	Blass, Friedrich, Albert Debrunner, and Robert W. Funk. *A Greek Grammar of the New Testament and Other Early Christian Literature.* Chicago: University of Chicago Press, 1961
BECNT	Baker Exegetical Commentary on the New Testament
Belief	Belief: A Theological Commentary on the Bible
BETL	Bibliotheca Ephemeridum Theologicarum Lovaniensium
BHT	Beiträge zur historischen Theologie

Bib	*Biblica*
BibSac	*Bibliotheca Sacra*
BMSEC	Baylor–Mohr Siebeck Studies in Early Christianity
BTB	*Biblical Theology Bulletin*
BZNW	Beihefte zur Zeitschrift für die neutestamentliche Wissenschaft und die Kunde der älteren Kirche
CBR	*Currents in Biblical Research*
CCT	Contours of Christian Theology
CNT	Commentaire du Nouveau Testament
ConBNT	Coniectanea Neotestamentica
COQG	Christian Origins and the Question of God
CTQ	*Concordia Theological Quarterly*
DJD	Discoveries in the Judaean Desert
EC	*Early Christianity*
EHS.T	Europäische Hochschulschriften: Reihe 23, Theologie
EKKNT	Evangelisch-katholischer Kommentar zum Neuen Testament
EvQ	*Evangelical Quarterly*
FB	Forschung zur Bibel
FRLANT	Forschungen zur Religion und Literatur des Alten und Neuen Testaments
GH	Gorgias Handbooks
HTR	*Harvard Theological Review*
HTS	Harvard Theological Studies
ICC	International Critical Commentary
Int	*Interpretation*
IThS	Innsbrucker theologische Studien
JBL	*Journal of Biblical Literature*
JCT	Jewish and Christian Texts
JETS	*Journal of the Evangelical Theological Society*
JSNT	*Journal for the Study of the New Testament*
JSNTSup	Journal for the Study of the New Testament: Supplement Series
JTI	*Journal of Theological Interpretation*
K&D	Keil, Carl Friedrich, and Franz Delitzsch. *Biblical Commentary on the Old Testament*. Translated by James Martin et al. 25 vols. Edinburgh, 1857–78. 10 vols. Repr., Peabody, MA: Hendrickson, 1996
KEK	Kritisch-exegetischer Kommentar über das Neue Testament (Meyer-Kommentar)
LCC	Library of Christian Classics
LCL	Loeb Classical Library
LD	Lectio Divina
LNTS	Library of New Testament Studies
MdB	Le Monde de la Bible
MNTS	McMaster New Testament Studies
NIB	*New Interpreter's Bible*
NICNT	New International Commentary on the New Testament
NICOT	New International Commentary on the Old Testament
NIGTC	New International Greek Testament Commentary
NovT	*Novum Testamentum*

NovTSup	Supplements to Novum Testamentum
NPNF[2]	*Nicene and Post-Nicene Fathers*. Series 2. Edited by Philip Schaff and Henry Wace. 1886–1900. 14 vols. Repr., Peabody, MA: Hendrickson, 1996
NSBT	New Studies in Biblical Theology
NTL	New Testament Library
NTR	New Testament Readings
NTS	*New Testament Studies*
ORA	*Oxford University Research Archive*
PBM	Paternoster Biblical Monographs
PNTC	Pillar New Testament Commentary
PPS	Popular Patristics Series
ProEccl	*Pro Ecclesia*
PRSt	*Perspectives in Religious Studies*
QC	*Qumran Chronicle*
SacScript	*Sacra Scriptura*
SBJT	*Southern Baptist Journal of Theology*
SBLMS	Society of Biblical Literature Monograph Series
SBLSP	Society of Biblical Literature Seminar Papers
SBT	Studies in Biblical Theology
ScEs	*Science et esprit*
SCJ	*Stone-Campbell Journal*
SecCent	*Second Century*
SNTSMS	Society for New Testament Studies Monograph Series
SP	Sacra Pagina
SubBi	Subsidia Biblica
ThH	Théologie historique
TynBul	*Tyndale Bulletin*
WBC	Word Biblical Commentary
WC	Westminster Commentaries
WCF	Westminster Confession of Faith
WLC	Westminster Larger Catechism
WMANT	Wissenschaftliche Monographien zum Alten und Neuen Testament
WSAMA.T	Walberberger Studien der Albertus-Magnus-Akademic, Mainz—Theologische Reihe
WSC	Westminster Shorter Catechism
WTJ	*Westminster Theological Journal*
WUNT	Wissenschaftliche Untersuchungen zum Neuen Testament
ZECNT	Zondervan Exegetical Commentary on the New Testament

Part 1

The Resurrection in Acts

1

The State of the Question

The Resurrection in Acts

A Universal Message

We begin in Acts 17. After Paul and Silas made their way to Thessalonica, they entered a synagogue, and for three Sabbaths Paul reasoned with those present about the suffering and resurrection of Jesus, who is the Christ (v. 3). Some of the Jewish people were convinced, along with many Greeks and leading women; these joined the movement Paul and Silas represented. Others fomented an uproar and tried to seize Paul and Silas.

Later in Acts 17 Paul and Silas arrived in Athens, that bastion of classical philosophy, which Paul considered to be a hotbed of idolatry. Having gained the ear of the philosophers of the day, Paul gave them something new (for indeed, they enjoyed new things): he preached the resurrection of Jesus (v. 18) and that there would be a day of righteous judgment by this man who had been raised from the dead (vv. 30–31).

Whether, then, it was in a Jewish synagogue or in history-rich Athens, Paul in Acts consistently drew attention to the resurrection of Christ.[1] In the synagogue, the resurrection is the crucial point for proving the messianic status of Jesus from the Scriptures. On trial before the Areopagus, the

---

1. See also Alan J. Thompson, *The Acts of the Risen Lord Jesus: Luke's Account of God's Unfolding Plan*, NSBT 27 (Downers Grove, IL: InterVarsity, 2011), 78–79; Stanley E. Porter, *The Paul of Acts: Essays in Literary Criticism, Rhetoric, and Theology*, WUNT 1/115 (Tübingen: Mohr Siebeck, 1999), 167.

resurrection of Jesus is proclaimed to those who are not steeped in the Jewish Scriptures. Jesus of Nazareth, according to Paul, has been raised from the dead, and this is a cosmic event with implications for all people.

Beyond Paul, we find a similar emphasis on the resurrection throughout Acts. Indeed, whether the audience was Jews or gentiles, Pharisees or Sadducees, kings or congregants, a remarkable consistency is found in the apostolic emphasis on the resurrection of Jesus. The resurrection is firmly rooted in the Jewish Scriptures, yet is also a message with universal relevance.

Acts 17 thus provides a preview for my argument. Simply put, in Luke's second volume, the resurrection of Jesus bears a weighty load, weighty enough to merit extended reflection.

The Resurrection and the Interpretation of Acts

It is not difficult to identify any number of knotty exegetical issues in Acts, and it may be that attending to the role of Christ's resurrection in Acts will help untangle some of these. Acts is, from one perspective, a *transitional* book, and many of the exegetical difficulties seem to be tethered to this unique period in the history of the church. At the same time, Acts is a *programmatic* book for subsequent generations of Christians, providing the apostolic basis for the early Christian message and delineating the life of the earliest community of Jesus followers. As a *transitional* book, Acts recounts a number of nonrepeatable events; as a *programmatic* book, Acts provides guidance for the church in subsequent ages. It therefore behooves the exegete to wrestle with which portions of Acts are transitional, unrepeatable moments in the history of salvation and which are programmatic events that believers today should emulate.[2]

Parsing out these distinctions is tricky. For example, in what sense was the coming of the Holy Spirit at Pentecost a qualitatively new event in the history of redemption, and in what sense ought we to see the Spirit's work as contiguous with divine activity in ages past? If the Holy Spirit comes to all people—Jews and gentiles—by Acts 10, then why had the Spirit not already fallen on the group of Ephesian believers in Acts 19? Similarly, why did the Samaritans not receive the Spirit when they believed? On a different note, why is so much attention devoted to the defenses of Paul in the latter chapters of Acts?

These issues have been variously addressed, and the number of thorny exegetical issues in Acts could easily be multiplied. No one volume would be sufficient to address them all. Nevertheless, in what follows I will argue

2. See also Dennis E. Johnson, *The Message of Acts in the History of Redemption* (Phillipsburg, NJ: P&R, 1997), 2–13.

that a robust appreciation of the resurrection of Christ in Acts—which is a prominent Lukan emphasis—provides a hermeneutical guide to help us untangle a number of knotty issues in Acts.

The Centrality of the Resurrection in Acts

In what follows I argue that the resurrection of Christ is one of the major emphases of Acts, which unifies and provides coherence for the theology of Luke's second volume.[3] By *resurrection* I simply mean the reality for Luke that Jesus of Nazareth had risen bodily from the dead to new life. Luke presents the resurrection of Christ as a singular turning point in the accomplishment of salvation that ushers in the age of the exalted Messiah. By focusing on the resurrection message of Acts, we are thus able to perceive with greater clarity the purpose(s) of Acts, and we are also better able to wrestle with questions related to the newness and contiguity of the gospel message with what has come before. My argument consists of two parts, which correlate to the two halves of this book. In part 1, I exegete relevant texts in Acts pertaining to the resurrection. In part 2, I explore the theological implications of the resurrection in more detail.

A few more words on these two divisions are in order. First, we need to appreciate how the resurrection is a major artery connecting various events and passages in Acts. To use another analogy, the resurrection of Christ serves as a powerful theological adhesive that contributes to the theological unity of Acts. For example, the resurrection is foundational to understanding the Lukan emphasis on the *kingdom*—which bookends Acts—and is also necessary to understand the rationale and timing(s) of the coming of the Holy Spirit. Additionally, the resurrection consistently plays a climactic role in the apostolic preaching. Indeed, I will also propose that the resurrection—though typically not an end in itself in the preaching—is often the logical key to the apostolic preaching in Acts,[4] since the resurrection explains the implications of the work of Christ like no other event. Thus, for example, though the

---

3. Following the strong and consistent evidence of the early church, I identify Luke to be the author of both the Gospel of Luke and the Acts of the Apostles. See, e.g., Irenaeus, *Haer.* 1.23.1; 3.1.1; 3.13.1–2; 3.10.1; 3.12.12; 3.14.1; 3.15.1; 3.17.2; 4.6.1; Martin Hengel, *The Four Gospels and the One Gospel of Jesus Christ: An Investigation of the Collection and Origin of the Canonical Gospels*, trans. John Bowden (Harrisburg, PA: Trinity Press International, 2000), 44–56; Joseph A. Fitzmyer, *The Acts of the Apostles: A New Translation with Introduction and Commentary*, AB 31 (New York: Doubleday, 1998), 47–51.

4. A point also made by Kevin L. Anderson, *"But God Raised Him from the Dead": The Theology of Jesus's Resurrection in Luke-Acts*, PBM (repr., Eugene, OR: Wipf & Stock, 2006), 197. See also the chart in Thompson, *Acts of the Risen Lord Jesus*, 91; Lidija Novakovic, *Raised*

apostolic speeches typically end in paraenesis,[5] the reason that the people must repent and believe is that Jesus *lives* (e.g., Acts 2:33–39; 13:37–41). My goal will thus be to show that at various key junctures of the apostolic preaching (including Paul's defenses), the conclusions and implications depend upon the resurrection of Jesus Christ. I will likewise argue for the key role of the resurrection more broadly in Acts, beyond the speeches.

Second, in addition to the *that* of the resurrection's centrality in Acts (part 1), we must consider the *why* and the *so what* of the resurrection in Acts. Therefore in part 2, I will linger over Luke's emphasis on the resurrection and consider some of its implications for Christian theology. To this end, I will address the way in which Jesus is and/or becomes Lord in Acts, the coming of the Holy Spirit, the Scriptures and the purpose of Acts, and the New Testament canon in light of early Christian theology. I will argue that the resurrection of Christ bears significantly on all of these issues.

Simply stated, my focus is intently on the resurrection and its implications in Acts and for Christian theology. Though, as the survey that follows will show, many have recognized the centrality of the resurrection in Acts, surprisingly few studies have traced out the implications of this observation in an integrated way, articulating its contribution to biblical and systematic theology.

I aim to make a bold case in this volume, because I am persuaded that so much in Acts hinges on the resurrection of Christ. We fail to do justice to the theological message of Acts if we give less attention to the resurrection than Luke himself does. To be clear, I will focus primarily on the resurrection of Christ himself, and not the general resurrection. Though the latter is also in view in Acts, I emphasize the cosmic and personal dimensions of Christ's resurrection, which certainly has consequential—indeed causal—implications for the general resurrection.[6] I also recognize that debates persist on the relationship of the resurrection to the ascension and enthronement of Jesus. These are all clearly important. Yet I will argue in chapter 5 that the resurrection seems to function for Luke as a *primus inter pares* (first among equals) when he is speaking of aspects of Christ's exaltation.

It will also be helpful to state what this book is and what it is not. Simply stated, this book is an investigation of the centrality of the resurrection of

---

from the Dead according to Scripture: The Role of Israel's Scripture in the Early Christian Interpretations of Jesus' Resurrection, JCT 12 (London: Bloomsbury T&T Clark, 2012), 197.

5. Cf. Herman N. Ridderbos, *The Speeches of Peter in the Acts of the Apostles* (London: Tyndale, 1962), 27.

6. Cf. Hans Conzelmann, *The Theology of Saint Luke*, trans. Geoffrey Buswell (London: Faber and Faber, 1960), 205–6.

Christ in Acts and its theological implications. This book is not an investigation of the *historicity* of the resurrection in Acts. Others have written with the goal of defending the veracity of the resurrection of Christ; that is not my aim.[7] Nevertheless, my argument does assume that the resurrection of Jesus described by Luke is historical.[8] Indeed, I believe the dichotomy between theology and history is artificial, which I will not assume. Questions pertaining to the historicity or nonhistoricity of particular events necessarily involve theological assumptions, since often such historical questions relate to how God does or does not intervene in history. Historicity is a theological issue for Luke as well. He affirms in the prologue of his Gospel that the events recounted can be traced back to eyewitnesses, so his readers can have certainty about the doctrines which they have been taught (Luke 1:1–4). To pose historical questions is therefore at the same time to pose theological questions; ultimately the two cannot be separated.

My method will be to look intently at the text of Acts and its role in the New Testament, taking a biblical-theological approach.[9] I will read Acts in light of Luke, assuming the hyphen in "Luke-Acts," though my argument does not hinge on one's assessment of the literary unity of the two books.[10] Indeed, as I argue in chapter 8, Acts is quite flexible in the canon and was placed alongside a variety of canonical books in the early centuries of the church. But while I will pay particular attention to the relevance of the Gospel of Luke for the interpretation of Acts, I will also read Acts in the context of and in light of the entire biblical canon. This approach assumes the macroscopic

7. E.g., N. T. Wright, *The Resurrection of the Son of God*, COQG 3 (Minneapolis: Fortress, 2003).

8. Cf. Joel B. Green, "'Witnesses of His Resurrection': Resurrection, Salvation, Discipleship, and Mission in the Acts of the Apostles," in *Life in the Face of Death: The Resurrection Message of the New Testament*, ed. Richard N. Longenecker, MNTS (Grand Rapids: Eerdmans, 1998), 244; C. K. Barrett, *A Critical and Exegetical Commentary on the Acts of the Apostles*, 2 vols., ICC (Edinburgh: T&T Clark, 1994–98), 2:xlix; Arthur Darby Nock, "A Note on the Resurrection," in *Essays on the Trinity and Incarnation*, ed. A. E. J. Rawlinson (London: Longmans, Green and Co., 1928), 47–50.

9. This is the same approach I discussed in *The Last Adam: A Theology of the Obedient Life of Jesus in the Gospels* (Grand Rapids: Baker Academic, 2017), 18.

10. For various perspectives, see Henry J. Cadbury, *The Making of Luke-Acts*, 2nd ed. (London: SPCK, 1958), 8–11; Robert C. Tannehill, *The Narrative Unity of Luke-Acts: A Literary Interpretation*, 2 vols. (Philadelphia and Minneapolis: Fortress, 1986–90), 2:6–8; Joseph Verheyden, "The Unity of Luke-Acts: One Work, One Author, One Purpose?," in *Issues in Luke-Acts: Selected Essays*, ed. Sean A. Adams and Michael W. Pahl, GH 26 (Piscataway, NJ: Gorgias, 2012), 27–50; Michael F. Bird, "The Unity of Luke-Acts in Recent Discussion," *JSNT* 29 (2007): 425–48; Jacob Jervell, *Die Apostelgeschichte: Übersetzt und erklärt*, KEK 3 (Göttingen: Vandenhoeck & Ruprecht, 1998), 91; Mikeal C. Parsons and Richard I. Pervo, *Rethinking the Unity of Luke and Acts* (Minneapolis: Fortress, 1993).

unity of the New Testament witness, which means that Luke's unique voice is not in fundamental disagreement with any other New Testament author.[11] This claim will not find universal assent, but fruitful vistas open before us if we approach the question of the resurrection in Acts in concord with, for example, Paul's letters. In addition, I am less interested than some other studies in questions of sources and underlying traditions, though to be sure, such questions do have their place.[12] My primary interests are more in the text of Acts itself and in Luke's narrative presentation.[13] I will, however, give particular attention to the Old Testament as a source, since the Old Testament is explicitly cited by Luke throughout.

State of the Question: The Resurrection in Acts

It is not novel to identify the resurrection as a key emphasis in Acts. Indeed, any number of articles, essays, commentaries, and monographs routinely note the importance of the resurrection for Luke's second volume.[14] Further, if the resurrection does occupy a substantial place in the theology of Acts, then it would be surprising if its significance had been little noted. However, it is much less common—in fact it is surprisingly rare—to find monographs or other book-length studies devoted to the resurrection in Acts.

11. Cf., e.g., Philipp Vielhauer, "On the 'Paulinism' of Acts," in *Studies in Luke-Acts: Essays Presented in Honor of Paul Schubert*, ed. Leander E. Keck and J. Louis Martyn (Nashville: Abingdon, 1966), 33–50, with the more recent assessment of Sigurd Grindheim, "Luke, Paul, and the Law," *NovT* 56 (2014): 335–58 (though Grindheim overplays the negative connotations of living according to the law).

12. I have written on this topic previously. See Brandon D. Crowe, "The Sources for Luke and Acts: Where Did Luke Get His Material (and Why Does It Matter)?," in Adams and Pahl, *Issues in Luke-Acts*, 73–95.

13. This is not to deny the importance of textual-critical issues (especially for Acts!). I will engage in such discussions where necessary throughout this study.

14. See, e.g., Jacob Jervell, *The Theology of the Acts of the Apostles* (Cambridge: Cambridge University Press, 1996), 31, 74, 77, 80, 90–91; Barrett, *Commentary on the Acts*, 2:xlix; Thomas R. Schreiner, *New Testament Theology: Magnifying God in Christ* (Grand Rapids: Baker Academic, 2008), 104–5; Dennis J. Horton, *Death and Resurrection: The Shape and Function of a Literary Motif in the Book of Acts* (Eugene, OR: Pickwick, 2009); C. F. D. Moule, "The Christology of Acts," in *Studies in Luke-Acts: Essays Presented in Honor of Paul Schubert*, ed. Leander E. Keck and J. Louis Martyn (Nashville: Abingdon, 1966), 165; H. Douglas Buckwalter, *The Character and Purpose of Luke's Christology*, SNTSMS 89 (Cambridge: Cambridge University Press, 1996), 114–18; Stefan Alkier, *The Reality of the Resurrection: The New Testament Witness*, trans. Leroy A. Huizenga (Waco: Baylor University Press, 2013), 141; Marion L. Soards, *The Speeches in Acts: Their Content, Context, and Concerns* (Louisville: Westminster John Knox, 1994), 30; Joshua W. Jipp, *Reading Acts* (Eugene, OR: Cascade, 2018), 17; Willie James Jennings, *Acts*, Belief (Louisville: Westminster John Knox, 2017), 14–15.

I do not intend here to survey all the research.[15] However, to situate the present work, it will be helpful to provide a brief, selective overview of some of the most significant works touching on the resurrection in Acts. To antici-pate the outcome of this survey: though much has been said, further study on the resurrection in Acts is warranted, especially studies that seek to think carefully about its implications.

Major Studies on the Resurrection in Acts

Pride of place among book-length treatments of the resurrection in Acts now goes to Kevin Anderson's *"But God Raised Him from the Dead": The Theology of Jesus's Resurrection in Luke-Acts*. To my knowledge this work, which originated as a PhD thesis, is the only recent, substantial monograph in English to give extended attention to the role of the resurrection in Acts.[16] An-derson provides an eminently capable treatment of the background and issues related to the resurrection, though his work also covers the Gospel of Luke. This makes for an ambitious project. Anderson points to Henry Cadbury as the first twentieth-century scholar to bring attention to the centrality of the resurrection for Luke and Acts,[17] yet Anderson is surprised that more has not yet been done on the subject.[18] In Anderson's estimation, a disproportionate amount of material has appeared on Luke's ascension accounts, which in part is due to the various ways that scholars have related the resurrection to the ascension in Lukan theology.[19] Anderson therefore steps into the gap and analyzes the prominence and theological role of the resurrection in Luke-Acts. For Anderson the resurrection has theological, christological, ecclesiological, and eschatological dimensions.[20]

Anderson has produced a fine study, and he is right to see the need for extended investigation of the resurrection in Acts. However, as I am sure

15. Surveys of research on Acts include François Bovon, *Luke the Theologian: Fifty-Five Years of Research (1950–2005)*, 2nd rev. ed. (Waco: Baylor University Press, 2006); W. Ward Gasque, *A History of the Interpretation of the Acts of the Apostles* (Peabody, MA: Hendrickson, 1989); Todd Penner, "Madness in the Method? The Acts of the Apostles in Current Study," *CBR* 2 (2004): 223–93; Eckhard J. Schnabel, "Fads and Common Sense: Reading Acts in the First Cen-tury and Reading Acts Today," *JETS* 54 (2011): 251–78.

16. Though see also Horton, *Death and Resurrection*.

17. Anderson, *"But God Raised Him from the Dead,"* 1; cf. Cadbury, *Making of Luke-Acts*, 278–80.

18. Anderson, *"But God Raised Him from the Dead,"* 1–2.

19. Anderson, *"But God Raised Him from the Dead,"* 5–10. This is a discussion I will contribute to in ch. 5.

20. Anderson, *"But God Raised Him from the Dead,"* 13.

Anderson himself would affirm, his study is not the last word; more angles and passages have yet to be considered. Additionally, Anderson's study takes the form of a dissertation, along with all its requisite constraints and expectations. I shall give more sustained focus to Acts than Anderson does in his work, but I walk a similar path.

Daniel Marguerat has written prolifically on the resurrection. Marguerat has published a short book on the resurrection more generally,[21] but he has also written a number of more focused essays on the resurrection in Luke and Acts. In perhaps his most relevant article for the present purposes (from 2001), Marguerat traces out some ways that the resurrection is the "heart of the message" in Luke-Acts.[22] These include the resurrection as the central hinge ("charnière centrale") of Luke-Acts, the requirement for apostles to be eyewitnesses to the resurrection, Luke's allocation of the most space of any evangelist to the resurrection of Christ (including chronological markers), the resurrection marking a recurring theme in the apologetic emphases of the missionary speeches in Acts, and the resurrection constituting a common motif to both Judaism and Christianity (cf. Acts 23:6).[23] In a 2012 essay, Marguerat considers the rhetorical role of the resurrection in Luke-Acts and argues that the resurrection is key ("clef") to the reading of history.[24] Here he argues that the resurrection is not the object, but the subject, of Luke's argumentation.[25] He further suggests that "the event of Easter is the lever that opens the meaning of the [Scriptures]."[26] Additionally, Marguerat has recently completed a two-volume commentary on Acts that I shall utilize throughout this study.[27]

21. Marguerat, *Résurrection: Une histoire de vie* (Poliez-le-Grand: Editions du Moulin, 2001).

22. Marguerat, "Luc-Actes: La résurrection à l'oeuvre dans l'histoire," in *Résurrection: L'après-mort dans le monde ancien et le Nouveau Testament*, ed. Odette Mainville and Daniel Marguerat, MdB 45 (Geneva: Labor et Fides, 2001), 195–214. Marguerat quotes "le coeur du message" (195) from François Bovon's French work *Luc le théologien: Vingt-cinq ans de recherche (1950–1975)*, 2nd ed., MdB 5 (Geneva: Labor et Fides, 1988), 132. This essay by Marguerat has since appeared in English: "Writing Acts: The Resurrection at Work in History," in *Paul in Acts and Paul in His Letters*, WUNT 1/310 (Tübingen: Mohr Siebeck, 2013), 130–47. The translations of French are my own.

23. Marguerat, "Luc-Actes," 195–96.

24. Marguerat, "Quand la résurrection se fait clef de lecture de l'histoire (Luc-Actes)," in *Resurrection of the Dead: Biblical Traditions in Dialogue*, ed. Geert Van Oyen and Tom Shepherd, BETL 249 (Leuven: Peters, 2012), 183–202.

25. Marguerat, "Quand la résurrection," 189.

26. Marguerat, "Quand la résurrection," 189. This is my translation of "L'événement de Pâques est le levier qui ouvre le sens des textes."

27. Marguerat, *Les Actes des Apôtres*, 2 vols., CNT 5a–b (Geneva: Labor et Fides, 2007–15), esp. 1:29.

Another significant voice is that of Robert F. O'Toole, SJ, whom Anderson considers to be the "veritable master of St. Luke's resurrection theology."[28] O'Toole's PhD dissertation focused on the resurrection in Acts 26 as the christological climax of Paul's defense.[29] He argues that the argument in Acts 26 is like a diptych, composed of two panels, with the end of each portion emphasizing the resurrection.[30] In addition, O'Toole has contributed several articles on the resurrection in Acts.[31] Among these is an important 1981 article in which he emphasizes the various ways that Acts assumes the ongoing work of the resurrected Christ.[32] For example, he argues that the risen Lord sends the Spirit and likely even picks Judas's replacement.[33] O'Toole's work is valuable, and I will give particular attention to his work on Acts 13 and Acts 26 in chapters 3 and 7.

Additional Studies on the Resurrection in Acts

Beyond these more extensive treatments, a wide array of other studies have recognized the key role of the resurrection in Acts, even if they are not entirely devoted to the topic. Alan Thompson's *The Acts of the Risen Lord Jesus* builds on the presupposition of the importance of the resurrection in Acts, as he proceeds to give a kingdom-centered exposition of Acts.[34] Another fine exposition of Acts that recognizes the key role of the resurrection is Dennis E. Johnson's *The Message of Acts in the History of Redemption*, cited earlier. Although this volume has not received the attention it deserves, Johnson recognizes the central role played by the resurrection (particularly in the speeches) and the important connections between the resurrection and the Scriptures.[35]

Among the many essays on the resurrection in Acts are I. Howard Marshall's contribution to a Festschrift for F. F. Bruce, in which he claims: "According

28. Anderson, *"But God Raised Him from the Dead,"* xviii.

29. O'Toole, *Acts 26: The Christological Climax of Paul's Defense (Ac 22:1–26:32)*, AnBib 78 (Rome: Biblical Institute Press, 1978), esp. v, 156–58.

30. O'Toole, *Christological Climax*, v, 30–32, 156–57; cf. O'Toole, "Christ's Resurrection in Acts 13,13–52," *Bib* 60 (1979): 369.

31. See especially O'Toole, "Activity of the Risen Jesus in Luke-Acts," *Bib* 62 (1981): 471–98; O'Toole, "Christ's Resurrection," 361–72; O'Toole, "Luke's Understanding of Jesus' Resurrection-Ascension-Exaltation," *BTB* 9 (1979): 106–14.

32. E.g., O'Toole, "Activity of the Risen Jesus," 471–72, 495.

33. O'Toole, "Activity of the Risen Jesus," 476, 485. This view is not unique to O'Toole; cf. Barrett, *Commentary on the Acts*, 2:xcv.

34. Thompson, *Acts of the Risen Lord Jesus*, esp. 48–54, 76–88.

35. See Johnson, *Message of Acts*, 144–46, 149–50; cf. 200.

to the theology expressed in the Acts of the Apostles the fundamental place in salvation history is to be assigned to the resurrection of Jesus Christ."[36] Marshall also expresses surprise "that no detailed attempt has been made to expound the theology of the resurrection [in Acts]"[37]—an observation that is perhaps only magnified these many years later, Anderson's monograph notwithstanding. Marshall concludes that the resurrection is, theologically, "the decisive act whereby in accordance with prophecy God exalted his Son to be the Lord and revealed him to chosen witnesses in order that they might preach the good news of forgiveness in his name."[38] This is a good start, and Marshall's essay is valuable. However, much more remains to be said theologically, as Marshall devotes more attention to questions of underlying tradition(s) than I shall in the present volume.

Another important essay comes from David G. Peterson.[39] Peterson also recognizes the centrality of the resurrection in Acts, and he traces out the implications further than many others. Peterson correctly notes that Peter's sermon at Pentecost already focuses on the resurrection, and this speech is programmatic for what follows in Acts.[40] Further, Peterson points to Jesus's resurrection as his "ultimate accreditation and vindication as God's servant and Messiah."[41] For Peterson, "the resurrection does not simply prove Jesus' divinity but inaugurates the End Time of prophetic expectation, a new world with the exalted Christ at its centre."[42] Peterson's essay accords with much of what I will argue more fully in the present volume.

Many others have recognized the importance of the resurrection as well. Bo Reicke in 1959, anticipating many later studies, suggested that Acts is about what "the risen Lord did for his church through his apostles."[43] Another study valuably considered passages that speak of the resurrection in Acts and related them to similar texts in some of the earliest noncanonical Christian

---

36. Marshall, "The Resurrection in the Acts of the Apostles," in *Apostolic History and the Gospel: Biblical and Historical Essays Presented to F. F. Bruce on His 60th Birthday*, ed. W. Ward Gasque and Ralph P. Martin (Grand Rapids: Eerdmans, 1970), 92. See also Marshall, *Luke: Historian and Theologian* (Grand Rapids: Zondervan, 1970), 42, 165.

37. Marshall, "Resurrection in the Acts," 92.

38. Marshall, "Resurrection in the Acts," 107.

39. Peterson, "Resurrection Apologetics and the Theology of Luke-Acts," in *Proclaiming the Resurrection: Papers from the First Oak Hill College Annual School of Theology*, ed. Peter M. Head (Carlisle: Paternoster, 1998), 29–57; cf. Peterson, *The Acts of the Apostles*, PNTC (Grand Rapids: Eerdmans, 2009), 53–97.

40. Peterson, "Resurrection Apologetics," 34–35.

41. Peterson, "Resurrection Apologetics," 35 (emphasis removed).

42. Peterson, "Resurrection Apologetics," 38.

43. Reicke, "The Risen Lord and His Church: The Theology of Acts," *Int* 13 (1959): 157–69.

writings.[44] Charles Talbert has considered the importance of the resurrection in Lukan theology.[45] Similarly, Joel Green writes that the resurrection of Jesus is "the central affirmation of the Christian message in the Acts of the Apostles."[46] Additionally, Jacob Jervell has argued that the resurrection is at the center of the gospel in Lukan theology.[47] Such studies show, for example, that the presupposition for the book of Acts is the ongoing work of the risen Jesus in the church, and a consistent emphasis of the speeches is the resurrection of Jesus.

Others have noted, in particular, the role of the resurrection in Paul's defenses. In addition to the work of O'Toole, Robert J. Kepple has argued that Paul's defense reveals three interrelated beliefs: (1) the resurrection of Jesus is part of Israel's scriptural hope; (2) the resurrection of Jesus fulfills this scriptural hope; (3) the resurrection of Jesus is necessarily tied to the broader belief in the resurrection of the dead.[48] Similarly, Klaus Haacker points out that Luke closely relates the resurrection of Jesus to the resurrection hope of Israel.[49] The resurrection does indeed play a key role in the defenses of Paul, and I shall have much more to say about this in due course.

When speaking of studies on the resurrection in the New Testament, one must also take note of N. T. Wright's formidable work *The Resurrection of the Son of God*. Wright demonstrates the uniqueness of the embodied resurrection envisioned by Judaism and early Christianity and provides expositions of key New Testament resurrection texts. Wright acknowledges the central role of the resurrection in Acts, yet he devotes only seven pages to Acts.[50]

All told, the resurrection is widely regarded to be important for the theology of Acts, which makes book-length treatments of the topic desiderata.

---

44. Everett F. Harrison, "The Resurrection of Jesus Christ in the Book of Acts and in Early Christian Literature," in *Understanding the Sacred Text: Essays in Honor of Morton S. Enlin on the Hebrew Bible and Christian Beginnings*, ed. John Reumann (Valley Forge, PA: Judson, 1972), 217–31.

45. Talbert, "The Place of the Resurrection in the Theology of Luke," *Int* 46 (1992): 19–30; cf. Talbert, *Luke and the Gnostics: An Examination of the Lucan Purpose* (Nashville: Abingdon, 1966).

46. Green, "Witnesses of His Resurrection," 227.

47. Jervell, *Theology of the Acts*, 90; cf. Jervell, *Luke and the People of God: A New Look at Luke-Acts* (Minneapolis: Augsburg, 1972), 75–112.

48. Kepple, "The Hope of Israel, the Resurrection of the Dead, and Jesus: A Study of Their Relationship in Acts with Particular Regard to the Understanding of Paul's Trial Defense," *JETS* 20 (1977): 231–41.

49. Haacker, "Das Bekenntnis des Paulus zur Hoffnung Israels nach der Apostelgeschichte des Lukas," *NTS* 31 (1985): 437–51, esp. 446.

50. Wright, *Resurrection of the Son of God*, 451–57.

Theological Dimensions of the Resurrection

Several studies discuss the theological dimensions of the resurrection in the New Testament. As we have seen, plenty of studies have noted the theological importance of the resurrection in Acts, yet fewer have provided a sustained and integrated consideration of Luke's contribution in light of the scope of biblical and systematic theology. Relevant in this regard is the work of Richard Gaffin, who did something like this for Paul's epistles. Gaffin has argued persuasively for the centrality of the resurrection in Pauline theology.[51] Gaffin argues that "the resurrection is *the* pivotal factor in the whole of the apostle's soteriological teaching."[52] Key texts for Gaffin include 1 Corinthians 15 and Romans 1:3–4.[53] The latter text contrasts "two successive stages of Christ's history, implying two successive modes of *incarnate* existence."[54] For Gaffin, the resurrection of Christ is in Paul the great climax of redemptive history and is of a piece with the resurrection of believers.[55] Significantly for the present study, Gaffin recognizes that Paul's sermon at Pisidian Antioch in Acts 13 (especially v. 33) is very close to Romans 1:4.[56] I believe this is correct, and in both passages the resurrection of Jesus is the lynchpin of the argument. Something similar to what Gaffin has offered for Paul remains to be done for Acts.

Looking Ahead

Despite widespread awareness of the importance of the resurrection for Acts, few sustained treatments of the theological dimensions of the resurrection have been offered in recent years. In what follows, I will provide a new synthesis and suggest some new possibilities in the way that the resurrection functions in Acts in the context of early Christian theology. The resurrection has implications for many aspects of Christian doctrine—including

51. Gaffin, *The Centrality of the Resurrection: A Study in Paul's Soteriology* (Grand Rapids: Baker, 1978). This was later released as a second edition with a different title: *Resurrection and Redemption: A Study in Paul's Soteriology*, 2nd ed. (Phillipsburg, NJ: P&R, 1987). See more recently Gaffin, "The Work of Christ Applied," in *Christian Dogmatics: Reformed Theology for the Church Catholic*, ed. Michael Allen and Scott R. Swain (Grand Rapids: Baker Academic, 2016), 268–90.

52. Gaffin, *Centrality of the Resurrection*, 135 (emphasis original).

53. See also Peter J. Scaer, "Resurrection as Justification in the Book of Acts," *CTQ* 70 (2006): 219–31.

54. Gaffin, *Centrality of the Resurrection*, 112 (emphasis original).

55. See, e.g., Gaffin, *Centrality of the Resurrection*, 112–13, 135.

56. Gaffin, *Centrality of the Resurrection*, 113.

Christology, soteriology, pneumatology, eschatology, and ecclesiology. By way of example, there have been any number of studies concerned with the eschatology of Luke.[57] One thinks of Hans Conzelmann's watershed work.[58] Yet, Conzelmann gives less attention than one might expect to the wide-ranging implications of Jesus's resurrection (he has more to say about the general resurrection).[59] Yet to speak of the eschatological age is to speak about the age of the resurrected and ascended Christ. This perennial question of Lukan eschatology, in other words, is necessarily tied to the resurrection of Jesus.

The Resurrection, the Apostles, and the Kingdom in Acts

As I conclude this opening chapter, I want to set the table for the context of the chapters to follow. In chapters 2–4, I give extended, though not exclusive, attention to *speeches* in Acts. However, as readers of Acts well know, there is much to the theology of Acts beyond the speeches; the narrative contours and narrator's comments are no less important for understanding the theology of Acts than are the speeches.[60] Three aspects of the theology of Acts, in particular, reveal the centrality of the resurrection: the divine necessity of the resurrection, the kingdom framework of Acts, and the role of the apostles as resurrection spokesmen.

The Resurrection and Divine Necessity

First, Luke emphasizes the divine necessity (*dei*; Gk. "it is necessary") of certain events that had to take place for the accomplishment of eschatological salvation.[61] As part of a broader theology of promise and fulfillment,[62] these *dei* statements are fairly diverse, but include the necessity of the resurrection. In the final three *dei* statements in Luke (24:7, 26, 46), the resurrection is

---

57. See, e.g., the survey of literature in Bovon, *Luke the Theologian*, ch. 1.

58. Conzelmann, *Theology of Saint Luke*; for the German title, see *Die Mitte der Zeit: Studien zur Theologie des Lukas*, 3rd ed., BHT 17 (Tübingen: Mohr Siebeck, 1960).

59. Cf. Conzelmann, *Theology of Saint Luke*, 204–6.

60. See, e.g., Beverly Roberts Gaventa, "Toward a Theology of Acts: Reading and Rereading," *Int* 42 (1988): 150; Fitzmyer, *Acts of the Apostles*, 96; Osvaldo Padilla, *The Acts of the Apostles: Interpretation, History and Theology* (Downers Grove, IL: IVP Academic, 2016), 88–107.

61. See further Crowe, *Last Adam*, 95, 103–7, and sources cited there.

62. See, e.g., Samson Uytanlet, *Luke-Acts and Jewish Historiography: A Study on the Theology, Literature, and Ideology of Luke-Acts*, WUNT 2/366 (Tübingen: Mohr Siebeck, 2014), 35–69; Mark S. Giacobbe, "Luke the Chronicler: The Narrative Arc of Samuel-Kings and Chronicles in Luke-Acts" (PhD diss., Westminster Theological Seminary, 2018), 259–64.

necessary, as it is in 9:22. Luke therefore highlights the necessity of the resurrection for eschatological salvation.

Likewise, several *dei* statements in Acts correspond to *dei* statements in Luke. Indeed, more details regarding the Scriptures that were necessary to be fulfilled, which are mentioned with minimal exposition at the end of Luke, are provided in Acts. Although *dei* terminology is not always used in the scriptural expositions of Acts, several *dei* statements do speak of the necessity of the resurrection in Acts. Acts 3:21, for example, speaks of the need for heaven to receive Jesus until the restoration of all things. Though this passage raises a number of interesting questions, the text quite clearly envisions the heavenly session of the resurrected Christ. Also presupposing the resurrection of Christ is the *dei* statement in 4:12: there is no other name given among men, apart from Christ, by whom it is necessary to be saved. The theological context for this proclamation is an exposition of the resurrection of Christ (cf. v. 10). Another relevant *dei* passage is 17:3, where Paul explains the Scriptures in Thessalonica, including the way that Christ had to suffer and rise from the dead. Additionally, the replacement for Judas (cf. 1:21–22) needed to be an eyewitness to the resurrection of Jesus.

I will have more to say about the Scriptures throughout this study; and in chapter 7, I will argue that Acts manifests a clear interest in showing how the resurrection is the fulfillment of the Old Testament Scriptures. At this point I simply point out that Luke's *dei* statements indicate the resurrection is (1) necessary for the fulfillment of the Scriptures and (2) necessary for salvation.

The Resurrection and Kingdom Frame

The kingdom of God is important in Acts, and the resurrection of Christ is foundational to the rationale of the kingdom.[63] This is not to say that the kingdom is *only* about resurrection; but Luke's presentation of the coming of the kingdom presupposes the resurrection of Jesus. To begin, Acts evidences a kingdom *inclusio*.[64] In Acts 1:3 the risen Christ discusses the kingdom of God with his disciples, and in verse 6 the disciples ask Jesus about the restoration of the kingdom of Israel. Jesus's response refocuses the question onto the coming empowerment by the Holy Spirit (vv. 7–8), but this is not something different from the kingdom. For, as I argue in chapter 2, the coming of the Holy Spirit is predicated upon the resurrection and ascension of Jesus as universal king.

---

63. See also G. K. Beale, *A New Testament Biblical Theology: The Unfolding of the Old Testament in the New* (Grand Rapids: Baker Academic, 2011), 239–40

64. Thompson, *Acts of the Risen Lord Jesus*, 44–48.

The other aspect of this *inclusio* can be found in the final two verses of Acts (28:30–31). At the end of Acts Paul preaches without hindrance the *kingdom of God*, teaching about matters concerning the Lord Jesus Christ. Here is a close connection, as readers would expect by this point in Acts, between the lordship of Jesus and the kingdom of God. Indeed, it is best to understand the message about the kingdom of God to be a message about the glorified Lord Jesus Christ. The kingdom *inclusio* in Acts is therefore a framework focused on the resurrected Jesus.

Further, it is highly significant that the content of the preaching often focuses on the kingdom and on the living, resurrected Christ as Lord (cf., e.g., 2:24–36; 3:15, 26; 4:2, 10–12). The kingdom message of Acts is built upon the conviction that Christ is the living Lord. This also corresponds to two other aspects. First, the kingdom is often associated with *glory* in Luke and Acts, and the glory of Jesus is seen preeminently in his resurrected state (cf. Luke 9:26; 21:27; 24:26; Acts 7:55; 22:11). Indeed, glory and dominion are in several New Testament texts taken as concomitants, which speaks again of the risen Lord's glory (1 Pet. 4:11; Rev. 1:6; cf. Jude 25). Second, closely tied to the kingdom framework of Acts is the reality of a coming judgment by the authoritative, resurrected Jesus (cf. Acts 10:42; 17:31). Repentance is therefore necessary (17:30; cf. 2:36–38; 3:14–21; 24:25).

The Resurrection and the Apostles

A final preliminary point to consider is the importance of the resurrection for the apostolate. The importance of the apostles in Acts needs no defense. With the defection of Judas arose the need to find a twelfth, faithful apostle (1:15–26). And, importantly for the present study, 1:21–22 states that Judas's replacement had to be an eyewitness to Jesus's resurrection (and his ministry).[65] Thus, the proofs that the risen Jesus offered to the apostles were most likely proofs of his resurrection (vv. 2–3).[66] It soon becomes apparent in Acts that this is not an idle requirement, for the apostles immediately begin to testify about the *resurrection* of Jesus and its implications (see again 2:24–36, esp. v. 32; cf. Luke 24:46–48). The apostles had to be eyewitnesses of the resurrection because in large measure their task was to testify about the resurrection of Christ. The apostles are central to the book of Acts, and central to the task of the apostles is their role as witnesses to the resurrection of Jesus.

---

65. This is widely recognized. See Green, "Witnesses of His Resurrection," 228–31; Peterson, "Resurrection Apologetics," 33; Johnson, *Message of Acts*, 20, 144–45; cf. Crowe, *Last Adam*, 146–47.

66. Marguerat, "Quand la résurrection," 193–95.

Conclusion

In this chapter I have laid the groundwork for a fuller study of the resurrection in Acts. The resurrection of Jesus is central in the book of Acts. As such, it requires extended reflection. In the remainder of the first half of this volume I will trace out where and how the resurrection functions in Acts. After that, I will turn in part 2 to consider in more detail the theological dimensions of the resurrection in Acts.

2

"Both Lord and Christ"

Peter and the Resurrection

The present chapter focuses on resurrection passages featuring Peter, the most prominent apostle in the opening chapters of Acts. Several Petrine passages—especially the speeches—are highly significant. In the opening chapter I noted the importance of the apostles as witnesses to the resurrection of Jesus in Acts 1:16–22 (especially vv. 21–22)—a text in which Peter was the speaker. Building on Acts 1, in this chapter I will consider Peter's first major speech at Pentecost, his speeches in Jerusalem in Acts 3–5, his interaction with Cornelius (ch. 10), his deliverance from prison (ch. 12), and his role at the Jerusalem Council (ch. 15). In all these passages the resurrection of Jesus is key. Indeed, though he states the matter a bit too extremely, the observation of Jacob Jervell anticipates my discussion: "In the speeches, the only thing the listeners do not seem to know about is Jesus' resurrection (2:24ff., 32; 3:15)."[1]

The Resurrection of Jesus in Peter's Pentecost Sermon (Acts 2)

The Importance of the Pentecost Sermon

It is widely agreed that Peter's Pentecost sermon (2:14–36) is crucially important for the narrative of Acts and is programmatic for what follows.[2]

1. Jervell, *The Theology of the Acts of the Apostles* (Cambridge: Cambridge University Press, 1996), 77.
2. See, e.g., C. K. Barrett, *A Critical and Exegetical Commentary on the Acts of the Apostles*, 2 vols., ICC (Edinburgh: T&T Clark, 1994–98), 1:130; Craig S. Keener, *Acts: An Exegetical*

One author considers this speech to be an "epitome of Lukan theology."[3] Darrell Bock goes even further, arguing that the Pentecost speech "is one of the most important theological declarations in the New Testament."[4] Peter's Pentecost sermon—his first major sermon in Acts—provides the foundational, and perhaps fullest, exposition of the resurrection of Jesus in Acts.[5] Additionally, it is here that Peter explains the outpouring of the Holy Spirit (which is also a *christological* point for Peter). Peter's Pentecost sermon, therefore, plays a crucial role in the narrative of Acts. It also serves as a major pillar in my argument that the resurrection is a central emphasis of Acts.

Another major pillar, which I will consider in chapter 3, is Paul's first major speech at Pisidian Antioch (13:16–41). As in Peter's first major speech, in Paul's first major sermon he emphasizes the role of the resurrection of Jesus (vv. 30–37).[6] Both Peter's Pentecost sermon and Paul's sermon at Pisidian Antioch are the first major sermons from each of these two major characters, and both are the longest sermons from each apostle.[7] To these two pillars we could add a third pillar for my argument regarding the resurrection of Christ, which is Paul's defense before Herod Agrippa II in Acts 26. There too I will argue that Paul's case hinges on the resurrection of Jesus.

Commentary, 4 vols. (Grand Rapids: Baker Academic, 2012–15), 1:872–73; Kevin L. Anderson, *"But God Raised Him from the Dead": The Theology of Jesus's Resurrection in Luke-Acts*, PBM (repr., Eugene, OR: Wipf & Stock, 2006), 200; Mark L. Strauss, *The Davidic Messiah in Luke-Acts: The Promise and Its Fulfillment in Lukan Christology*, JSNTSup 110 (Sheffield: Sheffield Academic, 1995), 131–32; cf. C. H. Dodd, *The Apostolic Preaching and Its Developments* (New York: Harper & Row, 1936), 7–35.

3. Richard F. Zehnle, *Peter's Pentecost Discourse: Tradition and Lukan Reinterpretation in Peter's Speeches of Acts 2 and 3*, SBLMS 15 (Nashville: Abingdon, 1971), 61–70.

4. Bock, *Acts*, BECNT (Grand Rapids: Baker Academic, 2007), 108.

5. Thus it has been argued: "The entire apostolic preaching can be described as ear- and eye-witness testimony to the resurrection . . . nowhere [is the emphasis on the resurrection] revealed more strongly than in the speeches of Peter." Herman N. Ridderbos, *The Speeches of Peter in the Acts of the Apostles* (London: Tyndale, 1962), 18.

6. Also noted by Anderson, *"But God Raised Him from the Dead,"* 197. Cf. G. K. Beale, *A New Testament Biblical Theology: The Unfolding of the Old Testament in the New* (Grand Rapids: Baker Academic, 2011), 240.

7. The number of words in each speech depends, of course, on what textual decisions one makes. Schnabel considers Peter's speech in Acts 2:14–36 to be 429 words, and Paul's at Pisidian Antioch in Acts 13 to be 470 words. See Eckhard J. Schnabel, *Acts*, ZECNT (Grand Rapids: Zondervan, 2012), 132. Following the printed text of NA[27], my own count of the Pisidian Antioch speech (13:16–41) comes to 426 words, and Paul's defense before Herod Agrippa II (26:2–23) comes to 421 words. The longest speech in Acts, with 1,000 words, is Stephen's (7:2–53), which I will address in ch. 4. For a helpful list of speeches in Acts, see Joseph A. Fitzmyer, *The Acts of the Apostles: A New Translation with Introduction and Commentary*, AB 31 (New York: Doubleday, 1998), 104.

We have in Acts, then, not simply a few isolated comments about the resurrection, but a sustained emphasis from the major (and also some minor) characters. Taken together the resurrection passages in Acts form no haphazard lean-to, but reveal a strong edifice built on three major resurrection pillars: Peter's Pentecost sermon, Paul's sermon at Pisidian Antioch, and Paul's longest defense. I will therefore give sustained attention in this chapter to Peter's Pentecost sermon; I will address Pauline resurrection passages in chapter 3.

The Spirit, the Resurrection, and the Latter Days (2:1–21)

Peter's Pentecost sermon is occasioned by the outpouring of the Spirit in Jerusalem. Much could be said about this event, but my focus is mainly on the connection between the Spirit and the resurrection of Jesus. The risen Jesus, who presented himself alive and gave many resurrection proofs to his disciples (Acts 1:3), commanded his disciples to wait for the promise of the Father, which would be the baptism of the Holy Spirit (vv. 4–5). It even appears that the risen Jesus's command to wait for the coming of the Spirit (v. 5) means that Jesus himself will grant the Spirit.[8] This is all the more likely if we connect the outpouring of the Spirit to the words of John the Baptist in Luke 3:16 that the stronger one (*ho ischyroteros* = Jesus) would baptize with the Holy Spirit and fire. To be sure, this connection is not certain, especially since Jesus does not mention the fire to which John the Baptist drew attention.[9] Nevertheless, it is likely that the words of Jesus in Acts 1:5 do recall Luke 3:16 and that the pouring-out of the Spirit in Acts 2:1–4—which is manifested as tongues like (*hōsei*) *fire*—is the initial fulfillment of John the Baptist's words in Luke 3:16.[10] If so, then this provides further support for the interpretation that it is the *risen Christ* who pours out his Spirit in Acts 2.

Regardless of whether Acts 2:1–4 fulfills Luke 3:16, several other elements of Acts 2 further support the connection between the risen Christ and the outpouring of the Spirit. The tongues like fire dispersed on the disciples lead to them speaking in other tongues about the mighty acts (*ta megaleia*) of God (2:11).[11] The confusion that results (cf. vv. 11–13) leads to Peter's speech,

8. So also Robert F. O'Toole, SJ, "Activity of the Risen Jesus in Luke-Acts," *Bib* 62 (1981): 485.

9. Cf. David G. Peterson, *The Acts of the Apostles*, PNTC (Grand Rapids: Eerdmans, 2009), 133; Fitzmyer, *Acts of the Apostles*, 238.

10. See Bock, *Acts*, 129; Barrett, *Commentary on the Acts*, 1:114; Richard B. Gaffin Jr., "Justification in Luke-Acts," in *Right with God: Justification in the Bible and in the World*, ed. D. A. Carson (Grand Rapids: Baker, 1992), 109–12; Sinclair B. Ferguson, *The Holy Spirit*, CCT (Downers Grove, IL: InterVarsity, 1996), 58–60; Zehnle, *Peter's Pentecost Discourse*, 116.

11. For discussions of these events, see G. K. Beale, *The Temple and the Church's Mission: A Biblical Theology of the Dwelling Place of God*, NSBT 17 (Downers Grove, IL: InterVarsity,

wherein we find even clearer connections between the risen Christ and the outpouring of the Spirit. Much of Peter's exposition of the events the people are witnessing is taken from the Old Testament. This focus on the Old Testament recalls Jesus's statements about the scriptural necessity (*dei*) of, among other things, the resurrection (Luke 9:22; 24:7, 26, 44–46).

This brings us to Peter's quotation of Joel 2:28–32.[12] As with the outpouring of the Spirit, much could be said about the quotation of Joel 2.[13] Yet my focus is how the quotation of Joel 2 relates to the resurrection of Jesus. In this light, the opening of the Joel quotation in Acts 2:17 is significant: *kai estai en tais eschatais hēmerais* ("and it will be in the latter days," whereas Joel 2:28—in the Greek of the LXX, with which Peter's quote mostly agrees—reads simply *kai estai meta tauta*: "and it will be after these things").[14] The phrase *en tais eschatais hēmerais* ("in the latter days," and variations of this phrasing) recalls any number of scriptural texts that speak about the coming blessings of the latter days (cf., e.g., Deut. 4:30; Isa. 2:2; Dan. 2:28; Hos. 3:5). Luke's inclusion of *en tais eschatais hēmerais* in the opening of the Joel 2 quotation thus indicates that the outpouring of the Spirit marks the coming of the latter days anticipated in Joel.[15] Additionally, Luke's phrasing may also call to mind the multitude of blessings associated with the latter days. This would include not only the outpouring of the Spirit but also the establishment of Mount Zion as the highest of the mountains, from where the word of the Lord would go forth (Isa. 2:2; Mic. 4:1; cf. Acts 1:8).[16] These additional blessings also include the restoration of Israel to the land,[17] evident here in the eclectic

---

2004), 201–16; Keener, *Acts*, 1:794–805. Might *ta megaleia* include the resurrection of Jesus—the mighty act of God par excellence? On the flexibility of *megas*, see BDAG, "μέγας," 623–24.

12. This is Joel 3:1–5 in the MT and LXX. For sake of simplicity, I will prefer the English versification of Joel.

13. See, e.g., C. M. Blumhofer, "Luke's Alteration of Joel 3:1–5 in Acts 2:17–21," *NTS* 62 (2016): 499–516; I. Howard Marshall, "Acts," in *Commentary on the New Testament Use of the Old Testament*, ed. G. K. Beale and D. A. Carson (Grand Rapids: Baker Academic, 2007), 532–36.

14. Some manuscripts (including B) instead read *meta tauta* in Acts 2:17, but this is almost certainly a harmonization to Joel 3:1 LXX.

15. So, e.g., Keener, *Acts*, 1:877–78; Marshall, "Acts," 534; Fitzmyer, *Acts of the Apostles*, 252; cf. Barrett, *Commentary on the Acts*, 2:lxxxiii.

16. See John Calvin, *Commentary on the Prophet Isaiah*, trans. William Pringle (repr., Grand Rapids: Baker, 2003), 1:92, 96–98; K&D, 7:74–76.

17. Noted by, e.g., Michael E. Fuller, *The Restoration of Israel: Israel's Re-gathering and the Fate of the Nations in Early Jewish Literature and Luke-Acts*, BZNW 138 (Berlin: de Gruyter, 2006), 257–64 (which focuses especially on the role of the Twelve); Alan J. Thompson, *Acts of the Risen Lord Jesus: Luke's Account of God's Unfolding Plan*, NSBT 27 (Downers Grove, IL: InterVarsity, 2011), 110–12, following Richard Bauckham, "The Restoration of Israel in

gathering of Jews in Jerusalem (Acts 2:5).[18] This is consistent with the wider context in Joel, where the next few verses promise the reversal of fortunes for God's people, who had been scattered among the nations (Joel 3:1–21 EVV / Joel 4:1–21 MT, LXX).

Significantly, this return to the land envisioned in Acts is communicated by resurrection language, especially building upon Ezekiel 36–37.[19] In Ezekiel we similarly find the collocation of the outpouring of the Spirit and the return of Israel to the land. Ezekiel 36 speaks about the Lord pouring out his Spirit (vv. 26–27), which is fulfilled on the day of Pentecost.[20] Moreover, this context in Ezekiel concerns the restoration of the people to the land and the attendant blessings spoken of in the Prophets.[21] Whereas the people were scattered because of their sins (cf. vv. 3–4, 17–21, 24–31), in the future God, for the sake of his holy name, will bring the people back to their land, cleanse them from their sins, and (significantly) grant them his Spirit (vv. 22–33).[22] This leads into the famous vision of the valley of dry bones in Ezekiel 37:1–14, which is likely also invoked in the opening verses of Acts 2.[23] In Ezekiel 37, the Spirit leads Ezekiel out and shows how the bones received the breath of life, which indicates the people returning to their land and receiving new life (cf. vv. 11–14). Ezekiel thus relates the work of the Spirit with restoration and

Luke-Acts," in *The Jewish World around the New Testament: Collected Essays I*, WUNT 1/233 (Tübingen: Mohr Siebeck, 2008), 358.

18. In this sense, it matters little whether 2:5 refers to Jewish residents in Jerusalem or only Jews who were visiting for the feast. For the former option, see Charles H. Talbert, *Reading Acts: A Literary and Theological Commentary on the Acts of the Apostles* (New York: Crossroad, 1997), 42; Keener, *Acts*, 1:833; Peterson, *Acts of the Apostles*, 135; Carl R. Holladay, *Acts: A Commentary*, NTL (Louisville: Westminster John Knox, 2016), 93. For the latter option, see Barrett, *Commentary on the Acts*, 1:118; Fitzmyer, *Acts of the Apostles*, 239; Bock, *Acts*, 100 (apparently); Bauckham, "Restoration of Israel," 357. These Jewish believers from every nation may also anticipate the gentile mission to every nation we encounter later in Acts.

19. Though, to be sure, Ezekiel is not the only OT text that forms the background for this understanding. See, e.g., the role of Isaiah, in David W. Pao, *Acts and the Isaianic New Exodus* (repr., Grand Rapids: Baker Academic, 2002), 111–46.

20. See, e.g., Peterson, *Acts of the Apostles*, 156; Schnabel, *Acts*, 148; cf. G. K. Beale, "The Descent of the Eschatological Temple in the Form of the Spirit at Pentecost, Part 1: The Clearest Evidence," *TynBul* 56.1 (2005): 85.

21. This is emphasized by N. T. Wright, *The Resurrection of the Son of God*, COQG 3 (Minneapolis: Fortress, 2003), 119–21.

22. On the Spirit in Ezek. 36–37, see Dennis E. Johnson, *The Message of Acts in the History of Redemption* (Phillipsburg, NJ: P&R, 1997), 57–58, 67nn10–11; cf. F. F. Bruce, *The Acts of the Apostles: The Greek Text with Introduction and Commentary*, 2nd ed. (Grand Rapids: Eerdmans, 1952), 81. Johnson rightly relates the Spirit in Ezekiel to the Spirit's work at creation; cf. Ezek. 36:33–36.

23. Noted by many, including Keener, *Acts*, 1:802; Peterson, *Acts of the Apostles*, 132; Bock, *Acts*, 96; Schnabel, *Acts*, 148, 150.

resurrection.[24] Later Jewish texts frequently drew upon Ezekiel 37 in ways that related the restoration of Israel to resurrection (e.g., 2 Macc. 7:22–23; *4 Macc.* 18:17; *Pseudo-Ezekiel*; *Sib. Or.* 4:181–82; *Liv. Pro.* 3:12; *T. Ab.* 18:11; possibly *2 Bar.* 50:1–3).[25]

In addition to promising the raising of dry bones, Ezekiel 37 also promises that the formerly scattered people will be united under one king (v. 22). This marks another shared emphasis with Peter's Pentecost sermon, since Peter will explain that Jesus is the heavenly king who reigns over the whole house of Israel (cf. Acts 2:24–36, esp. vv. 24, 36).[26] For Peter, the blessings of the latter days—including the outpouring of the Spirit, the forgiveness of sins, the regathering of Israel, and the unification of Israel under one king—have become a reality through the resurrection of Jesus, who is identified as the Lord of Joel 2 (cf. v. 21).

The Risen Lord Pours Out the Spirit (2:22–36)

After the quotation of Joel 2 comes a turning point in Peter's Pentecost sermon. From this point, Peter's exposition will focus more explicitly on the resurrection of Jesus, as he explains the identity of the Lord from the Joel quotation in Acts 2:21. The Lord for Peter is the resurrected Jesus, and it is because of Jesus's exaltation that the Holy Spirit is poured out. Here Peter relies again on the Old Testament, particularly the Psalms, to explain the events of Pentecost in relation to the resurrection of Jesus as the heir to the Davidic promises.

Once he has explained the death of Jesus in 2:22–23, Peter then moves to an exposition of the resurrection in verses 24–36.[27] Peter's first comment about

---

24. Ezekiel 37 is one of the most explicit OT passages speaking about the resurrection. See, e.g., Wright, *Resurrection of the Son of God*, 119–21; Anderson, *"But God Raised Him from the Dead,"* 55; C. D. Elledge, *Resurrection of the Dead in Early Judaism, 200 BCE–CE 200* (Oxford: Oxford University Press, 2017), 19; cf. Thomas R. Schreiner, *New Testament Theology: Magnifying God in Christ* (Grand Rapids: Baker Academic, 2008), 104–5; Thompson, *Acts of the Risen Lord Jesus*, 71–72.

25. For a discussion of such possibilities, see Anderson, *"But God Raised Him from the Dead,"* 55n18, 63–69; Richard Bauckham, "Life, Death, and the Afterlife in Second Temple Judaism," in *Life in the Face of Death: The Resurrection Message of the New Testament*, ed. Richard N. Longenecker, MNTS (Grand Rapids: Eerdmans, 1998), 91; Wright, *Resurrection of the Son of God*, 150–53, 188, 194; Michael Wolter, *Paul: An Outline of His Theology*, trans. Robert L. Brawley (Waco: Baylor University Press, 2015), 159 (§21); J. R. Daniel Kirk, *Unlocking Romans: Resurrection and the Justification of God* (Grand Rapids: Eerdmans, 2008), 30.

26. On "the whole house of Israel" in Acts and Ezek. 37:11, see Thompson, *Acts of the Risen Lord Jesus*, 128, following Bauckham, "Restoration of Israel," 358.

27. See, e.g., Robert F. O'Toole, SJ, "Acts 2:30 and the Davidic Covenant of Pentecost," *JBL* 102 (1983): 255.

the resurrection, which is the main point in this section, comes in verse 24: God raised (*anestēsen*) Jesus, having loosed (*lysas*) the birth-pains (*ōdinas*) of death,[28] because it was not possible for Jesus to be held (*krateisthai*) by death. Commentators have long discussed the background and meaning of the idiom "loosing the birth-pains of death."[29] The discussion often asks if the LXX translators have translated the Hebrew word for "cord" (*ḥebel*) as though it were the term for "birth-pain" (*ḥēbel*) (cf. 2 Sam. 22:6; Ps. 18:5 [18:6 MT/17:6 LXX]; 116:3 [114:3 LXX]).[30] On the one hand, Luke is following the LXX, but on the other hand he may well be aware of possible wordplays in Hebrew.[31] Additionally, "loosing the birth-pains of death," though it may sound like a mixed metaphor,[32] is an appropriate (and striking) idiom to refer to the resurrection.[33] Regardless of how one understands this phrase in Acts 2:24, the resurrection of Jesus is clearly in view. Luke's scriptural turn of phrase anticipates his fuller explanations from Psalms 16 [15 LXX] and 110 [109 LXX] in what follows. It is therefore fitting to focus primarily on Peter's explicit citations in this context.

To explain the resurrection in more detail Peter quotes Psalm 16:8–11 [15:8–11 LXX], which he attributes to David (Acts 2:25). As we will see, the Davidic dimensions of these psalms are key for Peter's argument. David expresses confidence that the Lord will sustain him in the midst of great trouble (v. 25); therefore David will rejoice, and his flesh will dwell in hope (v. 26). Historically, Psalm 16 probably speaks of a time when David was facing the threat of death. This passage can be read alongside Psalm 18—as it apparently is in Peter's speech, where "birth-pains of death" (*tou ōdinas tou thanatou*, 2:24) probably alludes to Psalm 18:5 [18:6 MT/17:6 LXX] (*ōdines hadou*)—which recounts the mortal threat of Saul against David.[34]

---

28. *Thanatou* is the more likely reading in this case than *hadou* (which is found in, e.g., D latt). The latter reading could be influenced by OT wording (Ps 17:6 LXX; 114:3 LXX). See also Barrett, *Commentary on the Acts*, 1:143.

29. See, e.g., Barrett, *Commentary on the Acts*, 1:143–44; Keener, *Acts*, 1:943–44; Strauss, *Davidic Messiah*, 135–40; Fitzmyer, *Acts of the Apostles*, 256; Bock, *Acts*, 122. See also BDAG, "ὠδίν," 1102.

30. See, e.g., Barnabas Lindars, *New Testament Apologetic: The Doctrinal Significance of the Old Testament Quotations* (London: SCM, 1961), 39–40.

31. So, e.g., Keener, *Acts*, 1:943–44. For possible influence of Aramaic, see J. R. Doeve, *Jewish Hermeneutics in the Synoptic Gospels and Acts* (Assen: Van Gorcum, 1954), 168–71.

32. Lindars, *New Testament Apologetic*, 39.

33. See especially Anderson, "But God Raised Him from the Dead," 203–8; Evald Lövestam, *Son and Saviour: A Study of Acts 13,32–37; With an Appendix: "Son of God" in the Synoptic Gospels*, ConBNT 18 (Lund: Gleerup, 1961), 44–45.

34. This is stated in the superscription of Ps. 18, though it is also consistent with the psalm's contents.

Similarly, Psalm 116 (though it does not include a Davidic superscription) seems to recall a similar situation in the close encounter with Sheol (v. 3). Further corroboration of this point comes in the latter half of the quotation of Psalm 16 in Acts 2:27–28: "For you will not abandon my soul to Hades, nor will you allow your holy one to see corruption. You have made known to me the paths of life, you will fill me with gladness with your presence." David therefore exulted in the provision of the Lord, who delivered him from (the threat of) death.

Yet if David rejoiced because his flesh would not see corruption, Peter points out an apparent inconsistency: David did indeed die and see corruption (Acts 2:29). This would not be surprising to Peter's audience, since the tomb of David was known to them.[35] Therefore David must have been speaking about someone other than himself, which is consistent with Peter's declaration that David was a prophet (v. 30).[36] David knew that God had sworn an oath to him that one of his descendants would sit on his throne (v. 30). And at this point Peter makes the crucial move: David's words in Psalm 16 were ultimately about the resurrection of the Messiah (2:31).[37] It is the Messiah who would ultimately not be abandoned to Hades; it is the Messiah whose flesh would not see corruption (v. 31).[38] The logic of Peter's reading of Psalm 16 thus assumes that David's deliverance anticipated a greater event in which the Lord would make good on his promise to raise up a son to sit on the throne of David (2 Sam. 7:12–13; Ps. 89:3–4 [89:4–5 MT/88:4–5 LXX]; 132:11 [131:11 LXX]).[39] As O'Toole has stated succinctly, "Luke sees the resurrection

---

35. Cf. Fitzmyer, *Acts of the Apostles*, 257.

36. See also Benjamin Sargent, *David Being a Prophet: The Contingency of Scripture upon History in the New Testament*, BZNW 207 (Berlin: de Gruyter, 2014), 62–66.

37. Jesus's resurrection is explicitly mentioned already in 2:30 in several manuscripts and traditions (e.g., E D* Ψ 33 1241 1739 𝔐 Harklean Syriac al.). After *horkō hōmosen autō ho theos ek karpou tēs osphyos autou* ("God swore to him an oath [that] from the fruit of his loins") and before *kathisai epi ton thronon autou* ("to set upon his throne") we encounter several options for the inclusion of *anastēsai/anastēsein ton Christon* ("to raise Christ"). Though the inclusion of the resurrection here is likely not original, it does reveal a common understanding that Peter's interpretation of Psalm 16 [15 LXX] hinges on the resurrection of Jesus. See also Anderson, *"But God Raised Him from the Dead,"* 211.

38. See Brandon D. Crowe, *The Last Adam: A Theology of the Obedient Life of Jesus in the Gospels* (Grand Rapids: Baker Academic, 2017), 194; cf. Martin Pickup, "'On the Third Day': The Time Frame of Jesus' Death and Resurrection," *JETS* 56 (2013): 533–34, which notes that decay was often viewed as a penalty for sin. The lack of decay in Jesus, therefore, implies his sinlessness.

39. Cf., e.g., Marshall, "Acts," 538; Fitzmyer, *Acts of the Apostles*, 250; Keener, *Acts*, 1:952; Strauss, *Davidic Messiah*, 139; Carl R. Holladay, "What David Saw: Messianic Exegesis in Acts 2," *SCJ* 19 (2016): 95–108. Contrast K. R. Harriman, "'For David Said concerning Him': Foundations of Hope in Psalm 16 and Acts 2," *JTI* 11 (2017): 250–51.

of Jesus as the realization of the promise made to David (2 Sam 7.12–16)."[40] Furthermore, Luke speaks of the kingdom of David as an everlasting kingdom, just as Gabriel promises Mary in Luke 1:32–33. From Psalm 16 Peter gleans the insight that David, being a prophet, spoke beforehand of the resurrection of the Messiah. Because he has been raised from the dead, the Son of David rules over an everlasting kingdom.[41]

The title Christ (*Christos*) is first encountered in Acts 2:31, and this term is strongly linked throughout Acts with the resurrection of Jesus, who reigns over this everlasting kingdom.[42] Indeed, the framework for understanding *Christ* in Acts (in light of the usage of the term in the Gospel of Luke) is the resurrected, Davidic Son who reigns over an everlasting kingdom.[43] The resurrection is thus implied—and frequently made explicit—in each occurrence of *Christos* in Acts.[44] In Acts 2 the Christ is identified specifically as Jesus of Nazareth, which is a common refrain throughout Acts (cf. 2:36; 3:6, 20; 4:10; 5:42; 18:5, 28). Jesus from Nazareth—a prophet mighty in word and deed (Luke 24:18–19; Acts 2:22)—is the heir to the Davidic promises, for God has raised him from the dead. Peter further draws attention to the role that he and the other apostles have as witnesses of Jesus's resurrection (2:32). The resurrection demonstrates that Jesus is the Christ.

Acts 2:32 also plays a crucial role in Peter's argument. Now that Jesus has been raised from the dead, he has been exalted to the right hand of God and pours out the Spirit (v. 33).[45] These latter two events follow logically upon the resurrection of Jesus (thus the *oun* in v. 33). The resurrection distinguishes Jesus as the Christ and enables him to reign from God's right hand. Peter supports this from Psalm 110 and possibly also Psalm 118:16.[46] A christological reading of Psalm 110 is familiar to readers of Luke's Gospel. Jesus uses this

---

40. O'Toole, "Acts 2:30," 253.

41. See, e.g., David G. Peterson, "Resurrection Apologetics and the Theology of Luke-Acts," in *Proclaiming the Resurrection: Papers from the First Oak Hill College Annual School of Theology*, ed. Peter M. Head (Carlisle: Paternoster, 1998), 37; Peterson, *Acts of the Apostles*, 149; O'Toole, "Acts 2:30," 254; Daniel Marguerat, *Les Actes des Apôtres*, 2 vols., CNT 5a–b (Geneva: Labor et Fides, 2007–15), 1:97–98.

42. I use *Christ* and *Messiah* interchangeably.

43. See also Strauss, *Davidic Messiah*, 140.

44. See especially 2:31, 36, 38; 3:6, 18–22; 4:10; 9:22, 34; 10:36; 17:3; 26:23; 28:31.

45. Cf. Keener, *Acts*, 1:957–59. Thus, Peter also speaks in his sermon about the ascension of Christ. My focus is on the resurrection of Christ, but I do not thereby intend to diminish the ascension of Christ. Instead, the resurrection and ascension are best viewed as being part of the same movement. I will say more about this in ch. 5.

46. For this latter option, see C. H. Dodd, *According to the Scriptures: The Substructure of New Testament Theology* (London: Nisbet, 1952), 99. Dodd also notes the next phrase in Ps. 117:17 LXX (*ouk apothanoumai alla zēsomai* ["I shall not die, but I shall live"]), which also points to the resurrection of Christ.

psalm to demonstrate that he is both David's Son and David's Lord (Luke 20:41–44). In Luke 20 Jesus speaks of his own authority over David, and likely his own preexistence.[47] As the Son of David, Jesus is not inferior to David, because he is also David's Lord. And by means of his resurrection, the Son of David achieves a reign superior to the reign of David himself. In Acts the lordship of Christ means that Jesus is exalted to the right hand of God, fulfilling Psalm 110. At Pentecost the heavenly enthronement of Jesus is demonstrated through the pouring-out of the Holy Spirit (2:33). The pneumatologically significant event of Pentecost is therefore at the same time *christologically* significant. The outpouring of the Spirit indicates that Jesus is the living, ascended king who reigns over all nations.

Further communicating the heavenly, exalted status of the resurrected Christ is the title Lord (*kyrios*). This title is relatively rare in the Gospels, perhaps since it is better reserved for the exalted Jesus. However, Luke is the exception, as *kyrios* is used for Jesus on a number of occasions before his heavenly exaltation (cf., e.g., Luke 1:43, 76; 2:11; 3:4; 7:13, 19; 10:1, 39–41; 11:39; 12:42; 13:15; 17:5–6; 18:6; 19:8, 31, 34; 20:42; 22:61; 24:3, 34).[48] Yet in Acts *Lord* is quite clearly related to the exaltation of Jesus. A key text in this regard is 2:36: "Therefore, let all the house of Israel know with certainty that God has made him both Lord and Christ, this Jesus whom you crucified."

Peter's climactic proclamation in 2:36 sums up his argument and explains the outpouring of the Spirit in relation to the heavenly exaltation of Jesus of Nazareth: he is both Lord and Christ.[49] As Lord, Jesus is the exalted, heavenly king who has conquered death. As Christ, Jesus has been resurrected from the dead and reigns over the promised kingdom of David, which will have no end. These two key terms for Peter—Lord and Christ—build on the foundational assumption of the resurrection. "This Jesus," as the one who fulfills Psalms 16 and 110 (among others), is a king superior to all others.

Though the heavenly, Davidic kingship of Jesus ends the sermon, the response of the people is also instructive. As we see throughout the sermons of Acts, if Jesus is the resurrected Lord, then the proper response is repentance (2:38). Repentance (along with baptism) is necessary because Jesus is not only the resurrected Lord but also the judge. Although Peter does not speak of

47. Cf. Simon J. Gathercole, *The Pre-existent Son: Recovering the Christologies of Matthew, Mark, and Luke* (Grand Rapids: Eerdmans, 2006), 236–38.

48. See especially C. Kavin Rowe, *Early Narrative Christology: The Lord in the Gospel of Luke*, BZNW 139 (2006; repr., Grand Rapids: Baker Academic, 2009).

49. For more on Acts 2:36, see my discussion in ch. 5.

Jesus as judge explicitly in Acts 2 (the point will be made explicit elsewhere; cf. 10:42; 17:31), it seems to be understood by the crowd. If Jesus is indeed the authoritative, Davidic king, then murdering him did not put an end to him, and he actually lives now and reigns over the Davidic kingdom. It therefore matters whether one submits to or opposes him.[50]

Finally, it is important to note the relationship of Jesus's obedience to his identity as Lord, Christ, and judge. Jesus is identified as righteous or the Righteous One in several places in Luke and Acts (Luke 23:47; Acts 3:14; 7:52; 22:14; cf. 13:10; 17:31). The resurrection is the vindication of Jesus's perfect obedience.[51] In earlier generations David professed that he would be delivered in accord with his righteousness (cf. Ps. 18:20–24 [18:21–25 MT/17:21–25 LXX]). The logic of Acts is that David, who in one sense was delivered from death in accord with his righteousness, anticipated a greater Son of David who would be more fully delivered from death because of his greater righteousness. If the resurrection is the divine answer to the human "no" to Jesus,[52] his obedience is also part of the explanation for *why* Jesus was resurrected.

Conclusion: Peter's Pentecost Sermon

Peter's first major sermon, in Acts 2, focuses intently on the resurrection of Jesus, and thus sets the precedent for following Petrine speeches in Acts. It therefore serves as a major resurrection pillar in Acts.

In Acts 2, Peter explains that the blessings of the latter days come to the people of God through the resurrection of the Davidic Messiah, who is the heavenly Lord. The outpouring of the Spirit is therefore built upon the christological foundation of the resurrection and exaltation of Jesus. The blessings of the latter days flow from the reality that Jesus of Nazareth lives—he is both Lord and Christ. Peter relies heavily on the Old Testament Scriptures to explain the resurrection, a topic I will explore more fully in chapter 7.

Many other texts in Acts speak of Jesus as either Lord or Christ, or as both. From a narratival perspective the foundational exposition of these terms (regardless of the speaker) comes in Acts 2, where they are explained in conjunction with Jesus's resurrection.

---

50. A point that echoes Ps. 2:1–2, which is quoted in Acts 4:25–26; cf. Ps. 2:7 in Acts 13:33, where the resurrection is explicitly in view.

51. See Crowe, *Last Adam*, ch. 7; see also below the discussion of Acts 13 in ch. 3.

52. So Charles H. Talbert, "The Place of the Resurrection in the Theology of Luke," *Int* 46 (1992): 22, following I. Howard Marshall, *Luke: Historian and Theologian* (Grand Rapids: Zondervan, 1970), 175.

The Resurrection Message in Jerusalem (Acts 3–5)

The Resurrection and Restoration of Life (3:1–26)

THE RESURRECTION AND THE RESTORATION OF ALL THINGS (3:1–21)

Soon after the events and speech at Pentecost, Peter again reflects at length on the resurrection of Jesus. As he and John go to the temple at the hour of prayer, they meet a lame man. Peter commands the man in the name of Jesus of Nazareth to rise and walk. Immediately the man rises, leaps up, enters the temple, and praises God (3:1–10).

The vocabulary utilized in this encounter (much like that used in the accounts of the later raising of Aeneas in 9:32–35, Dorcas in 9:36–43, and the lame man in Lystra in 14:8–10) is already suggestive, since the language of *rising* (egeirō, 3:7; possibly 3:6)[53] is the same language used frequently in Acts to refer to the resurrection of Jesus (3:15; 4:10; 5:30; 10:40; 13:30, 37; 26:8).[54] (*Anistēmi* is also used of Jesus's resurrection throughout Acts [2:24, 32; 3:22; 10:41; 13:33–34; 17:3, 31], and is used for the raising or healing of others in 9:34, 40–41; 14:10.) Although this language does not always refer to the resurrection of Jesus, it is suggestive that a healing done in the name of Jesus—who has himself been raised (3:13, 15, 26; cf. 2:31)—is portrayed in terms of being *raised*. The narrative use of these terms in Acts, in other words, relates the raising of the lame man to the resurrection of Jesus.[55] The reader consistently encounters resurrection language being used not only for Jesus himself but also for healings done in the name of Jesus (3:15–16). This keeps resurrection in the foreground. Additionally, apostolic healings in Acts are continuations and imitations of the ministry of Jesus himself (cf. Acts 1:1), who continues to act in Acts as the risen one.[56]

Even more importantly, the raising of the lame man provides Peter opportunity to explain in detail the resurrection of the one in whose name the

---

53. Acts 3:6 presents a difficult textual decision regarding the presence or absence of *egeirō*. Either way, the term is present in 3:7.

54. Cf. Barrett, *Commentary on the Acts*, 1:143.

55. Additionally, the healing of the lame man is explicitly called a sign (*sēmeion*) in 4:16, 22 (cf. 4:30). See also Dennis J. Hamm, SJ, "Acts 3:12–26: Peter's Speech and the Healing of the Man Born Lame," *PRSt* 11 (1984): 203, 212–13; Robert F. O'Toole, SJ, "Some Observations on *Anistēmi*, 'I Raise,' in Acts 3:22, 26," *ScEs* 31 (1979): 85–92; Thompson, *Acts of the Risen Lord Jesus*, 150–59.

56. See, e.g., Joel B. Green, "'Witnesses of His Resurrection': Resurrection, Salvation, Discipleship, and Mission in the Acts of the Apostles," in *Life in the Face of Death: The Resurrection Message of the New Testament*, ed. Richard N. Longenecker, MNTS (Grand Rapids: Eerdmans, 1998), 240; O'Toole, "Activity of the Risen Jesus"; Daniel Marguerat, "The Resurrection and Its Witnesses in the Book of Acts," in *Reading Acts Today: Essays in Honour of Loveday C. A. Alexander*, ed. Steve Walton et al., LNTS 427 (London: T&T Clark, 2011), 176.

man has been raised. Acts 3—which manifests a resurrection *inclusio* (see vv. 13, 26)[57]—includes several additional features pertaining to the resurrection of Jesus. In verse 13 Peter proclaims that God has glorified (*edoxasen*) his servant, Jesus. Here *glorify* must refer to the resurrection and/or ascension of Jesus, as Peter explains in the following verses.[58] Peter's sermon likewise features a servant (*pais*) *inclusio* for Jesus (vv. 13, 26), and the language of glorification very likely recalls the beginning of the fourth Servant Song (Isa. 52:13), in which the servant will be high and lifted up.[59] Yet, as is well known, in the fourth Servant Song the servant is a *suffering* servant.[60] Even so, the suffering servant will be exalted. This pattern of suffering yielding exaltation is thus presented as a pattern for the resurrection of Christ. Jesus was crucified under Pontius Pilate (Acts 3:13–14), but God raised him from the dead (v. 15). Additionally, *pais* is a Davidic title in Luke and Acts, as is established earlier in Luke in relation to the Davidic kingdom (Luke 1:69; cf. Acts 4:25).[61] And, as I argued in relation to Acts 2, the Davidic kingdom for Peter is an *everlasting* kingdom which is ruled by an everlasting king. In Isaiah *king* and *servant* are closely related concepts,[62] so it is not surprising that Peter combines kingdom language with servant language. Furthermore, if we broaden our perspective to include Isaiah 42:1 (the first Servant Song), then the servant is the one anointed with the Holy Spirit, as indeed Jesus himself is described in Acts (10:38). Later in his sermon, Peter further builds upon servant language to speak of the raising up(!) of a prophet like Moses (3:22, 26).

Two christological statements in 3:14–15 are of particular interest for the resurrection of Jesus. First, in verse 14 Jesus is described as the Holy and

---

57. Anderson, *"But God Raised Him from the Dead,"* 222.

58. See, similarly, Anderson, *"But God Raised Him from the Dead,"* 222–23. See also Barrett, *Commentary on the Acts*, 1:195; Hamm, "Acts 3:12–26," 202; O'Toole, "Some Observations on *Anistēmi*," 86.

59. So, e.g., Peterson, *Acts of the Apostles*, 174; Schnabel, *Acts*, 208; André Wénin, "Enracinement vétérotestamentaire du discours sur la résurrection de Jésus dans le Nouveau Testament," in *Resurrection of the Dead: Biblical Traditions in Dialogue*, ed. Geert Van Yen and Tom Shepherd, BETL 249 (Leuven: Peters, 2012), 9–11. For the relationship of high and lifted up in Isa. 6 and 53, as it pertains in a similar fashion in John's Gospel, see Richard Bauckham, *God Crucified: Monotheism and Christology in the New Testament* (Grand Rapids: Eerdmans, 1999), 50–51, 63–68. See also my discussion of Isa. 53 / Acts 8 in ch. 4.

60. Indeed, if there is an allusion here to the suffering servant of Isa. 53, then it could be one way Luke communicates that Jesus's death was substitutionary (cf. Acts 8:32–33). See further Peterson, *Acts of the Apostles*, 77–78; Johnson, *Message of Acts*, 146–49; Schnabel, *Acts*, 208–9.

61. Cf. Larry W. Hurtado, *Lord Jesus Christ: Devotion to Jesus in Earliest Christianity* (Grand Rapids: Eerdmans, 2003), 191–94.

62. Cf. Crowe, *Last Adam*, 140–53; Andrew T. Abernethy, *The Book of Isaiah and God's Kingdom: A Thematic-Theological Approach*, NSBT 40 (Downers Grove, IL: InterVarsity, 2016), 119–70.

Righteous One (*ton hagion kai dikaion*), "Holy" and "Righteous" likely being used here as christological titles.[63] As noted earlier, Jesus is identified several times in Luke and Acts as righteous, especially in relation to his crucifixion (see especially Luke 23:47; Acts 3:14; 7:52; cf. 22:14).[64] In verse 14 only one article is used for the two substantival adjectives, which underscores the close relationship between Jesus's holiness and righteousness. Righteousness is closely associated with the king in Isaiah (cf. Isa. 32:1), and the combination of righteousness and holiness in Acts 3—in a context featuring a *pais inclusio*—is language befitting the everlasting Davidic kingdom ruled over by Christ.[65] The language of holiness not only is a moral predication but also recalls the anointing of Jesus as king, as one who is set apart for a holy task (see again Isa. 42:1; Acts 10:38). Jesus is portrayed as the servant of God anointed by the Holy Spirit; he is thus set apart as holy and righteous.[66] As the Holy and Righteous One, Jesus was wrongfully crucified and was therefore raised from the dead. He has now ascended and reigns over an everlasting kingdom. Peter's logic assumes that Jesus was resurrected *because* he is the Holy and Righteous One.[67] Consistent with this are Peter's words in Acts 3:12, where he denies that either he or John was able to heal the lame man because of his own godliness or power. Instead, it is by the power of Jesus—the Holy and Righteous (and resurrected) One—that the lame man has been healed (v. 16).

Second, in 3:15 Peter refers to Jesus as *ton archēgon tēs zōēs*, which is commonly translated in English as "the author of life."[68] *Archēgos* occurs four

63. Among those that understand these terms as christological titles, see Fitzmyer, *Acts of the Apostles*, 286; Bock, *Acts*, 170–71; Bruce, *Acts of the Apostles*, 109; Schnabel, *Acts*, 209; Anderson, *"But God Raised Him from the Dead,"* 224; Keener, *Acts*, 2:1090–91; Jacob Jervell, *Die Apostelgeschichte: Übersetzt und erklärt*, KEK 3 (Göttingen: Vandenhoeck & Ruprecht, 1998), 94; Ulrich Wilckens, *Die Missionsreden der Apostelgeschichte: Form- und traditionsgeschichtliche Untersuchungen*, WMANT 15 (Neukirchen-Vluyn: Neukirchener Verlag, 1961), 168; Richard Belward Rackham, *The Acts of the Apostles: An Exposition*, 11th ed., WC (London: Methuen, 1930), 51; Rouven Genz, *Jesaja 53 als theologische Mitte der Apostelgeschichte: Studien zur ihrer Christologie und Ekklesiologie im Anschluss an Apg 8,26–40*, WUNT 2/398 (Tübingen: Mohr Siebeck, 2015), 182–83, 217–27; cf. Marguerat, *Actes des Apôtres*, 1:129. See also the discussion in Barrett, *Commentary on the Acts*, 1:195–96.

64. "Righteous One" may be an established messianic title. See Isa. 32:1; 53:11; Jer. 23:5; Zech. 9:9; *1 En.* 38:2; 53:6; *Pss. Sol.* 17:35; Peterson, *Acts of the Apostles*, 175.

65. Cf. Crowe, *Last Adam*, 145–50.

66. See Geerhardus Vos, *The Self-Disclosure of Jesus: The Modern Debate about the Messianic Consciousness*, ed. J. G. Vos, 2nd ed. (Grand Rapids: Eerdmans, 1953; repr., Phillipsburg, NJ: P&R, 2002), 109–11.

67. Crowe, *Last Adam*, 194.

68. So NRSV; ESV; NIV. CSB reads: "source of life"; KJV reads "prince of life." William L. Lane (*Hebrews 1–8*, WBC 47A [Dallas: Word, 1991], 56–57) prefers "champion."

times in the New Testament (Acts 3:15; 5:31; Heb. 2:10; 12:2) and is notoriously difficult to translate.[69] Though the term is used in the Old Testament, it is not clear that any particular usage from the Old Testament is determinative for how the term is used in Acts (or in Hebrews).[70] To determine the proper translation of *archēgos*, we must consider the New Testament contexts in which it is used. In Acts 3, Peter uses *archēgos* in connection with the resurrection of Jesus: as the one who has authority over life, Jesus was unable to be bound by death. This is consistent with the usage of "holy and righteous" in verse 14, whereby Jesus's resurrection is predicated upon his perfect holiness. Furthermore, as the term pertains to the healing of the lame man, Jesus is the *archēgos* of life, who brings greater wholeness to this man's experience of life. This is further consistent with Paul's statement in Acts 26:23, that Jesus is the first (*prōtos*) to rise from the dead.[71]

Jesus as *archēgos* is thus associated with life in Acts and elsewhere in the New Testament (Heb. 2:10; 12:2), particularly the life embodied by Jesus as the one who emerged victorious over death.[72] The notion of *solidarity* is also very much in view in the New Testament's use of *archēgos*.[73] Jesus is the one who has gone first through death and is now resurrected and exalted, who therefore is the authoritative life-giver. Further supporting the emphasis on the resurrection in connection to Jesus as *archēgos* in Acts 3:15 is Peter's statement that he and the apostles are witnesses of the resurrection, which again recalls the importance of the resurrection for the apostolic task (cf. 1:21–22). The resurrection is therefore key for understanding Jesus as the Holy and Righteous One and as the *archēgos* of life.[74] Thus it is prudent to translate *ton archēgon tēs zōēs* as either "Leader of life" or perhaps even "Champion

---

69. See BDAG, "ἀρχηγός ," 138–39; Paul-Gerhard Müller, ΧΡΙΣΤΟΣ ΑΡΧΗΓΟΣ: *Die religionsgeschichtliche und theologische Hintergrund einer neutestamentlichen Christusprädikation*, EHS.T 28 (Bern: Herbert Lang; Frankfurt: Peter Lang, 1973); Keener, *Acts*, 2:1097–99.

70. See, e.g., George Johnston, "Christ as Archegos," *NTS* 27 (1981): 381–85; J. Julius Scott Jr., "*Archēgos* in the Salvation History of the Epistle to the Hebrews," *JETS* 29 (1986): 47–54.

71. Wilckens, *Missionsreden der Apostelgeschichte*, 174; cf. Hans Conzelmann, *The Theology of Saint Luke*, trans. Geoffrey Buswell (London: Faber and Faber, 1960), 204–6; Rackham, *Acts of the Apostles*, 52.

72. See also Paul Ellingworth, *The Epistle to the Hebrews*, NIGTC (Grand Rapids: Eerdmans, 1993), 159; Keener, *Acts*, 2:1098; Anderson, *"But God Raised Him from the Dead,"* 225; Müller, ΧΡΙΣΤΟΣ ΑΡΧΗΓΟΣ, 256–57; Rackham, *Acts of the Apostles*, 52.

73. Geerhardus Vos, "The Priesthood of Christ in the Epistle to the Hebrews," in *Redemptive History and Biblical Interpretation: The Shorter Writings of Geerhardus Vos*, ed. Richard B. Gaffin Jr. (Phillipsburg, NJ: P&R, 1980), 133. Contrast Colin Hickling, "John and Hebrews: The Background of Hebrews 2:10–18," *NTS* 29 (1983): 113.

74. See also *2 Clem.* 20:5, where Jesus is identified as the *sōtēra kai archēgon tēs aphtharsias* ("Savior and Founder of immortality"). Cf. Müller, ΧΡΙΣΤΟΣ ΑΡΧΗΓΟΣ, 92–102, for a discussion of *archēgos* in early Christian texts.

of life."[75] Either way the emphasis falls on Jesus's authority over life and his solidarity with his people as the one who has emerged victorious over death through his resurrection.[76] All told, *archēgos* is a christological title that emphasizes the resurrection.

The logic of Jesus's resurrection may also help explain Peter's curious comment in 3:12 that the people should not be amazed by the healing of the lame man. Surely it was unusual and amazing for a man who was lame from birth suddenly to jump up and begin walking about the temple! But the logic of Peter's response reveals that he is shifting the focus from the formerly lame man to Jesus, whose glorification is far more impressive and consequential than anything Peter himself could do (cf. v. 23). If the greater is true—if Jesus has been raised from the dead (vv. 13, 15)—then one should not be surprised at the lesser: that a man could be healed who was lame from birth (v. 12). The latter is, to be sure, quite impressive, but is not as impressive or consequential as the resurrection of Jesus from the dead.

In what follows, Peter mentions the scriptural necessity that the Christ should suffer (3:18), even as his call to repentance assumes the resurrection (mentioned in vv. 13, 15). In addition, the phrase "times of refreshing . . . from the presence of the Lord" (v. 20),[77] which has often proven to be an opaque reference, is tethered to the return of Christ Jesus (v. 21) and the forgiveness of sins (v. 19). The future return of Jesus is another indication of the present, living status of the crucified one (cf. v. 18), and Jesus's location in relation to the *prosōpou tou theou* ("presence of God") and the statement that heaven must receive him (*hon dei ouranon men dexasthai*) for a given time (v. 21) further refer to Jesus's resurrected, living status, as Peter explained earlier in his exposition of Psalm 110 (Acts 2:33–35).

The duration of Jesus's heavenly reign is related more specifically to the times of the restoration of all things (*achri chronōn apokatastaseōs pantōn*, 3:21). The hapax legomenon *apokatastaseōs* has generated much discussion—

---

75. See, e.g., Müller, *ΧΡΙΣΤΟΣ ΑΡΧΗΓΟΣ*, 111–13, 255–58; Donald L. Jones, "The Title 'Author of Life (Leader)' in the Acts of the Apostles," *Society of Biblical Literature 1994 Seminar Papers*, SBLSP 33 (Atlanta: Society of Biblical Literature, 1994), 627–36; Hamm, "Acts 3:12–26," 202–3; for "champion," see Lane, *Hebrews 1–8*, 56–57. Anderson (*"But God Raised Him from the Dead,"* 224–26) understands the term to encompass leader, author, and champion.

76. There may also be echoes here of the exodus; Jesus himself connects his death to the exodus in Luke 9:31, in a context that anticipates his resurrection. The connections to the exodus would be in light of the Mosaic typology of the related term *archōn* ("ruler"), found in some texts (cf. Exod. 2:14 LXX; Acts 7:35). For these possibilities, see Keener, *Acts*, 2:1098; Müller, *ΧΡΙΣΤΟΣ ΑΡΧΗΓΟΣ*, 38.

77. Here *kyrios* refers to God the Father; see, e.g., Fitzmyer, *Acts of the Apostles*, 288.

what sort of *restoration* is in view?[78] One viable option is that it pertains to the reconstitution of Israel (cf. 1:6).[79] To be sure, Israel's reconstitution seems to be part of the blessings in view, as I have argued earlier in relation to Acts 2. However, on balance it is best here, especially in light of *pantōn* ("of all things"), to consider the restoration more broadly than only the restoration of Israel.[80] It refers to the restoration of all creation, which has been ruined by sin. The raising of the lame man thus anticipates the restoration of all things,[81] and this cosmic restoration is indissolubly tied to the resurrection of Christ.[82]

The reasons for relating the reconstitution of all things to the resurrection of Jesus are several.[83] First, Peter has already emphasized the resurrection of Jesus (3:13, 15), and he concludes by returning again to the resurrection (v. 26). Peter's sermon is thus christological through and through, and the key christological event in the sermon is the resurrection of Jesus. This is also consistent with the ongoing work of the risen and exalted Jesus, who healed the lame man. Second, the restoration of all things is necessary because of the deathly effects of sin (seen, for example, even in the lack of wholeness of the lame man; cf. Isa. 35:6).[84] There is an ethical problem with the universe due to the presence of sin, and that problem affects all of creation (including the man who could not walk).[85] But sin has been overcome through the resurrection of the Righteous One—the *archēgos* of life (Acts 3:14–15)—in whose name the lame man is healed (v. 16) and sins are blotted out (v. 19), and who will bring times of refreshing and the restoration of all things (vv. 20–21). This all depends on Jesus's resurrection.

Third, the restoration of all things is new-creational imagery, and the resurrection of Jesus marks the inauguration of new creation. The language of

---

78. See BDAG, "ἀποκατάστασις," 112.

79. Keener, *Acts*, 2:1111–12; Bauckham, "Restoration of Israel," 361–65.

80. See also Peterson, *Acts of the Apostles*, 182. Though Keener argues that 3:21 is mostly about Israel (*Acts*, 2:1112), he also notes the frequent associations of Israel's restoration with cosmic renewal. Cf. Richard Bauckham, *James*, NTR (London: Routledge, 1999), 105: "The renewal of Israel is the representative beginning of God's new creation of all things."

81. See Johnson, *Message of Acts*, 64–65; Hamm, "Acts 3:12–26," 210–11.

82. See also Beale, *New Testament Biblical Theology*, 139–40; Hans F. Bayer, "Christ-Centered Eschatology in Act 3:17–26," in *Jesus of Nazareth—Lord and Christ: Essays on the Historical Jesus and New Testament Christology*, ed. Joel B. Green and Max Turner (Grand Rapids: Eerdmans, 1994), 241–42.

83. See also Johnson, *Message of Acts*, 150–51.

84. Noted by, among others, Johnson, *Message of Acts*, 64–65; Peterson, *Acts of the Apostles*, 182; Hamm, "Acts 3:12–26," 200–201.

85. See, e.g., Herman Bavinck, *Reformed Dogmatics*, ed. John Bolt, trans. John Vriend, 4 vols. (Grand Rapids: Baker Academic, 2003–8), 3:710; cf. 3:423.

apokatastasis in 3:21 recalls other texts that evoke new-creational imagery—such as *palingenesia* ("regeneration") in Matthew 19:28—and that have creational connotations.[86] As C. K. Barrett has argued, the use of *apokatastasis* "implies a creation that has diverged from the condition in which it was intended to be; it is perverted and must be put right."[87] The way the world is "put right" or restored is through Jesus, who has been raised from the dead and continues to act as the exalted Lord who will return in the future.[88] The creational connotations of *apokatastasis* thus also recall the original created order in the days of Adam, whose sin led to the need for restoration.[89] Significantly, Jesus's resurrection is often related to his status as the last Adam in early Christianity.[90] As last Adam, Jesus possesses everlasting, glorious life, which stands in contrast to the entrance of sin and death through Adam's sin. Thus Paul argues that Christ's resurrection is the firstfruits of new creation, which overcomes the sin of Adam (1 Cor. 15:20–28, 45–49).[91] This is further related to the granting of the Holy Spirit (1 Cor. 15:45; 2 Cor. 3:17; cf. John 20:22), which is likewise related in Acts to the authority of the resurrected and exalted Christ. Paul's new-creational imagery, in conjunction with the language of firstfruits, corroborates the linkage of the renewal of creation to the resurrection of Christ in Acts.[92] This new-creational aspect is also consistent with the message of the holy prophets mentioned in Acts 3:21, since numerous prophetic texts speak of a cosmic renewal (e.g., Isa. 35:1–10; 65:17; 66:22; cf. *1 En.* 45:4–5; 96:3; *4 Ezra* 7:75; 13:26).[93]

Fourth, the restoration of all things in Acts 3:21 is related to the resurrection of Jesus because the coming age will see the eternal, messianic kingdom, which will coincide with the renewal of creation.[94] Peter in 2:22–36 argues for

---

86. So, e.g., Bruce, *Acts of the Apostles*, 112; Bock, *Acts*, 177; Fitzmyer, *Acts of the Apostles*, 289; Peterson, *Acts of the Apostles*, 182; Marguerat, *Actes des Apôtres*, 1:133. This imagery is not Stoic (nor is 2 Pet. 3:10); see Keener, *Acts*, 2:1110–12.

87. Barrett, *Commentary on the Acts*, 1:206.

88. See also Beale, *New Testament Biblical Theology*, 139–40.

89. Cf. the option noted by Keener (*Acts*, 2:1111): "What was ruined in Adam could be restored in the eschatological time." Keener also notes that this language in a Jewish context applies to the time of resurrection.

90. See Crowe, *Last Adam*, esp. 192–97; cf. Luke 3:38; Peter J. Scaer, "Resurrection as Justification in the Book of Acts," *CTQ* 70 (2006): 226–28.

91. See further Richard B. Gaffin Jr., *The Centrality of the Resurrection: A Study in Paul's Soteriology* (Grand Rapids: Baker, 1978), 78–92.

92. Cf. Gaffin, *Centrality of the Resurrection*, 39–40; Bock, *Acts*, 177; see also Rom. 8:18–23 (a text noted by Bock and many others).

93. Fitzmyer, *Acts of the Apostles*, 289; Bruce, *Acts of the Apostles*, 112; Keener, *Acts*, 2:1111; Peterson, *Acts of the Apostles*, 182; Johnson, *Message of Acts*, 65.

94. See, e.g., Bruce, *Acts of the Apostles*, 112; cf. Bruce, *The Book of Acts*, NICNT (Grand Rapids: Eerdmans, 1988), 85.

an everlasting, Davidic kingdom on the basis of the resurrection of Jesus. In chapter 3 he adds the dimension of the renewal of all things, but this is not separate from the lasting, messianic kingdom. This is again consistent with Paul's discussion of the resurrection and the lasting, messianic kingdom in 1 Corinthians 15:20–28, 42–58. Thus Paul writes in 15:24, "Then comes the end, when [Christ] delivers the kingdom to God the Father after destroying every rule and every authority and power" (ESV).[95] In sum, understanding the restoration of all things in Acts 3:21 to hinge upon the resurrection of Jesus fits snugly in the flow of thought of Peter's speech and is consistent with Paul's theology as well.

THE RAISING UP OF A PROPHET LIKE MOSES (3:22–26)

A transition in Peter's sermon comes in 3:22, where he provides more scriptural rationale for his argument. Returning to the servant imagery (which frames this speech), Peter again points to Moses, the servant of the Lord. Peter quotes Deuteronomy 18:15, 18–19, that the Lord would raise up (*anastēsei*) a prophet like Moses, to whom the people shall listen (Acts 3:23–26). The language of *raising* is particularly likely in this context of Acts 3 to evoke the raising of Jesus from the dead for at least four reasons.[96]

First, this statement is found in a context in which Peter expounds the resurrection of Jesus (cf. 3:13–21). Second, in 3:26 Peter explains that God has raised up (*anastēsas*) Jesus (from the dead), which explains the way in which the raising up of a prophet like Moses in Deuteronomy 18 is fulfilled.[97] Third, Deuteronomy 18:15 is also echoed in Luke 9:35 to underscore the eschatological message and mission of Jesus on the mount of transfiguration.[98] The transfiguration of Jesus is organically tied to—indeed it is a preview of—Jesus's exalted, resurrected state. Jesus is the glorious, authoritative one to whom the people (including Moses and Elijah) must listen. Luke thus provides several indications that the application of Deuteronomy 18 to Jesus entails Jesus being raised up—from the dead—as the bearer of eschatological

---

95. Likewise, Eph. 1:10 speaks of the summing up, or recapitulation (*anakephalaiōsis*), of all things in Christ, in association with his exaltation in the heavenly places (cf. 1:20–23). This argument likely also entails Adamic imagery (cf. Ps. 8).

96. See also O'Toole, "Some Observations on *Anistēmi*," 85–92; Jacques Dupont, *Nouvelles études sur les Actes des Apôtres*, LD 118 (Paris: Cerf, 1984), 75.

97. Hamm ("Acts 3:12–26," 213–14) suggests a double entendre here; cf. Wright, *Resurrection of the Son of God*, 454; Richard B. Hays, *Echoes of Scripture in the Gospels* (Waco: Baylor University Press, 2016), 219. *Pace* Wilckens, *Missionsreden der Apostelgeschichte*, 163; Barrett, *Commentary on the Acts*, 1:213.

98. And it is only in Luke 9:35 among the synoptic parallels that the word order *autou akouete* ("to him you will listen") mirrors the word order in Deut. 18:15 LXX, as also does Acts 3:22.

life and glory. Fourth, as with earlier speeches, the emphasis on Jesus's resurrection is designed to elicit a response. In this case, Peter explains that the raising up of Jesus is designed for blessing, that the covenant people might repent (3:26).[99] Yet, as we see in the next few verses, not everyone is favorably disposed to this resurrection message.

The Resurrection and the Sanhedrin (Acts 4–5)

THE RESURRECTION AND THE SANHEDRIN, PART 1: 4:1–31

The preaching of Peter leads to opposition, as we see with the Sadducees beginning in 4:1. The response of the Sadducees—and Peter's response to the Sadducees—draws further attention to the resurrection of Jesus. In verse 2 the Sadducees are greatly annoyed[100] by the preaching of the apostles, because they were preaching in Jesus the resurrection of the dead. Whether this last phrase means that the Sadducees' frustrations were because the apostles were preaching that Jesus had been resurrected from the dead or because they were preaching that in Jesus the general resurrection had begun[101]—either way the Sadducees resisted the resurrection preaching. Acts 4:2 thus confirms what we have already seen in Acts—namely, that Peter consistently emphasizes the resurrection of Jesus in his speeches. O'Toole correctly observes that the logic of 4:1–2 requires that the apostles had already been speaking about the resurrection.[102]

Here it will be helpful to recount briefly some of what we know about first-century Sadducees, especially since Acts 4 is not the only context in which Luke recounts a conflict with the Sadducees over the issue of the resurrection. Most important is the Sadducees' denial of the doctrine of the resurrection.[103]

---

99. Note *prōton* in 3:26, which reflects the movement of the gospel in Acts (i.e., from Jerusalem to the ends of the earth). See similarly Peterson, *Acts of the Apostles*, 185.

100. Thus reading *diaponoumenoi* (see BDAG, "διαπονέομαι," 235; Barrett, *Commentary on the Acts*, 1:219). The term found in D (*kataponoumenoi*) is stronger ("being tormented"; see BDAG, "καταπονέω," 525), though it is likely secondary.

101. The phrasing is ambiguous if one reads (with NA[28] and *ECM*) *katangellein en tō Iēsou tēn anastasin tēn ek nekrōn* ("proclaiming in Jesus the resurrection of the dead"). D reads: *anangellein ton Iēsoun en tē anastasei tōn nekrōn* ("proclaiming Jesus in his resurrection from the dead"). See also Barrett, *Commentary on the Acts*, 1:219–20.

102. O'Toole, "Some Observations on *Anistēmi*," 91–92 (noting especially Acts 3:22, 26).

103. See Josephus, *J.W.* 2.164–66; *Ant.* 18.16; N. T. Wright, *The New Testament and the People of God*, COQG 1 (Minneapolis: Fortress, 1992), 211–12; Wright, *Resurrection of the Son of God*, 131–40; Keener, *Acts*, 2:1129–32; Anthony J. Saldarini, *Pharisees, Scribes and Sadducees in Palestinian Society: A Sociological Approach* (Wilmington, DE: Glazier, 1988), esp. 298–308; Roland Deines, *Der Pharisäer: Ihr Verständnis im Spiegel der christlichen und jüdischen Forschung seit Wellhausen und Graetz*, WUNT 1/101 (Tübingen: Mohr Siebeck, 1997), 551; Daniel Marguerat, "Quand la résurrection se fait clef de lecture de l'histoire (Luc-Actes),"

This is stated explicitly in Luke 20:[104] the Sadducees, who deny there is a resurrection (v. 27),[105] try to trap Jesus with a reductio ad absurdum pertaining to levirate marriage and the resurrection (vv. 28–40). In Acts 4 the issues are even less theoretical: no longer is the debate about what might be in a hypothetical scenario; now the issue is whether the same Jesus who bested the Sadducees on the question of the resurrection (Luke 20:40) has himself *already, actually* been raised from the dead. Given the Sadducees' denial of the resurrection, as manifested in prior encounters with Jesus himself, it is not surprising that they are disturbed at the resurrection focus of the apostolic preaching.

This brings us to the apostles' arrest by the priestly leadership (cf. Acts 4:3). In response to the question of the authority by which the lame man was healed (cf. 3:1–10), Peter announces that the man was healed in the name of Jesus Christ of Nazareth (4:10). We have seen that *Christ* in Acts is understood as the ruler over the everlasting, Davidic kingdom. This is reconfirmed in Peter's speech that identifies Jesus Christ of Nazareth as the crucified and resurrected one (4:10).[106] Here Peter adds that Jesus's resurrection fulfills Psalm 118:22: the stone rejected by the builders has become the cornerstone (cf. Luke 20:17–18). This is another example of a psalm being used messianically, again in relation to the resurrection. The rejected stone corresponds to the crucifixion of the Messiah, and his becoming (*genomenos*) the cornerstone corresponds to his resurrection.[107] Building on this resurrection interpretation of Psalm 118, in 4:12 Peter sums up his argument: there is no other source for salvation apart from the resurrected Jesus. Moreover, it is intriguing that Peter speaks specifically of no other name *under heaven* among men by which we must (*dei*) be saved. On the one hand, "under heaven" may simply refer to all of

---

in *Resurrection of the Dead: Biblical Traditions in Dialogue*, ed. Geert Van Oyen and Tom Shepherd, BETL 249 (Leuven: Peters, 2012), 187; cf. C. D. Elledge, *Resurrection of the Dead in Early Judaism 200 BCE–CE 200* (Oxford: Oxford University Press, 2017), 102, interacting with Hippolytus, *Haer.* 9.24.

104. So Keener, *Acts*, 2:1129.

105. There is a text-critical question in Luke 20:27: Is the best reading *legontes* or *antilegontes*? James R. Edwards, *The Gospel according to St. Luke*, PNTC (Grand Rapids: Eerdmans, 2015), 576n79; Michael Wolter, *The Gospel according to Luke*, trans. Wayne Coppins and Christoph Heilig, 2 vols., BMSEC (Waco: Baylor University Press, 2016–17), 2:399, argue that *antilegontes* is the more difficult reading and therefore the better one. Either way, the presence of *mē einai* shows that the Sadducees do not believe in the resurrection.

106. Willie James Jennings (*Acts*, Belief [Louisville: Westminster John Knox, 2017], 47) avers that Peter, who again emphasizes the death and resurrection of Jesus, "has become like the great jazz master, Louis Armstrong. He states the melody and reveals the primordial blues structure that will become the home for endless variations, ever new but always familiar."

107. See I. Howard Marshall, "Acts," in *Commentary on the New Testament Use of the Old Testament*, ed. G. K. Beale and D. A. Carson (Grand Rapids: Baker Academic, 2007), 551; cf. 1 Pet. 2:4–8.

creation (cf. 2:5).[108] However, given the emphasis on the exalted, heavenly reign of Christ throughout Acts (e.g., 1:10–11; 2:34; 3:21; 7:55–56), could this be a contrast between the heavenly source of salvation and all other possibilities?[109] If so, it would again emphasize the exalted, reigning status of Jesus. Either way, Peter's speech in Acts 4 demonstrates that salvation is only found in the name of the risen, exalted Jesus.[110]

Peter's logic can thus be summarized: because only Jesus has been raised from the dead, salvation is only found in the name of Jesus. Indeed, the *name* of Jesus continues to draw attention in the response of the Jerusalem leadership, as the apostles are instructed not to preach or teach any further in the *name* of Jesus.[111] The response of Peter and John in 4:20 again recalls the task of the apostles as eyewitnesses of the resurrection (cf. 1:21–22): *ou dynametha gar hēmeis ha eidamen kai ēkousamen mē lalein* ("for we are unable *not* to speak [about] what we have seen and heard").

Following this encounter, Jesus is again spoken of as the servant (*pais*) in the prayer of 4:24–31 (cf. vv. 27, 30). I argued that in Acts 3, Jesus as *pais* recalls Jesus's anointed status as Christ (cf. 4:26)—the Davidic king who reigns over an everlasting kingdom. Jesus is the holy and righteous *pais* whose resurrection means that he is innocent of the charges that led to his death. He is therefore raised from death to rule over the Davidic kingdom forever. Ironically, though the Sadducees denied the resurrection of the body, their actions led directly to the resurrection-vindication of God's Messiah—even as they joined forces with the gentiles (4:27; cf. Luke 22:66)![112] Jesus's ongoing activity is further evident in the renewed filling of the believers by the Holy Spirit in the place of prayer (Acts 4:31), since the risen, exalted Lord Jesus pours out the Spirit.

Luke provides a fitting summary in 4:33: the apostles were, with great power, testifying to the resurrection of the Lord Jesus.

THE RESURRECTION AND THE SANHEDRIN, PART 2: 5:17–42

Further conflict with the Sadducees comes in Acts 5, where the apostles are arrested for preaching about the risen Jesus (5:17–18; cf. 4:19–20). The

---

108. So, e.g., Barrett, *Commentary on the Acts*, 232; Peterson, *Acts of the Apostles*, 192.

109. See also John Calvin, *Commentary upon the Acts of the Apostles*, ed. Henry Beveridge, 2 vols. (repr., Grand Rapids: Baker, 2003), 1:174–75; Matthew Sleeman, *Geography and the Ascension Narrative in Acts*, SNTSMS 146 (Cambridge: Cambridge University Press, 2009), 96.

110. O'Toole, "Activity of the Risen Jesus," 487–91. See also Acts 4:17–18.

111. Thompson (*Acts of the Risen Lord Jesus*, 159) suggests that *name* in Acts refers to "the active presence of Jesus in the fullness of his character as the means of receiving God's blessing."

112. So, e.g., Peterson, *Acts of the Apostles*, 200.

Sadducees' opposition is again due in large measure to the message of the resurrection. "The name" in which they accuse the apostles of teaching (5:28) must be the name of the risen Lord Jesus (cf. 2:38; 3:16; 4:10–12, 17–18, 30). This is further supported in 5:20 by the message of the angel, who led the apostles out of prison and instructed them to teach "all the words of this Life" (*panta ta rhēmata tēs zōēs tautēs*). As my translation indicates, *tēs zōēs tautēs* is perhaps best taken as a christological title for Jesus, who is earlier identified as the Leader (*archēgos*) of life (3:15).[113]

The apostolic response again focuses explicitly on the resurrection of Jesus. The apostles must obey God and speak about the resurrection of Jesus from the dead (5:29–30). God has raised (*egeirein*) Jesus from the dead and exalted him—the Leader (*archēgos*) and Savior—to his right hand (v. 31). As in 3:15, *archēgos* is used in 5:31 for Jesus in association with life (cf. v. 20) and the resurrection. Building on *archēgos* in 3:15, in 5:31 the apostles portray Jesus as the one who has defeated death and is therefore qualified to be Savior (cf. 4:10–12). Further confirming this resurrection focus of the apostles' response, they again speak of their role as *witnesses* (5:32; cf. 1:21–22). They are witnesses *to the resurrection of Jesus*.[114]

Earlier (in 4:2) the Sadducees were disturbed by the message of the resurrection. In 5:33 their reaction is even more visceral: the members from among the council were now furious (*dieprionto*) and wanted to kill the apostles. It is at this point that a Pharisee—no less than Gamaliel[115]—speaks up to fight back the fury of retribution. One gets the sense from Gamaliel's response—especially in light of what we know about the Pharisees (cf. 23:8)[116]—that Gamaliel is not a priori against the possibility that a dead man has been raised. Instead, his message is "wait and see." The language used by Gamaliel for false messiahs in Acts is further suggestive of the resurrection, since he speaks of the rising up (*anestē*) of Judas the Galilean (cf. 3:22). Here we have another Galilean figure who rose up but whose movement came to nothing because he perished (*apōleto*). It may therefore be that the rising up of Judas the Galilean—who did not rise from the dead—is contrasted with Jesus the Galilean,[117] who,

---

113. Cf. Fitzmyer, *Acts of the Apostles*, 9, 335; Rackham, *Acts of the Apostles*, 72. See, however, Acts 13:26, where "the word of this salvation" (*ho logos tēs sōtērias tautēs*) does not appear to be a christological title (cf. Keener, *Acts*, 2:1212).

114. Cf. Marguerat, *Actes des Apôtres*, 1:197; Ridderbos, *Speeches of Peter*, 17.

115. Rabban Gamaliel I, identified in Acts 22:3 as Paul's former teacher. See further Keener, *Acts*, 2:1222–23; 3:3215–20; Barrett, *Commentary on the Acts*, 1:292.

116. See, e.g., Keener, *Acts*, 2:1225–27.

117. In Acts Jesus is frequently identified as being from Nazareth, a town in Galilee. For Jesus's connection to Galilee most explicitly, see Acts 10:37; 13:31, and also the disciples in 1:11; 2:7.

though he died, was raised from the dead. And instead of Jesus's followers being scattered, like those of Judas the Galilean, they were first regathered in Jerusalem (cf. 2:5) before spreading out as bearers of the gospel message (cf. 1:8).[118] The apostles preached Jesus as the Messiah (5:42), and this message is predicated on the resurrection of Jesus, who reigns as the risen king.

The Resurrected Jesus Is Lord of All (Acts 10–11)

The next major Petrine speech comes in the encounter with Cornelius in Acts 10. This marks the gospel's advance among the gentiles (cf. 1:8) and thus a major turning point in both the narrative of Acts and the history of salvation.[119] I am particularly interested in Peter's exposition in 10:34–48, a speech in which he explains to Cornelius and those gathered the significance of Jesus of Nazareth. Peter begins with a phrase that is likely familiar to readers of the Scriptures today but that would have been a bombshell to the first (Jewish) disciples: truly, there is no partiality with God (*ep' alētheias katalambanomai hoti ouk estin prosōpolēmptēs ho theos*). The rest of Peter's speech teases out the rationale for this statement, which has much to do with the resurrection of Jesus.[120]

In 10:36 Peter speaks of Jesus Christ, whom he identifies as the one preeminently anointed with the Holy Spirit and power (v. 38). Though we do not know all that Cornelius and those gathered with him would have understood by the term *Christos*, it is clear for readers of Acts that it entails the kingship of the risen Jesus, who reigns over the everlasting Davidic kingdom. This perspective is further underscored in verse 36 when Peter proclaims that Jesus is Lord of

118. Though many disciples will be dispersed later (8:1, 4; 11:19), this is only after a foundational regathering. Further, the twelve apostles collectively are not dispersed (see Fuller, *Restoration of Israel*, 257–64; cf. Thompson, *Acts of the Risen Lord Jesus*, 103–24).

119. Some have identified the Ethiopian eunuch in Acts 8 as the first gentile believer in Jesus (cf. Eusebius, *Hist. eccl.* 2.1.13, noted in Fitzmyer, *Acts of the Apostles*, 410). However, given the historical connections between the Ethiopians and the Israelites, it is best to see the Ethiopian eunuch's conversion as anticipating the fuller inclusion of the gentiles; even more likely, he represents the marginalized among worshipers of God (Isa. 56:3–8). See further Fitzmyer, *Acts of the Apostles*, 412; Peterson, *Acts of the Apostles*, 291, following Luke Timothy Johnson, *The Acts of the Apostles*, SP 5 (Collegeville, MN: Liturgical Press, 1992), 160; see also Robert Louis Wilken, *The First Thousand Years: A Global History of Christianity* (New Haven: Yale University Press, 2012), 214–21.

120. Dennis J. Horton (*Death and Resurrection: The Shape and Function of a Literary Motif in the Book of Acts* [Eugene, OR: Pickwick, 2009], 74–77) has argued that Acts 10:24–48 portrays Cornelius's conversion as a death and resurrection, recalling Jesus's death and resurrection. Thus, Cornelius falls down at Peter's feet (10:25), recalling Ananias and Sapphira, who also fell at Peter's feet (5:5, 10). But in contrast to them, Peter raises (*ēgeiren . . . anastēthi*, 10:26) Cornelius to new life. I discuss Cornelius in more detail in ch. 6.

all (*houtos estin panton kyrios*). The lordship of Christ would likely have been viewed (especially to a Roman centurion) as antithetical to Caesar's purported lordship.[121] As universal Lord, Jesus rules over all that Caesar rules—and more. Additionally, the universal lordship of Christ is tightly tied to the logic of verse 34: because Christ is the universal Lord, it does not matter from what nation (or religious background) a person comes; it makes no difference what foods one eats. For the *people*—and not just the foods—that have previously been viewed as unclean have now been deemed acceptable in God's sight (cf. v. 28).[122] And the logic of this universality is also tightly tied to the resurrection of Jesus: Jesus is universal Lord, a truth demonstrated by his resurrection from the dead and heavenly reign.[123] The resurrection of Jesus therefore explains in large measure why and how the gospel goes to the gentiles: Jesus is not only Lord over Israel but Lord over all nations and peoples.[124]

Peter speaks even more explicitly about the resurrection in 10:39–42. The reference to the apostles as witnesses (*martyres*) in verse 39 seems to refer to the public ministry of Jesus, though the same language in verse 41 more obviously refers to the resurrection. Indeed, in 10:40 Peter draws explicit attention to the fact that God raised Jesus from the dead on the third day, and the resurrected Jesus appeared to the apostles who were designated witnesses.[125] Peter further connects the resurrection to a familiar theme in Acts: the resurrected Jesus—who is Lord of all—is set apart by God to be the judge of the living and the dead (v. 42; cf. 17:30–31).

In light of this emphasis on the resurrection to Cornelius and on the need for Peter to travel in person to bring this message to him and his associates, a further possibility arises. It appears that Cornelius was aware, at least to some degree, of the message of peace through Jesus (10:36) and possibly also of the powerful ministry of Jesus (vv. 37–38). Yet it appears that Cornelius was not well informed about the significant events of the end of Jesus's life, particularly his death and resurrection.[126] Both these elements are important for the gospel message that Peter delivers to Cornelius.[127] Moreover, Peter's

---

121. See C. Kavin Rowe, *World Upside Down: Reading Acts in the Graeco-Roman Age* (Oxford: Oxford University Press, 2009), 112.

122. See Mark 7:18–19; cf. Johnson, *Acts of the Apostles*, 190.

123. See also Marguerat, "Quand la résurrection," 199.

124. See further the discussion in ch. 5.

125. The corporeal nature of the resurrection is evident in Jesus's eating and drinking with his disciples (Acts 10:41); cf. Ign., *Smyrn.* 3.3.

126. Cf. Jervell, *Theology of the Acts*, 77; Jervell, *Apostelgeschichte*, 312.

127. Let it not be said that Luke's theology has no room for the cross. Here is one of the several places where we see that the death of Christ, and not *only* his resurrection, is important. For more on the relation between these, see the next chapter, on Acts 13.

speech ends with the reality of Christ as the risen judge of the living and the dead, in whose name repentance and forgiveness are found (vv. 42–43). Thus, for Cornelius to have an adequate apprehension of Jesus and his work, he must understand Jesus's death and resurrection and the coming judgment.[128]

Additionally, throughout Acts the results of Jesus's resurrection and ascension include the outpouring of the Holy Spirit. The outpouring of the Holy Spirit on the Jews who had gathered in Jerusalem for the day of Pentecost fulfills the covenantal promises to Abraham. Yet in 10:44–47 even the *gentiles* receive the Spirit—a shocking development to the circumcised believers who accompanied Peter. This underscores the theological insight of verses 28 and 34: truly there is no partiality with God. The risen, heavenly Lord pours out his Spirit even on the gentiles.[129]

The Resurrected Lord Delivers Peter (Acts 12)

Though it does not feature an extended exposition of the resurrection, the account of Peter's deliverance from prison in Acts 12 may contain echoes of the resurrection. The context is again Passover in Jerusalem (cf. Luke 22:1–23), and Peter (not unlike Jesus a few years before)[130] is seized by another Herod (Herod Agrippa I) and faces the prospect of death (Acts 12:1–2; cf. v. 19).[131] But instead of being brought out (for execution; see v. 4), Peter is delivered from prison by an angel. Thus the fate of Peter in this scenario is different from that of Jesus (who was not spared execution), even as the language recalls Jesus's own resurrection (*ēgeiren . . . anasta en tachei*, v. 7).[132] More specifically, it is an angel *from the Lord* that delivered Peter (vv. 7, 11, 17), and in this context "the Lord" may refer to Jesus himself—the resurrected Lord who continues to act powerfully from heaven. In contrast to the glorious

128. This may also be true of the statement in 10:36—Jesus is Lord of all by means of his resurrection and ascension, and this is likely also news to Cornelius.

129. Baptism is thus in the name of the *risen Christ*, who pours out his Spirit, and it is the *risen* Christ who commands baptism in Matt. 28:18–20.

130. The date of this event is likely sometime in 41–44—the date of Herod Agrippa I's reign (so Schnabel, *Acts*, 535). See further Fitzmyer, *Acts of the Apostles*, 486; Barrett, *Commentary on the Acts*, 1:592; Peterson, *Acts of the Apostles*, 368.

131. Note the violence of 12:1 and the comment that one of the apostles had already been killed (12:2).

132. Cf. Marguerat, "Quand la résurrection," 202; Horton, *Death and Resurrection*, 40–45; Johnson, *Acts of the Apostles*, 218–19; Michael D. Goulder, *Type and History in Acts* (London: SPCK, 1964), 43–44. It is possible that *pleuran* (side) in Acts 12:7 recalls traditional language about the side of Jesus, pierced at his death yet visible in his resurrected state (cf. John 19:34; 20:20, 25, 27).

reign of Christ (and indeed in contrast to the deliverance of Peter), the power of Herod Agrippa is portrayed as that of an ungodly ruler who takes counsel against the anointed Davidic king (cf. Ps. 2:1; Acts 4:27–28).[133] Herod carries himself as though he were a god (12:22) but is overtaken by a painful death (vv. 21–23; cf. Josephus, *Ant.* 19.343–51).[134] Herod—who is eaten by worms—is emphatically *not* Lord of all.[135] Instead, the risen Jesus, who continues to guide and protect his church, reigns supreme.

Peter's Final Speech: Salvation through the Lord Jesus (Acts 15:7–11)

Peter's final speech—and final appearance—comes at the Jerusalem Council in Acts 15:7–11. At stake is the role of the gentiles in the nascent church: to what degree must they follow the law of Moses to be full members (vv. 1–5)? Key for Peter's message is the encounter with Cornelius recorded in Acts 10. At the Jerusalem Council Peter explains that God has fully accepted the gentiles, as demonstrated by the outpouring of the Spirit on them. If the gentiles have received the covenant blessing of the Spirit, then they have equal standing alongside Jewish believers. This is the Spirit poured out by the risen Jesus (1:5; 2:33).

The clincher for Peter's sermon comes in 15:11: "But we believe that we will be saved through the grace of the Lord Jesus in the same way that they will" (*alla dia tēs charitos tou kyriou Iēsou pisteuomen sōthēnai kath' hon tropon kakeinoi*). Regardless of whether the "they" refers to gentiles or the more recent antecedent of "our fathers" in verse 10,[136] salvation is here linked to the lordship of Christ—the only one in whose name we can be saved, as Peter earlier proclaimed in 4:12. Additionally, the cleansing of the gentiles' hearts by faith (15:9) recalls similar statements made by Peter that relate forgiveness and cleansing to the resurrected status of Jesus (cf. 2:38; 5:30–31; 10:39–43).

In sum, though the final speech of Peter does not lay out all the details of the resurrection, its force is cumulative: readers of Acts have by this point encountered several Petrine speeches, which consistently draw attention to the resurrection of Jesus and its implications. This final Petrine speech is more

133. It is not coincidental that in 4:27 another Herod is explicitly mentioned—Herod Antipas (cf. Luke 23:7–12).

134. See Barrett, *Commentary on the Acts*, 1:590.

135. See Johnson, *Message of Acts*, 204–6. If the reference to worms (12:23) alludes to the wrathful worm of Isa. 66:24, this would evoke an important OT context pertaining to resurrection (66:22–24). Cf. Beale, *New Testament Biblical Theology*, 231–32.

136. See my discussion of this point in ch. 6.

occasional, dealing with the issue of gentile inclusion.[137] Peter's discussion of
the gentiles in Acts 15 recalls his earlier conviction regarding the full inclusion
of the gentiles (see 10:28, 34), which stems from his understanding that the
risen Jesus is Lord of all (vv. 36–43).

Conclusion

The Petrine passages in Acts demonstrate a strong and consistent focus on
the resurrection of Jesus. Already in Acts 1, Peter's first speech recognizes the
unique role of the apostles as eyewitnesses of the resurrection (vv. 21–22). In
Peter's first major sermon, at Pentecost—which lays out much of the theology
Acts—he makes much of Jesus's resurrection. Jesus's victory over death fulfills
Scripture and explains the outpouring of the Holy Spirit. As the message of
Jesus takes hold in Jerusalem, the apostles emphasize the reality of the resurrection of Jesus. The healing of the lame man occasions the explanation of
how the resurrected Jesus—the one who has been raised up as a prophet like
Moses—will lead to the restoration not just of one man but of all things. The
Sadducees object specifically to the message of the resurrection. Twice when
speaking of life Peter refers to Jesus as *archēgos*, which is a term particularly
suited to speak of Jesus's resurrection. Peter further recognizes that the reason
the gospel goes to the gentiles is that Jesus is Lord of all, and this by virtue
of his resurrection and ascension.

The resurrection is central to the Petrine passages of Acts. And as we will
see in the next chapter, the resurrection is key for the presentation of Paul
in Acts as well.

---

137. I will have more to say about the Jerusalem Council, and James in particular, in ch. 4.

$$3$$

"The Hope of Israel"

Paul and the Resurrection

I argued in the previous chapter that Peter's Pentecost speech was a major resurrection pillar in Acts. We now turn to the presentation of Paul in Acts. Here we find two additional major resurrection pillars: Paul's speech at Pisidian Antioch (13:16–41) and Paul's defense before Herod Agrippa II in Acts 26. In addition to these longer epitomes, Paul's other speeches from his missionary journeys reveal the centrality of the resurrection, not least his speech before the Areopagus in Acts 17. He also emphasizes the resurrection in his defenses more broadly.

In what follows I will therefore consider several Pauline texts from Acts 9–28 that bespeak the centrality of Jesus's resurrection. I will begin with the most substantial passages that speak of the importance of the resurrection—Paul's conversion (ch. 9), his sermon at Pisidian Antioch (ch. 13), his speech in Athens (ch. 17), and his defenses (chs. 21–26). Having covered these, I will attend to some other episodes that corroborate Paul's resurrection focus in Acts.

The Appearance of the Risen Christ to Paul (Acts 9)

When we first encounter Paul in Acts, he is not a follower of Jesus. Paul speaks about his one-time opposition to the Way in his letters (most notably Gal. 1:13–14; cf. 1:23), which is consistent with the portrayal of Paul as an early persecutor of the Way in Acts (7:58; 8:1–3; 9:1–2; 22:3–5; 26:9–11).[1] In Acts 9 Luke narrates Paul's encounter of the risen Christ on the road to Damascus, and twice more this event will be recounted in Paul's defenses in the latter chapters of Acts. It is significant that it is the *resurrected and exalted* Christ who appears to Paul.[2] This glorious appearance of the risen Christ is a watershed moment for Paul, and for early Christian theology. Thus, for example, Seyoon Kim has argued that the "origin of Paul's gospel" comes via the glorious Damascus road Christophany.[3] In this event we find in seed form the key features of Paul's Christology and theology of reconciliation.[4] As Kim observes, in the "Damascus road Christophany Paul realized that Jesus of Nazareth was not dead but alive, not cursed but exalted by God, and therefore that the Christian proclamation of him was correct."[5] Following Kim's argument, it is the vision of the *risen and living* Christ that so profoundly influenced Paul and the shaping of Christian theology.[6] On the Damascus road, Paul became convinced that the risen Christ is the guarantee of final salvation.[7]

In addition, this Christophany is most likely intended to demonstrate that Paul meets the requirements for being an apostle (cf. 14:14)[8]—Paul also is an eyewitness of Jesus's resurrection (cf. 1:21–22). After his calling and conversion,[9] Paul

---

1. It is unnecessary to posit a name change for Paul in Acts. Instead, *Saul* is best suited to a Jewish audience, and *Paul* to a gentile audience. See further Sean M. McDonough, "Small Change: Saul to Paul, Again," *JBL* 125 (2006): 390–91; Craig S. Keener, *Acts: An Exegetical Commentary*, 4 vols. (Grand Rapids: Baker Academic, 2012–15), 2:2017–22; F. F. Bruce, *The Acts of the Apostles: The Greek Text with Introduction and Commentary*, 2nd ed. (Grand Rapids: Eerdmans, 1952), 257; Martin Hengel, *Acts and the History of Earliest Christianity*, trans. John Bowden (London: SCM, 1979), 82; Richard Bauckham, "Paul and Other Jews with Latin Names in the New Testament," in *The Jewish World around the New Testament: Collected Essays I*, WUNT 1/233 (Tübingen: Mohr Siebeck, 2008), 371–92; Joseph A. Fitzmyer, *The Acts of the Apostles: A New Translation with Introduction and Commentary*, AB 31 (New York: Doubleday, 1998), 502–3; Michael J. Gorman, *Apostle of the Crucified Lord: A Theological Introduction to Paul and His Letters* (Grand Rapids: Eerdmans, 2004), 51.

2. So, e.g., G. K. Beale, *A New Testament Biblical Theology: The Unfolding of the Old Testament in the New* (Grand Rapids: Baker Academic, 2011), 241–44.

3. Kim, *The Origin of Paul's Gospel*, WUNT 2/4 (Tübingen: Mohr Siebeck, 1981; repr., Grand Rapids: Eerdmans, 1982).

4. See, e.g., the summaries in Kim, *Origin of Paul's Gospel*, 267–68, 329.

5. Kim, *Origin of Paul's Gospel*, 105.

6. For discussions of possible allusions to this event in the Pauline corpus, see Kim, *Origin of Paul's Gospel*, 3–31.

7. See Kim, *Origin of Paul's Gospel*, 73–74.

8. Cf. I. Howard Marshall, "The Resurrection in the Acts of the Apostles," in *Apostolic History and the Gospel: Biblical and Historical Essays Presented to F. F. Bruce on His 60th Birthday*, ed. W. Ward Gasque and Ralph P. Martin (Grand Rapids: Eerdmans, 1970), 105–7.

9. It is debated whether this is best described as a calling or a conversion. These should not be viewed as mutually exclusive. Paul's life is changed, and he is also given a calling. Cf. James

soon begins preaching from the Scriptures[10] that Jesus is the Son of God (9:20) and the Christ (v. 22). Readers of Acts are not left to guess the ways in which Paul made these claims, since we have ample indication of the sorts of things Paul would have preached about Jesus. Particularly important in this regard is Paul's first major speech at Pisidian Antioch.

Finally, it is possible that Paul's conversion is a death-and-resurrection scene that serves to identify him with the crucified and resurrected Christ.[11] In favor of such a reading is the descent of Paul into the darkness (of blindness) for a time, the command to rise (*anastēthi*) and enter Damascus (9:6), and his sight being restored (and his newness of life along with it) by Ananias. If this was Luke's intention, it is hard to demonstrate with any degree of certainty.[12]

The Resurrection in Paul's Pisidian Antioch Speech (13:16–41)

The Role of the Pisidian Antioch Speech in Acts

As with Peter in the previous chapter of this book, Paul's first major speech—at Pisidian Antioch (13:16–41)—expounds the logic and implications of Jesus's resurrection.[13] This is the longest Pauline speech overall, with Paul's final defense before Herod Agrippa II (26:1–23) being almost as long. These two major Pauline speeches rely on the logic of the resurrection, and in doing so they serve as two of three major pillars for my argument.[14]

D. G. Dunn, *Beginning from Jerusalem*, Christianity in the Making 2 (Grand Rapids: Eerdmans, 2009), 355–56; Kim, *Origin of Paul's Gospel*, 10.

10. The term *symbibazō* (9:22) likely refers to the bringing together of the *Scriptures* to make his point. See also Eckhard J. Schnabel, *Acts*, ZECNT (Grand Rapids: Zondervan, 2012), 454; David G. Peterson, *The Acts of the Apostles*, PNTC (Grand Rapids: Eerdmans, 2009), 314; C. K. Barrett, *A Critical and Exegetical Commentary on the Acts of the Apostles*, 2 vols., ICC (Edinburgh: T&T Clark, 1994–98), 1:465; Stephen S. Liggins, *Many Convincing Proofs: Persuasive Phenomena Associated with Gospel Proclamation in Acts*, BZNW 221 (Berlin: de Gruyter, 2016), 166.

11. For this possibility, see Dennis J. Horton, *Death and Resurrection: The Shape and Function of a Literary Motif in the Book of Acts* (Eugene, OR: Pickwick, 2009), 52–55, which follows Richard Belward Rackham, *The Acts of the Apostles: An Exposition*, 11th ed., WC (London: Methuen, 1930), 133, though Horton acknowledges that this view has not gained widespread acceptance; see also Michael D. Goulder, *Type and History in Acts* (London: SPCK, 1964), 34–51.

12. Although it is proper to consider conversion to be a sort of resurrection. Cf. Francis Turretin, *Inst.* 10.4.21.

13. For a history of interpretation, see John Eifion Morgan-Wynne, *Paul's Pisidian Antioch Speech (Acts 13)* (Eugene, OR: Pickwick, 2014), 1–33.

14. Cf. Stanley E. Porter, *The Paul of Acts: Essays in Literary Criticism, Rhetoric, and Theology*, WUNT 1/115 (Tübingen: Mohr Siebeck, 1999), 167, 171; cf. Keener, *Acts*, 1:256 and 256n204.

Consistent with the role of Peter's Pentecost sermon, Paul's Pisidian Antioch speech plays an important role in the narrative of Acts. This speech "has introductory and programmatic importance for Luke."[15] It is the first major speech on the first missionary journey and thus provides the first opportunity for readers to see the type of scriptural argument Paul will make to demonstrate that Jesus is the Son of God and the Christ—two emphases apparent in Paul's preaching from his conversion (cf. 9:20, 22).[16] At Pisidian Antioch the resurrection plays a central role in Paul's argument—both in terms of the identity of Christ and in the efficacy of his work.[17] Structurally, the speech can be divided into three movements, which are marked by vocative addresses to his audience: in 13:16 (*andres Israēlitai kai hoi phoboumenoi ton theon*), in verse 26 (*andres adelphoi, huioi genous Abraam, kai*[18] *hoi en hymin phoboumenoi ton theon*), and in verse 38 (*andres adelphoi*).[19] I will therefore take each of these sections in order, noting how each contributes to Paul's unpacking of the resurrection of Jesus.

Paul's Pisidian Antioch Speech, Part 1 (13:16–25)

The opening of Paul's speech provides a David-focused survey of God's actions to raise up a people and a king for his people. God chose the people's fathers and led them powerfully out of Egypt (13:17). He eventually gave the Israelites the inheritance of the promised land, along with judges to lead them until Samuel (vv. 18–21). The people soon asked for a king, and God gave them Saul (v. 21). But Saul was displaced and God raised up (*ēgeiren*) David for the people—a man after God's own heart who would do God's will (v. 22). In Paul's speech, David is the prototypical, royal figure from whom will come the people's ultimate Savior—Jesus (v. 23).

Paul moves more intently to the resurrection of Jesus in the second movement of his speech (13:26–37), but already in these opening verses the Lukan Paul is preparing his audience for the role of the resurrection of Jesus. We see

15. Mark L. Strauss, *The Davidic Messiah in Luke-Acts: The Promise and Its Fulfillment in Lukan Christology*, JSNTSup 110 (Sheffield: Sheffield Academic, 1995), 150; see also C. A. Joachim Pillai, *Early Missionary Preaching: A Study of Luke's Report in Acts 13* (Hicksville, NY: Exposition Press, 1979), 50–52.

16. See similarly Kevin L. Anderson, *"But God Raised Him from the Dead": The Theology of Jesus's Resurrection in Luke-Acts*, PBM (repr., Eugene, OR: Wipf & Stock, 2006), 235.

17. See also, among others, Morgan-Wynne, *Paul's Pisidian Antioch Speech*, 146; G. Walter Hansen, "The Preaching and Defence of Paul," in *Witness to the Gospel: The Theology of Acts*, ed. I. Howard Marshall and David Peterson (Grand Rapids: Eerdmans, 1998), 300–306.

18. 𝔓[45] and B do not include *kai*.

19. For surveys of how various scholars see the structure, and for the view that a threefold structure is to be preferred, see Morgan-Wynne, *Paul's Pisidian Antioch Speech*, 62–68.

this in several ways. First, in verse 17 Paul uses the verb *hypsoō* ("lift up" or "exalt") to speak of God's exaltation of his people in Egypt, and the adjective *hypsēlos* ("exalted") refers to God's power in the first exodus. The verb *hypsoō* is used throughout Acts to refer to the exaltation of Jesus (2:33; 5:31) and also refers to God's eschatological salvation through Christ in Mary's Magnificat (Luke 1:52). Given that redemption is presented as a new exodus in the New Testament (cf. Luke 9:31),[20] Paul's language of exaltation may anticipate the greater salvation through the lifting up of the Son of God in his death-resurrection-ascension.

Second, an even more likely possibility is that the language of God raising up (*egeiren*) David in Acts 13:22 anticipates the raising up of Jesus from the dead. As I argued in the previous chapter concerning Acts 3, the use of *egeirō* recalls the consistent Lukan use of this term for the resurrection of Jesus. Thus, whereas David was raised up as a man after God's own heart, Luke does not use the same verb for King Saul, who instead is described as having been "given" (*edōken*) to Israel. The use of *egeirō* for David thus associates him more closely with Jesus, his offspring (Acts 13:23), whereas Saul (the Benjamite) is not part of the messianic line.[21] Yet, even though David was a man who would do all the will of God (*hos poiēsei panta ta thelēmata* [*theou*]), David fell asleep, was added to his fathers, and saw corruption (cf. 13:36). Paul therefore will demonstrate in the second movement of his sermon that David is *not* the final Savior.

Indeed, already in the opening verses of the sermon Jesus is identified as the Savior (13:23). This brings us to a third possible way that Paul anticipates the resurrection in the first movement of his speech. In 13:23 there is a textual question about the main verb that speaks of God's establishing Jesus as Savior: is it *ēgagen* ("[God] brought") or *ēgeiren* ("[God] raised")? Most present-day editions of the Greek New Testament along with modern translations opt for the aorist of *agō*.[22] This makes a great deal of sense.[23] However, it is not an open-and-shut case; the possibility remains that *raised* (*ēgeiren*) is the

---

20. Cf. David W. Pao, *Acts and the Isaianic New Exodus* (repr., Grand Rapids: Baker Academic, 2002).

21. There is another Saul in this context who is also from the tribe of Benjamin—Paul himself! However, Paul's Benjamite heritage is not mentioned in Acts (cf. Rom. 11:1; Phil. 3:5).

22. *ECM*; NA[28]; THGNT; SBLGNT; English versions include CSB; ESV; NET; NIV; NRSV.

23. In terms of external evidence, *ēgagen* is supported by $\mathfrak{P}^{74}$, ℵ, B, 𝔐, Vulgate, Bohairic. These represent solid, early external evidence. In terms of transcriptional probability, since *egeirō* occurs in the previous verse (13:22) and in 13:30, 37, harmonization is likely in 13:23 (so, e.g., the passing comment of Barrett, *Commentary on the Acts*, 1:636). Likewise, ΗΓΑΓΕΝ could easily be mistaken for ΗΓΕΙΡΕΝ, especially in light of the frequent use of *egeirō* throughout this and other speeches in Acts.

best reading.[24] Luke does not write anywhere else that God *led* Jesus,[25] but Luke writes on at least eight occasions in Acts that God *raised* Jesus (3:15; 4:10; 5:30; 10:40; 13:30, 37; 26:8; cf. Luke 9:22; 24:6, 34).[26] Moreover, *egeirō* is especially common in speeches, and the *raising* of Jesus is elsewhere closely related to his status as *Savior* (Acts 5:30–31; cf. Luke 1:69).[27]

Yet on balance, the printed reading in the *Editio Critica Maior* and Nestle-Aland 28 (*ēgagen*) is most likely correct.[28] Even if *ēgeiren* is secondary, its presence in the manuscript tradition is easy to understand, for this term accords with the logic of Paul's speech and Luke's preference for this word to describe the resurrection of Christ. The alternate reading *ēgeiren* reveals the early reception of Acts 13:23—and this reception indicates that some early readers recognized in Paul's speech an emphasis on the resurrection of Jesus.

The Lukan Paul does emphasize the resurrection at Pisidian Antioch, although a careful reading of Paul's rhetorical strategy indicates that though Paul is preparing his audience for the resurrection of Jesus early on (cf. 13:22), he does not divulge *the way in which* the Davidic savior is established until the second movement of his speech.[29] The reference to Jesus in 13:23 is thus a preview of the fuller discussion of this Savior that is soon to come. Paul builds anticipation about the details of this Davidide in verses 16–25 before launching into a fuller discussion in verses 26–41, and especially verses 26–37, where Paul will finally reveal that Jesus is the Davidic savior by means of his resurrection.

24. So KJV ("raised"); Schlachter (*"erweckt"*); *Edition de Genève* (*"suscité"*); Daniel Marguerat, *Les Actes des Apôtres*, 2 vols., CNT 5a–b (Geneva: Labor et Fides, 2007–15), 2:45; Matthäus Franz-Joseph Buss, *Die Missionspredigt des Apostels Paulus im Pisidischen Antiochen: Analyse von Apg 13,16–41 im Hinblick auf die literarische und thematische Einheit der Paulusrede*, FB 38 (Stuttgart: Katholisches Bibelwerk, 1980), 46–47, following Jacques DuPont, "L'utilisation apologétique de l'Ancien Testament dans les discours des Actes," in *Études sur les Actes des Apôtres* (Paris: Cerf, 1967), 254n13. Though external evidence does favor *ēgagen*, one need not dismiss out of hand *ēgeiren*, which is found in Codex Bezae (D) and Ephraemi Rescriptus (C) along with Syriac and Sahidic witnesses.

25. Though see the quotation of Isa. 53:7 in Acts 8:32; cf. Luke 4:1.

26. This count would be nine if one opts for a second usage of *egeirō* in Acts 3:6.

27. *Sōtēra* is more likely than *sōtērian* in 13:23 (so, e.g., Barrett, *Commentary on the Acts*, 1:637—though in this case the external evidence in favor of *sōtēr* includes many of the same witnesses that support *ēgeiren* in the first half of the verse, including D, C, Syriac and Coptic [Sahidic] manuscripts, and Theodoret). The language of 13:23 is also similar to Judges 3:9, where the OG reads *ēgeiren kyrios sōtēra tō Israēl* ("the Lord raised up a savior for Israel"), and could thus be another reason to reject *ēgeiren* in Acts 13:23 due to harmonization. Cf. Bruce, *Acts of the Apostles*, 265.

28. So, e.g., Anderson, *"But God Raised Him from the Dead,"* 241n20; Barrett, *Commentary on the Acts*, 1:636; Peterson, *Acts of the Apostles*, 388n66.

29. If so, then perhaps internal evidence is not so strongly in favor of *ēgeiren* after all.

Paul's Pisidian Antioch Speech, Part 2 (13:26–37)

Paul has much more to say about the Davidic Savior—and his resurrection—in the second portion of his speech (13:26–37). Picking up on the language of salvation from verse 23, in verse 26 Paul begins to say more about how "this salvation" has come forth in the person of Jesus.[30] Though they should have known better, the religious leaders and the people put Jesus to death on a tree (vv. 26–29). Interestingly, Paul links this wicked act explicitly to their ignorance of *the prophets*.[31] Yet as the answer to the death of Jesus, Paul introduces the theological key to his speech in verse 30: God has raised the crucified one from the dead (*ho de theos ēgeiren auton ek nekrōn*).[32] The salvation mentioned in verse 26 (and v. 23) is offered because of the resurrection of Jesus—*because* Jesus has been raised from the dead, Paul preaches the good news which was promised to the fathers (v. 32).[33] Paul also concludes this section of the speech with reference to the resurrection of Jesus in verse 37—Jesus did not see corruption.[34]

Jesus's resurrection is also likely in view in 13:32–33: here Paul proclaims that he announces the good news that God has fulfilled the promise to the fathers, and this by raising up (*anastēsas*) Jesus in accord with Psalm 2. Here we must ask two questions: first, what was promised to the fathers, and second, in what sense was Jesus raised up? We start with the second issue—the sense of *anastēsas* in Acts 13:33. One possibility is that this refers to the "raising" of Jesus on the "stage of history."[35] One reason for this is that it is not explicitly stated that Jesus is raised "from the dead." However, as we see elsewhere in Acts, it is not necessary to find the entire phrase for the language of *egeirō* or *anistēmi* to refer to the resurrection.[36] I will say more about the use of Psalm 2:7 below (in relation to sonship), but it will suffice here to observe that (probably) most scholars do see the raising in 13:33 as a reference to the

---

30. For the argument that *salvation* is central in the theology of Luke, see I. Howard Marshall, *Luke: Historian and Theologian* (Grand Rapids: Zondervan, 1970), 92–93.

31. See further ch. 7.

32. D presents different phrasing for 13:30–31 but does not change the basic message.

33. See also Morgan-Wynne, *Paul's Pisidian Antioch Speech*, 37, which rightly sees the resurrection emphasized from 13:30 onward. In 13:30–31 the apostles are again identified as witnesses of Christ's *resurrection*. Cf. Dennis E. Johnson, *The Message of Acts in the History of Redemption* (Phillipsburg, NJ: P&R, 1997), 144.

34. See also Morgan-Wynne, *Paul's Pisidian Antioch Speech*, 67.

35. So Barrett, *Commentary on the Acts*, 1:645; see also Schnabel, *Acts*, 581.

36. So Morgan-Wynne, *Paul's Pisidian Antioch Speech*, 118–19; Evald Lövestam, *Son and Saviour: A Study of Acts 13,32–37; With an Appendix: "Son of God" in the Synoptic Gospels*, ConBNT 18 (Lund: Gleerup, 1961), 10; see also Gerhard Delling, "Die Jesusgeschichte in der Verkündigung nach Acta," *NTS* 19 (1972–73): 382–83. Note also the reading of D in 13:30, which understands *egeirō* as a reference to Jesus's resurrection but omits *ek nekrōn*.

resurrection of Jesus.[37] This resurrection interpretation is preferred since it best fits the context of Acts 13 as Paul explains *how* salvation has come—through the resurrection of Jesus.

This brings us back to the first issue—the content of the promise in 13:32. What specifically does Paul understand the promise to the fathers to be? And how does this relate to the resurrection of Jesus? The best way to answer this is not to oversimplify the matter, but to look at the wider context of the promises in Luke and Acts. When this is done, several aspects, which are all related, come into focus. I mention four here: (1) the promise of a lasting Davidic kingdom, (2) the outpouring of the Holy Spirit, (3) the forgiveness of sins, and (4) the resurrection of God's people.

First, and primarily in view in Acts 13, the promise must refer to the promise to David for an everlasting kingdom.[38] Consistent with the theology of Peter's speeches (cf. 2:24–32), Jesus is the Savior, the Davidic Son (13:22–23) who rules over an everlasting kingdom. As in Acts 2, in 13:35 Paul invokes Psalm 16:10 [15:10 LXX] in support of Jesus's resurrection. Paul's speech is founded on the promise of the Davidic covenant (13:16–25), which is fulfilled by means of Jesus's resurrection (cf. 2 Sam. 7:12).[39] God has delivered on his promise to David by raising Jesus from the dead.

So prominent is this Davidic emphasis in Acts 13 that we should linger over its implications a bit further. In addition to Psalms 2:7 and 16:10, Paul also invokes Isaiah 55:3 to speak of the Davidic blessings that accrue to Jesus on account of his resurrection—the "holy [and] sure [blessings] of David"[40] (*ta hosia Dauid ta pista*). What are these blessings?[41] Some have argued that

37. See, e.g., Anderson, *"But God Raised Him from the Dead,"* 244 (cf. 245–49); Darrell L. Bock, *Acts,* BECNT (Grand Rapids: Baker Academic, 2007), 456; Peterson, *Acts of the Apostles,* 392; Fitzmyer, *Acts of the Apostles,* 516; Robert F. O'Toole, SJ, "Christ's Resurrection in Acts 13,13–52," *Bib* 60 (1979): 366; Morgan-Wynne, *Paul's Pisidian Antioch Speech,* 146; Hansen, "Preaching and Defence of Paul," 302–3; Buss, *Missionspredigt des Apostels Paulus,* 89. One might also consider the possibility of a *double entendre*: God has raised Jesus in history and from the dead; cf. the horn of salvation God has raised up (*ēgeiren*) in Luke 1:69. Thanks to Josh Leim for this suggestion.

38. Cf. O'Toole, "Christ's Resurrection in Acts 13,13–52," 368–70.

39. On 2 Sam. 7 as the background here, see Anderson, *"But God Raised Him from the Dead,"* 244; Strauss, *Davidic Messiah,* 150–57; Morgan-Wynne, *Paul's Pisidian Antioch Speech,* 83–125.

40. So also ESV; NIV; the NRSV has "the holy promises made to David" (see also CSB). This is also correct, though the sense in Acts 13:34 is more the fulfillment of the promises rather than the promises themselves. Thus, the gloss of "blessings" seems to be more fitting. But see Anderson, *"But God Raised Him from the Dead,"* 252n62.

41. For surveys, see Strauss, *Davidic Messiah,* 168–74; Darrell L. Bock, *Proclamation from Prophecy and Pattern: Lucan Old Testament Christology,* JSNTSup 12 (Sheffield: JSOT Press, 1987), 252–54; Anderson, *"But God Raised Him from the Dead,"* 250–54.

they must refer to the resurrection itself.[42] However, this is not the best interpretation. Instead, as Mark Strauss and others have argued, "the holy and sure blessings of David" refers to the blessings of the Davidic kingdom, though these do indeed come by means of the resurrection of Jesus.[43] Bock helpfully summarizes two key components of the use of Isaiah 55:3 in Acts 13:34: "(1) the provision for an everlasting rule . . . and (2) the opportunity of deliverance through the Davidic son."[44] He continues, "Thus τὰ ὅσια Δαυίδ, is directly but not exclusively related to the resurrection. The resurrection is the provision that guarantees the eternal nature of the Davidic covenant."[45] I argue in what follows that the blessings of the Davidic covenant, which come to fruition through the resurrection of Jesus, are multifaceted.

It is further likely that the Davidic promises in Acts 13 recall the promises to Abraham to bless all the nations of the earth. In addition to the explicit mention of Abraham in the transition to this section of his speech (v. 26), Paul recognizes his own role as a light to the nations (13:47; cf. Isa. 49:6). The promise to Abraham of a land and a people that would bless all the nations of the earth (Gen. 12:1–3) is sluiced through the channel of the Davidic kingdom and flowers in the resurrection of Jesus, the ultimate Davidic king. Thus God's people—and the nations—are provided a lasting place in which to dwell securely in *everlasting* perpetuity. This is even clearer in Paul's response when he mentions eternal life (Acts 13:46, 48).

Thus Isaiah 55:3 is used in Acts 13:34 to speak about the certainty of the Davidic promises in light of the resurrection of the true Son of David.[46] The resurrection of Jesus is also proved from the citations of Psalm 2:7; 16:10 in Acts 13:33, 35.[47] Jesus is the true Son of David, but is also distinguished from David.[48] Whereas David was buried and saw decay, Jesus—who did all the will

---

42. E.g., J. R. Doeve, *Jewish Hermeneutics in the Synoptic Gospels and Acts* (Assen: Van Gorcum, 1954), 174. See also the discussion in Strauss, *Davidic Messiah*, 169.

43. Strauss, *Davidic Messiah*, 170–74; Hansen ("Preaching and Defence of Paul," 303) argues that the *hoti* that introduces the citation of Isa. 55:3 underscores the causal relationship between the resurrection and the certainty of the Davidic blessings. See similarly Barrett, *Commentary on the Acts*, 1:647.

44. Bock, *Proclamation from Prophecy and Pattern*, 254.

45. Bock, *Proclamation from Prophecy and Pattern*, 254 (though *everlasting* would be a better term in this case than *eternal*). See also Strauss, *Davidic Messiah*, 172.

46. See similarly Morgan-Wynne, *Paul's Pisidian Antioch Speech*, 122; Strauss, *Davidic Messiah*, 170–74; Lövestam, *Son and Saviour*, 79.

47. On the connections between Ps. 16:10 and Isa. 55:3, see, e.g., Anderson, *"But God Raised Him from the Dead,"* 249–50; Doeve, *Jewish Hermeneutics*, 173–74.

48. See also the discussion by Dupont of A. Loisy—who speaks of "le vrai David"—in Jacques Dupont, "ΤΑ ῸΣΙΑ ΔΑΥΙΔ ΤΑ ΠΙΣΤΑ (Actes 13,34 = Isaïe 55,3)," in *Études sur les Actes des Apôtres* (Paris: Cerf, 1967), 340.

of God (13:22)—was raised from the dead (13:34). As Evald Lövestam has shown, this exegetical approach is consistent with various strands of Davidic expectations among Jews in the first century concerning a lasting kingdom (e.g., Sir. 47:11–13; 1 Macc. 2:57; *Pss. Sol.* 17:4, 21; 4QFlor 1 I, 10–11).[49] Lövestam even argues that in the Old Testament and early Judaism "the promise to David was of *everlasting* dominion."[50] In such a context Paul explains that the everlasting, Davidic kingdom comes through the resurrection of Jesus. This is part of the way the promises to the fathers are fulfilled.

Second, the promise also refers to the outpouring of the Holy Spirit. The Gospel of Luke ends with Jesus commanding his disciples to wait for the promise of the Father (Luke 24:49), and Acts begins in much the same way (Acts 1:4). The Spirit is also the focus of the promise in Peter's Pentecost sermon (2:33, 39).[51] I argued in the previous chapter that the outpouring of the Spirit in Acts 2 is related to resurrection and restoration passages in the Old Testament. In Acts it is the *risen Jesus* who pours out the Spirit; because Jesus has been exalted at God's right hand, the Spirit is poured out anew on God's people.

Third, in Acts the promised good news to the fathers also includes the forgiveness of sins, which is specifically in view in 13:38–39. This is consistent with Peter's earlier speeches, where he emphasizes the offer of salvation because of the work of Christ (2:38; 5:31; 10:43).[52] The promised Savior brings forgiveness of sins (cf. 5:31; 13:23, 38). I will say more about forgiveness and justification in relation to the resurrection of Jesus below.

Fourth, the promise to the fathers includes the general resurrection of God's people, which is contingent upon the resurrection of Jesus himself.[53] That which was promised to the fathers in 13:32 thus includes not only the resurrection of the Son of David (vv. 33–35) but also what Paul later calls the "hope of Israel" (28:20)[54]—the resurrection of God's people. Jesus's resurrection is the necessary prerequisite for the resurrection of his people.[55] The

---

49. Lövestam, *Son and Saviour*, 8–87.

50. Lövestam, *Son and Saviour*, 72 (emphasis original).

51. Morgan-Wynne (*Paul's Pisidian Antioch Speech*, 186) correlates the promise in Acts 13 to Paul's discussion of the promised Holy Spirit in Gal. 3:13–14.

52. See also David A. deSilva, "Paul's Speech in Antioch of Pisidia," *BibSac* 151 (1994): 41; cf. Robert F. O'Toole, SJ, "Acts 2:30 and the Davidic Covenant of Pentecost," *JBL* 102 (1983): 254.

53. See similarly O'Toole, "Christ's Resurrection in Acts 13,13–52," 368, 371.

54. See also Acts 26:6, 8, noted by Anderson, *"But God Raised Him from the Dead,"* 257–58. Paul says more about the resurrection of Jesus as the foundation for the general resurrection later in Acts (24:15, 21; 26:22–23; cf. 17:18; 23:6).

55. See also Anderson, *"But God Raised Him from the Dead,"* 258–59; cf. Peterson, *Acts of the Apostles*, 393; Alan J. Thompson, *Acts of the Risen Lord Jesus: Luke's Account of God's Unfolding Plan*, NSBT 27 (Downers Grove, IL: InterVarsity, 2011), 83.

lasting kingdom of David thus includes the benefit of eternal, resurrection life for those who are citizens of this kingdom. This explains why Paul speaks of the reactions of his hearers in terms of being unworthy of or inheriting eternal life (13:46, 48). The message of Pisidian Antioch is about the resurrection, both that of Christ and, by implication, the general resurrection. Those who scoff at God's work in Paul's day (vv. 40–41; cf. Hab. 1:5) are those specifically who scoff at the resurrection.[56]

Thus the benefits of the resurrection of Jesus, the Son of David, are multifaceted. These four aspects of what was promised (13:32)—the establishment of the lasting Davidic kingdom, the outpouring of the Holy Spirit, the forgiveness of sins, and the resurrection of God's people—are all possible because of the resurrection of Jesus. In short, Jesus's resurrection from the dead ensures the salvation of his people.[57] Lövestam summarizes the matter nicely: "The resurrection and exaltation signify, as it were, the crowning of Jesus' work of salvation, the purpose of which is to save from sin and death and grant an inheritance in the kingdom of God."[58]

Paul's Pisidian Antioch Speech, Part 3 (13:38–41)

By this point in the speech, Paul has established the scriptural and historical importance of the resurrection of Jesus. The culmination comes in verses 38–41, where Paul unpacks the practical relevance of Jesus's resurrection for his audience.[59] Having just mentioned the resurrection in verse 37, Paul offers a promise and a warning. The offer is forgiveness and justification apart from the law of Moses (vv. 38–39; cf. Rom. 6:7);[60] the warning is not to scoff at God's (resurrection) work (Acts 13:40–41; cf. Hab. 1:5). God has indeed raised Jesus from the dead; the proper response is therefore faith in the God of their fathers (cf. Acts 13:32–33). To summarize the logic of Acts 13:16–41: because Jesus has been raised from the dead, justification and forgiveness of sins are freely offered; therefore beware of the scoffing that leads to judgment.[61] Paul's conclusion hinges on the resurrection of Jesus.

56. See Morgan-Wynne, *Paul's Pisidian Antioch Speech*, 130; Hansen, "Preaching and Defence of Paul," 305–6.
57. So O'Toole, "Christ's Resurrection in Acts 13,13–52," 368.
58. Lövestam, *Son and Saviour*, 86.
59. This climax is recognized by many, including John J. Kilgallen, "Acts 13,38–39: Culmination of Paul's Speech in Pisidia," *Bib* 69 (1988): 483–84; Schnabel, *Acts*, 583; Morgan-Wynne, *Paul's Pisidian Antioch Speech*, 37.
60. I say more about justification and forgiveness in the next section.
61. Lövestam's comprehensive summary (*Son and Saviour*, 87) is worth quoting: "When in Paul's sermon in Acts 13, Jesus is presented as the promised Saviour, in that after his suffering and death he was raised from the dead and by this installed in the permanent dominion promised

Ramifications of the Resurrection Derived
from Paul's Pisidian Antioch Speech

The resurrection of Jesus is the logical key to Paul's Pisidian Antioch speech.[62] Before moving on to another passage, it is necessary to tease out further some theological ramifications of the resurrection in this speech. Again we will consider four features relating to the resurrection: (1) the sonship of Jesus, (2) the relationship between Jesus's death and resurrection, (3) justification, and (4) implications for the gentile mission.

1. Resurrection and Sonship

First is the sonship in view in the quotation of Psalm 2:7 in Acts 13:33. I have argued that the raising of Jesus that the Lukan Paul connects with Psalm 2:7 is best taken as a reference to Jesus's resurrection, and not merely to his appearance in world history. The quotation of Psalm 2 reminds us that Jesus's resurrection is closely associated with his sonship. This recalls the correlation of sonship and resurrection in Romans 1:3–4, which is an important text to consider alongside Paul's sermon in Acts 13.[63] As in Romans 1, in Acts 13 the resurrection of Jesus is understood within a Davidic framework. The resurrection of Jesus is *at least* a confirmation of his messianic sonship, but we may be able to say even more than that.

Some have suggested that the resurrection marks the point at which Jesus *became* Son of God, strictly speaking.[64] However, this option must be ruled out for several reasons.[65] This view assumes discordance in various strata of tradition in Luke and Acts, with Luke at once (1) revising or taking over

---

to David for his seed, the whole wealth of the NT message of salvation is thus implied there: the forgiveness of sins and complete salvation, with freedom from death and all the powers of evil, and participation in the kingdom of God with the risen and exalted Jesus."

62. Joachim Pillai (*Apostolic Interpretation of History: A Commentary on Acts 13:16–41* [Hicksville, NY: Exposition Press, 1980], 40) calls the resurrection the "turning point in history" and says it "marks a new *kairos* and no doubt the most important in the history of salvation."

63. Cf. Richard B. Gaffin Jr., *The Centrality of the Resurrection: A Study in Paul's Soteriology* (Grand Rapids: Baker, 1978), 113; Bock, *Acts*, 456; Bruce, *Acts of the Apostles*, 270; cf. Peter J. Scaer, "Resurrection as Justification in the Book of Acts," *CTQ* 70 (2006): 219–31. See also N. T. Wright, *The Resurrection of the Son of God*, COQG 3 (Minneapolis: Fortress, 2003), 451. Contrast Barrett, *Commentary on the Acts*, 1:646.

64. See Philipp Vielhauer, "On the 'Paulinism' of Acts," in *Studies in Luke-Acts: Essays Presented in Honor of Paul Schubert*, ed. Leander E. Keck and J. Louis Martyn (Nashville: Abingdon, 1966), 44: "This Christology is adoptionistic, not a theology of preexistence" (this quote is also noted in Morgan-Wynne, *Paul's Pisidian Antioch Speech*, 146n25). Cf. Richard I. Pervo, *Acts: A Commentary*, Hermeneia (Minneapolis: Fortress, 2009), 338–39.

65. Cf. Herman Bavinck, *Reformed Dogmatics*, ed. John Bolt, trans. John Vriend, 4 vols. (Grand Rapids: Baker Academic, 2003–8), 2:275.

tradition to present Jesus as Son of God throughout Luke and Acts (e.g., Luke 1:32; 3:22, 38; 4:3, 9, 41; 10:21–22) and at the same time (2) failing to be consistent with his editorial/authorial procedure. It is further out of accord with articulations of the rule of faith (*regula fidei*) from the earliest days of the church, which consistently identified Jesus as the divine Son of God.[66] This adoptionistic view is thus not satisfactory historically or exegetically, and is the least persuasive option.[67]

A second option argues for the opposite perspective—that the sonship in view in Psalm 2:7 is eternal sonship, with the "today" of Psalm 2:7 construed as *eternal* begetting. Paul thus speaks in Acts 13:33 of the manifestation or confirmation of eternal sonship. Though this option is much less discussed in Acts scholarship today, it has a long pedigree in Christian exegetical tradition.[68] This view does not necessarily detract from the importance of the resurrection, though it may not find it in 13:33. For example, Reformed theologian Francis Turretin speaks of the "today" as two sided: it refers at the same time both to the eternal begetting of the Son of God and to the manifestation of that sonship when he was sent into the world, fulfilling the promises to the fathers.[69] Yet even if one affirms the eternal sonship (and eternal begetting) of the second person of the Trinity,[70] it is arguable whether the "today" of Psalm 2:7, in light of its use in Acts 13:33, refers to an "eternal present" in God's sight.[71] Further, as I argued above, the "raising" of Jesus in Acts 13:33 most likely refers to the resurrection. Thus no less than Calvin demurs to the view that the "today" of Psalm 2:7 is eternal begetting, and instead opts for an

66. For statements of the rule of faith, see Everett Ferguson, *The Rule of Faith: A Guide*, Cascade Companions (Eugene, OR: Cascade, 2015), 1–15. Indeed, the preexistence of Christ was a sine qua non for early Christian interpreters. See, e.g., Justin, *Dial.* 45, 48, 56, 59–63, 85, 87, 128; Irenaeus, *Haer.* 1.10.1; *Epid.* 12, 44–51, 91; *Diogn.* 7:1–9:1; Ign., *Eph.* 7:2; 19:3; *Magn.* 6:1; *Rom.* (salutation); *Smyrn.* 1:1; *Pol.* 3:2; 2 *Clem.* 9:5; cf. 1:1; *Barn.* 5:6, 10–11; 6:12, 16; Melito, *Peri Pascha*; Origen, *Princ.* preface 1.

67. See also Michael F. Bird, *Jesus the Eternal Son: Answering Adoptionist Christology* (Grand Rapids: Eerdmans, 2017).

68. See, e.g., the comments of Cyril of Alexandria and Bede in Francis Martin, ed., *Acts*, vol. 5 of *Ancient Commentary on Scripture: New Testament* (Downers Grove, IL: InterVarsity, 2006), 167.

69. Turretin, *Inst.* 3.29.8. For Turretin the raising of Christ in Acts 13:33 does not speak of the resurrection; that comes in texts like Acts 13:35; Rom. 1:4. See also Petrus van Mastricht, *Theoretical-Practical Theology*, trans. Todd M. Rester, ed. Joel R. Beeke, 7 vols. (Grand Rapids: Reformation Heritage, 2018–), 2:542–43. Mastricht relates Acts 13:33 more explicitly to the resurrection.

70. See recently Fred Sanders and Scott R. Swain, eds., *Retrieving Eternal Generation* (Grand Rapids: Zondervan, 2017).

71. See Augustine, *Enarrat. Ps.* 2:6; cf. D. A. Carson, "John 5:26: *Crux Interpretum* for Eternal Generation," in Sanders and Swain, *Retrieving Eternal Generation*, 91–92.

interpretation that highlights the "today" as the day of Jesus's resurrection (much like Rom. 1:4).[72]

Despite the strong pedigree of the second view and its correct theological perspective, it is prudent to consider other options. A third view understands Jesus already to be Son of God before his resurrection and sees the resurrection as confirming, manifesting, and/or vindicating his messianic-Davidic sonship. This is a common approach today.[73] This view rightly sees the resurrection not as the *beginning* of Jesus's sonship but as its vindication. This view is substantially correct, though Acts 13 encourages us to say even more about the sonship of Jesus.

This brings us to a fourth view, which combines the second and third views. This fourth view focuses primarily on the resurrection and royal enthronement of the messianic Son—which is Paul's point in the context of Acts—but it grounds Jesus's resurrection and enthronement in his preexistent, even eternal, sonship.[74] This sonship is thus something more (not less) than messianic sonship—it is preexistent, divine sonship on which the particularities of Jesus's messianic sonship are predicated.[75] Bock appears to hold a similar view, when he states: "Because Jesus was the incorruptible Son promised in Scripture, he must be raised."[76] To be sure, proponents of the third view (above) may also affirm the resurrection as the vindication of Jesus's *divine* sonship, but it is typically not emphasized. This fourth option understands the "today" of Psalm 2:7 in Acts 13:33 as the day of Jesus's resurrection (or

---

72. John Calvin, *Commentary upon the Acts of the Apostles*, ed. Henry Beveridge, 2 vols. (repr., Grand Rapids: Baker, 2003), 1:535–36; cf. Calvin, *Commentaries on the Epistle of Paul the Apostle to the Hebrews*, trans. John Owen (repr., Grand Rapids: Baker, 2003), 42. Calvin attributes this view to Augustine. For Calvin, the "today" of Ps. 2:7 could almost be called an "external begetting," since it is not about the hidden, internal actions of the Trinity but about the manifestation of the Son to humanity. See Calvin, *Hebrews*, 42; cf. Calvin, *Commentary upon the Acts*, 1:535.

73. So Keener, *Acts*, 2:2069–71; Peterson, *Acts of the Apostles*, 392; Anderson, *"But God Raised Him from the Dead,"* 247–49; Ben Witherington III, *The Acts of the Apostles: A Socio-Rhetorical Commentary* (Grand Rapids: Eerdmans, 1998), 412. Strauss, *Davidic Messiah*, 164, is similar.

74. See similarly Calvin, *Commentary upon the Acts*, 1:535; Bavinck, *Reformed Dogmatics*, 3:435, 442; Mastricht, *Theoretical-Practical Theology*, 2:542–43, 552, 554. Fitzmyer (*Acts of the Apostles*, 517) acknowledges that the use of Ps. 2 in the NT "lead[s] eventually to the Nicene Creed's confession about the Son as One in being with the Father" but also avers that this "mode of expression [was] not yet current in NT times." Similarly, Barrett (*Commentary on the Acts*, 2:lxxxvi) doubts that Luke speaks metaphysically here.

75. Cf. Geerhardus Vos, *The Self-Disclosure of Jesus: The Modern Debate about the Messianic Consciousness*, ed. J. G. Vos, 2nd ed. (Grand Rapids: Eerdmans, 1953; repr., Phillipsburg, NJ: P&R, 2002), 151; Turretin, *Inst.* 3.29.9. See alternatively Peterson (*Acts of the Apostles*, 392): "In this context, Paul says nothing about the preexistence of the Son of God."

76. Bock, *Proclamation from Prophecy and Pattern*, 249.

heavenly enthronement). Thus Luke's primary emphasis is the resurrection as constitutive of the accomplishment of salvation. But this salvific event must be understood in light of Luke's rich, nuanced christological portrait.

For example, as we saw with Luke 20:41–44 (appealing to Ps. 110 [109 LXX])—to which we could add the sunrise from on high in Luke 1:78—Luke manifests a preexistence Christology,[77] which is closely related to the Davidic contours of the Psalter (cf. Luke 20:41–44; Acts 2:25, 30; 4:25). Further, in the Gospel of Luke the *sonship* of Jesus transcends a merely temporal relationship (e.g., Luke 3:22; 9:35; 10:21–22). This is consistent with the broader New Testament witness. Beyond Luke-Acts, there is much to be said for preexistence Christology in the Pauline corpus,[78] and Psalm 2:7 is also used in Hebrews 1:5 in a way that bespeaks preexistence Christology. In the same context in Hebrews, the Son is said to be the radiance of the glory of God and the exact representation of his character (1:3) and the firstborn who, having completed his earthly work, enters the heavenly world (v. 6).[79]

Luke's preexistent Christology is thus consistent with other New Testament authors who see the messianic sonship of Jesus arising out of his preexistent sonship. It is not that Jesus was not Son before his resurrection, but the resurrection marks a new era of the eternal Son's messianic sonship—for "today" the preexistent Son is enthroned as the resurrected, victorious king of glory.

2. Cross and Resurrection

Second, Paul's speech at Pisidian Antioch raises the perennial question about the role of the death of Christ in Lukan theology. If indeed we find such a strong emphasis on the resurrection at Pisidian Antioch (and elsewhere), does this lessen the importance of the sacrificial death of Christ for Luke?[80] Though I do not have the space to answer this question thoroughly, I will briefly mention some aspects of Luke-Acts that manifest the importance of Christ's death for salvation. First, Luke does indeed place more emphasis on

77. See Simon J. Gathercole, *The Pre-existent Son: Recovering the Christologies of Matthew, Mark, and Luke* (Grand Rapids: Eerdmans, 2006), 231–42; contrast Ernst Haenchen, *The Acts of the Apostles: A Commentary*, trans. R. McL. Wilson (Philadelphia: Westminster, 1971), 91.

78. E.g., Phil. 2:6–7. Cf. Kim, *Origin of Paul's Gospel*, 111; Gordon D. Fee, *Pauline Christology: An Exegetical-Theological Study* (Peabody, MA: Hendrickson, 2007), 500–512.

79. Cf. William L. Lane, *Hebrews 1–8*, WBC 47A (Dallas: Word, 1991), 25–27. On *oikoumenēn* as the heavenly world in Heb. 1:6, see further Craig R. Koester, *Hebrews: A New Translation with Introduction and Commentary*, AB 36 (New York: Doubleday, 2001), 193; Paul Ellingworth, *The Epistle to the Hebrews*, NIGTC (Grand Rapids: Eerdmans, 2003), 117–18; and David M. Moffitt, *Atonement and the Logic of Resurrection in the Epistle to the Hebrews*, NovTSup 141 (Leiden: Brill, 2011), 53–118.

80. See, e.g., Hengel, *Acts and the History of Earliest Christianity*, 67.

the resurrection of Jesus than on the cross. But this emphasis does not necessarily entail a lessening of the importance of Jesus's death.[81] Both Jesus's death and resurrection are necessary for atonement.[82] Luke seems to focus on the saving work of Christ by emphasizing the outcome of Jesus's death—his resurrection—rather than the death per se.[83]

Additionally, Luke gives ample indication of standing squarely in the stream of early Christian theology (and Pauline theology!) that recognizes the importance of the cross. For example, at Pisidian Antioch Paul speaks of Jesus being put to death on a tree (*xylon* rather than *stauros*), which may recall the language of being cursed from Deuteronomy 21:23.[84] Indeed, this text from Deuteronomy was used by Paul to speak of Jesus's atonement-by-curse-bearing in Galatians 3:13 (cf. Acts 5:30; 10:39; 1 Pet. 2:24). Thus, though Paul's sermon at Pisidian Antioch says comparatively little about the death of Christ, it may reflect a setting similar to that of Galatians—a text in which Paul clearly emphasizes the salvific death of Christ (cf. 2:19 [2:20 EVV]; 3:13). Luke's account provides a great deal of historical verisimilitude. In addition, Luke consistently highlights the death of Jesus as the death of the "righteous one" (Luke 23:47; Acts 3:14; cf. 22:14) and presents the death in terms of the (Suffering) Servant of Isaiah (e.g., Isa. 53:7–8 in Acts 8:32–33).[85] Such allusions to the Old Testament provide sufficient evidence to conclude that Luke did indeed view Christ's death to be wrath-bearing.[86]

In sum, though Luke does give more attention to the resurrection of Jesus, this is by no means inconsistent with the view that the death of Christ is salvific in character. Luke may simply draw more attention to the resurrection

81. Cf. also Horton, *Death and Resurrection*, esp. 13–38; Robert C. Tannehill, *The Narrative Unity of Luke-Acts: A Literary Interpretation*, 2 vols. (Philadelphia: Fortress, 1986–90), 2:35n24.

82. See, e.g., John Murray, *The Epistle to the Romans*, 2 vols., NICNT (Grand Rapids: Eerdmans, 1959–65), 1:157; Lane G. Tipton, "Union with Christ and Justification," in *Justified in Christ: God's Plan for Us in Justification*, ed. K. Scott Oliphint (Fearn: Mentor, 2007), 37–38.

83. See also David P. Moessner, "Reading Luke's Gospel as Ancient Hellenistic Narrative," in *Reading Luke: Interpretation, Reflection, Formation*, ed. Craig G. Bartholomew, Joel B. Green, and Anthony B. Thiselton, Scripture and Hermeneutics Series 6 (Milton Keynes: Paternoster; Grand Rapids: Zondervan, 2005), 125–54.

84. See Thompson, *Acts of the Risen Lord Jesus*, 83–88; Peterson, *Acts of the Apostles*, 75–79; Johnson, *Message of Acts*, 146–49; Marshall, *Luke: Historian and Theologian*, 173. I am also indebted here to Charles Hill's Greek exegesis lectures on Galatians (Reformed Theological Seminary, Orlando, Florida, Spring 2005). Contrast Morgan-Wynne, *Paul's Pisidian Antioch Speech*, 187–89.

85. See also Benjamin R. Wilson, *The Saving Cross of the Suffering Christ: The Death of Christ in Lukan Soteriology*, BZNW 223 (Berlin: de Gruyter, 2016). Wilson argues at length for the originality of the textually uncertain Luke 22:19–20, which would provide additional evidence for a Lukan emphasis on the death of Christ.

86. Cf. Thompson, *Acts of the Risen Lord Jesus*, 95–96.

of Christ as the "great reversal" of Jesus's unjust death,[87] and through (and indeed *because of*) this resurrection, Jesus is exalted over all.

3. Resurrection and the Forgiveness of Sins

Third, how does the resurrection relate to the forgiveness of sins and the law of Moses in 13:38–39? Does Luke's account of Paul's speech shed light on the doctrine of justification, perhaps even in a way that is consistent with Paul's letters? In verses 38–39 Luke speaks of being justified by faith in Jesus (*en toutō pas ho pisteuōn dikaioutai*), in contrast to what it was not possible to be justified (*dikaiōthēnai*) from (*apo*) by the law of Moses. Despite the preference of many modern English translations, the language of *dikaioō* in verses 38–39 is best translated in terms of being justified, rather than being freed. *From what* is a person justified? It must be from sin. Paul uses similar language in Romans 6:7: "For the one who has died has been justified [*dedikaiōtai*] from [*apo*] sin."[88] The Lukan Paul in Acts 13 correlates justification by faith (v. 39) with the forgiveness of sins (v. 38). Significantly, this good news derives from Paul's exposition of the resurrection, which is apparent from *oun* and *dia touto* in Acts 13:38. These refer back to Jesus, who was raised and did not see decay (vv. 36–37).

But how close is the Pisidian Antioch speech in Acts to the Pauline doctrine of justification? Has Luke misunderstood, or only half understood, Paul?[89] Although Paul does speak of justification in contrast to the law of Moses (e.g., Gal. 2:16; 3:11; 5:4),[90] it is objected that Paul speaks less clearly about the correlation of forgiveness of sins to justification.[91] However, if the "we" passages of Luke are taken at face value to indicate that Luke accompanied

87. See Morgan-Wynne, *Paul's Pisidian Antioch Speech*, 188–89; cf. Ned B. Stonehouse, *The Areopagus Address* (London: Tyndale, 1949), 48.

88. See Bock, *Acts*, 459, which correctly notes that the supposed difficulties in English translations (is it "freed from" or "justified from"?) are not a problem in Greek. For "freed" see ESV; NASB; NRSV; for "justified" language see CSB; KJV; NIV (1984, 2011). Marguerat argues that Luke reserves for Paul the language of justification in Acts (*Actes des Apôtres*, 2:51, 96).

89. Dunn (*Beginning from Jerusalem*, 428n65) thinks that Luke has only "half grasped" Paul's theology at this point; see also Vielhauer, "On the 'Paulinism' of Acts," 41–42, 45–48. See further the survey of views in Kyle Scott Barrett, "Justification in Lukan Theology" (PhD diss., Southern Baptist Theological Seminary, 2012), 1–26.

90. I glean here again from Charles Hill's Greek exegesis lectures on Galatians (Reformed Theological Seminary, Orlando, Florida, Spring 2005); see also Johnson, *Message of Acts*, 155; Marshall, *Luke: Historian and Theologian*, 189–92; Bock, *Acts*, 459–60; Anderson, *"But God Raised Him from the Dead,"* 255–56; cf. Tannehill, *Narrative Unity*, 2:172.

91. E.g., Dunn, *Beginning from Jerusalem*, 428; Vielhauer, "On the 'Paulinism' of Acts," 41. See also Krister Stendahl, "The Apostle Paul and the Introspective Conscience of the West," *HTR* 56 (1963): 199–215; his approach has been recently engaged by Stephen Westerholm, *Justification Reconsidered: Rethinking a Pauline Theme* (Grand Rapids: Eerdmans, 2013), 5.

Paul on some of his travels (which remains the best view), then it beggars belief to think that Luke has misunderstood this key theological emphasis of an apostle he knew personally. A better view is that Acts 13:38–39 provides another angle on the ("Pauline") doctrine of justification, and one that supports the "older" perspective on Paul—namely, that one's right standing before God does not depend on one's adherence to the law of Moses and that justification entails the forgiveness of sins.[92]

Particularly pertinent for the present discussion is the relationship in Acts 13 between justification and Jesus's resurrection. The causal link between Jesus's resurrection and believers' justification in Paul's Pisidian Antioch sermon recalls similar connections in Paul's letters. For example, in Romans 4:24–25 believers are justified *because* of Jesus's resurrection.[93] Thus Romans speaks of justification on the basis of Christ's resurrection, in addition to justification on the basis of Christ's death (cf. 3:24–25). This variety of emphases in Paul further encourages readers of Acts not to misconstrue Luke's understanding of the atoning work of Christ—justification is not based upon *either* the death of Christ *or* his resurrection; it is based on Christ's *entire work*.

It is also noteworthy that Paul relates the resurrection of Christ to Adam in both Romans 5 and 1 Corinthians 15. In both cases, the obedience of the last Adam leads to life for those with faith in Christ (Rom. 5:12–21; 1 Cor. 15:20–49). These passages relate the obedience of Christ to his resurrection, which Luke also does. Not only does Luke clearly view Christ as a new Adam (cf. Luke 3:38),[94] but Jesus is consistently identified as the Holy and Righteous One (using the *dik-* word group; see Luke 23:47; Acts 3:14–15) who did not see decay. Jesus's resurrection in Acts is predicated in large measure upon his perfect obedience (see the use of Ps. 16 in Acts 2:24–36; 13:34–37; cf. 13:22), which is similar to Paul's Adam Christology (Rom. 5:18–19; 1 Cor. 15:21–22). Luke and Paul agree that justification comes through the resurrection of the perfectly righteous one.

4. Resurrection and Gentile Mission

A fourth insight from the resurrection emphasis in Paul's speech at Pisidian Antioch is its relation to the gentile mission. Bock has noted that Luke's

---

92. Paul's letters do occasionally speak of forgiveness of sins, especially if one includes disputed Pauline Letters (e.g., Rom. 4:7; Eph. 1:7; 4:32; Col. 1:14; 2:13; 3:13). Cf. Keener, *Acts*, 2:2074–77; Barrett, "Justification in Lukan Theology," 185–91.

93. See also Daniel Marguerat, "Quand la résurrection se fait clef de lecture de l'histoire (Luc-Actes)," in *Resurrection of the Dead: Biblical Traditions in Dialogue*, ed. Geert Van Oyen and Tom Shepherd, BETL 249 (Leuven: Peters, 2012), 200.

94. See further Brandon D. Crowe, *The Last Adam: A Theology of the Obedient Life of Jesus in the Gospels* (Grand Rapids: Baker Academic, 2017).

sus builds on the necessary framework of the scriptural
his dealings with humanity.[113] The proper response for
is not substantially different from the response called
n the synagogue: repent and believe in light of the resur-
ough some believe (v. 34), responses to the resurrection
are not uniformly positive (v. 32).[114] If Paul's appearance
us is a trial (which will not be the last in Acts!), Paul turns
sembly—they themselves will be subject to the resurrected
l.[115]

sion to Adam in 17:26 may also reflect Pauline scriptural
resurrection,[116] since in Paul's letters the resurrection is
to an Adam Christology, as we see in 1 Corinthians 15.
surrection entails the risen Christ's universal lordship and
, which pertains to all people descended from Adam. This
what we have already seen in Acts (cf. 10:36, 42): the resur-
ar the universal authority of Christ over all people, and in
rity is portrayed in adamic terms. To integrate the teachings
Corinthians 15: just as surely as all people come from one
h that one man death entered the world, so has God now (*nyn*,
d one new, righteous Man from the dead who has author-
anity. For Paul resurrection theology is Adam theology, and
in the Areopagus speech. Yet even clearer than this, Jesus's
he fulcrum for Paul's call to faith and repentance (vv. 30–31).

tion Elsewhere in Paul's Missionary Journeys (Acts 13–21)

e prominence of the resurrection in two Pauline speeches from
journeys, it will be helpful to consider some other Pauline
cts—both speeches and narratives—that further support the
f the resurrection. Though these are not as weighty as other

christological explanations from the Old Testament end with Paul's sermon at Pisidian Antioch, which then gives way to the gentile mission.[95] Indeed, it may even be that the speech itself provides the necessary momentum in Acts for the remainder of Paul's missionary journeys.[96] After this sermon Luke applies the language of serving as a light to the gentiles from Isaiah 49:6 to Paul and Barnabas in Acts 13:47.[97]

In light of the resurrection emphasis of Paul's speech, Luke may be indicating that the gentile mission is under way *because of* Jesus's resurrection. The apostolic preaching in Acts consistently emphasizes the resurrection,[98] and this message—rooted in the Old Testament Scriptures—is for gentiles as well. For if Jesus has been raised from the dead and exalted to God's right hand, then he truly is Lord of *all* (Acts 10:36). This explains the need for the gentile mission.

Acts 13: Conclusion

We have covered much ground in relation to Paul's important speech at Pisidian Antioch. The most important aspects can be itemized as follows.

1. Paul's speech hinges on the resurrection of Christ.
2. Jesus's resurrection fulfills the covenantal promises to David.
3. Because Jesus has been raised from the dead, justification and forgiveness of sins are offered.
4. Though Paul makes his case in large part from the Old Testament, his message is not only for Jews but for gentiles as well. The latter come more clearly into view when Paul visits Athens.

The Resurrection Message in Athens (Acts 17:16–34)

Of all the Pauline speeches in Acts, perhaps none has been more widely dissected than Paul's speech before the Areopagus in Acts 17.[99] How many studies ask what Athens has to do with Jerusalem? Martin Dibelius considered this speech to be a climax of the entire book of Acts.[100]

Stonehouse, *Areopagus Address*, 32; cf. C. Kavin Rowe, *One True Life: The
Christians as Rival Traditions* (New Haven: Yale University Press, 2016), 248.
N. Clayton Croy, "Hellenistic Philosophies and the Preaching of the Resurrec-
, 32)," *NovT* 39 (1997): 28.
we, *World Upside Down*, 39; see also N. T. Wright, *Paul: A Biography* (San
perOne, 2018), 193–207.
:26 as a reference to Adam, see Rowe, *World Upside Down*, 199n154; Barrett,
on the Acts, 2:842; Bock, *Acts*, 566; Bruce, *Acts of the Apostles*, 336; Fitzmyer,
ostles, 608–9; Schnabel, *Acts*, 734; Peterson, *Acts of the Apostles*, 496–97; Keener,
8.

95. Bock, *Proclamation from Prophecy and Pattern*, 211, 213, 215.
96. Cf. O'Toole, "Christ's Resurrection in Acts 13,13–52," 370–71.
97. See recently Holly Beers, *The Followers of Jesus as the "Servant": Luke's Model from Isaiah for the Disciples in Luke-Acts*, LNTS 535 (London: Bloomsbury T&T Clark, 2015), 154–64.
98. Note again the helpful chart in Thompson, *Acts of the Risen Lord Jesus*, 91.
99. See the bibliography on Acts 17 in Clare K. Rothschild, *Paul in Athens: The Popular Religious Context of Acts 17*, WUNT 1/341 (Tübingen: Mohr Siebeck, 2014), 157–60.
100. Martin Dibelius, *Studies in the Acts of the Apostles*, ed. Heinrich Greeven, trans. Mary Ling and Paul Schubert (London: SCM, 1956), 26.

I therefore will not be able to enter into all of the debates or explore all possible avenues relating to Acts 17. I will focus primarily on Jesus's resurrection in Paul's speech before the Areopagus (vv. 22–31). At Pisidian Antioch Paul emphasizes the implications of the resurrection and shows the resurrection to be a scriptural necessity. In Athens Paul's argument takes a bit of a different shape—and is more briefly recounted in Acts—but his argument again depends upon the resurrection.

At the beginning of Paul's visit to Athens—which appears to have been almost an afterthought in the context of his missionary journey—he was particularly distressed (*parōxyneto*) by the pervasiveness of idols (17:16). He therefore preached in the synagogue and publicly in the *agora* (v. 17). Though we do not have much information about either the synagogue sermon or the preaching summarized in verse 17 we do find strong indication in verse 18 that it was specifically the resurrection that led to the ruffling of theological feathers in Athens.[101] This resurrection emphasis is consistent with what readers of Acts have encountered by this point in Paul's synagogue sermons (e.g., in Pisidian Antioch, Thessalonica). We can therefore conclude that in the synagogue Paul would have been expounding the resurrection of Jesus from the Scriptures even before his Areopagus speech.[102]

But as in Thessalonica and Berea (cf. 17:2–3, 5–14), in Athens Paul's resurrection message was not met with universal approval. Paul was reviled as a *spermologos*—a term that derides the simplicity and apparent incoherence of Paul's message[103]—and a proclaimer of strange divinities (*xenōn daimoniōn*, v. 18) specifically because he was preaching "Jesus and the resurrection." This phrase has elicited much discussion. Are "Jesus" and "Resurrection" perceived to be two divinities preached by Paul?[104] Whatever misunderstanding may have accrued to this language in Paul's preaching, it is clear to readers of Acts, especially in light of the Areopagus address itself, that Jesus and his resurrection continue to be central in the Pauline *kērygma*.[105]

101. See also Stonehouse, *Areopagus Address*, 9–13.

102. See also Thompson, *Acts of the Risen Lord Jesus*, 90.

103. Thus the possible association with a common bird who picks up seeds and scraps. See Keener, *Acts*, 3:2595–96; Bruce, *Acts of the Apostles*, 333; Barrett, *Commentary on the Acts*, 2:830.

104. See, e.g., Wright, *Resurrection of the Son of God*, 456; also Fitzmyer, *Acts of the Apostles*, 605, which leaves open the possibility that *Anastasis* is understood by Paul's audience as a female deity balancing Jesus as a male deity. Barrett (*Commentary on the Acts*, 2:831) finds this unlikely in light of the language (i.e., the verbs) Paul uses elsewhere to describe the resurrection (*egeirō*, *anistēmi*).

105. So Stonehouse, *Areopagus Address*, 42, which observes that "Jesus and the resurrection" is "a most apt and succinct characterization of the preaching of Paul and Peter as reported in Acts."

In the address itself (
tion "to an unknown go
sensibilities, Paul expla
whom they do not know,
people.[106] Paul quickly m
in the first place—idolatry
not live in any temple ma
whom all people owe their e
a likely reference to Adam (v
solidarity of all humanity. A
verse 28,[108] Paul returns to t
common Creator and means
honor God appropriately (v.

Now comes the crucial mo
and the required response (17
been building all along.[109] Th
know about is neither Epicurus
recalled in Acts 17.[110] Instead, t
been raised from the dead and w
resurrection of Jesus, as Rowe ha
human history."[111] As we see else
repent in light of the resurrection.[1
Testament Scriptures, the framewo

106. C. Kavin Rowe, *World Upside Down*
Oxford University Press, 2009), 201n170, fo
gus Speech in the Composition of Acts," in
Rylaarsdam, Essays in Divinity 6 (Chicago: U
significance of eight occurrences of "all" (*pan*

107. See Rowe, *World Upside Down*, 199n1
on the Acts, 2:842; Bock, *Acts*, 566; Peterson,

108. See, e.g., Bruce, *Acts of the Apostles*, 3
Acts, 3:2657–61. See alternatively Schnabel, *Act*
use of Epimenides, proposing that Luke "fashic
popular traditions about [Epimenides]" (*Paul i*
also notes some suggestive sources viewing Epim
a sort of resurrection (cf. pp. 41, 48, 76, 114).

109. Rightly noted by many, including Wright,
"Preaching and Defence of Paul," 317.

110. Socrates was also tried in Athens for intro
mentary on the Acts, 2:824–31; Rowe, *World Upsid*

111. Rowe, *World Upside Down*, 40–41.

112. Again Rowe, *World Upside Down*, 41: "To a
[is] . . . to become a Christian."

---

the resurrection of J
account of God and
this gentile audienc
for by the message i
rection of Jesus. Th
and its implications
before the Areopag
the tables on the as
Jesus as judge of a

Paul's likely all
thinking about th
strongly tethered
The logic of the r
authority to judg
is consistent with
rection makes cl
Acts 17 this auth
of Acts 17 and 1
man, and throug
Acts 17:30) rais
ity over all hum
both are in view
resurrection is t

The Resurrec

Having seen th
his missionar
passages in A
importance

113. So also
Stoics and Earl
114. See als
tion (Acts 17:1
115. Cf. R
Francisco: Ha
116. For 1
Commentary
Acts of the A
Acts, 3:2645–

parts of the argument in this chapter, they do merit brief discussion before we move on to Paul's defenses in the last quarter of Acts.

I will organize my comments based on the traditional missionary journeys. Though this organizing feature is not without its problems—it's debatable how important these journeys are for the structure of Acts[117]—the journeys nevertheless provide helpful rubrics to categorize the events of Acts 13–21.

First Missionary Journey (Acts 13:1–14:28)

We have already considered in detail Paul's first major speech on the first missionary journey—the sermon at Pisidian Antioch—which gives sustained attention to the resurrection of Jesus. In light of the programmatic nature of this speech, it is not surprising that resurrection is characteristic of Paul's preaching on the first missionary journey. We see this, for example, in Paul's exploits in Iconium, Lystra, and Derbe (Acts 14). Three possible echoes of the resurrection resound in this chapter.

First, Paul and Barnabas preach in the synagogue at Iconium (14:1). After being run out of Iconium, they continue to preach in Lystra, Derbe, and the surrounding areas of Lycaonia (v. 6). After being stoned in Derbe and subsequently returning to Lystra, Iconium, and Pisidian Antioch (cf. v. 20), Paul preached the word in Perga and Attalia (in Pamphylia), before returning to Syrian Antioch (vv. 24–26). Though Luke does not provide anything like a summary of Paul's speeches in these locations, Paul's Pisidian Antioch sermon exemplifies the sort of argument Paul would have made. Given the prominence of synagogues in the diaspora,[118] Paul likely delivered many of his speeches on the first missionary journey in synagogues (cf. 13:5; 14:1) or at least to audiences with many Jewish listeners. This would explain the ire of many Jews who pursued Paul—especially from Pisidian Antioch and Iconium (14:19). They were no doubt disturbed to hear that a crucified, cursed man is God's chosen Messiah.[119]

Paul gives a different sort of speech in Lystra (14:8–18), where he and Barnabas go into crisis-prevention mode; they can scarcely stop the people

117. This is illustrated by the disagreement among commentators on where one ends and another begins. For example, is the Jerusalem council included in the first missionary journey? Does the second missionary journey end in 18:22 or 18:23? Should Paul's final journey to Jerusalem be part of the third missionary journey? See Thompson, *Acts of the Risen Lord Jesus*, 67–68; Fitzmyer, *Acts of the Apostles*, 121–22; Bock, *Acts*, 47–48. My own outline of the missionary journeys in what follows agrees with Thompson's.

118. On ancient synagogues, see Keener, *Acts*, 2:1298–302; Lee I. Levine, *The Ancient Synagogue: The First Thousand Years* (New Haven: Yale University Press, 2000), esp. 105–12; Anders Runesson, *The Origins of the Synagogue: A Socio-Historical Study*, ConBNT 37 (Stockholm: Almqvist & Wiksell, 2001).

119. Cf. Justin, *Dial.* 90, noted in Rowe, *One True Life*, 152.

from sacrificing to them in response to Paul's miraculous deed. This speech of Paul, therefore, is less an evangelistic sermon and more of an urgent plea for the people not to sacrifice to Paul and Barnabas (vv. 13–16). Yet even Paul's mention of "previous generations" (*en tais parōchēmenais geneais*, v. 16) may assume the epochal turning point that has arrived with the resurrection of Christ with its present-day implications for the audience in Lystra.[120] We also know that, as in Athens, Paul can emphasize the resurrection to a gentile audience.

Second, the healing of the man at Lystra who could not walk is another miraculous deed that builds on the resurrection of Christ. This conclusion follows from the similarity of the healing in Acts 14:8–11 with the healing of the lame man at the temple in 3:1–10.[121] Though no comparable statement to 3:6 is found in 14:8–11 (whereby the name of Jesus of Nazareth is expressly invoked in the healing), since Paul's healing recalls Peter's healing, the *means* of healing is the same as well.[122] If the healing of the lame man in Acts 3 is accomplished through an apostle by the risen Jesus, then the same is true of the Lystran man in Acts 14.[123] And if the raising of the lame man in Acts 3 was a sign of the resurrection, the same is likely true of the raising of the man in Acts 14.[124]

Third, Paul's experience of being stoned and left for dead in Lystra (14:19–20) may recall the resurrection of Christ.[125] Paul does not actually experience death. Nevertheless, he is thought to be dead by the mob, yet arises and returns into the city. Again Luke uses *anistēmi* to speak of someone rising in a way that recalls the raising of Jesus from the dead.

Second Missionary Journey (Acts 15:36–18:22)

Paul's resurrection-focused Areopagus speech comes on his second missionary journey. Not surprisingly, the resurrection features prominently elsewhere on this journey.

120. This statement recalls Acts 17:30. So Bock, *Acts*, 477.

121. E.g., Goulder, *Type and History in Acts*, 27, 107.

122. The term *anistēmi* is used for the healing of the Lystran man in 14:10, whereas *egeirō* is used for the man in Acts 3. However, as I argued in ch. 2, the "raising up" of a prophet like Moses that builds on the raising of the lame man employs *anistēmi*.

123. See also Robert F. O'Toole, SJ, "Activity of the Risen Jesus in Luke-Acts," *Bib* 62 (1981): 492.

124. See also Dennis J. Hamm, SJ, "Acts 3:12–26: Peter's Speech and the Healing of the Man Born Lame," *PRSt* 11 (1984): 203–4.

125. This has also been suggested by Horton, *Death and Resurrection*, 55–56; Goulder, *Type and History in Acts*, 47, 101. This stoning was apparently in response to Paul's word-and-deed ministry, which may also recall the ministry of Jesus (cf. Luke 24:19).

We begin in Philippi, the Roman colony (16:12) that would have been teeming with Roman (military) influence.[126] It is therefore fitting that Paul's encounter with Lydia recalls Peter's encounter with the Roman centurion Cornelius in Acts 10. Lydia is a worshiper of God (*sebomenē ton theon*, 16:14), whereas Cornelius is a devout (*eusebēs*) man who fears God (*phoboumenos ton theon*, 10:2). Despite the differences in terminology, the similarities between the two people are clear.[127] Like Cornelius, Lydia had knowledge of God's work of salvation that was incomplete apart from the apostolic message about Jesus. This is the implication of the Lord (Jesus) opening her heart to understand Paul's message (16:14). Surely Paul introduced Lydia to the work of Jesus, who fulfilled Scripture by dying and rising again—and therefore is Lord (cf. v. 15).

A similar scenario arises with the Philippian jailer. After the dramatic earthquake and the jailer's resulting desperation, Paul offers the man salvation in the name of the Lord Jesus (16:31). This summary proclamation, which we can assume would have been accompanied by further instruction from Paul (v. 32), also recalls the message to Cornelius about Jesus of Nazareth, who is Lord of all by virtue of his resurrection (10:36, 40–43). Paul's message to the Philippian jailer and his household was no doubt similar to Luke's presentation of Peter's message to Cornelius and his household.

Paul's activity in Thessalonica also bespeaks the importance of his resurrection message. As we saw in Pisidian Antioch, in Thessalonica Paul expounds the resurrection of Christ in the synagogue from the Scriptures (17:1–3). The response is again mixed (vv. 4–5), and in this case Paul and Silas are accused of preaching another king (v. 7). If Paul's synagogue sermons (note *three Sabbaths*, v. 2) were consistent with his synagogue sermon at Pisidian Antioch, then Paul preached Jesus as the promised Davidic king who reigns over an everlasting kingdom by means of his resurrection. The accusation, therefore, of "another king" (*basilea heteron*, v. 7) is not altogether wrong (cf. 10:36), though in Luke's larger presentation it is also clear that this new Jesus movement is not therefore a political threat to Rome.[128] The

---

126. As a *colonia*, Philippi would have been home to Roman citizens designed to bring stability to a new place, and soldiers would have been rewarded with land here (see Barrett, *Commentary on the Acts*, 2:780). Philippi was the site of the important Battle of Philippi, where Octavian and Marc Antony defeated Brutus and Cassius just over a hundred years prior to Paul's encounter with Lydia (42 BC). See also Keener, *Acts*, 3:2380–83.

127. Barrett, *Commentary on the Acts*, 2:783, rightly notes the relevance of 10:2 for understanding 16:14.

128. See Rowe, *World Upside Down*, 92–102; cf. the testimony of the heavenly nature of the kingdom attributed to the grandsons of Jude, as related by Eusebius, *Hist. eccl.* 3.20.

resurrected Jesus, as Lord over all humanity, reigns over a different sort of kingdom.

The responses to Paul and Silas in Thessalonica lead them to Berea, where again the resurrection looms large. The Bereans are famous for being more noble (*ēsan eugenesteroi*) than the Thessalonians, because they searched the Scriptures to see if Paul's preaching was true (17:10–12). Since in Acts the apostolic preaching focuses on the resurrection and its fulfillment of the Old Testament, the Bereans must have been searching the Scriptures for the resurrection (cf. Luke 24:44–47; Acts 26:22–23).[129]

Later (after visiting Athens) Paul comes to Corinth, where he spends eighteen months (18:11). Again Paul invests his time teaching in the synagogue that the Christ is Jesus (vv. 1–5). By this point in Acts it is clear that Jesus's identification as *Christ* means that he is the promised Son of David—the holy one who does not see decay by virtue of his resurrection.[130] While Paul is in Corinth he sees a vision of the risen and ascended Christ, who encourages Paul and provides assurance that he continues to reign over his church (cf. vv. 9–10). It is also in Corinth that Paul is brought before Gallio (vv. 12–17), where Paul's message is deemed to be a matter pertaining to Jewish law. This coheres with what we see elsewhere: Paul's resurrection message accords with the Jewish Scriptures.

Third Missionary Journey (18:24–21:16)

The resurrection must have also been emphasized on Paul's third missionary journey. Several factors indicate this. First, Paul spends extended time in Ephesus (19:8, 10; 20:31), where he reasons—surely from the Scriptures—with the Jews in Ephesus about the kingdom of God (19:8). *Kingdom* in Acts assumes the lordship of Jesus as the risen Christ, who reigns over an everlasting kingdom.

Toward the conclusion of his third missionary journey, Paul offers his farewell address to the Ephesian elders at Miletus (20:17–38). He reminds them of the message he expounded at greater length during his sojourn in Ephesus, including repentance and faith in the Lord Jesus Christ (v. 21; cf. 20:24, 35). Paul again mentions the kingdom that he preached among them (20:25), as indeed is recorded in Acts 19. These statements are shorthand ways for Paul to speak of the message of Christ and his resurrected authority that he no doubt expounded in greater detail during his three-year stay in Ephesus. Paul's reference to proclaiming "the whole counsel of God" (*pasan tēn boulēn tou*

---

129. See further the discussion in ch. 7.
130. Thus, for example, the quotations of Ps. 16 [15 LXX] in both Acts 2:25–28 and 13:35.

theou, 20:27) surely entails the resurrection as the fulfillment of the Scriptures (cf. Luke 24:44–47; Acts 26:22–23).

Second, the account of Paul's raising of Eutychus at Troas (20:7–12) also involves a resurrection trope.[131] It is best, as Barrett comments, to understand that Eutychus really was dead after falling out of the window (v. 9).[132] Though the details of Eutychus's revivification are vague (v. 10), what is clear is that a man who was dead[133] was proclaimed by Paul to be alive. The assumption is that Paul's action is the reason for Eutychus's return to life.[134] If Paul preached the resurrection and/or the ongoing reign of the risen Christ in his (lengthy) sermon in Troas (v. 7), then the raising of Eutychus may well have served as a sign of the spoken word.

In addition, the disciples at Troas were breaking bread together (20:7, 11). This eating is consistent with the sacramental eating of bread elsewhere in Acts, which also recalls the meal that Jesus gave his disciples. In Acts 20 they are again in an upper room (v. 8), though the term used here (*hyperōon*) is different from that used in the Gospel account (*katalyma*, Luke 22:11; *anagaion*, 22:12).[135] Readers of Acts may recall that the risen Christ was made known at Emmaus in the breaking of the bread. The meal at Troas is the meal of the *risen* Jesus. As with the raising of Dorcas, earlier in Acts (9:36–43), the raising of Eutychus shows the power of Jesus to raise the dead and ultimately points readers to the resurrection of Jesus himself.

Summary: Missionary Journeys

These additional aspects of Paul's missionary journeys corroborate the centrality of the resurrection in Acts. It bears repeating that two significant portions of Paul's missionary journeys have already been considered in detail: his initial sermon at Pisidian Antioch and the Areopagus speech in Athens. The resurrection looms large in both these speeches. These major speeches are not isolated examples of resurrection preaching, but are representative of the sort of message that Paul would have consistently delivered in a variety of contexts.

131. Horton, *Death and Resurrection*, 65–68; Goulder, *Type and History in Acts*, 101, 107; cf. Marguerat, "Quand la résurrection," 202.
132. Barrett, *Commentary on the Acts*, 2:954. He notes that Luke says elsewhere that someone (i.e., Paul) was *thought* to be dead when he really was not (see 14:19).
133. Or at least, who appeared to be dead.
134. So Barrett, *Commentary on the Acts*, 2:955, on 20:10 (interpreting Paul's words): "His life is now, in virtue of my action, within him."
135. For further discussion, see Horton, *Death and Resurrection*, 67, following Johnson, *Acts of the Apostles*, 358.

The Resurrection and Paul's Defenses (Acts 21–26)

Overview

Thus far we have considered two of three major resurrection pillars in Acts: Peter's first major speech, at Pentecost, and Paul's first major speech, at Pisidian Antioch. Both of these speeches hinge on the resurrection of Jesus. We come now to the third major resurrection pillar: Paul's defense before Herod Agrippa II in Caesarea (Acts 26), in conjunction with the defenses that dominate the last quarter of Acts (especially chs. 21–26). In these defenses Luke consistently draws attention to two theological issues: (1) Jesus has been raised from the dead, and (2) Paul's preaching does not contradict the Old Testament Scriptures, but coheres with them.

I will give primary attention in what follows to the resurrection message and in chapter 7 will consider in more detail the implications of Paul's appeal to the Old Testament.

Paul in Jerusalem (Acts 21–23)

We must not miss *why* Paul is on trial in the first place. Not unlike Jesus (and to some degree Stephen) before him, Paul is on trial because of a theological fisticuffs centering on the temple. After purifying themselves, Paul and four Jewish acquaintances entered the temple (21:26). When this happened, some Jews from Asia fomented an uproar in the temple against Paul—claiming he was overturning the law and defiling the temple (vv. 27–28). As the preceding narrative and the subsequent trials of Paul will make clear (cf. v. 29), however, these accusations were bogus; Paul had done no such thing.[136] Neither was Paul the Egyptian who led four thousand men out into the wilderness (v. 38). Instead, Paul confirms he is a Jew, from Tarsus in Cilicia (v. 39).

This provides Paul an opportunity to make his first defense in Jerusalem, just outside the temple (21:40–22:21).[137] In this initial defense, Paul appeals for the first time to his encounter with the risen Christ on the road to Damascus, an event to which he will return again in his climactic defense before Herod Agrippa II (26:12–18). On both these occasions, the appearance of the risen Christ to Paul is decisive for his conversion from persecutor of the Way to being a follower and messenger of the Way. In Acts 22 Paul emphasizes the

---

136. For the well-known inscription warning against bringing gentiles into the temple, see Bruce, *Acts of the Apostles*, 395; Rowe, *World Upside Down*, 63; Peterson, *Acts of the Apostles*, 589–90; cf. Schnabel, *Acts*, 892–93.

137. At this point, Paul is likely just outside the temple on the steps leading up to the Antonia Fortress. See Schnabel, *Acts*, 887; Keener, *Acts*, 3:3161–62, 3166–67.

brightness of the light accompanying the vision of the exalted Jesus (vv. 6, 9). The bright light is the glory of the risen and exalted Jesus, anticipated in his transfiguration (Luke 9:29). Paul further draws attention to his Jewish pedigree (Acts 22:3).

Paul's inclusion of Ananias—a devout man according to the law (Acts 22:12)[138]—further supports the consistency of Paul's belief in the resurrected Christ with the faith of his fathers. For though Ananias was a follower of the Way, neither had he departed from the faith of his fathers (v. 14). Ananias identifies the Jesus that Paul encountered as the Righteous One (*ton dikaion*, v. 14), which surely would have been a stark contrast to Paul's earlier understanding of Jesus and confirms that the followers of Christ were not blasphemers for following a crucified Messiah.[139] This is a hallmark of Paul's defenses—the faith he proclaims in the resurrected Jesus is not a transgression of the traditions of the fathers, but is in fact their fulfillment (cf. 23:6). Furthermore, Ananias tells Paul that his conversion is for the purpose that he might be a witness to what he has seen and heard (22:15). As we have seen throughout Acts, the role of the apostles as witnesses has primary reference to the resurrection of Jesus (1:21–22),[140] which is part of the reason why Paul must encounter the *risen* Christ.

Paul concludes by recounting a follow-up vision of Christ in which he was commanded to go and take the gospel to the gentiles (22:21).[141] This may have exacerbated the issue at hand, which was the charge that Paul had defiled the temple by bringing gentiles into forbidden areas (21:37). With this, Paul's defense outside the temple is ended, and he is taken off to the barracks.

At this juncture Paul introduces something into the equation that has led to not a little discussion and debate: the issue of his Roman citizenship.[142] Paul has already invoked his citizenship at Philippi to avoid unlawful punishment (16:37–38), and he does so again in Jerusalem (22:25–29). This appeal propels the narrative forward, as Paul will now have more occasions to explain the faith he propounds—to gentiles, kings, and the children of Israel (cf. 9:15).

138. 𝔓[74], A, Vulgate omit *eulabēs* ("devout").
139. It is quite plausible that the cursing of Jesus on the tree (cf. Deut. 21:23) would have been one indication to Paul that Jesus could not have been the true Messiah. His later teaching on this point (cf. Gal. 3:13) would therefore reveal a significant change of mind. Cf., e.g., Dunn, *Beginning from Jerusalem*, 339–40.
140. Paul is called an apostle in Acts 14:14.
141. On the grammatical starkness of this episode, see Barrett, *Commentary on the Acts*, 2:1043–44.
142. See the classic study of A. N. Sherwin-White, *Roman Society and Roman Law in the New Testament* (Oxford: Oxford University Press, 1963; repr., Eugene, OR: Wipf & Stock, 2004), 57–70.

Paul next appears before the Sanhedrin (22:30), like Peter and the Jerusalem apostles before him (4:5). Here the resurrection comes even more clearly into focus. Consistent with the resurrection message of Peter in Acts 4, Paul immediately turns to the resurrection as the issue for which he is on trial (23:6). To be sure, Paul also focuses on the resurrection because of the diverging views of the Pharisees and Sadducees (23:8). Invoking the resurrection therefore provided Paul with a reprieve, though this was not *merely* a rhetorical ploy.[143] Instead, Acts makes it abundantly clear that the resurrection was indeed the defining issue for Paul's message and ministry. As Alan Thompson has rightly observed, Paul is "doing more than throwing a strategic grenade into the proceedings . . . he *is* on trial for his 'hope in the resurrection of the dead.'"[144] In this context the resurrection of the dead most likely refers largely to the general resurrection of God's people, as was sometimes the case in earlier apostolic preaching (cf. 4:2) and as Paul will later emphasize before Felix (24:15). Even so, the rationale for this general resurrection is predicated upon the resurrection of Christ as the first to rise from the dead. This will be explicit in Paul's speech before Agrippa II (cf. 26:23).

Put simply, Paul is on trial because of his belief in the resurrection of Jesus.[145] This confirms the importance of the resurrection for Paul's preaching throughout Acts, and is consistent with major speeches in Pisidian Antioch, Athens, Jerusalem, and Caesarea.

Paul in Caesarea (Acts 24–26)

PAUL BEFORE FELIX (ACTS 24)

When Paul arrives under guard in Caesarea, he has the opportunity after five days to provide another defense to the governor: Claudius Antonius Felix (24:1–2).[146] Felix not only was the governor of Judea but also had a rather good grasp of the Way (v. 22), as he was married to Drusilla, the sister of Herod Agrippa II (v. 24; cf. 26:27). Two features of Paul's defense before Felix stand out. First, Paul confirms at the outset that he, though a follower of the Way, is teaching nothing else than what is written in the Law and the Prophets

143. Contrast Pervo, *Acts*, 574.

144. Thompson, *Acts of the Risen Lord Jesus*, 79 (emphasis original); see also Robert W. Wall, "The Acts of the Apostles: Introduction, Commentary, and Reflection," in vol. 10 of *NIB* (Nashville: Abingdon, 2002), 310–11.

145. See also Hansen, "Preaching and Defence of Paul," 321–22; Joshua W. Jipp, *Reading Acts* (Eugene, OR: Cascade, 2018), 118–20.

146. Sometime in the range of 52 to 59, depending on the dates one assigns to Felix as governor of Judea. For discussions of Felix, see Keener, *Acts*, 3:3329–31, 4:3430–32; Schnabel, *Acts*, 936; Bruce, *Acts of the Apostles*, 416–17; Barrett, *Commentary on the Acts*, 2:1080–81.

(24:14; cf. v. 16). Second, Paul specifically identifies the issue at hand as the resurrection of the dead (v. 15). Here again Paul likely has in view the general resurrection, which is contingent upon the resurrection of Christ as the first to rise from the dead.[147] Paul confirms this in his concluding statement to Felix in verse 21: "With respect to the resurrection of the dead I am on trial before you today" (*peri anastaseōs nekrōn egō krinomai sēmeron eph' hymōn*).[148] Rowe correctly comments on this passage, "From first to last, the Way is about the resurrection."[149]

Another, shorter defense of Paul before Felix is recorded later in Acts 24, when Felix's Jewish wife Drusilla (v. 24) was present. Again Paul spoke about faith in Christ Jesus.[150] Consistent with what we have seen in major aspects of Paul's preaching thus far, this faith in Christ would certainly have included the resurrection of Christ. This is corroborated by Paul's discussion of the coming judgment (v. 25), which Paul elsewhere attributes to the resurrected Jesus (17:31; cf. 10:42). In the end, Felix left Paul in prison to curry favor with the Jews (24:27).

Paul before Festus (Acts 25)

Felix was succeeded by Porcius Festus, who quickly gave Paul a hearing. In the short account of Acts 25, Paul emphasized familiar themes: he had not committed any crime against the law, the temple, or the emperor (v. 8). While he does not mention the resurrection explicitly, it probably was part of Paul's argument, especially in light of the defenses he made to Felix and later to Agrippa II. The clearest indication that Paul emphasized the resurrection to Festus comes in verse 19, where Festus informs the visiting Herod Agrippa II that Paul's case could be summarized by Paul's view that Jesus, who had been dead, was now alive.

This report from Festus to Agrippa II, however, comes after Festus refuses to take definitive action in Paul's favor. Instead, he, like Felix, desired to do the Jews a favor, this time by sending Paul back to Jerusalem (25:9). This prospect leads Paul to appeal to Caesar, and he will in due course set sail for Rome.

---

147. Cf. Wright, *Resurrection of the Son of God*, 453–54, 456.

148. My translation reflects the word order of the Greek, where the prepositional phrase concerning the resurrection is fronted following *hoti*. Some manuscripts read *hypo* in place of *epi*, but this issue does not affect the emphasis on the resurrection in 24:21. Charles Talbert identifies an A-B-A'-B' pattern in this speech, with each section concluding with the resurrection (see also below on the structure of Acts 26). Talbert, *Reading Acts: A Literary and Theological Commentary on the Acts of the Apostles* (New York: Crossroad, 1997), 206.

149. Rowe, *World Upside Down*, 78.

150. The preposition *eis* + the accusative makes it explicit that Paul is speaking about faith *in* Christ Jesus (*peri tēs eis Christon Iēsoun pisteōs*).

Paul before Herod Agrippa II (Acts 25–26)

Before Paul travels to Rome, he presents an extended defense to Herod Agrippa II (along with Bernice). This is the second-longest Pauline speech in Acts (26:2–23) and the third major resurrection pillar for my argument.[151] Acts 26 is a significant passage for understanding Acts, and it focuses on the resurrection of Jesus. In the words of Robert O'Toole, "The whole fabric of the speech hangs on the resurrection of the dead."[152] Key also is the re- lationship of Jesus's resurrection to the Old Testament Scriptures.[153] Paul's speech begins, after the opening pleasantries (*captatio benevolentiae*), with the main issue in verses 6–8: God raises the dead (v. 8), and this represents Paul's hope in the promise God made to the fathers (vv. 6–7). Paul returns to the resurrection at the end of his speech, and again relates the resurrection to the fulfillment of Scripture (vv. 22–23).[154] These two aspects—the importance of the resurrection and its relation to the faith of the fathers—provide the outline for my discussion.

First to be considered are the ways that Paul highlights the importance of the resurrection. Paul initially identifies the reason for his trial as the hope given to the fathers (26:6), and then clarifies that it should not be surprising that God raises the dead (v. 8). Notably, Paul does not say that God *can* raise the dead or God *will* raise the dead, but that God *raises* the dead—the im- plication being that this has already happened in Jesus.[155] Paul's statements in verses 6–8 round out the first movement of his speech, which culminates in discussion of the resurrection.[156]

Following the transition in 26:9, more discussion of the resurrection comes in verses 9–23. This includes Paul's second recounting of his conversion on the road to Damascus (vv. 12–18). This account, which includes additional information not found in Luke's prior discussions of Paul's conversion, is another opportunity for Paul to emphasize his encounter with the glorious, living—and *risen*—Lord Jesus. As in Acts 22, the crucial event for Paul is meeting the exalted Jesus, who changes the course of his life (cf. 26:19). In- cluded in this recounting of his Damascus road encounter is the call for Paul

---

151. By way of reminder, the other two are Peter's Pentecost sermon and Paul's sermon at Pisidian Antioch.

152. O'Toole, SJ, *Acts 26: The Christological Climax of Paul's Defense (Ac 22:1–26:32)*, AnBib 78 (Rome: Biblical Institute Press, 1978), 5.

153. See also Bock, *Acts*, 714.

154. O'Toole, *Christological Climax*, v, refers to this as a "diptych."

155. The raisings of Tabitha/Dorcas and Eutychus also point to this present reality.

156. For this structure, see O'Toole, *Christological Climax*, 28. O'Toole sees each major section of the speech being marked by *men oun* (26:4, 9); cf. Talbert, *Reading Acts*, 211–13.

to be a witness (*martyra*, v. 16), most likely to the resurrection of Jesus,[157] as we have seen in 22:15 and throughout Acts (cf. 1:21–22). But, unique in this account, it is the *Lord Jesus* who tells Paul he will be a witness, whereas earlier it was Ananias who said this (22:15). Yet Paul also emphasizes that his change of heart does not entail a rejection of his ancestral faith. Instead, as he continues, Jesus is the *first* (*prōtos*) to rise from the dead (26:23), which is the fulfillment of the Prophets and Moses (v. 22).[158] It is to this fulfillment that Paul testifies, with the term *martyreō* again recalling the task of witnessing to the *risen* Jesus.[159] Paul thus begins and ends his speech with reference to the resurrection of Jesus.[160]

Paul's emphasis on the resurrection in his speech elicits a rather strong response from Festus (26:24). Paul's reply to the charge that he is crazy (*mainē*, *mania*, v. 24) is that his logic makes perfect sense if one believes in the prophets (v. 27).[161] Paul further points to the public nature of the events he recounts (v. 26). Paul most likely has in view the events pertaining to the ministry, death, and resurrection of Jesus—the origins of Christianity.[162] It might also include the message of Jesus going forth to the gentiles (v. 23).[163] The singular "this" (*touto*) that has not been done in a corner (v. 26) very likely then refers to the resurrection of Jesus, which holds primacy of place in Paul's speech (vv. 2–23), though it may simply be a way to speak summarily of the work of Christ.[164] Either is possible, though the former is to be preferred.[165] The work of Christ—and specifically his resurrection—was a public event, which corresponds to the nonnefarious nature of the church in Acts.[166]

157. See also Peterson, *Acts of the Apostles*, 667; Fitzmyer, *Acts of the Apostles*, 759.

158. Ulrich Wilckens, *Missionsreden*, 174, connects the language of *first* here to Jesus's identity as *archēgos* in Acts 3:15; 5:31. If so, it may provide further support for understanding *archēgos* firmly in resurrectional terms, as I argued in the previous chapter. Wilckens, *Die Missionsreden der Apostelgeschichte: Form- und traditionsgeschichtliche Untersuchungen*, WMANT 15 (Neukirchen-Vluyn: Neukirchener Verlag, 1961), 174.

159. See O'Toole, *Christological Climax*, 104.

160. So, e.g., O'Toole, *Christological Climax*, 30–32. He further observes that 26:23 is a summary of the apostolic preaching (113).

161. On the charge of madness, see Abraham J. Malherbe, "'Not in a Corner': Early Christian Apologetic in Acts 26:26," *SecCent* 5 (1985–86): 206–7.

162. See here Barrett, *Commentary on the Acts*, 2:1168–69.

163. So Peterson, *Acts of the Apostles*, 674; Schnabel, *Acts*, 1016.

164. As is commonly noted, the language of doing something in a corner is proverbial. See Bruce, *Acts of the Apostles*, 448–49; Malherbe, "'Not in a Corner,'" 201–2; O'Toole, *Christological Climax*, 139n45; Fitzmyer, *Acts of the Apostles*, 764; Schnabel, *Acts*, 1016. See especially Epictetus, *Diatr.* 2.12.17.

165. See, e.g., Rowe, *World Upside Down*, 86.

166. See also Malherbe, "'Not in a Corner,'" 202, following Haenchen, *Acts of the Apostles*, 691–92.

Agrippa further challenges Paul, asking if in such a short span (*en oligō*) he thinks he can persuade Agrippa to become a Christian (*Christianos*, 26:28).[167] It is worth remembering that "Christian" originated as a term of derision (cf. Acts 11:26; 1 Pet. 4:16), which is probably the sense in which Agrippa uses the term in 26:28.[168] For the present purposes it is highly significant that Paul's speech centers on the resurrection as the heart of the message about Christianity. The resurrection plays a preeminent role in Paul's explanation of the work of Christ, and in response to the resurrection Agrippa apparently resists Paul's attempts to convince him.

Second to be considered in Paul's defense before Agrippa II are the ways that Paul relates the resurrection to his ancestral faith. Paul mentions his background as a Pharisee, a member of the strictest of the Jewish sects of the day (26:5). This strictness included zeal for the law of God,[169] as we see elsewhere in Acts (e.g., 22:3).[170] What is more, Paul relies on his heritage to bolster his argument that the resurrection is not something out of accord with his ancestral traditions but that he is now aware that the hope the Pharisees hold to—that is, the hope in the resurrection (cf. 23:8)—has come to fruition through Jesus. The hope that the fathers sought to attain (*katantēsai*) has been confirmed, and indeed granted through the resurrection of Jesus. Jesus's resurrection does not contradict God's covenant promises, but fulfills what is anticipated night and day (26:7). Paul further alludes to the power of God to raise the dead (v. 8). Anyone familiar with the Old Testament Scriptures—including Agrippa—would likely know that God is the Creator (Gen. 1–2), who has the power to kill and make alive (Deut. 32:39).[171] Even more to the point, God had already raised the dead through the mighty acts of Elijah and Elisha even before the ministry of

167. This phrase is notoriously difficult to translate. So, e.g., Rowe (*World Upside Down*, 230n227): "The sentence resists entirely felicitous translation," and Barrett (*Commentary on the Acts*, 2:1169): "Agrippa's words to Paul are perhaps the most disputed, as regards to their construction and meaning, in Acts."

168. So, e.g., Rowe, *World Upside Down*, 131; Bock, *Acts*, 723.

169. See Josephus, *J.W.* 2.162, noted by Fitzmyer, *Acts of the Apostles*, 756.

170. Cf. Isaac W. Oliver, *Torah Praxis after 70 CE: Reading Matthew and Luke-Acts as Jewish Texts*, WUNT 2/355 (Tübingen: Mohr Siebeck, 2013).

171. On the prominence of Deut. 32 in the ancient world, see the tables in Brandon D. Crowe, *The Obedient Son: Deuteronomy and Christology in the Gospel of Matthew*, BZNW 188 (Berlin: de Gruyter, 2012), 48–49, 150–51, 156; on the unique, life-giving prerogative of the biblical God, reflected in Deut. 32:39, see Richard Bauckham, *God Crucified: Monotheism and Christology in the New Testament* (Grand Rapids: Eerdmans, 1999), 11n10; Bauckham, *The Testimony of the Beloved Disciple: Narrative, History, and Theology in the Gospel of John* (Grand Rapids: Baker Academic, 2007), 242–50.

Jesus, and others had been brought back from the precipice of death.[172] Jesus himself alludes to the covenant promises to Abraham, Isaac, and Jacob in Luke 20:27–40—resurrection life was implied by the yet unfulfilled promises given to the patriarchs.[173]

Paul is even more explicit at the end of his speech, where he points to the resurrection as the realization in history of what the Prophets and Moses said would happen (26:22). Paul clarifies that he has in view the suffering of Christ, his resurrection, and the message going forth to the gentiles (v. 23); the defense of the Lukan Paul here corresponds closely to insights provided by the risen Jesus in Luke (Luke 24:25–27, 44–47).[174] Here again we find a logical connection between the resurrection of Christ and the mission to the gentiles. The Prophets are also in view in Paul's response to Agrippa's resistance—if Agrippa did indeed believe the Prophets, then he should also believe in the resurrection—which has now begun in Christ (26:23). The resurrection should not have been a significant stumbling block for Agrippa if he believed the prophets (v. 27).

These two aspects of Paul's speech—the resurrection and its relation to his ancestral faith—can be summed up as the realization of the *hope of Israel*. The terminology for hope (*elpis, elpizō*) is used seven times in Acts to refer to the resurrection; three of these occurrences come in 26:6–7, and two come elsewhere in Paul's defenses (23:6; 24:15).[175] Indeed, in 23:6 the phrasing *peri elpidos kai anastaseōs nekrōn* equates hope (*elpidos*) with the resurrection of the dead (*anastaseōs nekrōn*).[176] This is consistent with the hope expressed in Acts 2:26, citing Psalm 16:9 [15:9 LXX]: "My flesh will dwell *in hope*" (*hē sarx mou kataskēnōsei ep' elpidi*). Already in Acts 2 the foundational exposition of the resurrection correlates hope with the resurrection. Later, in Paul's penultimate speech, the resurrection is again understood in terms of hope—specifically "the hope of Israel" (*elpidos tou Israēl*, 28:20). If the apostolic preaching has as its focus the resurrection of Jesus, then this resurrection

---

172. For example, Jonah and Hezekiah. I return to these examples in ch. 7.

173. In Luke Jesus's answer on the resurrection confounds his hearers, and from that point no one dares ask him any more questions (Luke 20:40).

174. In Acts 26:22 Paul does not mention the Psalms explicitly as does Jesus in Luke 24:44 (though see Luke 24:27). But given the prominence of the Psalms for Paul's explanations of the resurrection to this point in Acts, one can hardly doubt their importance for Paul. It is also quite possible that the Prophets for Paul would have included the Psalms (cf. Acts 2:30).

175. See also O'Toole, *Christological Climax*, 89–95, which I have found helpful for the following discussion; K. R. Harriman, "'For David Said concerning Him': Foundations of Hope in Psalm 16 and Acts 2," *JTI* 11 (2017): 249.

176. This is hendiadys; see BDF §442.16; Barrett, *Commentary on the Acts*, 2:1063; Fitzmyer, *Acts of the Apostles*, 718.

is rightly summed up using the language of *hope*.[177] And this hope is not unexpected, but is built on the promises given to the fathers in Scripture.[178]

Conclusion: Paul's Defenses

Paul is on trial because of the resurrection (24:21). This entails not only the general resurrection (23:6; 24:15) but more fundamentally the resurrection of Jesus Christ as the foundation for the general resurrection (26:23). This should not be viewed as a threat either to Judaism or to the emperor, for Paul is speaking simply about the fulfillment of the Old Testament Scriptures (24:14–15; 26:3–8, 22–23, 27), and Roman officials consistently find Paul to be free from fault (cf. 25:25; 26:32). The resurrection is not an unforeseen *novum*; rather, it is the fulfillment of the Old Testament Scriptures that has irrupted in history. This was at the heart of Paul's gospel, and as such, it was at the heart of Paul's defenses.

Resurrection and Paul's Message in Rome (Acts 27–28)

Paul makes much of the resurrection in his defenses before the Sanhedrin, Felix, Festus, and Herod Agrippa II. After his appeal to Caesar, Paul journeys to Rome, where he again relates the resurrection to the hope of Israel (28:20). Moreover, Luke may even portray Paul's journey to Rome in death-and-resurrection terms.

Echoes of the Resurrection in Paul's Journey to Rome?

Luke's account of Paul's voyage to Rome raises many interesting questions. My interest is how it may function as a resurrection trope within Acts. The peril surrounding Paul leads readers to marvel at the way Paul's life was spared so that the word of God might continue to grow. Might Luke be presenting Paul's escape from near death as a sort of resurrection experience, one that recalls the greater experience of Jesus? Many scholars have suggested just such a connection.[179]

---

177. The collocation of hope and resurrection is consistent with what we know of Paul's letters. For example, see Rom. 4:18–25; 2 Cor. 1:9–10; cf. Ign., *Trall*. (salutation).

178. Cf. Jacob Jervell, *The Theology of the Acts of the Apostles* (Cambridge: Cambridge University Press, 1996), 90–91, 97–98. I discuss the scriptural basis of resurrection in more detail in ch. 7.

179. See, e.g., Horton, *Death and Resurrection*, 56–59; Goulder, *Type and History in Acts*, 39, 61; A. J. Mattill Jr., "The Purpose of Acts: Schneckenburger Reconsidered," in *Apostolic History and the Gospel: Biblical and Historical Essays Presented to F. F. Bruce on his 60th Birthday*,

Several reasons arise for viewing Paul's journey as a death-and-resurrection. One is that shipwreck is understood by some to be a "common ancient metaphor for death."[180] Consistent with this is the equation of waters with death, which finds a precedent in the biblical story of Jonah (Jon. 2:1–9).[181] In Luke's Gospel Jesus invokes the sign of Jonah to refer to his own resurrection (Luke 11:29–32).[182] Additionally, Paul announces on board the ship that the lives of those on board are in grave danger (Acts 27:10), underscoring the prospect of imminent death. Yet after the ship has a particularly perilous time and it appears all is lost (v. 20),[183] Paul tells those aboard that an angel has appeared to him and no lives will be lost (vv. 23–24). The angel is specifically identified as the angel of the God whom Paul worships. This is the God who raises the dead, as Paul has made clear before Agrippa II (26:8).[184] True to the revelation Paul received (27:24), Paul's life is spared, as are the lives of all those with him. Perhaps the breaking of bread on board the boat (27:35) is another reminder of life in the face of death, since the risen Christ is made known when he eats bread with his disciples (Luke 24:30–31; cf. 22:19). Despite the peril facing Paul, his life and the lives of those with him were spared—not only from shipwreck but from the soldiers (Acts 27:42–44). This deliverance from what appeared to be certain destruction to the men in the moment may well be used by Luke to present Paul's new lease on life as an echo of the resurrection of Jesus. Yet if Luke intends Paul's shipwreck to be an echo of the resurrection of Christ, then we must admit it is subtle.[185]

Beyond Paul's deliverance from death at sea, another possible resurrection episode is Paul's escaping what should have been certain death from the serpent bite on Malta (28:1–6).[186] Had Paul been spared from death at sea

ed. W. Ward Gasque and Ralph P. Martin (Grand Rapids: Eerdmans, 1970), 121; cf. Marguerat, "Quand la résurrection," 202. Goulder even states, "As the climax of the Gospel is the death and resurrection of Christ, so the climax of Acts is the *thanatos* and *anastasis* of Paul" (39).

180. Horton, *Death and Resurrection*, 57, quoting (though not verbatim) Richard I. Pervo, *Luke's Story of Paul* (Minneapolis: Fortress, 1990), 92. Pervo also includes prison as an ancient metaphor for death.

181. See again Horton, *Death and Resurrection*, 57.

182. See further my discussion of the sign of Jonah in ch. 7.

183. Note also the language of *hope* (*elpis*) and being *saved* (*sōzō*) in 27:20—two words often used to speak of the resurrection in Acts (e.g., 2:26; 4:12; 5:30–31).

184. In Acts God is consistently viewed as the agent who raised Jesus from the dead (2:24, 32; 3:15, 26; 4:10; 5:30; 10:40; 13:30, 33–34, 37; 17:31; 26:8).

185. For a critique of the view that Acts 27 is a death-and-resurrection scene, see Eckhard J. Schnabel, "Fads and Common Sense: Reading Acts in the First Century and Reading Acts Today," *JETS* 54 (2011): 274–75. See also the discussion in Keener, *Acts*, 4:3568–69n128.

186. This possibility is not discussed by Horton (*Death and Resurrection*), who argues for death-and-resurrection in the shipwreck. For this encounter as a "resurrection scene," see Willie James Jennings, *Acts*, Belief (Louisville: Westminster John Knox, 2017), 241.

only to then meet his end on land? Had Justice (*hē dikē*) found him out? Paul should have died from such a bite; his deliverance was miraculous.[187] Paul's callousness to the deadly bite recalls Jesus's statement in Luke 10:18–19 that the seventy (or seventy-two) disciples sent out would have authority over serpents (*opheōn*) and scorpions. These represent the authority of the devil, whom Jesus saw falling like lightning from heaven.[188] Though the terminology for the serpent is different in Acts 28 (*echidna*), Paul's deliverance from the serpent must be an indication of the authority granted by the risen Christ to Paul, especially in fulfillment of the mission given to him (cf. 9:15).[189]

A more remote possibility is that the sting of the serpent's bite has been rendered impotent by the work of Christ—who has defeated the devil (cf. Luke 10:18) and thus extinguished the sting of death. This possibility emerges particularly because of the association of Satan with serpent imagery in the New Testament (2 Cor. 11:3; Rev. 12:9; 20:2; cf. Rom. 16:20; 1 Tim. 2:14). Interestingly, in 1 Corinthians 15:55–56 Paul speaks of the sting (*kentron*) of death being overcome through Christ (following Hos. 13:14). The term for sting (*kentron*) is typically used of a stinger, as in a scorpion (cf. Rev. 9:10).[190] Though *kentron* is not used in Acts 28, perhaps we have here a conceptual parallel to 1 Corinthians 15: through the death and resurrection of Christ, death's venomous power is overcome. If so, Acts may present Paul's preliminary experience of the resurrection through the miraculous avoidance of certain death via poison. Because Christ has faced the sting of death from the diabolic serpent, he is able to grant Paul deliverance from a poisonous serpent in a way that gives Paul the opportunity to continue witnessing to the risen Jesus. Conceptually this makes sense, though admittedly such a view is difficult to demonstrate given the paucity of explicit verbal links.

It is certainly worth considering whether Luke presents Paul's harrowing experiences in terms of death-and-resurrection in order to remind readers of the resurrection of Christ and his ongoing authority. Ultimately, however, an interpretation emphasizing Paul's death and resurrection in Acts 27–28 must remain tentative. Luke's resurrection emphasis in Acts is much clearer in other texts, such as his account of Paul in Rome.

187. So rightly Barrett, *Commentary on the Acts*, 2:1222.

188. For a discussion of this passage, see Crowe, *Last Adam*, 159–61. Note also the longer ending of Mark (esp. 16:18), which may well be influenced by the account in Acts. See also Barrett, *Commentary on the Acts*, 2:1223; Keener, *Acts*, 1:397.

189. Cf. Jipp, *Reading Acts*, 128–29.

190. This is also the term for the goads in Acts 26:14, where it appears to be proverbial (see Barrett, *Commentary on the Acts*, 2:1158).

The Hope of the Resurrection in Rome

We are on firmer ground to see the resurrection playing an important role in Paul's final words in Acts. Paul opens his first speech in Rome by again denying he has done anything against his ancestral, Jewish traditions (28:17–19). In 28:20 Paul announces that he is in chains because of the hope of Israel. There can be little question for readers of Acts that this hope refers to the resurrection of the dead that has begun in Jesus (cf., e.g., 23:6; 24:15; 26:6–7).[191] Paul is apparently not prolix at this juncture concerning the details of this hope, but a day is established to give Paul an opportunity to state his case. At the appointed time, Paul again refers to the Scriptures (28:23), no doubt to defend the scriptural necessity of the Messiah's resurrection in a way that's consistent with what readers of Luke and Acts have already encountered in several passages (cf. Luke 24:44–47; Acts 26:22–23).

The resurrection's importance is also apparent in the kingdom emphasis of these last few verses of Acts. I noted in chapter 1 that Acts manifests a kingdom *inclusio* (1:3–8; 28:31). I have further argued that the kingdom of God is predicated upon the resurrection of Jesus, who reigns as the heavenly Lord. Thus, when Paul speaks about the kingdom of God in his final appearance in Acts (28:23, 31), this must be the kingdom of the risen Jesus.

Consistent with this, Paul speaks not only about the kingdom of God but also about the Lord Jesus Christ (28:31). Luke uses *Lord* as a title of honor for the risen and exalted Jesus, and as *Christ*, Jesus is the anointed Son of David who does not see decay (cf. 2:36). Thus the collocation of *kingdom* and *Lord* Jesus *Christ* brings to mind the kingdom of the resurrected and ascended Jesus. The freedom of Paul to preach this gospel without hindrance (28:31) may also recall the reigning power of Jesus, who, we may conclude, has delivered Paul from death[192] and enables him to witness before gentiles, kings, and the sons of Israel (9:15). Indeed, the mission to the gentiles, as we have also seen, not only is part of the scriptural necessity that had to be fulfilled (cf. 26:23) but also assumes that the resurrected Jesus is the Lord of *all* nations (10:36). The resurrection is indeed the hope *of Israel*, but it is not the hope only *for Israel*. This hope of Israel is the hope for gentiles as well.

As Paul's speeches and the book of Acts conclude, it is clear that the resurrection is not simply one event among many but is the quintessential way

---

191. See also Thompson, *Acts of the Risen Lord Jesus*, 82. Barrett (*Commentary on the Acts*, 2:1240) unnecessarily dichotomizes between messianic salvation and the resurrection of the Messiah.

192. Though Acts 27:20 mentions only that an angel of God announced to Paul that he would be spared from death, we see throughout Acts that the risen Jesus guides and reigns over his church.

that Scripture is fulfilled and is the means by which Jesus as Messiah is Lord of all. The resurrection, in short, is the "hope of Israel," and this hope has broken into history through Jesus of Nazareth.

Conclusion: Paul and the Resurrection

This chapter on Paul and the resurrection is the longest in the present study. Extended discussion of Paul is necessary because of the wealth of material Luke includes on the resurrection in conjunction with Paul. I have outlined several ways that Pauline passages in Acts reveal Luke's emphasis on the resurrection.

First, it is the risen Christ who confronts Paul on the road to Damascus, and this encounter is subsequently emphasized by Paul in two of his defenses.

Second, Paul's synagogue sermon at Pisidian Antioch and other speeches (such as the Areopagus speech) manifest a keen interest in the resurrection, which is often portrayed as the fulfillment of Old Testament Scriptures.

Third, the resurrection is consistently the fulcrum on which Paul's argument hinges in his defenses. He even identifies the resurrection as the reason he is on trial (23:6; 24:21).

Fourth, Luke possibly includes other narrative cues that present Paul's experience in terms of death-and-resurrection in ways that recall other, more prominent features of the resurrection message in Acts.

With the conclusion of this chapter, we now have seen that resurrection is central for both Peter and Paul. There are, of course, other figures in Acts as well, whom we will consider in the following chapter.

4

"I Will Rebuild the Tent of David"

Other Resurrection Voices in Acts

In addition to Peter and Paul, other characters play important roles in Acts, though they may not receive as much attention. In this chapter I will consider the role of James of Jerusalem—an important figure in the early church, whose speech at the Jerusalem Council in Acts 15 corroborates the importance of Christ's resurrection in Acts. Next I will look at the account of Stephen—which includes the longest speech in Acts (7:2–53)—and what it has to say about Christ's resurrection. I will also consider Philip's ministry and the activities of other minor characters in Acts that reveal Luke's interest in the resurrection. This chapter will be briefer than the previous two but will nevertheless make an important contribution to understanding the resurrection in Acts.

James and the Resurrection (Acts 15)

I have already addressed Peter's role at the Jerusalem Council; we come now to the role of James, who makes the decisive speech at the council (15:13–21), leading to the apostolic pronouncement letter (vv. 23–29). James's speech is of particular interest. In studies of James's speech—and there is no shortage— the issue that often looms largest is the usage of Amos 9:11–12 in Acts 15:16– 18. Though not the main point of James's speech per se (note the *dio* in 15:19), the logic of Amos 9 on the lips of James does give the rationale for the actions taken by James and the apostles. But what does Amos 9 refer to? And to what degree does the Lukan James mean the same thing as the shepherd of Tekoa? But before we look at the context of Amos 9, we need to consider in more detail the contours of Acts 15.

The Jerusalem Council addresses the role of gentiles among followers of the Way. At this juncture in Acts readers have already encountered Paul's first missionary journey, on which, as we have seen, Paul's resurrection message finds eager reception among many gentiles. But what about circumcision and the law of Moses? Are gentiles required to abide by these (cf. 15:5)? Peter narrates his experience preaching the gospel to the gentiles and recounts that the Holy Spirit has been poured out even on the gentiles (v. 8), who are also saved by the grace of the Lord Jesus (cf. v. 11).[1] Peter's speech is corroborated by the testimony of Paul and Barnabas, who relate the signs and wonders God has done through them among the gentiles (v. 12). At this point James makes his speech.

James agrees with (Simeon) Peter, Paul, and Barnabas that God is working among the gentiles; the task before them is to determine how practically Jews and gentiles will coexist in the messianic community. James finds support for inclusion of the gentiles in Amos 9. The way this text is used in Acts 15 has led to not a little dissension and debate. Among the first order of questions that must be addressed are the textual differences between Acts 15, the Old Greek, and the Masoretic Text. Luke does not simply follow what we know as the Septuagint (though his text is mostly similar). And a related question: How does the Masoretic Text square with the Septuagint? Does it? The most striking difference is the change from "possess" (*yāraš*) in Amos 9:12 MT to "seek" (*ekzēteō*) in the Septuagint (which Luke follows in Acts 15:17). Thus, whereas in the Masoretic Text the *remnant of Edom* (which stands synecdochically for all the nations)[2] will be *possessed* by the people of God,[3] in the Septuagint (and in Acts), the *remnants of all the nations* will *seek* (the Lord).[4]

Though I will not engage this particular debate at length, the best way to understand the reception of the Masoretic Text tradition in the Septuagint (which assumes they can be reconciled) is to correlate *seeking the Lord* to *being possessed by the people of God*—or perhaps better, being incorporated into the people of God.[5] The context of Amos supports this. In Amos

1. For more on 15:11, see the discussion in ch. 6.
2. I discuss this further below.
3. See, e.g., Douglas Stuart, *Hosea–Jonah*, WBC 31 (Nashville: Nelson, 1988), 398.
4. Luke includes "the Lord," whereas most LXX manuscripts omit these words.
5. See further Richard Bauckham, "James and the Gentiles (Acts 15.13–21)," in *History, Literature, and Society in the Book of Acts*, ed. Ben Witherington III (Cambridge: Cambridge

it is not only the nations that stand exposed to God's judgment; so do the people of Israel and Judah. In fact, most of Amos comprises rebukes against the faithlessness of God's people. Amos exhorts God's people to seek him, that they might live (cf. Amos 5:4, 6, 14).[6] The prospect of judgment is thus given as a warning not only to the nations but also to the people of God, with the prospect that in the future the kingdom—identified in Amos as the *sinful kingdom* (MT: *[ham]mamlākâ haḥaṭṭāʾâ*; LXX: *tēn basileian tōn hamartiōn*)—would be wiped out (9:8–9). Just as the call to repent is not only for Israel/Judah but for all the nations, so in Amos the prospect of life on the other side of judgment includes the implicit possibility that the nations will seek the Lord and live. This comes not through any foreign power (cf. 1:3–2:3) but by being "possessed" by God's people—a prospect anticipates the intervention of God's judgment. Amos is overall a book of warning, with only the last five verses of the book (9:11–15) holding out an explicit word of hope. Yet even in these last verses the Davidic dynasty will need rebuilding on the other side of judgment (v. 11).

This leads to a key question: What specifically does Luke intend by "rebuilding the tent of David" (*anoikodomēsō tēn skēnēn Dauid*) in Acts 15:16? It appears to be related to the resurrection of Christ. But how? One's answer must give sufficient attention to the context of Acts 15, where the gentile question looms large. To this end, it is not uncommon for commentators to understand the renewed tent to refer to the restoration of true Israel, generally understood to be composed of both Jews and gentiles.[7] A related possibility is that the rebuilt tent of David refers to restoration to the land.[8] This is an

---

University Press, 1996), 154–84. Though his view is slightly different from my own, Bauckham argues that Luke (or his underlying tradition) manifests a nuanced understanding of Amos and knowledge of the Hebrew text.

6. "Seek" in Hebrew is *dāraš*; building on this in Amos 9:11, *yāraš* may be a wordplay recalling the earlier context of Amos 5 and the collocation of *seeking* the Lord unto life. If so, then the LXX translators could have been aware of such connections. The LXX reads *ekzēteō* ("seek out") only in Amos 5:4, 6, 14 and 9:12.

7. See, e.g., Joseph A. Fitzmyer, *The Acts of the Apostles: A New Translation with Introduction and Commentary*, AB 31 (New York: Doubleday, 1998), 555–56; see also Jacob Jervell, *Luke and the People of God: A New Look at Luke-Acts* (Minneapolis: Augsburg, 1972), 51. For surveys, see Mark L. Strauss, *The Davidic Messiah in Luke-Acts: The Promise and Its Fulfillment in Lukan Christology*, JSNTSup 110 (Sheffield: Sheffield Academic, 1995), 187–92; John Eifion Morgan-Wynne, *Paul's Pisidian Antioch Speech (Acts 13)* (Eugene, OR: Pickwick, 2014), 169–75; W. Edward Glenny, "The Septuagint and Apostolic Hermeneutics: Amos 9 in Acts 15," *BBR* 22 (2012): 16–20.

8. See Richard Bauckham, "The Restoration of Israel in Luke-Acts," in *The Jewish World around the New Testament: Collected Essays I*, WUNT 1/233 (Tübingen: Mohr Siebeck, 2008), 325, 357, 359, 366, though Bauckham understands Amos 9 in Acts 15 with particular reference to the eschatological temple (cf. 366). See also Michael E. Fuller, *The Restoration of Israel:*

emphasis of Amos 5, where in 5:2 Israel is fallen on her land, no more to rise (MT: *qûm*; LXX: *anastēnai*); there is no one to raise her up (MT: *məqîmāh*; LXX: *anastēsōn*). In contrast, when the Davidic tent is restored the cities will be restored and the people replanted in their land, which will teem with blessings (9:13–15). Given Luke's interest in restoration (cf. Acts 2:5), a focus on the land may be in view in Acts 15:16. These possibilities, however, focus more on *implications* of the rebuilt tent of David rather than the identity of the rebuilt tent itself.

Others, often following the argument of Richard Bauckham, find in Acts 15:16 a reference to the rebuilding of the eschatological temple.[9] For Bauckham, the resurrection of Christ cannot be in view since Luke avoids *anistēmi* from Amos 9:11 LXX and instead employs *anoikodomeō*—which must refer to the restoration of a building.[10] Nor, for the same reason, does the rebuilt tent refer to the rebuilt Davidic dynasty.[11] Instead, for Bauckham, James envisions the eschatological temple of the Christian community, composed of both Jews and gentiles.[12] Bauckham's view merits serious consideration; given that *anistēmi* is frequently used in Acts to refer to Jesus's resurrection, its absence in the quotation of Amos 9 is striking.

Nevertheless, it is best to understand the rebuilt tent of David to refer to the restoration of the Davidic dynasty.[13] This is rather close to 4QFlorilegium, which also relates Amos 9 to 2 Samuel 7, and refers to the rebuilt tent of David as the Davidic Messiah who would arise to save Israel (4QFlor 1 I, 10–13).[14]

Israel's Re-gathering and the Fate of the Nations in Early Jewish Literature and Luke-Acts, BZNW 138 (Berlin: de Gruyter, 2006), though Fuller does not discuss Acts 15.

9. See especially Bauckham, "James and the Gentiles"; Sabine Nägelle, *Labhütte Davids und Wolkensohn: Eine auslegungsgeschichtliche Studie zum Amos 9,11 in der jüdischen und christlichen Exegese*, AGJU 24 (Leiden: Brill, 1995), 89–90; cf. Eckhard J. Schnabel, *Acts*, ZECNT (Grand Rapids: Zondervan, 2012), 639.

10. Bauckham, "James and the Gentiles," 157.

11. Bauckham, "James and the Gentiles," 157.

12. Bauckham, "James and the Gentiles," 165.

13. So also Strauss, *Davidic Messiah*, 190; David G. Peterson, *The Acts of the Apostles*, PNTC (Grand Rapids: Eerdmans, 2009), 431; Craig S. Keener, *Acts: An Exegetical Commentary*, 4 vols. (Grand Rapids: Baker Academic, 2012–15), 3:2255–56; Darrell L. Bock, *Acts*, BECNT (Grand Rapids: Baker Academic, 2007), 504; Alan J. Thompson, *The Acts of the Risen Lord Jesus: Luke's Account of God's Unfolding Plan*, NSBT 27 (Downers Grove, IL: InterVarsity, 2011), 122–23; Glenny, "Septuagint and Apostolic Hermeneutics," 18; Robert C. Tannehill, *The Narrative Unity of Luke-Acts: A Literary Interpretation*, 2 vols. (Philadelphia and Minneapolis: Fortress, 1986–90), 2:188–89.

14. Cf. Fitzmyer, *Acts of the Apostles*, 556 (though Fitzmyer does not see strong similarity between 4QFlor and Acts 15 on this point); Keener, *Acts*, 3:2256. For 4QFlor (4Q174), see John M. Allegro, ed., *Qumrân Cave 4:I, 4Q158–4Q186*, DJD 5 (Oxford: Clarendon, 1968), 53–57; transcriptions with translations can be found in Florentino García Martínez and Eibert J. C. Tigchelaar, eds., *The Dead Sea Scrolls Study Edition*, 2 vols. (Leiden: Brill, 1997–98), 1:352–53.

For Luke, the Davidic dynasty is restored through the resurrection of Christ. Thus, while it is not entirely wrong to say that the rebuilt tent of David refers to the resurrection,[15] we must not frame this rebuilding in such a way that it is disconnected from the kingdom focus of the resurrection.[16] For this reason the rebuilt tent of David is best taken as a reference to the establishment of the Son of David on his throne—which comes by means of Jesus's resurrection/ glorification—and this universal enthronement explains the unity of Jew and gentile in the Christian community.[17]

The language of "rebuild" instead of "raise" is not decisive against this view, since the metaphor used by James in Acts lends itself well to "rebuilding" language. Jesus's resurrection is the means by which the fallen tent of David is restored.[18] Luke's language might thus be explained as Davidic language from the Old Testament, in which David's dynasty is established (see especially in 2 Sam. 7).[19] In 2 Samuel 7:13 the Septuagint employs both *oikodomeō*[20] and *anorthoō*: "He will build [*oikodomēsei*] for me a house for my name, and I will raise up [*anorthōsō*] his throne forever [*heōs eis ton aiōna*]."[21] These verbal parallels provide more evidence that James is speaking of the reestablishment of the Davidic kingdom by means of the resurrection of Christ.[22]

Further, the implications of Davidic restoration include not only restoration to the land but also the inclusion of gentiles in a fuller way. This restoration is couched in eschatological temple language, and elsewhere in the New Testament Jesus's resurrection is communicated in temple language (cf. John

15. Irenaeus, *Epid.* 38, 62; Ernst Haenchen, *The Acts of the Apostles: A Commentary*, trans. R. McL. Wilson (Westminster: Philadelphia, 1971), 448.

16. As does Haenchen (*Acts of the Apostles*, 448).

17. Thus, James's speech manifests a logic similar to that of Peter's speech to Cornelius and of Paul's speeches at Pisidian Antioch and Athens.

18. Note also that James mentions plural *prophets* (Acts 15:15). Thus we should expect to find other texts that fit with James's interpretation of Amos 9. Many OT texts speak of the establishment of David's kingdom (e.g., Isa. 11:1–10; Ezek. 37:1–28; Dan. 2:44; Obad. 21), along with the inclusion of the gentiles. On this latter point, see the texts listed in Bock, *Acts*, 503.

19. See here Glenny, "Septuagint and Apostolic Hermeneutics," 19. Also recall the importance of 2 Sam. 7 for Paul's speech at Pisidian Antioch in Acts 13:16–41.

20. Glenny ("Septuagint and Apostolic Hermeneutics," 19–20) plausibly concludes that the *ana-* prefix in Acts 15 points to the *re*-building of David's house. See also 1 Chron. 17:12; 22:10. Interestingly, the same combination is found in Prov. 24:3.

21. The everlasting reign of the Davidic dynasty in 2 Sam. 7 is also included in 4QFlor 1 I, 10–11 (noted by Bauckham, "Restoration of Israel," 346).

22. Additionally, some have related the restoration of Acts 3:21 to (among other texts) Amos 9:11–12. See Dennis J. Hamm, SJ, "Acts 3:12–26: Peter's Speech and the Healing of the Man Born Lame," *PRSt* 11 (1984): 210; see also Hans F. Bayer, "Christ-Centered Eschatology in Acts 3:17–26," in *Jesus of Nazareth—Lord and Christ: Essays on the Historical Jesus and Christology*, ed. Joel B. Green and Max Turner (Grand Rapids: Eerdmans, 1994), 247–48. I argued in ch. 2 that Acts 3:21 assumes the priority of the resurrection of Christ.

2:18–22). As G. K. Beale argues, Jesus's resurrection marks the beginning of the fulfillment of Amos 9:11–12, which speaks of Jesus as the eschatological temple who is the locus of worship for believing Jews and gentiles.[23]

Luke's use of tent (*skēnē*) terminology in eschatologically charged contexts is also significant. In the transfiguration Peter's misplaced suggestion about making three booths (*skēnas*, Luke 9:33) misses the newness of the coming of Christ in contrast to the ages of Moses and Elijah. This is dramatically manifested in the glory of Christ that is revealed on the mountain, which anticipates Jesus's resurrection glory. Later, in the parable of the unjust steward, the climax comes in 16:9: "Make friends for yourselves by unrighteous mammon, so that when it fails they may receive you into eternal tents" (*heautois poiēsate philous ek tou mamōna tēs adikias, hina hotan eklipē dexōntai hymas eis tas aiōnious skēnas*). Though this is undoubtedly one of the most difficult of Jesus's parables, a likely interpretation is that Jesus's disciples should have an eschatological orientation that informs their use of money.[24] The future, denoted by "eternal tents," should guide their actions in the present. In the transfiguration and the parable of the unjust steward, Luke uses the term *skēnē* to guide our attention toward eschatological-resurrection life. Luke's two other uses of *skēnē* are found on the lips of Stephen in Acts 7 and will be considered in the next section.

Not to be missed among the plenteous debates surrounding Acts 15 is the purpose for which the Davidic dynasty has been rebuilt, stated in verse 17 (note *hopōs*): the inclusion of the gentiles among the eschatological people of God.[25] This is emphasized in another change between Amos 9:12 LXX / Acts 15:17 and Amos 9:12 MT. Whereas Amos 9:12 MT has God's people possessing the remnant *of Edom* (*'ĕdôm*), in the Septuagint and Acts it is the remnants *of the people* (*tōn anthrōpōn*) who seek the Lord.[26] This change may seem strange, but is not terribly difficult to understand when we consider that in the context of Amos 9, Edom stands synecdochically for the nations; a couple of minor changes in vowel pointing (though excluding a consonantal vowel [*mater lectionis*])—changing Edom (*'ĕdôm*) to Adam (*'ādām*)—simply

---

23. Beale, *The Temple and the Church's Mission: A Biblical Theology of the Dwelling Place of God*, NSBT 17 (Downers Grove, IL: InterVarsity, 2004), 233. Beale also relates this rebuilding in Acts 15:16 to the resurrection of Jesus (*Temple and the Church's Mission*, 233–36).

24. See, e.g., Klyne R. Snodgrass, *Stories with Intent: A Comprehensive Guide to the Parables of Jesus* (Grand Rapids: Eerdmans, 2008), 415–18.

25. See G. K. Beale, *A New Testament Biblical Theology: The Unfolding of the Old Testament in the New* (Grand Rapids: Baker Academic, 2011), 685–86.

26. The Greek for "remnant" is plural (*hoi kataloipoi*), but the plural can easily be translated in the singular as "rest" or "remainder": the plural is not a major difference from the Hebrew singular. See BDAG, "κατάλοιπος," 521.

make explicit the universal reference to Edom already present in Amos.[27] Further, in Luke's writings Jesus is clearly the Savior for all people, as we see in Luke's Adamic genealogy (Luke 3:38).[28] The more universal reference to "peoples" in Acts 15:17 fits with the emphases of both Amos and Luke.[29]

Both Amos 9:12 LXX and Acts 15:17 include the language "they will seek" (*ekzētēsōsin*), though in Amos 9 LXX the object of that seeking—which must be the Lord—remains unstated.[30] In Acts, James explicitly identifies the Lord as the object of seeking. But who is the Lord in Acts 15:17? Jesus is consistently identified as the exalted Lord in Acts, though this does not preclude the identification of God the Father as Lord as well. Yet a couple of features suggest that *kyrios* in 15:17 is the exalted Jesus.

First, the resurrection of Jesus is squarely in view in connection with the rebuilt tent of David; and the rebuilt dynasty precipitates the fuller inclusion of the gentiles. Second, the fuller inclusion of gentiles among the people of God is tied to the universal lordship of Christ throughout Acts. However, this is not an open-and-shut case, for a few reasons. Chief among these is the second reference to "Lord" in 15:17, which most likely does not refer to Jesus, especially if we find an allusion to Zechariah 8:22.[31] In the end, *kyrios* in 15:17 could refer either to Jesus or to God the Father.[32] Regardless of one's decision on this matter, it is clear that the blessings in view come by means of the resurrection of Jesus, which is the means by which the fallen kingdom of David has been reestablished. This is good news for both Jews and gentiles. Amos 9 thus explains that James's decision is to welcome the gentiles into the people of God, not burdening them more than necessary.

To summarize this rather long discussion: the tent of David is best taken as a reference to the restored Davidic kingdom, which comes by means of the resurrection of Jesus Christ. This restoration entails many blessings for the

27. See also Keener, *Acts*, 3:2257n506.

28. See further Brandon D. Crowe, *The Last Adam: A Theology of the Obedient Life of Jesus in the Gospels* (Grand Rapids: Baker Academic, 2017).

29. Contrast C. K. Barrett, *A Critical and Exegetical Commentary on the Acts of the Apostles*, 2 vols., ICC (Edinburgh: T&T Clark, 1994–98), 2:727, where he says that in Luke's rendering, "the meaning of [Amos 9:12] is almost reversed."

30. As noted earlier, the MT of Amos 9:12 does not include "they will seek," but says "they will possess [*yîrəšû*] the remnant of Edom."

31. On a possible allusion to Zech. 8:22, see Bauckham, "James and the Gentiles," 162; Schnabel, *Acts*, 640.

32. Though Rowe (*World Upside Down: Reading Acts in the Graeco-Roman Age* [Oxford: Oxford University Press, 2009], 112) argues that this use of *kyrios* refers "doubly" to the Father and to Jesus.

people of God, including the inclusion of the gentiles.[33] Though he receives comparatively little attention in Acts itself, James's central role in the earliest decades of Christianity is well established, which highlights the importance of his speech in Acts. In Acts 15 we have a third foundational, apostolic figure making a major speech expositing the resurrection of Jesus.[34] If the three major resurrection pillars of my argument are Peter's Pentecost speech, Paul's Pisidian Antioch speech, and Paul's defense before Herod Agrippa II, then one could supplement this by highlighting Peter, Paul, and James as three apostolic pillars who bear witness to the resurrection in Acts.

Stephen and the Resurrection (Acts 7)

The longest speech in the book of Acts comes not from Peter, Paul, or James, but from Stephen. With a tally of a thousand words,[35] Stephen's speech is more than twice as long as the next-longest speech in Acts (Paul's speech at Pisidian Antioch, 13:16–41). Stephen responds to the charges in Acts 6 that he was blaspheming Moses and God (v. 11) and had disparaged the temple (*tou topou tou hagiou*) and the law of Moses (vv. 13–14). In response, Stephen emphasizes that worship of God has never been tied to one place (*topos*) and shows how Moses, though rejected by his own people, was nevertheless God's deliverer (7:35–36). Moreover, Moses himself testified that he was not the final prophet, but spoke of another prophet who would come after him (v. 37; cf. Deut. 18:15). It would therefore be mistaken, and indeed out of accord with what Moses himself said, to limit God's saving and revealing activity to the work of Moses hundreds of years earlier. The resurrection of Christ features prominently in Stephen's defense—more prominently than may appear at first glance.

The first, and most obvious, way that the resurrection of Christ figures in the Stephen episode comes at the conclusion of his speech, when Stephen gazes into heaven and sees the glory of God, with the risen and ascended Jesus standing at his right hand (7:55–56).[36] This vision of the Son of Man recalls Jesus's own statements about his vindication before his crucifixion (Luke 22:67–70) and portrays Jesus as the righteous, vindicated heavenly Lord (cf.

---

33. See Charles H. Talbert, *Reading Acts: A Literary and Theological Commentary on the Acts of the Apostles* (New York: Crossroad, 1997), 140.

34. See similarly Strauss, *Davidic Messiah*, 192–93.

35. Though this count could fluctuate depending on textual decisions and on whether one includes Stephen's final words in 7:56, 59–60.

36. See also Kevin I. Anderson, *"But God Raised Him from the Dead": The Theology of Jesus's Resurrection in Luke-Acts*, PBM (repr., Eugene, OR: Wipf & Stock, 2006), 197.

23:47), who stands to vindicate Stephen's unjust death.[37] This heavenly vision is consistent with Paul's emphasis on Jesus as the risen judge (Acts 17:30–31). Additionally, Stephen's vision of Christ is the first vision of the heavenly Christ in Acts, following his ascension in Acts 1:9.[38] Stephen's speech not only vindicates Stephen himself but also further vindicates Jesus. In spite of his unjust death, Jesus, the Righteous One, now reigns from heaven. Stephen's unjust death and vindication by the living Christ echo the unjust death and resurrection of Jesus himself (cf. Luke 23:34, 46; Acts 7:52, 59–60).[39]

Second, the role of Moses in Stephen's speech testifies to the importance of the resurrection of Jesus. Moses spoke of a prophet whom God would raise up (*anastēsei*) after him (7:37, quoting Deut. 18:15). As with Peter in Acts 3:22, in Acts 7 Stephen correlates this raising up of a prophet like Moses preeminently to the resurrection of Jesus. In Acts 3:22 Peter also invokes Deuteronomy 18 to make this point. Therefore, when Deuteronomy 18 is again quoted, this time on the lips of Stephen, Luke has already made it clear that Jesus is the eschatological prophet, who has been raised up by means of his resurrection.[40] Like Moses, Jesus was God's chosen deliverer who was rejected by his own people (cf. Acts 7:35). But unlike Moses, Jesus is the greater prophet who has been raised from the dead. The biblical voice of Moses also anticipates the resurrection in the way that Exodus 3:6 is interpreted in Luke and Acts. In Luke 20 Jesus bests the Sadducees in a debate about the resurrection by invoking God's covenantal promises to Abraham, Isaac, and Jacob (vv. 37–40)—God is not the God of the dead, but of the living. For Moses to participate in Abraham's blessing must entail the institution of resurrection—which we know comes by means of Jesus—since Moses himself did not inherit the land in his own day. It is also suggestive that in Acts 7:32 Stephen quotes the same passage that Jesus uses with the Sadducees to demonstrate the resurrection: Exodus 3:6. By this point readers of Luke and Acts have encountered Exodus 3:6 as scriptural support for the resurrection both in Luke 20:37–40 and Acts 3:13—in the latter case to demonstrate that God has glorified Jesus. Though

37. See Bock, *Acts*, 311–12; Fitzmyer, *Acts of the Apostles*, 392–93; Schnabel, *Acts*, 390; Keener, *Acts*, 2:1441–42.

38. Other appearances of the heavenly Christ include Paul's vision of Jesus on the Damascus road (9:3–5; recounted twice [22:6–8; 26:12–18]), Paul's vision at Corinth (18:9–10), and his vision of Christ in the temple (22:17–21).

39. Luke's Gospel does not include the temple charge at the trial of Jesus, but this accusation would surely have been known to many of Luke's readers (cf. Matt. 26:60–61; Mark 14:58; John 2:18–22). See Barrett, *Commentary on the Acts*, 1:328; Michael D. Goulder, *Type and History in Acts* (London: SPCK, 1964), 42–43.

40. Both Moses and Jesus are identified as prophets mighty in word and in deed (Luke 24:19; Acts 7:22).

these latter two uses of Exodus 3:6 are not as explicitly tied to the resurrection as in Luke 20, they may nevertheless recall the scriptural foundation for the resurrection.

Third, Stephen's relativizing of the temple[41] is built upon the presupposition of Jesus's resurrection. The climax of Stephen's historical interpretation comes in 7:47–50,[42] where Stephen boldly proclaims that even though Solomon built God a house, the Most High does not dwell in temples made with human hands (*cheiropoiētois*). Stephen thus uses the language of idolatry ("made with hands") to speak of Solomon's temple, leveling the charge of idolatry against those who opposed his message.[43] Jesus himself is the temple not made with hands (cf. Mark 14:58). God's covenantal promises to David (especially from 2 Sam. 7) are highly important in Luke's writings, and the promise of a lasting, Davidic kingdom features prominently in Acts.[44] This affects one's understanding of the Solomonic temple, since no human-made temple is the ultimate realization of God's promise to David. Instead of David building God an everlasting house, God promises to build David a house by raising up a son to reign forever. This lasting kingdom comes by means of Jesus's resurrection from the dead.[45] God's presence was never limited to one place. Thus Stephen shows the biblical logic of understanding the temple to anticipate Christ as the fulfillment of the temple, for in Acts Jesus is consistently portrayed as the resurrected Lord over all peoples and places. This perspective is corroborated by the quotation of Isaiah 66:1–2 in Acts 7:49–50. No earthly temple would suffice as a house for God.[46] Instead, God has raised up Jesus (from the dead) to be the Davidic king in perpetuity, and the temple that he builds corresponds to Jesus's resurrected body.

Further underscoring the importance of the resurrection for Stephen's speech are correlations between Stephen's speech and James's speech in Acts 15.[47] I argued above that James's use in Acts 15 of "rebuilding the tent of David" (cf. Amos 9:11–12) refers most fundamentally to the rebuilt Davidic dynasty that comes by means of Jesus's resurrection. Stephen's speech likewise builds upon Amos 5:25–27 in Acts 7:42–43, in large measure pick-

41. Similar language is used by Thompson, *Acts of the Risen Lord Jesus*, 169.
42. So Beale, *Temple and the Church's Mission*, 217–18.
43. See also Thompson, *Acts of the Risen Lord Jesus*, 169.
44. See, e.g., Peter's Pentecost speech; Paul's Pisidian Antioch speech; James's Jerusalem speech.
45. See also 2 Cor. 5:1, where the resurrection body is identified as *acheiropoiētos*. See F. F. Bruce, *The Acts of the Apostles: The Greek Text with Introduction and Commentary*, 2nd ed. (Grand Rapids: Eerdmans, 1952), 176.
46. Here and what follows, see also Beale, *Temple and the Church's Mission*, 217–18.
47. See Tannehill, *Narrative Unity*, 2:189.

ing up on Amos's critique of God's people for worshiping the nonambulatory god Molech—who was indeed made with hands (*cheiropoiētos*). In the Septuagint—with which Luke mostly agrees—the Israelites are forced to take up the tent of Molech, which was made according to an earthly image (*typos*). In contrast, the tent of meeting was built on a heavenly pattern from the living God (Acts 7:44). Whereas seeking the Lord leads to life (cf. Amos 5:4, 6, 14[48]), Molech can neither speak nor give life.

Amos 5 anticipates Amos 9 in several ways, including paving the way for the Septuagint's correlation of seeking the Lord unto life in 9:12. Stephen's speech thus prepares the reader of Acts for James's speech. Both appeal to Amos, both speak of the proper mode of worship in light of the coming of Christ, and both assume the resurrection of Christ. Stephen's speech anticipates this last point, which finds more emphasis in James's speech, by introducing the language of tent (*skēnē* [7:43–44], also *skēnōma* [7:46]), which James will use to refer to the Davidic dynasty. Stephen's speech is less explicit in this regard, but he does contrast idolatry with God's final purposes in Christ. By relativizing the Solomonic temple in light of redemptive history, Stephen shows that the tent of David must be more than a singular, holy place. It must correspond to the house that God builds for David (2 Sam. 7:11–14).[49] James's point—that the rebuilt booth of David comes by means of Jesus's resurrection—follows upon the foundation laid by Stephen in the context of Acts. The resurrection of Jesus is the means by which the kingdom and true worship are established.

Much more could be said about Stephen's speech; and there may be more even to explore in connection to Jesus's resurrection. But the sum of the matter is clear: Stephen's speech necessitates the centrality of Jesus's resurrection.[50]

Philip and the Resurrection (Acts 8)

Following Stephen's speech comes the ministry of Philip the evangelist (Acts 8:1–40; cf. 21:8), which is also relevant for the resurrection in Acts. The first episode involving Philip is his preaching of the word of Christ in Samaria

48. Amos 5:26 is read alongside Amos 9:11 in CD VII, 14–15. See Barrett, *Commentary on the Acts*, 1:368; Fitzmyer, *Acts of the Apostles*, 382.

49. The language of tent (LXX: *skēnē*), in conjunction with God's place of dwelling, also appears in 2 Sam. 7.

50. It has also been argued that Stephen himself serves to further the death-and-resurrection schema in Acts. See Dennis J. Horton, *Death and Resurrection: The Shape and Function of a Literary Motif in the Book of Acts* (Eugene, OR: Pickwick, 2009), 49–51; Goulder, *Type and History in Acts*, 74, 93. However, on this point I remain unpersuaded.

(8:4–5). What Luke mentions in passing—Philip was preaching the Christ—is filled out in more detail elsewhere in Acts. To preach the *Christ*, as we see in Peter's Pentecost sermon, is to preach Jesus as the chosen Davidic king who reigns over an everlasting kingdom. Even though Luke does not include these details in Acts 8, readers of Acts should read the shorter, summary statements in light of the fuller expositions, which prominently feature the resurrection.

Another angle of Philip's preaching to consider—though here again we are left to reconstruct what Luke leaves unstated—is whether he preached Jesus as the prophet like Moses from Deuteronomy 18:15, 18. Allusions to Deuteronomy 18 are common in Luke's writings (Luke 9:35; Acts 3:22; 7:37),[51] and these allusions correlate to Luke's emphasis on Jesus's resurrection as the means by which this prophet is established. Such an emphasis on Deuteronomy 18 coheres not only with Luke's emphases elsewhere but also with the Samaritans' acceptance of the Torah as Scripture and their likely expectation of the *Taheb*—or restorer—based on Deuteronomy 18.[52] This question, however, cannot be answered confidently. Philip may have preached Jesus as the Christ from texts outside the Torah, such as 2 Samuel 7 or Psalm 16, as we see elsewhere in Acts (regardless of his audience's views of those texts). But it would be fitting for him to have included Jesus's fulfillment of Deuteronomy 18, by means of his resurrection, as part of his message. Philip's confrontation with Simon Magus may provide a further clue to the content of Philip's preaching. This exchange is precipitated by Philip's preaching of the good news of the *kingdom* and the *name of Jesus Christ* (8:12). These two elements—the messiahship of Jesus and his lasting kingdom—presuppose Jesus's resurrection (cf. 8:16).

The second episode featuring Philip—his encounter with the Ethiopian eunuch—further bespeaks the importance of Jesus's resurrection. This encounter centers upon the interpretation of Isaiah 53:7–8 (Acts 8:32–33), which was being read (presumably aloud) from the Ethiopian's chariot. The portion of Isaiah 53 quoted emphasizes the death of the suffering servant figure.[53] Indeed, though it is commonly recognized that Luke does not emphasize the cross of Christ as much as some other New Testament authors, this should

---

51. For more on the use and circulation of Deuteronomy in the ancient world, see Brandon D. Crowe, *The Obedient Son: Deuteronomy and Christology in the Gospel of Matthew*, BZNW 188 (Berlin: de Gruyter, 2012), 39–117.

52. See Keener, *Acts*, 2:1497; Ben Witherington III, *The Acts of the Apostles: A Socio-Rhetorical Commentary* (Grand Rapids: Eerdmans, 1998), 282–83; see also the cautions of Stephen Haar, *Simon Magus: The First Gnostic?*, BZNW 119 (Berlin: de Gruyter, 2003), 166.

53. A point emphasized by Rouven Genz, *Jesaja 53 als theologische Mitte der Apostelgeschichte: Studien zur ihrer Christologie und Ekklesiologie im Anschluss an Apg 8,26–40*, WUNT 2/398 (Tübingen: Mohr Siebeck, 2015), e.g., 123.

not be misconstrued to imply that Luke had no interest in or no place for the death of Christ as sin-bearing.[54] The inclusion of servant passages from Isaiah—especially from Isaiah 53—buttresses the argument that Luke also understands the cross of Christ to be salvific and substitutionary. Even so, one must not lose sight of the *exaltation* of the suffering servant figure in Isaiah 52:13–53:12.[55] The servant not only suffers but is vindicated (cf. Isa. 52:13; Acts 3:13, 26). In Acts the resurrection-vindication of Jesus is a major emphasis, which provides ample reason to conclude that the exaltation or vindication of the servant is part of the message that Philip would have preached to the eunuch—just as he presumably did in Samaria. For Philip to have explained *only* the suffering of the servant might imply that Jesus remains dead; this is certainly not Luke's view. To speak only of the suffering would be to focus on the injustice to the exclusion of the vindication. But Luke tends to emphasize the vindication of the death of Jesus as the righteous servant (cf. Luke 23:47; Acts 3:13, 26; 4:27).[56]

It is even possible that the portion of Isaiah 53 read by the Ethiopian eunuch refers to the resurrection/ascension of Christ. The quotation of Isaiah 53:7 in Acts 8:33 ends with the following: "His life is taken away from the earth" (*airetai apo tēs gēs hē zōē autou*). Some have argued that this phrase refers to the resurrection and ascension of Jesus as Lord, who now reigns as the king exalted over death.[57] This is not certain, however, since *airō* sometimes clearly refers to death in Luke-Acts (Luke 23:18; Acts 21:36; 22:22; cf. Acts 20:9).[58]

All told, it would be artificial to bifurcate the suffering and the vindication of the servant in Acts; Luke speaks of both. Thus, by quoting the passage about the servant's suffering, in a larger work emphasizing the resurrection

54. See also my discussion in ch. 3 (under section "2. Cross and Resurrection") on the cross in relation to Paul's Pisidian Antioch speech.

55. This point is brought out well in Richard Bauckham, *God Crucified: Monotheism and Christology in the New Testament* (Grand Rapids: Eerdmans, 1999), 47–51.

56. For those that emphasize vindication, see Tannehill, *Narrative Unity*, 2:111–12; Robert F. O'Toole, SJ, *Luke's Presentation of Jesus: A Christology*, SubBi 25 (Rome: Editrice Pontificio Istituto Biblico, 2004), 108; cf. Darrell L. Bock, *Proclamation from Prophecy and Pattern: Lucan Old Testament Christology*, JSNTSup 12 (Sheffield: JSOT Press, 1987), 228–29.

57. See Daniel Marguerat, "The Resurrection and Its Witnesses in the Book of Acts," in *Reading Acts Today: Essays in Honour of Loveday C. A. Alexander*, ed. Steve Walton et al., LNTS 427 (London: T&T Clark, 2011), 178, building especially on *airō*. He further argues that the eunuch will be restored like Christ, the resurrected one (179). If so, this would be consistent with the view of restoration built upon the foundation of Christ's resurrection in Acts 3:21. Others note the similarity of *airō* to *epairō* in Acts 1:9: e.g., Dietrich Rusam, *Das Alte Testament bei Lukas*, BZNW 112 (Berlin: de Gruyter, 2003), 388; Richard Glöckner, OP, *Die Verkündigung des Heils beim Evangelisten Lukas*, WSAMA.T 9 (Mainz: Matthias-Grünewald-Verlag, 1975), 211.

58. So Genz, *Jesaja 53*, 99–100, 128.

of Christ as servant, Luke most likely intends readers to understand the importance of *both* the death *and* resurrection of Christ from Isaiah 53.

The Resurrection Elsewhere in Acts

We are approaching the end of the exegetical section of this volume. To this point we have considered resurrection contributions in Acts of Peter, Paul, James, Stephen, and Philip, along with Luke's narrative cues. In what follows I consider what some of the minor characters in Acts add to the conversation.[59] I have already referred to some of these, such as the temple beggar, Aeneas, Dorcas,[60] the Lystran lame man, and Eutychus. I will not repeat those discussions. The following comments focus on those characters I have not yet covered that I consider to be most relevant: (a) Ananias and Sapphira, (b) Gamaliel, and (c) an important trio in Ephesus and Corinth (Priscilla, Aquila, and Apollos).

Ananias and Sapphira (5:1–11)

Among the more intriguing episodes in Acts is the account of Ananias and Sapphira (5:1–11), not least because of the swift judgment they meet for lying to the apostles about money. By lying to the apostles they had lied to God (v. 4). We would be warranted to discuss here the foundational authority of the apostles or the nods to the personality and deity of the Spirit (cf. vv. 3–4). But my focus is on the way the death of Ananias and Sapphira is an inverted resurrection story.[61] Instead of meeting the apostles and experiencing life, as the temple beggar did, Ananias and Sapphira instead face Peter and breathe their last.[62] Here is a warning for the new community to heed the authority of the apostles and not to test the Spirit of the Lord (v. 9).[63] That Lord is the resurrected Jesus, who continues to guide his church by his Spirit. In this case, he metes out judgment on those whose actions obstruct the Way.[64]

59. See also Horton, *Death and Resurrection*, 61–78.

60. Believing in the name of the Lord in Acts 9:42—immediately after the raising of Dorcas—assumes belief in the Lord who raises the dead.

61. See also Horton, *Death and Resurrection*, 91–93.

62. Might there be a contrast to the reception of the Spirit in this language of *ekpsychō* (5:5, 10)? Whereas the Spirit is the breath of life (Gen. 2:7) and the resurrected Jesus in John breathes out (*emphysaō*) and commands his disciples to receive the Holy Spirit (20:22; cf. Gen. 2:7; Ezek. 37:9), in Acts 5 Ananias and Sapphira resist the Spirit and their breath expires. See also Crowe, *Last Adam*, 32–33, 51, 134n61, 196.

63. There may be a hint of irony in the young men "rising up" (*anastantes*, 5:6) to bury Ananias's dead body.

64. Later in Acts another one who worked against the Way will be converted (i.e., Paul). Interestingly, it is another Ananias who serves as the means of Paul's restoration to life. See also Horton, *Death and Resurrection*, 52–55.

Gamaliel I (5:34–39)

Earlier I mentioned the Pharisee Gamaliel and his hesitation to neutralize the apostolic resurrection message, in contrast to the Sadducees, who were a priori—and in practice—opposed to the resurrection. This Gamaliel is most likely Rabban Gamaliel I (the Elder), the esteemed Hillelite teacher of Paul (cf. 22:3).[65] Certainly in Luke and the Gospels more broadly, Jesus had many theological disagreements with the Pharisees. Yet despite many popular, negative conceptions of the Pharisees wholesale, it remains that a background in Pharisaism (as we see in Acts) seems to be fertile ground for becoming a follower of the Way.[66] For example, believing Pharisees are present at the Jerusalem Council (15:5).

One reason for this apparent compatibility must have been the Pharisaic openness to the resurrection, such as we see in the cautious approach of Gamaliel in Acts 5:34–39. How many Sadducees would have suggested that to oppose the resurrection message would be to oppose God (cf. v. 39)? Thus Gamaliel rose (*anastas*!) in defense of the apostles—or at least he did not dismiss the resurrection out of hand. Later his student—Paul of Tarsus—meets the resurrected Christ on the road to Damascus. Gamaliel serves in Acts as an important witness to the scriptural fidelity of the resurrection message, a topic to which we will return in chapter 7.

Priscilla, Aquila, and Apollos (18:24–28)

In Acts 18 we meet Apollos, an Alexandrian Jew well trained in the Scriptures. Though Apollos spoke rightly about Jesus, he did not know of Jesus's death and resurrection, but only of the baptism of John (vv. 24–25). After hearing Apollos in the synagogue, Priscilla and Aquila instructed him and he went to Achaia (= Corinth). Here Apollos demonstrated from the Scriptures that the Christ was Jesus (v. 28). Consistent with the preaching we have seen throughout Acts, Apollos's training from Priscilla and Aquila likely would have included instructions about the Davidic kingdom established through the resurrected and ascended Christ. That he could demonstrate this from the Scriptures is also consistent with the plenteous scriptural arguments in Acts relating Jesus as the risen and exalted Messiah to the fulfillment of Scripture.

65. See the discussions in Barrett, *Commentary on the Acts*, 1:292; Keener, *Acts*, 2:1222–25.
66. See Martin Hengel, *Acts and the History of Earliest Christianity*, trans. John Bowden (London: SCM, 1979), 95; cf. Robert Maddox, *The Purpose of Luke-Acts*, FRLANT 126 (Göttingen: Vandenhoeck & Ruprecht, 1982), 40–42.

Conclusion to Part 1: Where We Are and Where We Are Going

We have come to the end of part 1, which lays out the exegetical foundation for the centrality of the resurrection in Acts. Though we could scarcely claim with the preacher that "all has been heard" (Eccles. 12:13)—surely some stones remain yet unturned—it should be clear that the resurrection is a major emphasis for Luke. Since so much ground has been covered, a brief summary will be helpful.

In chapter 1, I argued that the resurrection holds universal significance and is consistently the logical key to the speeches in Acts. Chapter 2 is devoted to Petrine passages in Acts, with particular emphasis on the first major resurrection pillar: Peter's Pentecost sermon. Peter's speeches reveal an interest in Jesus as the anointed Davidic Son who has been raised from the dead to reign over an everlasting kingdom. Jesus is the prophet like Moses who has been raised up from the dead and will eventually restore all things. In chapter 3, I considered two more resurrection pillars (Paul's Pisidian Antioch sermon and his defense before Herod Agrippa II), along with Paul's conversion, his preaching ministry, and his missionary journeys (and journey to Rome). It is striking how often Paul appeals to the resurrection. In chapter 4, I have argued that the speeches and preaching of James, Stephen, Philip, Gamaliel, and Apollos also emphasize the resurrection. Ananias and Sapphira serve as a foil to the fullness of resurrection life offered by Jesus the Lord.

With this exegetical foundation in place, we look ahead to part 2, where I will provide more synthesis. What does it mean now that Jesus is exalted Lord? How does the newness of the resurrection relate to the faithfulness of God and his saving actions throughout history more broadly? These topics will occupy chapters 5–6. And how does the newness of the resurrection relate to the Scriptures of Israel? This is the topic of chapter 7. Finally, how does the importance of the resurrection in Acts relate to the emergence of the New Testament canon, and how does the resurrection speak to the distinctiveness of early Christian beliefs? These questions will conclude the volume in chapter 8.

The Theological Significance of the Resurrection in Acts

5

The Resurrection and the Accomplishment of Salvation (*Historia Salutis*)

I n part 2, I will synthesize the exegetical insights from part 1 to draw out more systematically what Luke sets forth in narrative form.

In this chapter I consider the resurrection as the great turning point in the history of salvation. If the coming of Christ, broadly speaking, marks the decisive act in the history of salvation, then the resurrection marks the denouement of the coming of the kingdom, in anticipation of the kingdom's ultimate consummation (cf. Acts 1:11). To speak of the accomplishment of salvation I will employ the Latin phrase *historia salutis* ("history of salvation"), which speaks of the accomplishment of salvation in history.[1] *Historia salutis* therefore gives attention to unique events in the history of redemption, and the resurrection marks the signal turning point in that history. By focusing on the resurrection through the lens of *historia salutis*, I consider what is new in the history of salvation. In the next chapter, I will consider

---

1. This term apparently originates with Herman Ridderbos, "The Redemptive-Historical Character of Paul's Preaching," in *When the Time Had Fully Come: Studies in New Testament Theology* (Grand Rapids: Eerdmans, 1957), 48–49, noted by Richard B. Gaffin Jr., *"By Faith, Not by Sight": Paul and the Order of Salvation* (Waynesboro, GA: Paternoster, 2006), 18–19n2; cf. Gaffin, *Perspectives on Pentecost: New Testament Teaching on the Gifts of the Holy Spirit* (Phillipsburg, NJ: P&R, 1979), 22, 25–26; Gaffin, "Pentecost: Before and After," *Kerux* 10.2 (1995): 3–4.

in more detail the experience of salvation (i.e., "order of salvation," *ordo salutis*). There I will argue that, despite the newness of the accomplishment of salvation in Acts, we also find a great deal of consistency with respect to salvation across the ages.

The present chapter will proceed in the following way. I will first explain how the resurrection of Christ, as the great turning point in *historia salutis*, helps us parse out the relationship between Jesus's resurrection, ascension, and exaltation, which has long been a topic of interest in studies of Lukan eschatology. Though these are different events, they are best viewed collectively as part of one movement of Jesus's experience of glory. Next I will consider the newness of Christ's experience of lordship in light of the preexisting reality that Jesus was Lord already at his birth (cf. Luke 2:11). Then I will consider the newness of the outpouring of the Holy Spirit beginning at Pentecost. Finally, I will consider some redemptive-historical shifts that have taken place in light of the resurrection, especially pertaining to the temple, Sabbath, food laws, circumcision, and worldwide mission.

The Resurrection, Salvation, and Lukan Eschatology

The Resurrection and Ascension: A Debated Relationship

In part 1, I emphasized that the resurrection of Christ is a key element of Lukan theology. Some may be wondering about the role of the ascension, another Lukan emphasis.[2] We could further inquire about the relationship between the resurrection, ascension, and enthronement (or exaltation) of Jesus. On the relationship between these, no consensus has emerged,[3] though one could argue that a disproportionate amount of attention in recent years has been devoted to the ascension, with less attention devoted to Christ's resurrection.[4] Though I have said comparatively little about the ascension

2. See, e.g., Hans Conzelmann, *The Theology of Saint Luke*, trans. Geoffrey Buswell (London: Faber and Faber, 1960), 204.

3. See, e.g., Robert F. O'Toole, SJ, "Luke's Understanding of Jesus' Resurrection-Ascension-Exaltation," *BTB* 9 (1979): 106–14; Arie W. Zwiep, "*Assumptus Est in Caelum:* Rapture and Heavenly Exaltation in Early Judaism and Luke-Acts," in *Christ, the Spirit and the Community of God: Essays on the Acts of the Apostles*, WUNT 2/293 (Tübingen: Mohr Siebeck, 2010), 60–63; Kevin L. Anderson, *"But God Raised Him from the Dead": The Theology of Jesus's Resurrection in Luke-Acts*, PBM (repr., Eugene, OR: Wipf & Stock, 2006), 5–10, 41–47; cf. the survey in François Bovon, *Luke the Theologian: Fifty-Five Years of Research (1950–2005)*, 2nd rev. ed. (Waco: Baylor University Press, 2006), 1–85.

4. Anderson, *"But God Raised Him from the Dead,"* 5–6. See recently, e.g., David K. Bryan and David W. Pao, eds., *Ascent into Heaven in Luke-Acts: New Explorations of Luke's Narrative Hinge* (Minneapolis: Fortress, 2016).

thus far, there should be no objection that the ascension is highly significant for Acts. At the same time, for Luke it is first of all Christ's resurrection that marks the great transition of redemptive history from Jesus's humiliation to his exaltation.

Yet this does not mean that we should separate the resurrection from the ascension and exaltation of Jesus. On the one hand, these epochal events must be integrally related to one another, since Luke moves between them inconspicuously in his narratives.[5] For example, in Acts 2:33–36 the answer to the death of Jesus is the way that God has made Jesus both Lord and Christ. Certainly this passage has in view the enthronement of Jesus, since the Spirit is poured out as proof of the exaltation of Christ (note the quotation of Ps. 110:1 [Ps. 109:1 LXX]). Peter also contrasts the heavenly reign of Christ with the earthly reign of David (v. 34). But Jesus's heavenly enthronement assumes his resurrection as well, since a dead Jesus would not be a reigning Jesus. Indeed, Peter's speech includes not only the enthronement of Jesus but the resurrection of Jesus as well (cf. vv. 24, 31–32). The resurrection, ascension, and enthronement of Christ mark three aspects of Jesus's experience of glory.

On the other hand, one is cautioned against simply equating these events as though Luke makes *no* distinction between them.[6] Nor would it be sufficient to say that for Luke the resurrection is about the heavenly lordship of Christ.[7] Luke specifically emphasizes Jesus's resurrection in several passages, which was necessary according to Scripture (Luke 9:22; 24:6–7, 46). And it is the resurrection that marks the vindication of Christ and his unjust death (cf. Luke 23:47). We run the risk of attenuating Luke's narrative presentation if we flatten Jesus's experience of glory; Luke would have us see several landmarks along the way to Jesus's heavenly enthronement (and in anticipation of his return; cf. Acts 1:11). This is not to say that all of our questions are necessarily

5. Cf. Joel B. Green, "'Witnesses of His Resurrection': Resurrection, Salvation, Discipleship, and Mission in the Acts of the Apostles," in *Life in the Face of Death: The Resurrection Message of the New Testament*, ed. Richard N. Longenecker, MNTS (Grand Rapids: Eerdmans, 1998), 232; I. Howard Marshall, "The Resurrection in the Acts of the Apostles," in *Apostolic History and the Gospel: Biblical and Historical Essays Presented to F. F. Bruce on His 60th Birthday*, ed. W. Ward Gasque and Ralph P. Martin (Grand Rapids: Eerdmans, 1970), 92; Herman Bavinck, *Reformed Dogmatics*, ed. John Bolt, trans. John Vriend, 4 vols. (Grand Rapids: Baker Academic, 2003–8), 3:442–43.

6. Cf. Anderson, *"But God Raised Him from the Dead,"* 41–47. See also Stanley E. Porter, "The Unity of Luke-Acts and the Ascension Narratives," in *Ascent into Heaven in Luke-Acts: New Explorations of Luke's Narrative Hinge*, ed. David K. Bryan and David W. Pao (Minneapolis: Fortress, 2016), 120–24; Carl R. Holladay, "What David Saw: Messianic Exegesis in Acts 2," *SCJ* 19 (2016): 106–8.

7. Cf. Howard Clark Kee, *Good News to the Ends of the Earth: The Theology of Acts* (London: SCM; Philadelphia: Trinity Press International, 1990), 11.

answered. For example, mystery remains as to "from where" Jesus appears to his disciples in his resurrected state. As Herman Bavinck has argued, Jesus in his resurrected state appears to be withdrawing from the present world but is transitioning to "another way of living and working."[8] Rather, the point of distinguishing aspects of Jesus's experience of glory is to appreciate that the appearances of the resurrected Christ to his disciples, including on the road to (and at) Emmaus, precede the singular ascension experience from the Mount of Olives recorded in Luke 24:50–53; Acts 1:9–11. It is not facile to observe that in Luke-Acts we encounter a progression of events: the resurrection (Luke 24:1–49; cf. Acts 1:3–5), followed by the ascension (Luke 24:50–53; Acts 1:9–11), and subsequently the proof of the heavenly exaltation/enthronement of Jesus is seen in the pouring-out of the Holy Spirit at Pentecost (Acts 2:1–4; cf. 2:33–36).[9] We must be sensitive to Luke's narrative presentation and be careful of superimposing upon Luke's works an eschatological reconstruction that is either too complex or simplistic, which we could scarcely have expected the original audience to understand.[10]

To this end, I will consider in this section, first, the role of the resurrection as the vindication of Jesus's perfect obedience. Second, I will consider in more detail the nature of the unity of the resurrection, ascension, and enthronement of Christ.

Resurrection as Vindication

First, to understand the role of Jesus's resurrection in marking a transition to his experience of glory, it is important to appreciate that Jesus's resurrection is the vindication of his perfect obedience. As such, it is constitutive of the accomplishment of salvation (*historia salutis*). The resurrection accounts of the Gospels (including Luke) resolve the final conflict faced by Jesus in the crucifixion. Without the resurrection the narratives would be unresolved; it would seem that the enemies of Jesus had indeed defeated him.[11] The resur-

8. Bavinck, *Reformed Dogmatics*, 3:443. He continues: "The forty days, accordingly, were of the utmost importance for the disciples. In that period they were introduced to the practice of communion with the—indeed—living but at the same time glorified Lord. They were becoming accustomed to the idea that in the future Christ would exist and work in another mode and another form (μορφη)" (3:444).

9. For a survey of various construals, see Anderson, *"But God Raised Him from the Dead,"* 6–10.

10. See similarly Anderson, *"But God Raised Him from the Dead,"* 41–47.

11. See Brandon D. Crowe, *The Last Adam: A Theology of the Obedient Life of Jesus in the Gospels* (Grand Rapids: Baker Academic, 2017), 192–97; cf. W. D. Davies and Dale C. Allison Jr., *A Critical and Exegetical Commentary on the Gospel according to Saint Matthew*, 3 vols., ICC (Edinburgh: T&T Clark, 1988–97), 3:673.

rection is the great "amen" to the sacrificial life and death of Jesus.[12] It not only demonstrates the veracity of Jesus's predictions of his own resurrection (Luke 9:22; 18:33; cf. 24:6–7, 26, 46) but also proves that Jesus—and his message—were "in the right." Therefore, the resurrection is the justification of Jesus because by it Jesus's punishment and condemnation are overcome, and he is raised to eternal life.[13] Further, as I have argued from Paul's Pisidian Antioch sermon, the resurrection is part of the grounding of Jesus's followers' justification as well (Acts 13:37–39).[14] I have also argued that what Luke gives in the Pauline speech imbedded in his narrative is consistent with what we find in Paul's letters (cf. Rom. 4:24–25). Because Jesus is the holy one of God, wholly without sin, he was raised to new life over sin and death. He therefore reigns over an everlasting kingdom and is able to grant freedom from sin for all those who repent and believe (cf. Acts 2:38; 3:19; 13:39).

In terms of *historia salutis* resurrection marks what theologians have often called the transition from Jesus's state of humiliation (e.g., incarnation, life under the law, subject to death) to his state of glory (e.g., raised to new life, ascension, enthronement, future return).[15] In the words of Bavinck, Jesus's "entire state of exaltation from the resurrection to his coming again for judgment is a reward for the work that he accomplished as the Servant of the Lord in the days of his humiliation."[16] Bavinck continues: "[What Christ obtained for himself in the state of exaltation] consisted in the exaltation itself, in the resurrection, ascension, seating at God's right hand, and the return for judgment; in other words, in the mediatorial glory to which he was raised in both natures. He did not possess that glory beforehand but obtained it at his exaltation."[17] Consistent with an understanding of Jesus's resurrection

12. See, e.g., Louis Berkhof, *Systematic Theology*, 4th ed. (Grand Rapids: Eerdmans, 1941), 349.

13. Geerhardus Vos, *Reformed Dogmatics*, ed. Richard B. Gaffin Jr., 5 vols. (Bellingham, WA: Lexham, 2012–16), 3:201; Vos, *The Pauline Eschatology* (Grand Rapids: Eerdmans, 1953), 151, quoted in Richard B. Gaffin Jr., *The Centrality of the Resurrection: A Study in Paul's Soteriology* (Grand Rapids: Baker, 1978), 122; cf. Geerhardus Vos, "The Eschatological Aspect of the Pauline Conception of the Spirit," in *Redemptive History and Biblical Interpretation: The Shorter Writings of Geerhardus Vos*, ed. Richard B. Gaffin Jr. (Phillipsburg, NJ: P&R, 1980), 109.

14. I will say more about this in the next chapter. For a landmark study on this issue (focusing largely on Paul), see Gaffin, *Centrality of the Resurrection*; cf. Heidelberg Catechism, question and answer 45.

15. See Francis Turretin, *Inst.* 13.9; 13.17; Bavinck, *Reformed Dogmatics*, 3:339, 424–36; Vos, *Reformed Dogmatics*, 3:201, 219–30; Berkhof, *Systematic Theology*, 350; WCF 8.4; WLC 51; WSC 28.

16. Bavinck, *Reformed Dogmatics*, 3:433.

17. Bavinck, *Reformed Dogmatics*, 3:434. Bavinck here expresses the view prevalent in Reformed theology (and elsewhere) that the Mediator was exalted according to both his human nature and divine nature. See also Vos, *Reformed Dogmatics*, 3:219.

as his justification, Jesus's experience of glory was the reward for his perfect obedience and was the demonstration of his Father's approval.[18]

Bringing these two aspects together—the resurrection as the seal of Jesus's perfect obedience and the beginning of his experience of glory—it is striking that Jesus's resurrection is often portrayed in Adamic terms. Jesus's resurrection is thus the answer to Adam's disobedience and corresponds to the right to eternal life. Since Jesus's obedience excels Adam's disobedience, his experience of glory is the answer to the futility of creation that emerged after the sin of Adam. Such a correlation is certainly true for Paul, where he, in texts like Romans 5–8 and 1 Corinthians 15, compares and contrasts Christ's work resulting in resurrection life to Adam's sin resulting in death.[19] Something similar is operative in Acts as well.

To be sure, Luke often tethers the resurrection of Christ to a strong Davidic Christology, whereby Christ reigns over the everlasting (Davidic) kingdom. Yet before David in the biblical narrative, Adam is portrayed as a king who should have reigned forever.[20] In terms of redemptive history, it also appears that David himself recognized the royal dimensions of Adam's created state.[21] The Davidic kingdom is thus predicated upon a royal investiture of humanity, focused first of all in Adam. Luke's Davidic Christology does not preclude an Adamic Christology, but Luke's Christology draws together the Davidic and Adamic. The latter can be seen, for example, in Luke's genealogy (cf. Luke 3:38), in his usage of "Son of Man," and in his multiple allusions to Genesis (e.g., 13:10–17).[22] A particularly relevant Adamic resonance in Luke is found in the account of the transfiguration, where Jesus's experience of glory stands in contrast to the glory that Adam never attained.[23] Significantly, the transfiguration also anticipates Jesus's resurrected estate of glory.

Jesus's pouring-out of the Spirit in Acts (Acts 2:33) is also Adamic. Elsewhere in the New Testament the giving of the Spirit is correlated to Adam Christology (John 20:22; 1 Cor. 15:45),[24] which draws upon the association of the Spirit with the creation of Adam (Gen. 2:7). Yet whereas Adam was

---

18. See, e.g., Vos, *Reformed Dogmatics*, 3:220–23; Berkhof, *Systematic Theology*, 345.

19. I have discussed this further in "The Passive *and* Active Obedience of Christ: Retrieving a Biblical Distinction," in *The Doctrine on which the Church Stands or Falls: Justification in Biblical, Theological, Historical, and Pastoral Perspective*, ed. Matthew Barrett (Wheaton: Crossway, 2019), 437–64.

20. See, e.g., Gen. 1:26–28; cf. 3:22. See further Crowe, *Last Adam*, 56–61, 151.

21. See especially Ps. 8, which includes a Davidic superscription and speaks of the royal dignity of humanity, echoing Gen. 1.

22. For defense and further discussion, see Crowe, *Last Adam*, 23–53, 104–5.

23. See Crowe, *Last Adam*, 49–50. The transfiguration also manifests the *divine* glory of Jesus. See Vos, *Reformed Dogmatics*, 3:6–9.

24. On similarities between Luke and 1 Corinthians 15 on the resurrection, see Daniel Marguerat, "Quand la résurrection se fait clef de lecture de l'histoire (Luc-Actes)," in *Resurrection*

receptive in creation, Christ has the authority to pour out the Spirit and give life.[25] As resurrected, life-giving last Adam, Christ has inaugurated a new age, which can be summarized as the age of the Spirit.[26] The Spirit rested on Christ in his incarnate work in a special way (Luke 1:35; 3:16, 22; 4:1, 18; 10:21; cf. 9:34–35; 11:20; Acts 10:37–38), and through this messianic work the new-creational age of the Spirit—the age of the last Adam—is inaugurated.[27] This new age is also identified as the age of the resurrection, and we have seen that Jesus's own resurrection marks the beginning of the resurrection anticipated by God's people. Indeed, in Jesus's encounter with the Sadducees in Luke 20:27–40 he speaks of two ages—"this age" (*tou aiōnos toutou*, v. 34) and the age of the resurrection.[28] For Luke the "coming age" (*tou aiōnos ekeinou*, v. 35) is marked by resurrection—a perspective that is echoed in Paul's defense in Acts 26:6–8, 22–23. Thus, for Jesus to have been raised from the dead is for the eschatological age of the Spirit to have dawned—the resurrection age. The resurrection of Christ thus marks not only the transition from Jesus's state of humiliation to his state of exaltation but concomitantly the transition from age of anticipation to age of fulfillment.

The resurrection of Christ, therefore, is central to Luke's understanding of *historia salutis*. The resurrection as the justification of Christ secures the salvation of his people and marks the transition to the age of the Spirit.[29] It is the "beginning of a new '*Heilsepoche*'" ("salvation epoch").[30] Since it is the key to the righteousness and justification of his people, we should therefore not be surprised that the resurrection consistently marks a logical key to the speeches in Acts (e.g., in Peter's Pentecost sermon [Acts 2:31–32, 36], after the healing of the lame man at the temple [3:13, 15], and in Paul's sermon at Pisidian Antioch [13:30, 32–33, 37–39]). In Acts, as in Paul's letters, the resurrection demonstrates the Adamic glory and righteousness of Christ and is the result and seal of his perfect work in the state of humiliation.

---

of the Dead: Biblical Traditions in Dialogue, ed. Geert Van Oyen and Tom Shepherd, BETL 249 (Leuven: Peters, 2012), 187–88, 193.

25. See also Vos, "Eschatological Aspect," 107. Vos notes the term *zōopoieō* in 1 Cor. 15:45, but the life-giving authority of the resurrected Christ is clear in Acts even though this term is not used (cf. Acts 3:1–10, 21).

26. See similarly Vos, "Eschatological Aspect," 101–11.

27. See especially Vos, "Eschatological Aspect," 96, 107. Vos here comments on 1 Cor. 15. He says much less about Acts in this watershed article (cf. 100).

28. Cf. Darrell Bock, *Luke*, 2 vols., BECNT (Grand Rapids: Baker Academic, 1994–96), 2:1622; Joel B. Green, *The Gospel of Luke*, NICNT (Grand Rapids: Eerdmans, 1997), 720–21.

29. On the soteriological aspect of the Spirit, see Vos, "Eschatological Aspect," 102, 108–21.

30. Following Richard Glöckner, OP, *Die Verkündigung des Heils beim Evangelisten Lukas*, WSAMA.T 9 (Mainz: Matthias-Grünewald-Verlag, 1975), 224. Glöckner speaks here of the *Erhöhung* ("exaltation") of Jesus, though he understands the resurrection and exaltation to be very closely related (218–22).

Unity of Resurrection and Ascension in Historia Salutis

Second, having considered the singular significance of the resurrection for *historia salutis*, we now must consider the unity of the elements constitutive of Christ's estate of glory. The key transition moment for *historia salutis* comes with the resurrection, but the resurrection is only one aspect of Christ's state of exaltation. Also included are his ascension, his exaltation at the right hand of the Father, and his coming again in glory. These aspects—in addition to the resurrection—are clearly present in Acts (ascension: Acts 1:9–11; cf. Luke 24:50–53; exaltation: Acts 2:33–34; 5:31; 7:55–56; cf. Luke 22:69; promise of future return: Acts 1:11; 3:21). While our gaze has been focused attentively in this volume on the resurrection of Jesus, this need not (indeed, *must* not) obfuscate other aspects of Christ's state of exaltation.[31] Though some have seen a dichotomy between Luke's accounts of Jesus's resurrection and ascension,[32] these are best viewed as being of a piece with a broader theology of Christ's exaltation. They are distinct, but not separate.

There is no disjunction, then, between the risen Jesus and the exalted Jesus. Instead, Luke moves seamlessly between the various aspects of Jesus's estate of glory, so that it is difficult at times to distinguish sharply between various aspects (see, e.g., Acts 3:13). Yet the resurrection holds a position as *primus inter pares* as the first—and therefore transitional—phase of Jesus's state of glory in the economy of redemption. Such a view may be found in Luke 24:26, where the resurrected Christ speaks of the necessity (*dei*) of his suffering and entering into his glory. At this point Christ has not yet ascended, but he speaks already of the present reality of his experience of glory. It would not be wrong to speak of Jesus's ascension as his glorification, but the experience of glory has already begun before Jesus's ascension.[33]

The Lord of *Historia Salutis*

As the transition from Christ's state of humiliation to glory, the resurrection also marks a new experience of Christ's lordship. Acts 2:36 states that God has made Jesus "both Lord and Christ." This *making* should not be taken in an absolute sense, as though Jesus were not already Lord (or Christ) before his

31. As Bavinck notes (*Reformed Dogmatics*, 3:445), "The ascension, as much as the resurrection, was a constituent of the faith of the church from the beginning."

32. Cf. Bovon, *Luke the Theologian*, 79.

33. See also Conzelmann, *Theology of Saint Luke*, 203n2, though it is not quite right to say that Luke "sharply divides" the resurrection appearances of Christ on earth from his heavenly ascension.

resurrection. For indeed Luke applies the title *kyrios* to Jesus during his earthly ministry much more frequently than the other evangelists.[34] Already at his birth (and indeed even *before* his birth) Jesus is identified as both Lord and Christ (Luke 2:11; cf. 1:31–33, 35, 43). And yet Acts speaks of a new experience of Christ's lordship beginning with his resurrection. This is what Peter refers to in his Pentecost sermon (Acts 2:36): by exalting Jesus, God has made (*epoiēsen*) him both Lord and Christ in a new sense. That new sense is best taken, in connection with the resurrection, as the exaltation of Christ that corresponds to the perfection of his work in the state of humiliation. This is emphatically *not* a new ontological experience of lordship. It is rather a new experience of lordship in redemptive-historical terms in the context of the accomplishment of redemption.[35] Having completed his work and conquered death, Jesus is now exalted as the heavenly Lord. There is, then, a real exaltation of Christ that is inaugurated with the resurrection.[36] This new status of lordship certainly involves an epistemological shift—now, in his state of exaltation, Christ's exaltation is no longer veiled but "radiates outward for all to see."[37] Yet there is more than *only* an epistemological shift; the estate of lordship Christ entered by means of his resurrection corresponds to the real accomplishment of salvation in the economy of redemption (*historia salutis*). Here I depart from the engaging contribution of Kavin Rowe, who emphasizes the fundamental unity of Christ's lordship throughout Luke-Acts.[38] While I agree with much of Rowe's argument (including his denial of a newness in ontology at the resurrection),[39] we are compelled by the epochal shift that corresponds to the resurrection of

34. See especially C. Kavin Rowe, *Early Narrative Christology: The Lord in the Gospel of Luke*, BZNW 139 (2006; repr., Grand Rapids: Baker Academic, 2009).

35. Cf. Turretin, *Inst.* 3.23.31: "Christ was made Lord after the resurrection (Acts 2:36), not in essential dominion (which he had even from the foundation of the world as the maker of all things) . . . but in personal and economical dominion." Translation from Francis Turretin, *Institutes of Elenctic Theology*, ed. James T. Dennison Jr., trans. George Musgrave Giger, 3 vols. (Phillipsburg, NJ: P&R, 1992–97), 1:290. See also Keener, *Acts*, 1:964; Fitzmyer, *Acts of the Apostles*, 260.

36. See especially Bavinck, *Reformed Dogmatics*, 3:435, which is worth quoting at length: "At the resurrection he received the glory that according to his Godhead he already had before (John 17:2, 24), became the Lord of glory (1 Cor. 2:8), the power of God (1 Cor. 1:24), obtained a name above every name, that is, the name of 'Lord' (κυριος) (John 20:28; Acts 2:36; 1 Cor. 12:3; Phil. 2:9–10), and thereby the κυριοτης, the right, the authority, and the power to exercise lordship over all creatures as mediator, prophet, priest, and king, to subdue his enemies, to gather his people, and to regain the fallen creation for God (Pss. 2, 72, 110; Matt. 28:18; 1 Cor. 15:21ff.; Eph. 1:20–23; Phil. 2:9–11; Heb. 1:3f.; 1 Pet. 3:22; Rev. 1:5; etc.). In the resurrection God openly appointed him Son of God, Lord, King, Mediator, saying to him: 'You are my Son; today I have begotten you' (Acts 2:33, 36; 3:15; 5:31; 13:33; 17:31; Heb. 1:5)."

37. Bavinck, *Reformed Dogmatics*, 3:435.

38. Rowe, "Acts 2:36 and the Continuity of Lukan Christology," *NTS* 53 (2007): 37–56.

39. Rowe, "Acts 2:36 and the Continuity," 54.

Christ to posit more than only an epistemological shift. The resurrection of Christ introduces a new aspect to his execution of lordship beyond what was true before his completion of his work of humiliation.[40]

In this sense, *poieō* in Acts 2:36 ("God *made* [*epoiēsen*] him both Lord and Christ") is best taken as an installation to the place of honor at God's right hand.[41] This is consistent with Paul's outlook in Romans 1:3–4, where Jesus the Lord is declared (*horisthentos*) Son of God in power by his resurrection from the dead. The new experience of Christ in Romans 1 is not a newness of ontological sonship but the glorified experience of sonship that corresponds to his resurrected, Spiritual life.[42] The same is true for Christ as Lord in Luke-Acts: though he was already Lord at his birth (and indeed, even when crucified, Jesus is Lord! [Luke 24:3]),[43] a new experience of lordship is inaugurated with Christ's resurrection and entrance into the state of glory. The everlasting kingdom that is a persistent focus of Luke-Acts is established by the resurrection of Christ, the universal Lord, who is both David's son and David's Lord (Ps. 110:1; Luke 20:41–44; Acts 2:34).

Lord is thus the most fitting term to communicate the exalted work of Christ in the context of *historia salutis*. Because Jesus has conquered death and accomplished salvation, his experience of lordship shifts after the resurrection. Moreover, this new experience of glorified lordship not only affects Jesus as Mediator but marks several epochal shifts in salvation history. These include the outpouring of the Holy Spirit, a shift with respect to the Jerusalem temple, the relativizing of some key marks of Judaism (especially the Sabbath, dietary laws, and circumcision), and greater emphasis and clarity of worldwide mission. We will look at each of these in turn.

The Outpouring of the Holy Spirit

One of the most prominent epochal shifts following upon Christ's resurrection in Acts is the outpouring of the Holy Spirit. We have already considered the christological reasons that the Spirit was poured out, especially the exaltation of the resurrected Christ to the right hand of God (cf. Acts 2:22–36). In

40. Rowe sees the resurrection as providing the vindication of Jesus's prior status as Lord ("Acts 2:36 and the Continuity," 54–55).

41. See Keener, *Acts*, 1:964; cf. Herman N. Ridderbos, *The Speeches of Peter in the Acts of the Apostles* (London: Tyndale, 1962), 21–22.

42. I capitalize "Spiritual" to highlight the connection of the resurrection body of Christ with the Holy Spirit. See further Gaffin, *Centrality of the Resurrection*, 78–86. See also my discussion in ch. 3 (under section "1. Resurrection and Sonship").

43. Cf. Rowe, *Early Narrative Christology*, 184–89.

this section I argue for the newness of the role of the Spirit in the context of *historia salutis*, which is consistently emphasized in Acts. This will provide the foundation for my discussion of the Spirit in the next chapter, where I will also argue for continuity of the Spirit's work across the ages.

To begin, it is important to understand the association of the Spirit with Christ himself. This is clear throughout Luke-Acts, even from the days of Jesus's conception by the power and holiness of the Spirit (Luke 1:35). From his baptism (3:22), to his obedience in the face of temptation (4:1, 14), to the opening sermon of his ministry (4:14, 18), to his powerful working of miracles (cf. 11:20 with Matt. 12:28), Jesus was anointed, guided, and empowered by the Holy Spirit (cf. Isa. 11:2).[44] It is thus not surprising that Peter in Acts 10:36–38 summarizes that Jesus was anointed by God with the Holy Spirit and power, doing good and healing those oppressed by the devil.[45] The Spirit is so closely identified with Christ himself that we can in fact refer to the Spirit as the Spirit of Christ.[46]

If Jesus himself pours out the Spirit in Acts (cf. Luke 3:16; Acts 2:33), then it makes sense that Jesus is presented as being in full possession of the Spirit. Yet it is only after his resurrection and ascension that Jesus pours out the Spirit, which corresponds to the correlation of the Spirit and the age of resurrection. I introduced this concept in the first part of chapter 2, where I considered the role of texts such as Ezekiel 36–37 and Joel 2–3 for understanding the prophetic hopes of restoration and resurrection. It is therefore fitting that Jesus's experience of the resurrection is identified elsewhere in the New Testament as a *Spiritual* existence—that is, Paul refers to Jesus's resurrected body as a *Spiritual* (*pneumatikon*) body (1 Cor. 15:44; cf. v. 46). To be sure, this language is much debated—what does Paul mean by a "s/Spiritual body"? A thorough discussion of this passage is beyond my present purposes, but in brief the best answer is that a Spiritual body is a body characterized by the age of the Spirit, which is also the age of (bodily) resurrection.[47] This is seen in 1 Corinthians 15:45 and the presentation of Christ as last Adam, who has inaugurated the age of the Spirit, and it is the glorified Jesus himself who pours out the Spirit.[48]

44. Cf. Bavinck, *Reformed Dogmatics*, 3:435; Vos, "Eschatological Aspect," 96.
45. See also Crowe, *Last Adam*, 72–74, 146–47.
46. So Sinclair B. Ferguson, *The Holy Spirit*, CCT (Downers Grove, IL: InterVarsity, 1996), 35–56.
47. Cf. Gaffin, *Centrality of the Resurrection*, 67–68, 78–92; Vos, "Eschatological Aspect," 101–11.
48. On Christ's resurrection and his role as last Adam and as "life-giving Spirit," see Gaffin, *Centrality of the Resurrection*, 87–88; cf. Benjamin L. Gladd, "The Last Adam as the 'Life-Giving Spirit' Revisited: A Possible Old Testament Background on One of Paul's Most Perplexing Phrases," *WTJ* 71 (2009): 297–309; Crowe, *Last Adam*, 33; Bavinck, *Reformed Dogmatics*, 3:436.

This leads us to the observation that Christ's pouring-out of the Spirit, in conjunction with his resurrection and exaltation, marks the coming of the eschaton. Though the consummation of the eschaton remains future (when Christ returns), this consummate reality has already irrupted into the present age.[49] Just as the Spirit was active in a special way at creation (cf. Gen. 1:2), so is the Spirit especially active in re-creation, beginning signally with the resurrection of Christ.[50] As Geerhardus Vos has stated succinctly, "The Spirit and the resurrection belong together."[51] The emphasis on the coming of the Spirit in Acts highlights the fulfillment of God's promises and the accomplishment of salvation (*historia salutis*).[52] The connection between, for example, the outpouring of the Spirit and prophecy in Acts (cf. Acts 2:3–4, 17–18) indicates this newness of the resurrection age.[53]

Luke thus emphasizes the newness of the coming of the Spirit in conjunction with the glorification of Jesus; there should be little debate on this. And yet Luke also has much to say about the work of the Spirit before the resurrection (e.g., the Spirit's presence with Simeon [Luke 2:25–27]). In light of such texts, the newness of the Spirit in Acts must be relative rather than absolute.[54] In the next chapter I will consider how we square the perennial presence and work of the Spirit through the ages with the manifest newness of the Spirit's work following Jesus's resurrection.

Redemptive-Historical Shifts of the Resurrection Age

We turn now to some significant redemptive-historical shifts in Acts. While these may seem obvious today to those familiar with Christian tradition, these each represent major developments in a first-century Jewish context. Something significant must have happened to precipitate such changes. This is indeed what we find in Luke-Acts. The resurrection of Jesus precipitates significant shifts in some major features of spiritual praxis.

Temple

Luke manifests a particular interest in the temple. The Gospel of Luke opens (following the prologue) with Zechariah in the temple (cf. 1:9, 21–22).

49. See Vos, "Eschatological Aspect."
50. Vos, "Eschatological Aspect," 93–95.
51. Vos, "Eschatological Aspect," 101. Vos deals particularly with Pauline theology, but this is also true for Acts. See also Gaffin, *Perspectives on Pentecost*, 20.
52. See similarly Vos, "Eschatological Aspect," 100.
53. See Alan J. Thompson, *The Acts of the Risen Lord Jesus: Luke's Account of God's Unfolding Plan*, NSBT 27 (Downers Grove, IL: InterVarsity, 2011), 132–33.
54. Cf. Turretin, *Inst.* 3.30.22; 12.7.45; cf. 12.5.15.

It is in the temple that the infant Jesus encounters the aged Simeon and Anna (2:27–28, 36–38), and later in his childhood Jesus is found in the temple asking insightful questions of the teachers (2:46). Whereas the final temptation in the Matthean temptation account involves all the kingdoms of the world (Matt. 4:8), in Luke the climactic temptation involves the temple (4:9–11). Luke ends with the disciples in the temple praising God (24:53), which forms an *inclusio* with the temple at the beginning of the Gospel.

In Acts the temple continues to loom large. The disciples gather at the temple (2:46; 3:1; 5:20); after his Damascus road experience Paul prays in the temple, where he sees a vision of the risen Christ (22:17–18); and Paul later brings an offering to the temple (21:26). At the temple the apostles speak about Christ and his resurrection (3:11–26; 5:20–26, 42). James presents Jesus's resurrection in Acts 15 as central to the restoration of the Davidic dynasty, and he does so with temple language.[55] It is not the physical temple but Jesus himself who is the locus of worship.[56] Stephen speaks of the Jerusalem temple in idolatrous terms, leaving little doubt that the temple is no longer to be considered the center of worship for God's people (7:42–43; cf. 17:24).

By mentioning the temple at key points in his two-part narrative, Luke does not intend to underscore the abiding centrality of the Jerusalem temple. Instead, he relativizes it.[57] This is clearer in Acts than in Luke, for in Acts the completed work of Christ receives extended exposition. Indeed, the centrality of the Jerusalem temple in Luke seems to underscore the more minor role of the temple in Acts; in Acts Luke focuses on the move away from the physical temple. He instead envisions a different sort of a temple—a spiritual temple composed of believers in Christ. This is implied in the resurrected and glorified Christ's pouring out his Spirit on the church at Pentecost. G. K. Beale has argued that the events of Pentecost are portrayed with temple imagery.[58] The effusion of the Spirit from the exalted Christ incorporates and builds up God's people into a living temple.[59] In conjunction with this corporate understanding of temple, I argued in the

---

55. See ch. 4 (under section "James and the Resurrection") for more on this.

56. G. K. Beale, *The Temple and the Church's Mission: A Biblical Theology of the Dwelling Place of God*, NSBT 17 (Downers Grove, IL: InterVarsity, 2004), 233–36.

57. Note, e.g., the lack of emphasis on the temple in the apostolic speeches of Acts. Even where, for example, Paul prays in the temple (22:17–21), the risen Christ instructs him to *leave* Jerusalem.

58. On this point, and for what immediately follows, see esp. Beale, "The Descent of the Eschatological Temple in the Form of the Spirit at Pentecost, Part 1: The Clearest Evidence," *TynBul* 56.1 (2005): 73–102.

59. See also Dennis E. Johnson, *The Message of Acts in the History of Redemption* (Phillipsburg, NJ: P&R, 1997), 59.

previous chapter that Jesus's resurrection is envisioned by Luke as part of the matrix of imagery relating to the rebuilt, eschatological temple (Amos 9:11–12; Acts 15:16–18).[60] If so, then the shift in Luke is not simply *away* from the temple, but the focus shifts from the physical temple to the spiritual temple composed of God's people, under the leadership of the restored (resurrected) Davidic king.[61]

Further supporting this perspective are possible echoes of Psalm 68 in Acts 2:33.[62] This has been a common suggestion, given the likely verbal parallels between the two texts. Jesus's ascent on high (*hypsōtheis*) seems to echo language used for God in Psalm 67:19 LXX (68:18 EVV) (*anebēs eis hypsos*). Further, the receiving (*labōn*) of the promised Holy Spirit from the Father and then pouring him out (*execheen*) likely recalls God's receiving gifts (*elabes domata*, Ps. 67:19 LXX) among people (cf. Acts 2:38: *lēmpsesthe tēn dōrean tou hagiou pneumatos*).[63] In addition to likely verbal parallels, conceptually Psalm 68 and Acts 2 are quite close. In Psalm 68 God, the great king, is presented as a victorious warrior who receives the victory spoils.[64] In Acts 2, Jesus is the resurrected king who receives the promised Holy Spirit as proof of his victory and subsequently pours out the Spirit. We should recall that before Jesus pours out the Spirit, Luke has emphasized the Spirit's accompaniment of Jesus throughout his incarnate existence. The notion that a victorious king would grant spoils to his people in the wake of victory was a common trope across cultures of the ancient world (cf. 2 Cor. 2:14).[65] In

---

60. See again Beale, *Temple and the Church's Mission*, 233.

61. Thus temple imagery is used for both Christ and the church in Acts.

62. Cf. Barnabas Lindars, *New Testament Apologetic: The Doctrinal Significance of the Old Testament Quotations* (London: SCM, 1961), 44; cf. 51–59; I. Howard Marshall, "Acts," in *Commentary on the New Testament Use of the Old Testament*, ed. G. K. Beale and D. A. Carson (Grand Rapids: Baker Academic, 2007), 541; Jacques DuPont, *Nouvelle études sur les Actes des Apôtres*, LD 118 (Paris: Cerf, 1984), 202–9; G. K. Beale, "The Descent of the Eschatological Temple in the Form of the Spirit at Pentecost, Part 2: Corroborating Evidence," *TynBul* 56.2 (2005): 69–72; cf. the discussion of Barrett, *Commentary on the Acts*, 1:149–50. Those who are not convinced include Robert F. O'Toole, SJ, "Acts 2:30 and the Davidic Covenant of Pentecost," *JBL* 102 (1983): 246–47; Darrell L. Bock, *Proclamation from Prophecy and Pattern: Lucan Old Testament Christology*, JSNTSup 12 (Sheffield: JSOT Press, 1987), 181–83 (though he does admit that Ps. 68 was important for the outpouring of the Spirit in early Christianity; cf. 352n92). More recently Bock (*Acts*, BECNT [Grand Rapids: Baker Academic, 2007], 133; noted also by Eckhard J. Schnabel, *Acts*, ZECNT [Grand Rapids: Zondervan, 2012], 149n91) suggests a *conceptual* parallel to Ps. 68 may be operative.

63. This connection is noted by Beale, "Descent of the Eschatological Temple, Part 2," 69.

64. Cf. Todd A. Scacewater, "The Divine Builder: Psalm 68 in Jewish and Pauline Tradition" (PhD diss., Westminster Theological Seminary, 2017), 86–92.

65. A Roman audience might think of the generosity of Julius Caesar, who (though he did *not* position himself publicly as a king [cf. the second-century work of Suetonius, *Jul.* 79]) bestowed gifts on his soldiers and the people following his victories (see Suetonius, *Jul.* 38, 83).

this light, in Acts the Spirit is poured out in a new way that corresponds to the new accomplishment of salvation. And this outpouring has particular reference to the equipping of God's people (as the new temple dwelling) for the task of ministry.

This view—that the resurrected, exalted Christ pours out the Spirit for equipping the saints in the renewed, spiritual temple, especially in light of a possible allusion to Psalm 68—is also consistent with the citation of Psalm 67:19 LXX [68:18 EVV] in Ephesians 4:7–10. As in Acts 2, the focus in Ephesians 4 is on the outpouring of the Spirit in the context of *historia salutis*— salvation accomplished (e.g., Eph. 1:7–10, 20–23; 3:11). And in Ephesians the gifts given to the church are gifts of the Holy Spirit—constitutive of the victory of Christ—whereby the church is built up (4:11–14). Additionally, temple themes and imagery are important in Ephesians, not least in terms of the role of the Holy Spirit (cf. 2:19–22). This emphasis is consistent with Psalm 68, where the gifts given/received are likely gifts for the temple.[66] Likewise, in Acts the focus on the outpouring of the Spirit corresponds to the new temple composed of God's people throughout the world. This fulfills Numbers 11, where Moses expressed the desire that all of God's people would be prophets, filled with the Spirit (v. 29). Luke's citation of Joel 3:1–5 LXX (2:28–32 EVV) in Acts 2:17–21 shows that this is being fulfilled—now all of God's people are receiving the Spirit, from the oldest to the youngest, male and female, rich and poor. Prophethood is now extended to all of God's people. Acts and Ephesians share the perspective that the exalted Christ pours out his Spirit on his people as a result of his victorious, incarnate work.[67] These are the contours of the Spirit's newness in Acts—it is a new equipping for ministry in the eschatological, spiritual temple of God.[68] And all these gifts are predicated on the resurrection of Christ, who has emerged as the messianic king victorious over death, exalted at God's right hand.

Another shift with respect to the temple relates to the forgiveness of sins. The ministries of John the Baptist and Jesus show starkly that forgiveness of sins is not tied to a particular place (cf. Luke 1:77; 3:3; 5:20–24; 7:47–49). Indeed, Jesus states in Luke 24:47 that forgiveness of sins is preached in Jesus's

---

66. Scacewater, "Divine Builder," 78–93, 228–39, 264–69.

67. Another possibility is that Luke intends the Ephesian town clerk's appeal to the heavenly stone that fell to Ephesus—home of the famous Temple of Artemis—to be taken by the informed reader as an ironic echo of the heavenly kingdom-temple stone of Dan. 2:34–35. Stone language is frequently used to speak of the resurrection of Christ in the NT—including in Luke and Acts (Matt. 21:42; Mark 12:10; Luke 20:17; Acts 4:10–11; 1 Pet. 2:6–8; cf. Ps. 118:22 [117:22 LXX]; Isa. 28:16). This is particularly intriguing if Ephesians was actually sent to Ephesus (cf. the thorny text-critical issues in Eph. 1:1).

68. See similarly Beale, "Descent of the Eschatological Temple, Part 1," 94.

name beginning *from* Jerusalem.[69] Thus the message of forgiveness goes *out* from the place that many would have considered to be the place they would come *to* for forgiveness—the temple in Jerusalem (cf. 1 Kings 8:28–53). In light of the traditional role of the temple and its institutions, the emphasis on forgiveness in Jesus's name in Acts 2:38—in conjunction with baptism and the reception of the Spirit—indicates that the Jerusalem temple's role in the mediation of forgiveness is no more.[70] A new era has come. This move away from the physical temple does not mean, however, that true forgiveness of sins is an entirely new phenomenon with the resurrection of Christ. As I will argue in the next chapter, forgiveness of sins was already a reality in the Old Testament, which also necessitates that the Spirit was already at work before Pentecost.

Sabbath, Dietary Laws, Circumcision

Sabbath

The resurrection of Christ marks a shift not only in the role of the temple but also with respect to some of the defining marks of first-century Judaism, especially Sabbath observance, food laws, and circumcision.[71] We begin with Sabbath, which was traditionally celebrated on the seventh day of the week, hearkening back to creation (cf. Gen. 2:1–3; Exod. 20:11). By all accounts, Sabbath observance was a distinctive mark of the Jewish people.[72] It is therefore remarkable that we may find evidence in Acts for the early followers of Jesus gathering together not on the traditional Sabbath day but on Sunday. The key passage in Acts 20 relates Paul's seven-day visit with the believers in Troas and their breaking bread together on the "first day of the week" (*en . . . tē mia tōn sabbatōn*, v. 7). This language clearly echoes the day of Jesus's resurrection in Luke (cf. Luke 24:1: *tē mia tōn sabbatōn*).[73]

Is this episode evidence for disciples of Jesus gathering on the day of the resurrection in the first century? It is difficult to say with certainty, since we

---

69. There is a question about the proper punctuation in 24:47, but the point remains that there is a centrifugal move away from Jerusalem.

70. See Beale, "Descent of the Eschatological Temple, Part 2," 80–81.

71. These are the three Jewish identity markers addressed by Isaac W. Oliver, *Torah Praxis after 70 CE: Reading Matthew and Luke-Acts as Jewish Texts*, WUNT 2/355 (Tübingen: Mohr Siebeck, 2013), e.g., 41.

72. See, e.g., N. T. Wright, *The New Testament and the People of God*, COQG 1 (Minneapolis: Fortress, 1992), 237; James D. G. Dunn, "Works of the Law and the Curse of the Law (Galatians 3:10–14)," *NTS* 31 (1985): 523–42.

73. Thus, the context for Eutychus's raising in Acts 20:7–12—however one construes the specific day—recalls the day of Jesus's resurrection.

consistently find Jewish disciples of Jesus respecting Sabbath traditions in Acts.[74] It could be that Paul simply meets with fellow believers after visiting a synagogue on Saturday, which bled over into the next day.[75] At the same time, by the second century it becomes increasingly clear that Christians met together on Sunday, the day of the resurrection (Ignatius, *Magn.* 9:1; *Barn.* 15:9; Justin, *1 Apol.* 67).[76] Though there is the danger of reading second-century sources back into the first century,[77] there is also the danger of underplaying newness in Acts. We have seen that the temple is relativized, and I suggest something similar is true of a seventh-day Sabbath observance.[78] Though Luke does not denigrate the traditional Sabbath (i.e., Saturday) and the characters in Acts frequently adhere to it, there is a shift away from the *necessity* of its observance in light of the new-creational, eschatological-era-inaugurating resurrection of Christ.[79] It therefore seems more likely that the disciples gathered together on a Sunday in Acts 20:7.[80] Even *if* Sunday were to be construed as beginning the night before,[81] the day the disciples gather is the day of the resurrection.

Food Laws

Another distinctive characteristic of first-century Judaism is adherence to traditional food laws, which distinguished between clean and unclean foods.[82] These are also recalibrated in light of the resurrection of Jesus. Despite recent

74. See especially Oliver, *Torah Praxis after 70 CE*, 192, 203–4, 234–35; Keener, *Acts*, 3:2965–66.

75. See the extended discussion of Oliver, *Torah Praxis after 70 CE*, 222–32; cf. Keener, *Acts*, 3:2967–68.

76. See also Michael J. Kruger, *Christianity at the Crossroads: How the Second Century Shaped the Future of the Church* (Downers Grove, IL: InterVarsity Academic, 2018), 98–99, to whom I am indebted for the resurrection reference in Justin. Keener (*Acts*, 3:2965n138) also notes Irenaeus, *On Easter* (according to fragment 7 in *ANF* 1:569–70).

77. So Keener, *Acts*, 2:2965.

78. Even Oliver (*Torah Praxis after 70 CE*, 192) notes that it is unlikely that gentiles were expected to observe the Sabbath.

79. Cf. Turretin, *Inst.* 11.14. See also 1 Cor. 16:2; Rev. 1:10. *Pace* Markus Vinzent, *Christ's Resurrection in Early Christianity and the Making of the New Testament* (Farnham, Surrey: Ashgate, 2011), 195–97, 203–4.

80. So Keener, *Acts*, 3:2967–68; Ben Witherington III, *The Acts of the Apostles: A Socio-Rhetorical Commentary* (Grand Rapids: Eerdmans, 1998), 606; David G. Peterson, *The Acts of the Apostles*, PNTC (Grand Rapids: Eerdmans, 2009), 557; Bock, *Acts*, 619–20.

81. See, e.g., Oliver, *Torah Praxis after 70 CE*, 230. Keener, however, notes the common position that "Luke uses the typical non-Jewish method of reckoning days from dawn to dawn" (*Acts*, 3:2967).

82. See, e.g., Oliver, *Torah Praxis after 70 CE*, 241–51; Keener, *Acts*, 3:1768–74; James D. G. Dunn, *Beginning from Jerusalem*, Christianity in the Making 2 (Grand Rapids: Eerdmans, 2009), 392–96.

objections,[83] one of the clearest texts in this regard is the vision of Peter and his subsequent interaction with Cornelius in Acts 10. Three times in a vision Peter sees a sheet being lowered from heaven full of unclean animals, which Peter is commanded to eat. Three times Peter refuses (vv. 9–16). Surely Peter thought this was some sort of a test. After this vision, however, Peter recognizes that all *people* are clean, leading to the fuller inclusion of the gentiles (v. 28; cf. v. 17), with the Roman centurion Cornelius serving as a stark paradigm.[84] I argued earlier (in ch. 2) that the rationale for this fuller inclusion of the gentiles is tethered to the universal, resurrected lordship of Jesus (cf. v. 36). If Peter's vision indicates that God shows no partiality between peoples (vv. 34–35), then it follows that there need no longer be perpetual, necessary dietary distinctions between peoples that are equally members of the messianic community (cf. 11:17).[85] This reality is consistent with Peter's vision in Acts 10.[86]

To be sure, debate ensues on this issue in Acts, and the implications of Peter's vision (and of the outpouring of the Holy Spirit on the gentiles) remain to be worked out. This leads us to the Jerusalem Council. It is best to understand the council's prohibition against things sacrificed to idols, blood, and things that have been strangled (15:29; cf. v. 20)—which most likely relate to food[87]—to be either a prohibition especially against idolatrous feasts[88] or a prohibition against certain types of food that were particularly important for fellowship in the church between gentiles (who did not follow traditional food laws) and Jewish believers, many of whom still adhered to food laws.[89] This

83. Oliver, *Torah Praxis after 70 CE*, 337–45.

84. On Cornelius, see the extensive discussion in Keener, *Acts*, 2:1732–55.

85. Oliver recognizes that gentiles would not have been required to observe food laws (*Torah Praxis after 70 CE*, e.g., 244, 396).

86. Of course, this is likely the point made by Jesus in Mark 7:19—a text that rightly informs the way one reads Acts 10 when taking a biblical-theological approach that reads the NT documents as mutually interpretive (contrast the approach of Oliver, *Torah Praxis after 70 CE*, 32, 256, 275). This point may already be anticipated in Luke 10:8, where the itinerant disciples are told to eat what is set before them. See similarly David E. Garland, *Luke*, ZECNT (Grand Rapids: Zondervan, 2011), 427.

87. See especially Oliver, *Torah Praxis after 70 CE*, 365–98.

88. See especially Witherington, *Acts of the Apostles*, 460–67, followed by Thompson, *Acts of the Risen Lord Jesus*, 186–87; see also Bavinck, *Reformed Dogmatics*, 4:542. One downside to Witherington's view is that it is difficult to restrict the prohibition against *porneia* primarily to cultic concerns (so rightly Keener, *Acts*, 3:2271–75; cf. Roland Deines, "Das Aposteldekret—Halacha für Heidenchristen oder christliche Rücksichtnahme auf jüdische Tabus?," in *Jewish Identity in the Greco-Roman World / Jüdische Identität in der griechisch-römischen Welt*, ed. Jörg Frey, Daniel R. Schwartz, and Stephanie Gripentrog, AJEC 71 [Leiden: Brill, 2007], 383–86). Bock (*Acts*, 506, 513) plausibly suggests that idolatry is in view, but not exclusively so, and that the more cultic elements come first in the list of Acts 15:29.

89. E.g., Oliver, *Torah Praxis after 70 CE*, 370–98.

would have been particularly appropriate for the transitional era recounted in Acts. For the sake of the peace of the nascent church, gentiles were to make a concession by avoiding blood, in order not to give undue offense to Jewish believers who continued to follow such laws.[90] And they were to avoid sexual immorality, which is consistently prohibited throughout the New Testament.[91]

The directives of the Jerusalem Council are thus consistent with the insights of Acts 10—the resurrected lordship of Jesus over all peoples renders perpetual, thoroughgoing dietary distinctions unnecessary.

CIRCUMCISION

A further defining mark of Judaism is circumcision. Luke mentions circumcision on several occasions in his two volumes, beginning with John the Baptist (Luke 1:59) and then Jesus himself, who is circumcised on the eighth day (2:21). Stephen mentions circumcision briefly in his speech (Acts 7:8), but it is in the encounter with Cornelius that circumcision emerges as a divisive issue. After recounting the outpouring of the Spirit on Cornelius and those who heard Peter's report (10:44), Luke refers to the Jewish believers from circumcision (*hoi ek peritomēs pistoi*, v. 45) who were amazed at what had happened. In what follows Peter is critiqued by others from among the circumcised (*hoi ek peritomēs*, 11:2). Yet in both cases, the skeptical are convinced by the outpouring of the Spirit even among the gentiles (10:45–47; 11:17–18).

However, these initial acceptances of the uncircumcised by the circumcised do not solve all the issues; they must be addressed at the Jerusalem Council (cf. 15:1–2). We have seen that the Jerusalem Council spoke to issues of idolatry and/or food laws and sexual immorality. It is striking that what precipitates the council—the question of circumcision—is not explicitly mentioned in the council's letter. The silence in this case rings clear: circumcision is not required for gentiles to be fully integrated as followers of the Way.[92] Instead the outpouring of the Spirit and the closely related practice of Christian baptism (see 2:38; 10:47–48; 11:15–17; cf. 1:5) mark out God's people (cf.

---

90. So, e.g., Turretin, *Inst.* 11.14.14; 11.25.17, 20–21; Bock, *Acts*, 506; cf. Keener, *Acts*, 3:2277. One's understanding of the background of this decree will inform one's decision here. Keener (*Acts*, 3:2260–69) gives four options for the background: general moral obligations, prohibitions against idolatry, regulations for sojourners in the land (from Lev. 17–18), and the so-called Noahide laws pertaining to all humanity. My present point stands regardless of the view one takes on this matter. It is noteworthy that Luke devotes a great deal of space to matters of food in Acts 10–11; cf. 11:3.

91. E.g., 1 Cor 6:18; Gal. 5:19; Eph. 5:3; 1 Thess. 4:3–6; Rev. 2:21.

92. As in Acts 10–11, in Gal. 3–4 the outpouring of the Spirit among the gentiles is the mark of God's covenantal blessing, demonstrating that gentiles are not required to be circumcised.

10:45; 15:7–9). Furthermore, as we have seen, the resurrected and ascended Christ pours out the Spirit on his people (cf. 1:5; 2:33). This outpouring is an eschatological, covenantal blessing experienced by both Jews and gentiles.[93] This newness, following directly upon the epochally significant resurrection and exaltation of Jesus, relativizes circumcision, which had for thousands of years been a defining mark of God's covenant people.

Worldwide Mission

The era of the exalted Christ is also the era of the fuller, worldwide mission.[94] We have already seen this adumbrated in the discussion above,[95] given the outpouring of the Holy Spirit on all people, the shift away from the Jerusalem temple, and the recalibration of traditional, distinguishing marks. Whereas Christ and his message moves toward Jerusalem in Luke (cf. Luke 9:51), a centrifugal movement away from Jerusalem is apparent in Acts (Luke 24:47; Acts 1:8; cf. Isa. 2:3; Mic. 4:2). This development corresponds to the transition away from the Jerusalem temple and the empowering outpouring of the Holy Spirit (Luke 24:48–49; Acts 1:4–5, 8), which are predicated upon the resurrection of Jesus. And as I have argued throughout this volume, the message preached by the apostles itself prominently features the resurrection of Jesus.

The resurrection is thus not only an impetus for mission but also a key component of the content of the message. By means of his resurrection and ascension Jesus is demonstrated to be Lord of all (Acts 10:36), and this universal lordship grounds the universal mission. Paul can even say before Agrippa that Christ, being the first to rise from the dead, would proclaim light both to the Jews and to the gentiles (26:23). What was anticipated in Luke's infancy narrative—that the Savior of Israel would be a light to the gentiles (cf. 2:29–32)—comes to fruition through the resurrection. Because Jesus is the resurrected judge of the whole world, the clarion call is now for all people, everywhere, to repent (17:30–31).

93. On the Spirit as eschatological, covenantal blessing, see, e.g., Vos, "Eschatological Aspect"; Gaffin, *Perspectives on Pentecost*, 20–21; Peterson, *Acts of the Apostles*, 156.

94. Others who relate mission to the resurrection include Charles H. Talbert, "The Place of the Resurrection in the Theology of Luke," *Int* 46 (1992): 28–30; G. K. Beale, *A New Testament Biblical Theology: The Unfolding of the Old Testament in the New* (Grand Rapids: Baker Academic, 2011), 16; John Calvin, *Inst.* 2.11.12. C. Kavin Rowe (*World Upside Down: Reading Acts in the Graeco-Roman Age* [Oxford: Oxford University Press, 2009], 121) notes the matter starkly: "It would not be too much . . . to say that the resurrection of Jesus is the reason for mission."

95. See also the comments on mission in light of Acts 13 in ch. 3 (under section "4. Resurrection and Gentile Mission").

Conclusion

This chapter has been devoted to the way the resurrection serves as the turning point in salvation history (*historia salutis*), which explains the installation of Christ as victorious Lord, the outpouring of the Holy Spirit, the move away from the Jerusalem temple, a relativization of traditional, distinguishing marks among God's people, and the fuller, worldwide mission. These developments, however, must not be taken to indicate absolute newness of salvation, since Luke also speaks of continuity across the ages. Thus, despite the new experience of lordship, Christ was already Lord at his birth (Luke 2:11), and the Holy Spirit was already at work before the ministry of Jesus even began (1:15, 35, 41, 67; 2:25–27).

This raises a question that must be addressed: How does the newness precipitated by Christ's resurrection in the context of *historia salutis* relate to continuity across the ages, particularly with respect to the experience of salvation? I will address this question in more detail under the rubric of *ordo salutis* in the next chapter.

6

The Resurrection and the Experience of Salvation (*Ordo Salutis*)

In the previous chapter I addressed the newness of Christ's resurrection in the context of *historia salutis*. Yet Luke also recognizes a strong degree of continuity across the ages, even with regard to some of those elements that are highlighted as "new." In what follows I consider in more detail what measure of continuity across the ages we may find in Luke-Acts, despite the newness of the resurrection. For this purpose I employ the phrase *ordo salutis* ("order of salvation"). Whereas *historia salutis* refers to the accomplishment of salvation in history, *ordo salutis* is more concerned with the application or subjective experience of salvation. This term, however, has often been questioned. I will first, therefore, offer a brief definition and defense of *ordo salutis*, after which I will consider some elements of continuity across the ages in Lukan theology. Despite Luke's clear emphasis on *historia salutis*, his interest in the continuity of salvation renders it necessary to consider questions of *ordo salutis* as well. Otherwise we risk attenuating the richness of Luke's theological contributions.

One additional preliminary word is necessary. In this chapter I will say a bit less about the resurrection itself. Instead, my aim is to look at those things that do not fundamentally change despite the newness precipitated by the resurrection of Christ. Yet this chapter is crucial for my overall argument, not least because it argues that we must appreciate the emphasis on continuity of salvation in Acts, in spite of Luke's clear penchant for emphasizing the newness of the resurrection age. Continuity and discontinuity are complementary for Luke. But in both cases—in terms of both discontinuity (*historia salutis*—the new) and continuity (*ordo salutis*—the consistent)—the resurrection of Christ is key.

The Role of *Ordo Salutis*

Ordo Salutis: *Preliminary Definition*

Use of the phrase *ordo salutis* is likely more common than *historia salutis*, yet its frequency does not reflect universal acceptance.[1] Indeed, the concept of an *ordo salutis*—especially in relation to Pauline theology—is commonly dispensed with as foreign to the New Testament.[2] However, despite some legitimate concerns that may arise in response to some construals of the *ordo salutis*,[3] some sort of an order is necessary to consider sufficiently the various aspects of the New Testament teaching on salvation.[4] I am not able to interact with every objection to the *ordo salutis* here, but will make three brief points.

First, *ordo salutis* can be used more narrowly or more generally. More narrowly, it refers to the logical order (= *ordo*) of various aspects of salvation derived from the teaching of Scripture.[5] More generally, *ordo salutis* can refer

1. For a survey of the subjective experience of salvation in Luke's writings—including the question of an *ordo salutis*—see François Bovon, *Luke the Theologian: Fifty-Five Years of Research (1950–2005)*, 2nd rev. ed. (Waco: Baylor University Press, 2006), 305–28. See also Sinclair B. Ferguson, *The Holy Spirit*, CCT (Downers Grove, IL: InterVarsity, 1996), 97–100; Richard B. Gaffin Jr., "The Work of Christ Applied," in *Christian Dogmatics: Reformed Theology for the Church Catholic*, ed. Michael Allen and Scott R. Swain (Grand Rapids: Baker Academic, 2016), 271–72; David B. Garner, *Sons in the Son: The Riches and Reach of Adoption in Christ* (Phillipsburg, NJ: P&R, 2016), 219–53, 287–314.

2. See recently Matthew W. Bates, *Salvation by Allegiance Alone: Rethinking Faith, Works, and the Gospel of Jesus the King* (Grand Rapids: Baker Academic, 2017), 168–72. Additional objections are addressed by Ferguson, *Holy Spirit*, 98–100; Ferguson, "*Ordo Salutis*," in *New Dictionary of Theology*, ed. Sinclair B. Ferguson and David F. Wright (Downers Grove, IL: InterVarsity, 1988), 480–81; Gaffin, "Work of Christ Applied," 271–72.

3. Some reservations are noted by Garner, *Sons in the Son*, 220–23.

4. So rightly Ferguson, "*Ordo Salutis*," 481; Ferguson, *Holy Spirit*, 100; John Murray, *Redemption Accomplished and Applied* (Grand Rapids: Eerdmans, 1955), 80.

5. See discussions in Louis Berkhof, *Systematic Theology*, 4th ed. (Grand Rapids: Eerdmans, 1941), 415–22; Ferguson, "*Ordo Salutis*," 480; Ferguson, *Holy Spirit*, 96–97; cf. Herman Bavinck, *Reformed Dogmatics*, ed. John Bolt, trans. John Vriend, 4 vols. (Grand Rapids: Baker Academic, 2003–8), 3:522–28, 564–68, 589–90, 593–95; 4:249.

to the experience or application of salvation. I use this broader definition in what follows. Even so, the narrow definition is legitimate as well.

Second, *ordo salutis*, as the application of redemption, brings into focus the salvific benefits experienced by faith in union with Christ.[6] As such, they are christologically grounded and inseparable.[7] Thus *ordo salutis* is not best understood primarily as *temporal* order.[8] For indeed, even glorification is already a reality for those in Christ in an already/not yet sense.[9] It is thus not necessary to speak of the *ordo salutis* as a "*sequential progression*," nor of justification as a "discrete additional step" within the *ordo salutis*.[10] Instead, the benefits of Christ, in union with him, are a unified, package deal.[11] To be united to Christ by faith is to receive all his redemptive benefits.[12] It is a complex of distinct but inseparable benefits that *ordo salutis* has in view (e.g., justification, sanctification, adoption, and so forth).

Third—and particularly relevant—the union that is in view in the *ordo salutis* is union with the *resurrected Christ*.[13] The *ordo salutis* deals with the work of the Spirit in the application of redemption. Since it is Jesus in his risen

6. See the foundational statement in John Calvin, *Inst.* 3.1.1; cf. Ferguson, *Holy Spirit,* 100–106; Richard B. Gaffin Jr., *"By Faith, Not by Sight": Paul and the Order of Salvation* (Waynesboro, GA: Paternoster, 2006), 43; Lane G. Tipton, "Union with Christ and Justification," in *Justified in Christ: God's Plan for Us in Justification*, ed. K. Scott Oliphint (Fearn: Mentor, 2007), 23–49. Unfortunately, Bates (*Salvation by Allegiance Alone*, 168n6) misconstrues this crucial point in Murray's *Redemption Accomplished and Applied*, stating that Murray views union with Christ as a step in the *ordo salutis*. However, Murray explicitly denies that union with Christ is a *step* in the application of redemption (161, 165; cf. 80). Instead, union with Christ for Murray "underlies every step of the application of redemption" (161).

7. See also Ferguson, *Holy Spirit*, 102–3; Garner, *Sons in the Son*, 237–53; cf. Murray, *Redemption Accomplished and Applied*, 83, 161; Robert Letham, *Union with Christ: In Scripture, History, and Theology* (Phillipsburg, NJ: P&R, 2011), 90; Bavinck, *Reformed Dogmatics*, 4:249; Berkhof, *Systematic Theology*, 416; Francis Turretin, *Inst.* 17.1.

8. There is some debate on this point. On chronological order in the *ordo salutis*, see Richard A. Muller, *Dictionary of Latin and Greek Theological Terms: Drawn Principally from Protestant Scholastic Theology* (Grand Rapids: Baker, 1985), 215; Bates, *Salvation by Allegiance Alone*, 168–69; cf. Garner, *Sons in the Son*, 220–23.

9. See Ferguson, *Holy Spirit*, 103; Gaffin, *Centrality of the Resurrection*, 133–34; cf. Letham, *Union with Christ*, 90.

10. Bates, *Salvation by Allegiance Alone*, 172 (emphasis original). Though I must disagree with some of his points, Bates is correct to note the importance of union with Christ (*Salvation by Allegiance Alone*, 166–75).

11. Cf. Gaffin, "Work of Christ Applied," 283; Tipton, "Union with Christ and Justification," 24–38; Sinclair B. Ferguson, *The Whole Christ: Legalism, Antinomianism, and Gospel Assurance—Why the Marrow Controversy Still Matters* (Wheaton: Crossway, 2016), 42–52.

12. Cf. Calvin, *Inst.* 3.1.1; Gaffin, "Work of Christ Applied," 285.

13. See Ferguson, *Holy Spirit*, 103–8; Gaffin, *Centrality of the Resurrection*, 129–31; Gaffin, "Work of Christ Applied," 274–83; Tipton, "Union with Christ and Justification," 25–27.

state of glory who pours out the Spirit, we can therefore describe the *ordo salutis* as "the work of Christ in his state of exaltation."[14] Though Acts may say less about union with Christ, Acts does provide much of the framework for the Pauline exposition of the resurrection, and does so in soteriologically charged contexts.[15]

Relating Ordo Salutis *to* Historia Salutis

I thus believe in the biblical and theological legitimacy of the more technical sense of *ordo salutis*. However, in this chapter I employ *ordo salutis* in the broader sense, with reference more generally to the experience of salvation. It is of particular interest that the *ordo salutis* considers the application of salvation to God's people across the ages; what is in view is the shared experience of God's people that does not fundamentally change.[16] *Ordo salutis* therefore asks different questions than *historia salutis*, though the two cannot be separated. As I argued in the previous chapter, *historia salutis* deals with the accomplishment of salvation in history. *Ordo salutis* deals with the application of salvation to all believers—whether Old Testament or New Testament believers, whether Abraham or Paul. Yet whatever salvific benefits are experienced by believers—even before the coming of Christ in history—these must ultimately depend upon the completed work of Christ. In this sense one could say that *ordo salutis* depends upon *historia salutis*. This means that justification in days before the coming of Christ (e.g., Abraham; cf. Gen. 15:6) rests on the completed work of Christ no less than justification in the New Testament. This can be a fine line to walk, since justification is an eschatological doctrine that receives fuller exposition in the New Testament in light of the work of Christ.[17] And yet it is striking that Paul uses both Abraham and David—two Old Testament believers—as paradigms of justification by faith for New Testament believers (cf. Rom. 4:1–25).[18] This assumes and necessitates the fundamental unity of the experience of justification (i.e., in terms of *ordo salutis*) across the ages.[19]

---

14. Gaffin, "Work of Christ Applied," 269 (emphasis removed); cf. Turretin, *Inst.* 13.9.

15. See further the discussions in ch. 8.

16. Gaffin, "Work of Christ Applied," 288; cf. Ferguson, "*Ordo Salutis*," 480.

17. On justification as an eschatological doctrine see G. K. Beale, *A New Testament Biblical Theology: The Unfolding of the Old Testament in the New* (Grand Rapids: Baker Academic, 2011), 469–526; Herman N. Ridderbos, *Paul: An Outline of His Theology*, trans. John Richard De Witt (Grand Rapids: Eerdmans, 1975), 161–66.

18. Cf. Calvin, *Inst.* 2.10.11, 23; Francis Turretin, *Inst.* 12.5.7, 15; 12.7.19.

19. Cf. Calvin, *Inst.* 2.10.4; Turretin, *Inst.* 12.5.12; 12.9; 12.10.23; Bavinck, *Reformed Dogmatics*, 3:223.

Relating *ordo salutis* to *historia salutis* is not only an issue for Paul's letters, but is crucial for interpreting Luke's writings. The bulk of this volume has been devoted to underscoring the role of the resurrection, which is the key transitional point of *historia salutis*. And yet Luke also emphasizes continuity across the ages. Interpretations of Acts suffer when *ordo salutis* questions are asked of passages that emphasize *historia salutis*. It is not exegetically prudent to extrapolate from unique events in the history of redemption universal principles of *how* one comes to experience salvation. This means, for example, that the episodes in Samaria (Acts 8), with Cornelius (Acts 10), and with the disciples of John the Baptist in Ephesus (ch. 19) are less about delineating a normative, subjective order of events that compose the experience of salvation and are more about unique, transitional moments in the history of redemption.[20] For this reason I will use *ordo salutis* more broadly to speak of the continuity of salvation across the ages.

Understood in terms of continuity of participation in salvation, *ordo salutis* is manifested by Luke in a number of ways. Five brief examples will illustrate this point. First, in the opening chapters of Luke salvation is framed as the fulfillment of God's covenant promises, highlighting the relation of the new to the old. This is particularly evident in the Magnificat (cf. Luke 1:50, 54–55) and the Benedictus (cf. 1:68–75). There even appears to be a fulfillment *inclusio* that brackets the Gospel of Luke (1:1; 24:44).[21]

Second, along with an emphasis on covenant continuity, Luke recognizes the continuity of salvation among the faithful remnant of God's people, such as aged Zechariah, Elizabeth, Simeon, and Anna—the first three of whom are explicitly identified as righteous (cf. Luke 1:6; 2:25–32).[22] I will argue later that Cornelius may also be included in this category (Acts 10:2, 22).

Third, Peter's speech at the temple in Acts 3 closely correlates the present realities of salvation in Christ with the blessings already experienced in the Abrahamic covenant (v. 25; cf. 2:39).[23]

Fourth, in Acts 4:12 it is the resurrected Jesus who bears the name by which all people must be saved (cf. v. 10)—yet this universal focus (*oude gar onoma estin heteron hypo ton ouranon to dedomenon en anthrōpois*) must somehow

---

20. See similarly Gaffin, *Perspectives on Pentecost: New Testament Teaching on the Gifts of the Holy Spirit* (Phillipsburg, NJ: P&R, 1979), 22–28.

21. See Brandon D. Crowe, *The Last Adam: A Theology of the Obedient Life of Jesus in the Gospels* (Grand Rapids: Baker Academic, 2017), 94–95.

22. This is implied for Anna as well (2:36–38).

23. See Calvin, *Inst.* 2.10.23; Turretin, *Inst.* 12.5.15; Bavinck, *Reformed Dogmatics*, 3:223.

also include those who lived chronologically before the incarnate work of Christ.[24]

Fifth, an emphasis on the continuity of salvation can also be seen in the promise of eternal life. In the controversy with the Sadducees about the resurrection in Luke, Jesus emphasizes the continuity of God's covenant promises even to those who had died: "God is not the God of the dead, but of the living" (*theos de ouk estin nekrōn alla zōntōn*, Luke 20:38). Surely the consummate experience of everlasting life comes in the resurrected state (cf. Luke 14:14; John 5:24–25), and the resurrection promises are contingent upon the resurrection of Christ in terms of *historia salutis* (cf. Acts 26:22–23). Nevertheless, despite this consummate state of glorified existence that lies still in the future for God's people, some kind of ongoing life was already experienced by Old Testament believers (cf. Luke 20:37).[25] This hope of eternal life explains why, in Stephen's speech, Abraham received no lasting inheritance in Canaan despite the promises given to him (Acts 7:3–5).[26] The patriarchs must have experienced continued life, even before the resurrection of Jesus.

Luke thus sees a continuity of *ordo salutis* even as he emphasizes the newness of *historia salutis*. Furthermore, it is striking that many of Luke's emphases on continuity come in passages that speak of Christ's resurrection. The preceding examples are given by way of orientation; I discuss additional texts in what follows. At this point it is enough to note that Jesus's accomplishment of salvation (including prominently his resurrection) enables a continuity of *ordo salutis* experience across the ages.

Ordo Salutis, Forgiveness of Sins, and Justification

Central to the application of salvation is justification, which entails the forgiveness of sins. Some of the texts that I consider below have already been included in discussions pertaining to the newness of Christ's work. Those discussions should be kept in mind as I argue below for continuity of the experience of salvation. By highlighting continuity of *ordo salutis* in Acts, I do not intend to undermine the newness of what Christ has done in terms of *historia salutis*. Yet it is striking that Luke emphasizes continuity *even in texts that highlight the newness of Christ's work*. This phenomenon underscores

---

24. Cf. Turretin, *Inst.* 12.5.6, 12; Bavinck, *Reformed Dogmatics*, 3:223.

25. See the seminal discussion of Calvin, *Inst.* 2.10.7–23. Calvin's entire discussion of the unity and differences in the old covenant and new covenant repays careful reading. Note also the much-discussed parable of the rich man and Lazarus (Luke 16:19–31).

26. Following Calvin, *Inst.* 2.10.13.

the importance of distinguishing the closely related concepts of *historia salutis* and *ordo salutis*.

Forgiveness of Sins

First to be considered are texts that speak of the continuity of forgiveness of sins. Forgiveness is not only something that was offered to God's people after the death and resurrection of Christ, but was a reality even before Christ embarked upon his public ministry. This is apparent in several passages. We have seen that Zechariah, Elizabeth, and Simeon are described as righteous in Luke 1–2.[27] I have also suggested, but not yet pursued, the possibility that Cornelius also fits into this category (Acts 10:2, 22). A full consideration of righteousness and related concepts is beyond the scope of the present study. Yet it should not be overlooked that Noah is the first person explicitly identified in Scripture with the term "righteous" (LXX: *dikaios*; MT: *ṣadîq*; Gen. 6:9; cf. 7:1), which is correlated with his blamelessness (LXX: *teleios*; MT: *tāmîm*). This is consistent with the way that righteousness is contrasted with sin throughout the Old Testament—a point memorably stated at the opening of the Psalter (Ps. 1:5). To be characterized as righteous is diametrically opposed to being characterized by sinfulness. This must be true not only in the righteous person's ethical avoidance of sin but also in the righteous person's cleansing from sin—the two are related (cf. Ps. 32:1–2 [31:1–2 LXX]). Thus, from their being described as righteous before the coming of Christ it can be inferred that Zechariah, Elizabeth, and Simeon were not only living according to the law (albeit imperfectly) but also forgiven for their sins.

The ministry of John the Baptist offers another example of forgiveness being offered before the initiation of Christ's public ministry. Luke states that John's baptism was a baptism of repentance for the forgiveness of sins (Luke 3:3). To be sure, John's ministry is closely and uniquely related to the coming of Jesus; he came in the power and spirit of Elijah to prepare the way for the Lord (cf. 1:17, 76–77). And yet John—who, despite his role in the coming of eschatological salvation, himself belongs to the old order (7:28; 16:16)—proclaimed the forgiveness of sins *before* Christ's ministry had begun. This is not surprising, given the promises and provisions for forgiveness found throughout Scripture before the coming of Christ (among many, see Exod. 34:7; Lev. 4:20, 26, 39; 5:10; Num. 14:19; 1 Kings 8:34–36, 46–51; 2 Chron. 7:14; Ps. 32:1, 5 [31:1, 5 LXX]; 103:3, 12 [102:3, 12 LXX]; Isa. 1:18; 33:24).[28]

---

27. See also Richard B. Hays, *Echoes of Scripture in the Gospels* (Waco: Baylor University Press, 2016), 207–8.

28. See also Turretin, *Inst.* 12.7.45; 12.10.

The Scriptures require us to say that true forgiveness of sins was already a reality in the Old Testament.[29]

We also find, however, that John's message is not sufficient after the coming of Christ. However one takes the unique events of the rebaptism of the disciples of John in Acts 19:1–7—and we must recognize the uniqueness of the moment in terms of *historia salutis*—at least two things must be true. First, John spoke of the present possibilities of repentance and forgiveness even before the coming of Christ. Second, John's message and ministry were provisional and anticipatory; his was not the final word.[30] Even if someone in this transitional phase in the days of John experienced the blessings of salvation without full knowledge of Christ and his work, we nevertheless see the need throughout Acts for the message of Christ (and his resurrection) to be made known, now that Christ has come (cf. 19:5).

This view is confirmed by the preceding events pertaining to Cornelius in Acts 10. I argued in chapter 2 that the knowledge that Cornelius and his household lacked pertained to the work of Christ, including his resurrection (vv. 40–42). At the same time, Peter emphasizes to Cornelius the continuity of God's promises across the ages: the prophets already spoke of forgiveness in previous generations (v. 43).[31] The coming of Christ is not an unexpected development, but is the hope to which the prophets looked.[32] Peter emphasizes both the newness of the work of Christ and its continuity with what the prophets spoke. This is consistent with the exposition of Jesus at the end of Luke, which understands the Old Testament to be inherently christological (Luke 24:44–47).[33] What is more, it is not simply forgiveness in the abstract that the prophets bear witness to, but forgiveness *in God's chosen Messiah* (Acts 10:43).[34] This underscores the continuity of the experience of salvation

29. So Calvin, *Inst.* 2.10.4; Turretin, *Inst.* 12.5.15; 12.7.45; 12.8.14; 12.10; Bavinck, *Reformed Dogmatics*, 3:221–24. We also find Jesus offering forgiveness during his ministry, even before his death and resurrection (cf. Luke 5:20; 7:47).

30. See, e.g., Richard B. Gaffin Jr., "The Holy Spirit," *WTJ* 43 (1980): 65; Gaffin, *Perspectives on Pentecost*, 14–16; Geerhardus Vos, *Biblical Theology: Old and New Testaments* (1948; repr., Edinburgh: Banner of Truth, 1975), 317.

31. This is a favorite passage of Turretin. See Turretin, *Inst.* 2.8.11, 20; 12.5.9, 14–16; 12.8.18; 15.12.20; Bavinck, *Reformed Dogmatics*, 3:223; 4:105.

32. Cf. Turretin, *Inst.* 12.7.45; 12.10–12; WCF 7.5–6.

33. So Richard B. Gaffin Jr., "Justification in Luke-Acts," in *Right with God: Justification in the Bible and in the World*, ed. D. A. Carson (Grand Rapids: Baker, 1992), 121. Gaffin further argues here that Cornelius must be righteous (*dikaios*, 10:22; cf. Luke 7:1–10) like other OT-era believers, including Zechariah, Elizabeth, Simeon, and Anna.

34. Taking *toutō* as masculine at the beginning of 10:43. For a discussion of possibilities, see Joseph A. Fitzmyer, *The Acts of the Apostles: A New Translation with Introduction and Commentary*, AB 31 (New York: Doubleday, 1998), 466; cf. C. K. Barrett, *A Critical and Exegetical Commentary on the Acts of the Apostles*, 2 vols., ICC (Edinburgh: T&T Clark, 1994–98), 1:528.

for God's people across the ages: "Old Testament religion is Christ-centered religion."[35] The forgiveness that was spoken of already by the prophets finds its ultimate grounding in the completed work of Christ.[36]

It is thus best to understand Cornelius already to be a true believer in Israel's God when Peter meets him, even if he has not yet been fully enfolded into the community—and even if his experience is quite exceptional. Several features of Luke's description suggest this perspective. Luke writes that Cornelius was a godly, righteous man who feared God (10:2, 22) and whose prayers had been heard (v. 4).[37] When Peter arrives he recognizes that God shows no partiality and that those like Cornelius—who (already!) fear God and do what is right in his sight—are no less to be numbered among the people of God than the Jewish believers (vv. 34–35). Yet Cornelius was in a curious position—he had not yet heard of the resurrection or experienced the outpouring of the Holy Spirit. Even so, this gentile appears to be part of God's righteous remnant.[38] At the same time, Cornelius's specific experiences are not programmatic for future generations, since he occupied a unique place in the outworking of redemption.[39] Few others in history have been in Cornelius's position—believing

35. Gaffin, "Justification in Luke-Acts," 121.

36. This is likely the best way to take Acts 17:30, which speaks of times of ignorance that God overlooked (*tous . . . chronous tēs agnoias hyperidōn ho theos* ["the . . . times of ignorance God overlooked"). It is not that sins were in no way punished in previous generations, but that sin is dealt with definitively (in terms of *historia salutis*) in the death of Christ. In light of the resurrection (and the new age it inaugurates), the message is now for all people to repent. This, however, does not negate the *ordo salutis* reality that forgiveness was already possible before the coming of Christ. Cf. Turretin, *Inst.* 12.10.19; Dennis E. Johnson, *The Message of Acts in the History of Redemption* (Phillipsburg, NJ: P&R, 1997), 198; David G. Peterson, *The Acts of the Apostles*, PNTC (Grand Rapids: Eerdmans, 2009), 501–2.

37. Further supporting this interpretation is the identification of Zechariah as righteous (Luke 1:6) and as one whose prayers had been heard (1:13). Additionally, in likely contrast to Zechariah and Cornelius, the Pharisee of Luke 18, though he prays, is not justified. See also John 9:31. Cf. the comments in Joel B. Green, *Conversion in Luke-Acts: Divine Action, Human Cognition, and the People of God* (Grand Rapids: Baker Academic, 2015), 50: "Many gentiles within the narrative of Acts need no conversion to the God of Israel per se but, like the exemplary Cornelius (10:1–4), already worship this God."

38. See the discussions in Ben Witherington III, *The Acts of the Apostles: A Socio-Rhetorical Commentary* (Grand Rapids: Eerdmans, 1998), 341–44; Craig S. Keener, *Acts: An Exegetical Commentary*, 4 vols. (Grand Rapids: Baker Academic, 2012–15), 2:1750–55, 1781.

39. See also Gaffin, "Justification in Luke-Acts," 121; Guy Prentiss Waters, *A Study Commentary on the Acts of the Apostles*, EP Study Commentary (Pistyll, Holywell, UK: Evangelical Press, 2015), 251; Peterson, *Acts of the Apostles*, 328; John Calvin, *Commentary upon the Acts of the Apostles*, ed. Henry Beveridge, 2 vols. (repr., Grand Rapids: Baker, 2003), 1:406–7 (which notes that "Cornelius had a church in his house"); Petrus van Mastricht, *Theoretical-Practical Theology*, trans. Todd M. Rester, ed. Joel R. Beeke, 7 vols. (Grand Rapids: Reformation Heritage, 2018–), 1:84. This point stands, even though 11:14 speaks about a word that must be spoken to Cornelius in order that he (and his household) might be saved. As I argued in

in God's covenant promises as a gentile at the turn of the ages. Indeed, Cornelius (no less than John's disciples) had to hear the message of Christ and his resurrection to be saved (cf. 11:14), which is illustrated in Peter's mission to speak with him. Though Cornelius's experiences are unique, this need for Jesus to be preached and for people to respond in faith is an abiding pattern for today. The forgiveness of sins that Cornelius apparently already knew is only possible because of the work of Christ, and this was already anticipated by the prophets (cf. 10:43).

In light of Luke's perspective that forgiveness of sins was a reality before the coming of Christ, it is striking that the Lukan Paul at Pisidian Antioch emphasizes that forgiveness of sins is preached because of the resurrection of Jesus Christ (Acts 13:37–39). This is a curious statement if forgiveness was already a reality before the coming of Christ. Yet Paul himself relates his message to the continuity of what has come before (cf. v. 32).[40] The best answer to this is that the *ordo salutis* reality of the forgiveness of sins ultimately depends on the accomplishment of salvation in history (*historia salutis*). This would also apply to the mention of forgiveness in 5:31, which emphasizes *historia salutis*. It is not that there was no forgiveness prior to the coming of Christ; instead forgiveness in any age is contingent upon the death and resurrection of Christ. In light of such texts, we can conclude that the blessing of forgiveness of sins experienced before the coming of Christ must be a benefit of the work of Christ in history. To be sure, this can be difficult to parse out, but it shows us the necessity of thinking carefully, synthetically, and systematically about the phenomena encountered in the task of exegesis.

Justification

Closely related to the forgiveness of sins in Paul's Pisidian Antioch speech—and a closely related concept in theological discourse more broadly—is justification (cf. Acts 13:38–39). As with forgiveness, justification was already a reality in terms of *ordo salutis* before the incarnate work of Christ. This must be true even if one describes justification as an eschatological doctrine that finds its fuller exposition in the New Testament. A fuller, newer exposition of justification is appropriate in light of the accomplishment of Christ in terms of *historia salutis*. Yet again Luke's emphasis on continuity constrains us to wrestle with how justification was already a reality before the incarnate

---

ch. 2, knowledge of Christ's death and resurrection is necessary for salvation now that he has come (cf. 10:37–41). Contrast Hans Jörg Sellner, *Das Heil Gottes: Studien zur Soteriologie des lukanischen Doppelwerks*, BZNW 152 (Berlin: de Gruyter, 2007), 301–3.

40. So Turretin, *Inst.* 12.5.15; cf. 12.10.21.

work of Christ. At least three reasons point to the *ordo salutis* continuity of justification in Luke-Acts.

Justification during Jesus's Ministry

First, Luke's Gospel already speaks of the possibility of justification during the ministry of Christ, before the consummation of his work. One has to be nuanced at this point, since not every usage of *dikaioō* in the New Testament refers monolithically to the technical theological doctrine of justification by faith (e.g., Matt. 12:37), which traditionally has been gleaned largely from Paul's letters. Even so, Luke's Gospel uses the terminology of justification in a way that is quite close to Paul's usage.

In addition to Acts 13:39, two texts from the Gospel of Luke stand out. First, the parable of the good Samaritan is precipitated by the question of a lawyer who is seeking to justify himself (*ho de thelōn dikaiōsai heauton*, 10:29). This entire episode (vv. 25–37) is bracketed by uses of *poieō*,[41] and verse 28 (*touto poiei kai zēsē*) likely alludes to the principle of "do this and live" from Leviticus 18:5. This principle of living by works is best taken in contrast to the principle of living by faith.[42] Jesus challenges the man's self-righteousness by pointing out the broad contours of who is one's neighbor, along with the moral imperative to *be a neighbor* to those in need, as the Samaritan is in the parable. The question from the lawyer assumes it was indeed possible to be justified in a preresurrection context; this is consistent with the examples of Zechariah, Elizabeth, and Simeon. But Luke 10:25–37 also assumes that Jesus is the one who was uniquely able to "do this and live." Interestingly, if the lawyer's question about eternal life is tantamount to "What must I do to participate in the resurrection of the righteous?,"[43] then it serves as a striking contrast to Jesus. The inability of any natural person to be justified by works is answered by the perfect work of Christ, whose perfect righteousness (cf. 23:47) results in his resurrection from the dead. This is the foundation in terms of *historia salutis* for the experience of justification in terms of *ordo salutis*. In terms of *ordo salutis*, the lawyer occupied a different position than Zechariah, Elizabeth, or Simeon.

Second is the parable of the tax collector and Pharisee (Luke 18:9–14). This is another uniquely Lukan parable featuring justification language. Whereas

---

41. So Klyne R. Snodgrass, *Stories with Intent: A Comprehensive Guide to the Parables of Jesus* (Grand Rapids: Eerdmans, 2008), 349.

42. See Crowe, *Last Adam*, 179–82; cf. Turretin, *Inst.* 12.7.32–33.

43. Cf. Darrell L. Bock, *Luke*, 2 vols., BECNT (Grand Rapids: Baker Academic, 1994–96), 2:1023; Crowe, *Last Adam*, 180.

the Pharisee trusted in his own righteousness (vv. 9–12), the tax collector recognized his need for mercy and forgiveness (v. 13). It is the tax collector, and not the Pharisee, who went home justified (*dedikaiōmenos*, v. 14). We must not miss the correlation between forgiveness of sins and justification in this parable (vv. 13–14), which we have encountered elsewhere in Luke's writings. At the same time, we must be wary of overreliance on specific words. Just as not every usage of *dikaioō* denotes the technical theological concept of justification, neither does the absence of the term indicate the absence of the concept. With this in mind, we most likely have an illustration of the justified tax collector in the ensuing account of the tax collector Zacchaeus (19:1–10). Despite the protestations of those who grumbled (v. 7), Jesus goes to Zacchaeus's house (v. 5) and subsequently proclaims that salvation has come to his house (v. 9). By reading the episode of Zacchaeus in light of the parable of the Pharisee and the tax collector, we can conclude that Luke correlates mercy, forgiveness, justification, and salvation (cf. 18:13–14; 19:9). The justification of Zacchaeus, like that of the tax collector in the parable, assumes the possibility of justification and forgiveness before the consummation of Christ's work.

Justification and Forgiveness of Sins

A second way we see the continuity of justification in Luke's writings is in its correlation to the forgiveness of sins. This is not only found in Luke 18:13–14 but assumed throughout Luke's writings. If we have established that forgiveness was possible before the finished work of Christ, then this necessarily means that the correlating reality of justification was also possible. We are again speaking in terms of *ordo salutis*. Here we can consider the role in Luke-Acts of Abraham, who features prominently throughout the New Testament as a man who was righteous by faith (cf. Gen. 15:6).[44] Though Luke does not explicitly relate Abraham to justification, his emphasis on Abraham as a man of faith is evident throughout. For example, both Mary's Magnificat (Luke 1:55) and Zechariah's Benedictus (v. 73) recall God's covenant promises to Abraham. Stephen makes much of Abraham's role in redemptive history (cf. Acts 7:2–8; 7:32). John the Baptist's ministry assumes that those who repent and bear fruit are true children of Abraham (Luke 3:8). When Zacchaeus responds favorably to Jesus (and is justified!), he is identified as a true son of Abraham (19:9). Further, Abraham is associated with eschatological life in a number of contexts (13:28; 16:19–31; 20:37; cf. Acts 3:13). It is therefore

---

44. To be righteous and to be justified share a root in Greek (*dik-*).

fitting that Paul presents his message of salvation at Pisidian Antioch to the children of Abraham (Acts 13:26), since he will discuss how one is *forgiven* and *justified* apart from the law of Moses (vv. 38–39). In light of the rich associations of Abraham's faith with justification throughout the New Testament, Luke's consistent appeal to Abraham likely assumes the continuity of justifying faith across the ages (cf. *1 Clem.* 32:4).

JUSTIFICATION AND THE JERUSALEM COUNCIL

A third possibility that speaks of the continuity of justification is found in Peter's words at the Jerusalem Council. Peter does not speak of justification explicitly, but of being saved apart from the yoke of the law (Acts 15:10–11). Already in Acts Paul has spoken of justification and forgiveness apart from the law (13:38–39).[45] It is therefore appropriate to conclude that the salvation by grace, apart from the law, that Peter has in view in 15:10–11 could be glossed as *justification*.[46]

A key question with respect to the issue of continuity of justification is, Who are the "they" in view in 15:11 who will be saved by the grace of the Lord Jesus just as "we" (i.e., a group that includes Peter) will? Does "they" refer to gentile believers, or to the more recent antecedent of "our fathers" (*hoi pateres hēmōn*) in v. 10? The latter option would mean that Peter is comparing the way of salvation in the Old Testament—which was also through the grace of the Lord Jesus!—to the way of salvation in the New Testament. To be sure, this would be a striking point for Peter to make given the clear interest in the gentile question at the Jerusalem Council and in the newness of salvation in light of the resurrection of Christ. This is a difficult exegetical decision, and it is not surprising that most commentators take "they" to be gentiles as a matter of course.[47] Indeed, the reference to the "them" who receive the Holy Spirit in v. 8 is almost certainly a reference to the gentiles who have received the Spirit, and it is the gentiles as well as the Jews whose hearts are cleansed by faith in v. 9.

45. See also the discussion in ch. 3 (under section "Resurrection and the Forgiveness of Sins"), and the importance of the resurrection for this point.

46. This is consistent with the correlation of salvation, justification, forgiveness, and mercy with respect to the parable of the Pharisee and tax collector and the realization of this correlation with Zacchaeus.

47. See Fitzmyer, *Acts of the Apostles*, 548; Rudolf Pesch, *Die Apostelgeschichte*, 2 vols., EKKNT (Zürich: Benzinger; Neukirchen-Vluyn: Neukirchener Verlag, 1986), 2:78; Richard Belward Rackham, *The Acts of the Apostles: An Exposition*, 11th ed., WC (London: Methuen, 1930), 252–53; Keener, *Acts*, 3:2238–39; Peterson, *Acts of the Apostles*, 427; Darrell L. Bock, *Acts*, BECNT (Grand Rapids: Baker Academic, 2007), 501; Henry Alford, *The Greek Testament*, vol. 2, *Acts, Romans, Corinthians*, rev. Everett F. Harrison (Chicago: Moody, 1958), 165.

Yet the possibility remains that the "they" Peter has in view in 15:11 are his ancestral fathers, especially since he draws explicit attention to the law that neither first-century Jewish believers nor prior generations had been able to bear.[48] If so, then Peter would be commenting explicitly on the continuity of salvation by faith for God's people throughout the ages.[49] If this is Peter's point, it would also necessarily include the conclusion that gentiles are saved by faith apart from the law.[50] Acts 15 is thus another possible text that speaks of the continuity of *ordo salutis* across the ages. On this view, the newness of the justification in view at Pisidian Antioch (cf. 13:36–39) is tempered by the continuity that Peter emphasizes in 15:10–11.[51] This latter text would also stand close to the continuity of forgiveness spoken of in 10:43.

In sum, Luke clearly understands that although justification is accomplished by the work of Christ (with special emphasis on Christ's resurrection; cf. Acts 13:37), forgiveness of sins, and therefore justification, were already realities before the coming of Christ. Yet it is also clear that forgiveness of sins and justification are accomplished by the work of Christ. This apparent tension requires us to consider both *historia salutis* and *ordo salutis*. In terms of *historia salutis*, forgiveness and justification requires the work of Christ in history. Yet in terms of *ordo salutis*, God's people could experience forgiveness and justification even before this work was accomplished in history.

This, however, leads to another perplexity: How should we understand the role of the Holy Spirit in Luke-Acts *before* Pentecost? To be sure, Pentecost is an epochally significant moment, especially in terms of *historia salutis*. And yet the benefits of salvation—such as justification—require the work of the Holy Spirit. How then are we to understand the work of the Holy Spirit before Pentecost? This brings us to our next topic.

Ordo Salutis and the Role of the Holy Spirit

In light of the continuity of salvation in Luke and Acts, we turn now to consider how Luke perceives the Holy Spirit's operations across the ages. As

---

48. Following here Calvin, *Commentary upon the Acts*, 2:58–60; Calvin, *Inst.* 3.5.4; cf. 2.10.23; Turretin, *Inst.* 12.5.11; cf. 11.23.10; 11.24.14; 12.5.9; 12.7.36; 17.2.16; Bavinck, *Reformed Dogmatics*, 3:223; 4:105; Mastricht, *Theoretical-Practical Theology*, 1:158. See further discussions in Barrett, *Commentary on the Acts*, 2:720; Waters, *Study Commentary on the Acts*, 357.

49. Cf. Ign., *Magn.* 8:2.

50. So Turretin, *Inst.* 12.5.11.

51. Calvin (*Commentary upon the Acts*, 57–59) avers that the yoke of the law in Acts 15:10 has two cords, consisting in Lev. 18:5 and Deut. 21:23. Calvin most likely gleans these from Paul's argument in Gal. 3:10, 12.

we do, it is important to recall the manifest newness of the Spirit's activity covered in the previous chapter. Luke clearly emphasizes the new work of the Holy Spirit following Pentecost. This newness corresponds to the newness of the accomplishment of salvation (*historia salutis*). But Luke's emphasis on continuity of *ordo salutis* requires us also to consider the possibility that the Holy Spirit's role in the application of salvation is not fundamentally different in the age characterized by the resurrection of Christ. Continuity of salvation requires some measure of continuity in the application of salvation, which is a question about the role of the Holy Spirit.[52] Put starkly, in what follows I will consider some ways that the work of the Holy Spirit is *not* new in Acts.

It is important to consider the ways that Luke speaks of the presence and work of the Holy Spirit before the coming of Christ (and thus before Pentecost).[53] This should not be controversial, since Luke's Gospel includes several references to the Spirit before the initiation of Christ's public ministry (Luke 1:15, 35, 41, 67; 1:80[?];[54] 2:25–27). As I argued earlier, Luke strongly associates the Spirit with Christ himself (e.g., Luke 1:35; 3:16; 4:1, 14, 18; 10:21; cf. Isa. 61:1; Acts 2:33; 10:38; cf. 1:5), such that we can refer to the Spirit as the Spirit of Christ.[55] Furthermore, Luke's early references to the Spirit should be taken in conjunction with the coming of eschatological salvation, so that (for example) even Elizabeth's being filled with the Holy Spirit is organically related to the coming of Christ (cf. Luke 1:41). And yet the Spirit is not *only* present with Christ himself. Luke indicates the Spirit had already been active among God's people. Stephen, for example, correlates the recalcitrance of his accusers with the recalcitrance of their fathers who always resisted the Holy Spirit (*hymeis aei tō pneumati tō hagiō antipiptete hōs hoi pateres hymōn kai hymeis*, Acts 7:51).[56] Resisting the Holy Spirit in Stephen's day was not fundamentally different from resisting the Holy Spirit in earlier days of covenant history.[57]

The contrasting perspective to Acts 7:51 may be intended in 5:32, where Peter states that the Holy Spirit is given to those who obey God (*to pneuma*

52. See, e.g., Turretin, *Inst.* 3.30.22; 12.5.6, 15–16; 12.7.19, 45; cf. Bavinck, *Reformed Dogmatics*, 2:277.

53. Cf. Barrett, *Commentary on the Acts*, 2:lxxxiii–lxxxiv.

54. On the possibility of a reference to the Holy Spirit in Luke 1:80, see John Calvin, *A Harmony of the Evangelists*, trans. William Pringle, 3 vols. (repr., Grand Rapids: Baker, 2003), 1:79; Turretin, *Inst.* 15.15.16; Joel B. Green, *The Gospel of Luke*, NICNT (Grand Rapids: Eerdmans, 1997), 120.

55. See Ferguson, *Holy Spirit*, 35–56.

56. Cf. Jacob Jervell, *The Theology of the Acts of the Apostles* (Cambridge: Cambridge University Press, 1996), 44–49, 65.

57. This also underscores the continuity of the message of salvation in previous eras (cf., e.g., Acts 3:25; 10:43; 26:22–23).

to hagion ho edōken ho theos tois peitharchousin autō). If the Holy Spirit could be resisted throughout covenant history (i.e., before Pentecost), then it is possible that Peter's comments about the gift of the Holy Spirit, which is given to those who obey God, are also true across the ages.[58] This, however, is not certain, especially given the *historia salutis* focus on resurrection (v. 31) and the emphasis on the role of the Holy Spirit as a *witness* (along with the apostles) in verse 32—a concept that Luke ties consistently to the resurrection of Christ (cf. 1:3). Peter may thus be speaking of the newness of the Spirit's work in 5:32.

More certain indication of the continuity of the Spirit's work is found in the Spirit's inspiration of Scripture (cf. 1:16; 4:25; 28:25). This is consistent with the continuity of the message of salvation noted earlier in this chapter and will be relevant again in the next chapter, where I devote more attention to the resurrection and the Scriptures.[59]

If Luke portrays the Holy Spirit as active before the completed work of Christ, it is fitting further to consider how the continuity of the Spirit's work relates to the continuity of forgiveness and justification, considered above. Put simply, if there is justification and the forgiveness of sins already before the resurrection of Christ, then the Holy Spirit must have been active with respect to the application of salvation (*ordo salutis*) before the epochal events of *historia salutis* recounted in Luke-Acts. This can be seen, first, in Luke-Acts. Second, corroboration for this Lukan perspective is found throughout the biblical canon. I will address these in order.

First, for Luke one's relation to the Holy Spirit is indicative of one's salvation. This conclusion follows from considering the implications of various texts we have already considered. For example, the inspired message of the prophets deals with the coming of Christ, and their message was already one of forgiveness (Acts 10:43; cf. 3:25). The Holy Spirit was also active among God's righteous people (e.g., Zechariah, Elizabeth, Simeon) even before Pentecost. According to Stephen, to resist the Holy Spirit—whether in previous generations or in the first century—was to oppose God (7:51). Peter also correlates the reception of the Spirit with salvation in 5:32.[60] Further, Luke associates the forgiveness of sins with the work of the Holy Spirit (Luke 3:3,

---

58. See also Jervell, *Theology of the Acts*, 47.

59. Luke's view of the Spirit's work with respect to both newness and continuity might find an analogy in Luke's use of *Lord* for Jesus. Though Jesus was already Lord at his birth (Luke 2:11), he is nevertheless also described as Lord in a new sense after his resurrection and ascension (cf. Acts 2:36).

60. Even if Peter has primarily in view the newness of the Spirit, one could still argue that the principle is true across the ages in light of Stephen's speech in 7:51.

16; 4:18–19; 12:10; Acts 2:38; 5:31–32). To be sure, many of these statements refer to the coming of eschatological salvation, which place forgiveness in the context of *historia salutis*.[61] Nevertheless, if for Luke forgiveness and justification were already realities before the coming of Christ, and if forgiveness and justification are communicated by the Holy Spirit, then it must follow that the Holy Spirit was already active unto salvation before Pentecost. From the perspective of *ordo salutis*, this continuity means that the Holy Spirit must have been applying the benefits of Christ's work even before Christ completed his work in history.[62]

This perspective is not common in contemporary studies of Luke-Acts given Luke's clear penchant for emphasizing *historia salutis*. Yet Luke's emphasis on the continuity of salvation makes questions about the continuity of the Spirit's work inescapable. The newness of the Spirit's activity for Luke—which is also inescapable—has its limits. This newness must be relative rather than absolute.[63] In the previous chapter I argued for a new era of the Holy Spirit's work particularly with respect to an eschatological outpouring that equips the people of God for service. On the other hand, the continuity of the Spirit's work means that any newness of justification, forgiveness, or spiritual enlivening is not absolute.[64]

Second, the method of the present study, which considers the entire biblical witness, also helps in understanding the role of the Holy Spirit across the ages. When we ask questions of *ordo salutis*, we are reformulating Luke's statements in a systematic way.[65] At this point we are considering a variety of texts as well as their implications (i.e., "good and necessary consequences" of texts).[66] We have seen, for example, that Luke emphasizes the continuity of forgiveness by means of the message of the prophets (cf. Acts 10:43). It is thus prudent to ask: What prophetic texts speak about forgiveness in tandem with the work of the Holy Spirit? A prominent section of Scripture in this

---

61. See, e.g., I. Howard Marshall, "The Resurrection in the Acts of the Apostles," in *Apostolic History and the Gospel: Biblical and Historical Essays Presented to F. F. Bruce on his 60th Birthday*, ed. W. Ward Gasque and Ralph P. Martin (Grand Rapids: Eerdmans, 1970), 103; David G. Peterson, "Resurrection Apologetics and the Theology of Luke-Acts," in *Proclaiming the Resurrection: Papers from the First Oak Hill College Annual School of Theology*, ed. Peter M. Head (Carlisle: Paternoster, 1998), 43.

62. See Turretin, *Inst.* 12.5.6, 15–16; 12.7.19, 45; cf. 5.2.10; 12.10.23; 15.5.20; WCF 3.6; 7.3, 5; 8.6; 11.4, 6; 13.1–3; 17.1–2.

63. So, e.g., Turretin, *Inst.* 3.30.22; 12.5.15; 12.8.18, 21; Richard B. Gaffin Jr., "Pentecost: Before and After," *Kerux* 10.2 (1995): 24.

64. For this last point, cf. G. K. Beale, "The Descent of the Eschatological Temple in the Form of the Spirit at Pentecost: Part 1: The Clearest Evidence," *TynBul* 56.1 (2005): 94.

65. Reformulation, however, does not necessarily entail misconstrual. As we know from everyday life, there can be accurate and inaccurate rearticulations of someone's position.

66. See WCF 1.6.

regard is Ezekiel 36–37. In Ezekiel 37:11–14 the Spirit breathes new life into dead bones, enabling them to live. As I have argued earlier, this is an image of restoration and resurrection for God's people that provides part of the scriptural background for Peter's Pentecost speech.[67] Yet it also has implications for *ordo salutis*. Calvin, for example, uses Ezekiel 37 to speak of the continuity of salvation across the testaments.[68]

Similarly, both a corporate and individual focus is also entailed in Ezekiel 36. Luke 1:6 may allude to Ezekiel 36:27, with respect to righteous Zechariah and Elizabeth walking in the statutes of the Lord.[69] Though Ezekiel has in large measure an eschatological future in view in which God's people are empowered to walk in his ways, it is nevertheless striking that Zechariah and Elizabeth are already viewed as obedient.[70] An allusion to Ezekiel 36:27— which speaks of the indwelling Spirit enabling obedience—would likely assume the Spirit's internal work, even before Pentecost.[71] This may also support reading Acts 5:32 as a reference to the giving of the Holy Spirit to all who obey God, even to pre-Pentecost believers like Zechariah and Elizabeth, who are characterized by obedience.

There is much more that could be said for Luke's contribution to the role of the Holy Spirit in relation to *ordo salutis*. But in sum, if the experience of salvation requires new life, and this new life must come from the Holy Spirit, then it follows that all of God's people who have been justified through the ages have been renewed by the Holy Spirit.[72] Luke does not spell out all these details, but his contribution adds to the overall picture that occupies the work of systematic theology.

Conclusion and Synthesis: *Historia Salutis* and *Ordo Salutis*

Luke is a narrative theologian; to understand his theology, we must pay attention to the way he presents his narratives. And yet one does not necessarily

---

67. See especially ch. 2, under section "The Spirit, the Resurrection, and the Latter Days."

68. See Calvin, *Inst.* 2.10.21.

69. See the marginal note in NA[28].

70. Cf. Geerhardus Vos, "The Eschatological Aspect of the Pauline Conception of the Spirit," in *Redemptive History and Biblical Interpretation: The Shorter Writings of Geerhardus Vos*, ed. Richard B. Gaffin Jr. (Phillipsburg, NJ: P&R, 1980), 96–97. See also John 3:3, 5–8, where Jesus tells Nicodemus that he must be born again by water and s/Spirit in order to see the kingdom of God. This is likely an allusion to the water and Spirit of Ezek. 36:25–27, applied at a personal level (*tis* ["someone"], John 3:3, 5).

71. See also Steven R. Coxhead, "The Cardionomographic Work of the Spirit in the Old Testament," *WTJ* 79 (2017): 77–95.

72. See again Turretin, *Inst.* 12.5.6, 15–16; 12.7.19, 45.

do injustice to these narratives by organizing and explaining them in various ways. In this chapter and the previous chapter I have considered Acts from the perspectives of *historia salutis* and *ordo salutis*. Far from being contraventions of Luke's narrative presentations, such syntheses of the events he narrates are actually encouraged by the narratives themselves. On the one hand, Luke speaks of the new developments of salvation history, as we saw in chapter 5. In this regard, the resurrection of Christ serves as the key fulcrum. On the other hand, Luke also speaks clearly about the unity of the salvation wrought by the covenant-keeping God. If we only gave attention to the newness of *historia salutis*, we would not do justice to Luke's many statements of continuity. Focusing on continuity using the category of *ordo salutis* thus appears to be a prudent and necessary step to ascertain how Luke's sometimes apparently disparate statements cohere.

A few caveats regarding *ordo salutis* may also help at this point. First, the continuity of *ordo salutis* does not mean either (a) that the subjective experience of salvation is always the same for each person to whom salvation is applied or (b) that true believers from the Old Testament had exactly the same experience of salvation as believers in the New Testament. Indeed, systematic theologians who emphasize the continuity of *ordo salutis* have often also made the point that many things in the New Testament are quite different from earlier eras. This is true for much of the Reformed tradition.

For example, in one of the most helpful hermeneutical sections of Calvin's *Institutes* (1559) he devotes one chapter to the continuity between the Old Testament and New Testament (2.10) and one chapter to differences between the two (2.11). Among the similarities are the substantial unity of God's covenant dealings, the emphasis on the future hope, the same Holy Spirit given to believers in the Old and New Testaments, and salvation by grace.[73] Calvin also recognizes a number of differences, including more of a focus on earthly concerns in the Old Testament, the presence of figures instead of the reality to which they pointed, the relative obscurity of the message, and the greater fear and bondage in the Old Testament.

The Westminster Confession of Faith (1646) gives nuanced attention to both the similarities and differences in salvation and its effects across the ages, noting one plan of salvation in various administrations (WCF 7.4–6; 11.6) while also acknowledging the greater boldness and freedom believers have in the new covenant (WCF 20.1).

---

73. Note the helpful headings in the Ford Lewis Battles edition of Calvin's *Institutes*: *Institutes of the Christian Religion*, ed. John T. McNeill, trans. Ford Lewis Battles, 2 vols., LCC 20–21 (Philadelphia: Westminster, 1960), 1:428–64 (*Inst.* 2.10–11).

Francis Turretin (1623–87) is also sensitive to both continuity and discontinuity. He not only emphasizes the continuity of the Spirit's work across the ages[74] but also discusses the difference of the Spirit being given "drop by drop" in previous eras, whereas in the New Testament the Spirit is poured out more effusively.[75] Turretin also recognizes the fuller "tranquility of conscience" that accrues to believers after the ransom and resurrection of Christ.[76]

Similarly, Herman Bavinck (1854–1921) also speaks of both continuity and discontinuity: "It would be foolish to think that the benefits of forgiveness and sanctification, of regeneration and eternal life, were . . . nonexistent in the days of the Old Testament. They were definitely granted then as well by Christ, who is eternally the same. But the consciousness and enjoyment of those benefits were far from being as rich in the Old Testament as in the time of the New Testament."[77]

We can sum up the interface of *historia salutis* and *ordo salutis* for Luke by returning to his rich teaching on the Holy Spirit. As I argued in the previous chapter, the Holy Spirit is the *eschatological* Spirit, and his sphere of activity is the coming age.[78] With the resurrection of Jesus comes the turning of the ages, and the Spirit is now poured out more effusively. Therefore, the Spirit's work in renewing his people is a mark of the coming eschaton that has intruded into the present age. This *historia salutis* reality, however, also has implications for *ordo salutis*, since already under the administration of the Old Testament, the presence and activity of the Spirit among God's people was an eschatological reality, anticipating the fuller glory that comes after the resurrection of Christ.

Sinclair Ferguson captures it well, with a far-reaching summary: "As in the Old Testament era, so in the New, [the Holy Spirit's] activity is soteriological, communal, cosmic and eschatological, and involves the transformation of the individual, the governing of the church and the world, and the bringing in of the new age."[79] If Abraham was justified by faith already in Genesis 15,

74. See, e.g., Turretin, *Inst.* 3.30.32; 12.5.6, 15.
75. See Turretin, *Inst.* 12.5.45; 12.8.21. Quotation (from 12.5.45) comes from Francis Turretin, *Institutes of Elenctic Theology*, ed. James T. Dennison Jr., trans. George Musgrave Giger, 3 vols. (Phillipsburg, NJ: P&R, 1992–97), 2:205.
76. Turretin, *Inst.* 12.10.26 (in Giger trans., 2:255). For more differences according to Turretin, see *Inst.* 12.7–8; 12.10.8, 20. Many of these passages also note continuity as well.
77. Bavinck, *Reformed Dogmatics*, 3:221.
78. See Vos, "Eschatological Aspect," 95–97. See also Gaffin, *Perspectives on Pentecost*, for a further extension of Vos's thinking on the Spirit in Acts. For a helpful anthology of Vos, see Danny E. Olinger, *A Geerhardus Vos Anthology: Biblical and Theological Insights Alphabetically Arranged* (Phillipsburg, NJ: P&R, 2005). See also Benjamin Breckenridge Warfield, "The Spirit of God in the Old Testament," in *Biblical and Theological Studies*, ed. Samuel G. Craig (Philadelphia: P&R, 1968), 127–56.
79. Ferguson, *Holy Spirit*, 93–94.

then this should be understood as a Spirit-enabled, eschatological reality that Abraham experienced before the coming of Christ.

The situation of believers today is not altogether different: justification is a Spirit-enabled, eschatological reality that anticipates the consummation. Yet believers today have even more freedom of conscience than believers in the Old Testament. From this angle, one might then appreciate the *differences* in *ordo salutis*, despite the fundamental unity, along with the *continuity* of *historia salutis*, despite elements of discontinuity.

The newness of *historia salutis* for Luke is inescapable, whereas differences in terms of *ordo salutis* are relative rather than absolute. Admittedly, the persuasiveness of my argument will hinge to a significant degree on the measure of continuity or discontinuity one perceives between the two Testaments. But Luke clearly sees a great deal of continuity between what he writes and what has come before. The resurrection not only is the great fulcrum of *historia salutis*, which ensures the realities of *ordo salutis*; it also preeminently demonstrates the veracity of the Old Testament Scriptures. In the next chapter I consider this aspect in much more detail.

7

The Resurrection as
Apologia Pro Scriptura

In the previous chapter we considered the continuity of salvation across the ages, which also speaks to the continuity of the Scriptures across the ages. We are now in a position to consider the way that Luke employs the resurrection to defend the veracity of the Scriptures. In this chapter I propose a new approach to Acts in light of the continuity of Scripture and the resurrection of Christ. I will argue that one of Luke's primary aims in Acts is to present an *apologia pro scriptura* ("defense of Scripture"), and one of the main ways he does this is by his frequent, scriptural appeals to the necessity of the resurrection of Christ. Stated differently, Luke understands the resurrection of Jesus to be the fulfillment of and definitive demonstration of the Scriptures' truthfulness. Luke's thoroughgoing focus on the resurrection is therefore also a thoroughgoing defense of Scripture.

My argument begins by reviewing some key passages in Acts that explain the resurrection by invoking the Old Testament. Next I consider the implications of the end of Luke's Gospel, where Jesus speaks of the scriptural necessity (*dei*) for the Christ to be resurrected. I will then consider how Luke's stated and modeled hermeneutical approach opens up other Old Testament texts that speak of the resurrection of the Christ, but which Luke does not quote directly. Finally, I will argue that Luke's pervasive use of the Old Testament in support of the resurrection serves as an *apologia pro scriptura*, and that

149

understanding this aspect of Luke's purpose enriches our understanding of the purpose of Acts.

The Resurrection and the Old Testament: A Glance Back

In part 1, I devoted extensive space to the resurrection in Acts, particularly with respect to the apostolic preaching. Not only does the resurrection occupy a prominent place in the apostolic preaching, but the resurrection message is consistently supported by appeals to the Old Testament. The message is not simply that Jesus has been raised from the dead but that his resurrection fulfills the Scriptures and thus calls for belief. It is not my intention to repeat my exegesis from part 1, but it will be helpful to provide a selective summary as we consider the role of the Old Testament in support of the resurrection.

Peter

Peter's programmatic Pentecost sermon appeals to several Old Testament texts to support the resurrection of Jesus. These include Psalm 16 [15 LXX], which states that God will not allow his holy one to see decay (Acts 2:25–28), and Psalm 110 [109 LXX], which supports the reality that the resurrected Christ is seated at the right hand of God (Acts 2:34–35). Additionally, Ezekiel 36–37 likely serves as background to Luke's statements about restoration (Acts 2:5, 17–21; cf. 1:6; 3:21) and provides part of the prophetic background for the reunification of the people under one king (2:24–36). Other psalms alluded to in support of the resurrection include Psalm 18:5 (18:6 MT/17:6 LXX) and Psalm 116:3 (114:3 LXX) in Acts 2:24, and Psalms 89:4 and 132:11 in Acts 2:30–31. The glorification of Jesus in Acts 3:13 may draw upon Isaiah 52:13, but also upon the raising up of a prophet like Moses from Deuteronomy 18 (Acts 3:22, 26). Additionally, the *apokatastasis* (Acts 3:21) recalls the original created order, which, though marred by sin, is beginning to be set right because of the resurrection of Jesus. Peter's defense of the resurrection before the Sanhedrin in Acts 4:11 appeals to the rejected stone of Psalm 118:22 [117:22 LXX], who has become the cornerstone. To Cornelius Peter mentions that Jesus was raised on the third day (Acts 10:40), and it is this Jesus to whom the prophets bear witness (v. 43).

Paul

After his conversion, Paul immediately begins to preach in Damascus that Jesus is the Son of God (9:20) and the Christ (v. 22). That he does so from the Old Testament Scriptures is clear from the context of the synagogue, his Jewish audience(s), and the likely connotation of *symbibazō* (v. 22) to refer to Scriptural arguments. Paul also preaches the resurrection in his first major sermon of Acts (at Pisidian Antioch, 13:16–41). Here Paul contextualizes the resurrection of Christ in relation to Israel's history, and in the second movement of this speech (vv. 26–37) he relates the resurrection of Christ explicitly to a number of specific Old Testament texts (cf. vv. 30–35). These include Psalm 2:7 (Acts 13:33), Isaiah 55:3 (Acts 13:34), and Psalm 16:10 [15:10 LXX] (Acts 13:35). In addition, 2 Samuel 7 hovers over the entire speech.

Beyond explicit quotations, we also find more universal references to the Old Testament with respect to the resurrection. In Acts 17 the Bereans were more noble than the Thessalonians because they searched the Scriptures to see if the Paul's resurrection preaching passed muster (v. 11). No Old Testament quotations are present at Paul's speech in Athens, but Paul's resurrection argument (vv. 18, 29, 31) relies on a scriptural worldview (cf. vv. 24–26).

Even more substantial are Paul's frequent appeals to the Scriptures and his ancestral traditions in his defenses, particularly with respect to the resurrection. In Jerusalem Paul appeals to the resurrection not simply to divide the Pharisees and Sadducees but also to appeal to his belief in the resurrection as the fulfillment of the hope of his fathers (Acts 23:6). In Caesarea Paul assures Felix that his resurrection message is nothing other than what was written in the Law and Prophets (24:14–15). Similarly, before Festus Paul reiterates that he has committed no crime against the law or the temple (25:8). In Paul's longest defense speech, before Herod Agrippa II, he again appeals to the Scriptures to demonstrate his guiltlessness—the resurrection is not out of accord with the Law, the Prophets, or the traditions of his fathers (26:6–8, 22–23, 27). Paul's final words in Acts again deal with the faithfulness of his resurrection message to the traditions of Israel (28:17–20). Indeed, Paul's reference to the *hope of Israel* (v. 20) is best taken as a reference to the resurrection in particular (cf. 2:26; 23:6; 24:15; 26:6–7).

Stephen, James, and Others

Stephen's speech recalls the prophet like Moses that God would raise up (Deut. 18:15 in Acts 7:37), which is accomplished through the resurrection of Jesus (cf. Acts 3:22). Additionally, Stephen's appeal to Amos 5:25–27 (Acts 7:42–43) and the language of *tent* prepare readers for the mention of the tent of Amos 9:11–12 in James's speech, which refers to the Davidic dynasty restored and established by means of the resurrection.

James also appeals to the Old Testament in support of the resurrection of Christ. Though there is debate about the use of Amos 9:11–12 in Acts 15:16–18, I have argued that the rebuilding of the tent of David refers to the restoration of the Davidic dynasty, which comes by means of the resurrection of Christ.

In Philip's encounter with the Ethiopian eunuch, his explanation of Isaiah 53:7–8 (Acts 8:32–33) possibly also alludes to the exaltation of the Messiah (cf. Isa. 52:13 in Acts 3:13).

Finally, Apollos's appeal to the Old Testament to demonstrate Jesus is the Christ (Acts 18:25–28) almost certainly includes the demonstration of Christ's resurrection.

Conclusion

This brief review underscores how frequently characters in Acts appeal to the Old Testament in support of the resurrection. Many passages cite the Old Testament explicitly, while others appeal more generally to the Old Testament. Yet both types of appeal reveal how important the Old Testament is for the resurrection message of Acts.

The Resurrection and the Old Testament according to Luke

Luke finds support for the resurrection in the Old Testament by way of both explicit citation and general appeal. Since the Old Testament features so prominently in this regard, it will be helpful to consider in more detail the hermeneutical approach Luke exhibits and its implications vis-à-vis the resurrection in the Old Testament. I will begin with Luke 24:44–47, in which the Lukan Jesus explains the scriptural necessity of the resurrection (among other aspects of his work). Then I will consider how this lines up with some important texts that speak of the resurrection in the Gospel of Luke. Next I will give attention to how these statements in the Gospel of Luke, together with his explicit quotations, open up many potential Old Testament resurrection avenues. I will thus entertain additional texts that are not directly quoted in Luke but are consistent with what we find elsewhere in Luke-Acts.

Admittedly what follows will be, at points, suggestive, but I contend that Luke's explicit statements compel us to consider his more maximal approach to finding the resurrection in the Old Testament.[1] Luke reads the entire Old

---

1. For a concise survey of views on Luke's use of the OT, see Dietrich Rusam, *Das Alte Testament bei Lukas*, BZNW 112 (Berlin: de Gruyter, 2003), 15–26.

Testament christologically, and he certainly would find references to the resurrection throughout the Old Testament, beyond the texts that he cites explicitly.

The Old Testament and the Resurrection in the Gospel of Luke

THE TEACHING OF THE RESURRECTED CHRIST (LUKE 24:13–27, 44–47)

Perhaps the clearest text in Luke or Acts that outlines Luke's approach to the Old Testament is found in Luke 24:44–47. In 24:44 Jesus speaks of the necessity (*dei*) that everything written about him in the law of Moses, the Prophets, and the Psalms be fulfilled. Three things in particular are identified as necessary, indicated by three infinitival clauses: the Christ must suffer (*pathein*), he must rise from the dead on the third day (*anastēnai ek nekrōn*[2] *tē tritē hēmera*),[3] and the message of repentance and forgiveness must be preached (*kērychthēnai*) in his name (vv. 46–47). Several aspects of these verses bear on the present argument.

First, it was necessary not only for the Christ to suffer but also to rise from the dead.[4] This coheres with Luke's emphasis on the resurrection in Acts. Second, the message of forgiveness and repentance must go forth in Jesus's name. We have seen in Acts that the preaching of the apostles features the resurrection quite prominently and that the message of forgiveness is related to the resurrection of Christ (cf. Acts 13:38). Third, Luke's inclusion of "everything" (*panta*) written about Jesus (*peri emou*) implies that there is much in the Old Testament that speaks directly of Jesus.[5] This is the case regardless of whether or not Luke 24:44 refers to a threefold division of Scripture (which is not certain).[6] The Lukan Jesus speaks of Moses and all the prophets (24:27;

---

2. *Ek nekrōn* is omitted by D and Coptic (Sahidic), but even so the resurrection is mentioned.

3. These statements recall the earlier statements of the two radiant figures at the empty tomb (24:6–7).

4. This is commonly recognized.

5. See similarly Alan J. Thompson, *The Acts of the Risen Lord Jesus: Luke's Account of God's Unfolding Plan*, NSBT 27 (Downers Grove, IL: InterVarsity, 2011) 74; cf. Jacob Jervell, *The Theology of the Acts of the Apostles* (Cambridge: Cambridge University Press, 1996), 47–48; Richard B. Gaffin Jr., "Justification in Luke-Acts," in *Right with God: Justification in the Bible and the World*, ed. D. A. Carson (Grand Rapids: Baker, 1992), 121.

6. Notice the single article used for Prophets and Psalms in 24:44. So Michael Wolter, *The Gospel according to Luke*, trans. Wayne Coppins and Christoph Heilig, 2 vols., BMSEC (Waco: Baylor University Press, 2016), 2:567–68; cf. Rusam, *Das Alte Testament*, 259–62. See alternatively Daniel B. Wallace, *Greek Grammar beyond the Basics: An Exegetical Syntax of the New Testament* (Grand Rapids: Zondervan, 1996), 287; Darrell L. Bock, *Luke*, 2 vols., BECNT (Grand Rapids: Baker, 1994–96), 2:1936; James R. Edwards, *The Gospel according to Luke*, PNTC (Grand Rapids: Eerdmans, 2015), 733. For possible examples of a threefold division of Scripture, see esp. 4QMMT C 10–11; Sir., prol.; 2 Macc. 2:13; Philo, *Contempl. Life* 25; Josephus,

cf. Acts 28:23) and, more pleonastically, of the law of Moses, the prophets, and the Psalms (Luke 24:44). However he construes the canonical divisions, it is clear that all the Scriptures are to be understood christologically.

Drawing these together we can conclude that Luke understands the totality of the Old Testament to be about Jesus, specifically his death, resurrection, and the message that must go forth in his name. This is also apparent earlier, on Jesus's journey to Emmaus (esp. Luke 24:25–27). Here Jesus speaks of a twofold necessity (*edei*): the Christ had to suffer, and then enter into glory (24:26). As I argued earlier, this entering into glory likely refers to the resurrection, which commences Jesus's experience of the state of glory. Such a view also coheres with Jesus's more explicit statement in Luke 24:46. Similarly, in 24:27 Jesus speaks of himself from the Old Testament, beginning from "Moses and all the prophets"—a phrase that corresponds to "the law of Moses, and the prophets, and the psalms" in 24:44.[7] Jesus further chastises his audience for being foolish and slow to understand the prophets (24:25), underscoring Luke's perspective that the Old Testament speaks with sufficient clarity about the sufferings and glories of the coming Christ. His view is quite the opposite of the sentiment that the "resurrection is certainly not something which could have been arrived at by reflection on the Old Testament."[8]

Yet in Luke 24, Luke does not identify specific Old Testament texts that Jesus fulfills in his resurrection. Indeed, it might be lamented that we do not know which biblical texts Jesus covered on the journey between Jerusalem and Emmaus that led the disciples' hearts to burn within them (v. 32). However, Luke quotes an array of biblical texts in the first half of Acts, many of which speak of the resurrection. If we consider these quotations in light of Luke 24, then we can make some informed hypotheses about other Old Testament texts that may speak of the resurrection of Christ that Luke does not cite explicitly.[9] In other words, the rather universal statements with

---

Ag. Ap. 1.39–40. These are discussed in Edmon L. Gallagher and John D. Meade, *The Biblical Canon Lists from Early Christianity: Texts and Analysis* (Oxford: Oxford University Press, 2017), 7–17. Yet, as Rusam notes (*Das Alte Testament*, 260–61), in no case is a third division specifically identified by the moniker "Psalms." However we construe the divisions of the Old Testament, David is clearly important for Luke's writings (e.g., explicit mention of the psalms in 24:44, the role of David as prophet in Acts 2:30, and the Davidic covenant in Acts 13:34).

7. Luke clearly understands David to be a prophet (Acts 2:30).

8. C. F. Evans, *Resurrection and the New Testament*, SBT 2/12 (Naperville, IL: Alec R. Allenson, 1970), 14. For a recent defense of the resurrection in the OT, see Claude Cohen-Matlofsky, "Resurrection, from the Hebrew Bible to the Rock-Cut Tombs: An Inscribed Concept," *QC* 23 (2015): 101–27.

9. See similarly Jacques Dupont, "L'utilisation apologétique de l'Ancien Testament dans les discours des Actes," in *Études sur les Actes des Apôtres*, LD 45 (Paris: Cerf, 1967), 246–47; note also his chart on pp. 281–82.

respect to the Old Testament in Luke 24:25–27, 44–47 mean that Luke likely does not have in mind only a limited subset of christological texts from each of these sections of the Old Testament—such as Deuteronomy 18 from the Law, 2 Samuel 7 from the Prophets, and Psalm 16 from the Psalms. Instead, the focus is on *all* the Scriptures.

Luke's maximalist christological reading of the Old Testament evident in Luke 24—especially with respect to the resurrection—coheres well with later statements in Acts that are also more general with respect to the resurrection in the Old Testament (e.g., 26:22–23).[10] Since Luke views the entire Old Testament as christological in some sense, his approach is not limited to texts he cites explicitly. Instead, those texts that are cited explicitly must be representative and illustrative of Luke's broader approach to the Old Testament. We turn next to examine this theory with respect to the other key texts in the Gospel of Luke, working backward through the Gospel.

Controversy with Sadducees on the Resurrection (Luke 20:27–40)

An important debate between Jesus and the Sadducees is found in Luke 20 in an episode revolving around how the Old Testament is to be interpreted. Luke explicitly states that the Sadducees denied the resurrection (Luke 20:27; cf. Acts 23:8), and in their view the words of Moses could not be squared with the resurrection (Luke 20:28; cf. Deut. 25:5–6). In response Jesus challenges their understanding of marriage in the resurrection age and retorts that Moses himself does indeed speak of the resurrection. Jesus points specifically to the passage about the (burning) bush, quoting Exodus 3:6 (Luke 20:37; cf. Exod. 3:15–16). Though Exodus 3 does not include the terminology of resurrection, Jesus's argument assumes that God's covenantal promises to the patriarchs remain in force, even though the patriarchs died (cf. Luke 20:28). If the latter is true, then it must mean that God will fulfill his promises to the patriarchs; this time of fulfillment must refer to the resurrection age (cf. v. 27). Once Jesus had proved the resurrection from the Old Testament,[11] the scribes—who were literate in the Scriptures[12]—expressed their approval (v. 39), and no one dared ask him any more questions (v. 40).[13]

---

10. Contrast, e.g., C. D. Elledge, *Resurrection of the Dead in Early Judaism, 200 BCE–CE 200* (Oxford: Oxford University Press, 2017), 88. For more on Luke's interaction with the Old Testament, see Richard B. Gaffin Jr., "'For Our Sakes Also': Christ and the Old Testament in the New Testament," in *The Hope Fulfilled: Essays in Honor of O. Palmer Robertson*, ed. Robert L. Penny (Phillipsburg, NJ: P&R, 2008), 70–75.

11. Cf. Matt. 22:29; Mark 12:24: they know neither the *Scriptures* nor the power of God.

12. On scribes, see Craig S. Keener, *The Gospel of Matthew: A Socio-Rhetorical Commentary* (Grand Rapids: Eerdmans, 2009), 537–38; Edwards, *Gospel according to Luke*, 164.

13. Cf. John Calvin, *Inst.* 2.10.21–23.

The Rich Man and Lazarus (Luke 16:19–31)

Another Lukan passage that relates the resurrection to the Old Testament is the parable of the rich man and Lazarus. There are many questions to ask of this parable, but my focus is on the final five verses. The rich man pleads with father Abraham to be allowed to return to his kindred and warn them of the perils of torment (16:27–28). The response of Abraham is telling: they already have Moses and the Prophets. The rich man protests that his family would believe if only someone would rise from the dead (v. 30). Abraham resists this sentiment, concluding that if they do not believe Moses and the Prophets, neither would they believe if someone rose from the dead (v. 31). Though this passage is not a defense of Jesus's resurrection directly, its logic suggests that the message of Scripture is sufficiently clear and that hard-heartedness against Scripture would not be overcome even if someone rose from the dead. This exchange may even anticipate the scriptural contours of the resurrection message that Luke will expound in Acts.

Even clearer is the correlation of this statement to the events of Acts. In Acts we do find a scriptural message about a man raised from the dead. But the opposition encountered by those who preach and hold to this message in Acts demonstrates that those who do not believe in the man raised from the dead will not believe in the Scriptures either (cf. Acts 13:36–40). To believe Scripture is to believe in the resurrection; to resist Scripture is to resist the resurrection.

Sign of Jonah (Luke 11:29–32)

The inability of the resurrection to convince those with hard hearts is likewise in view in the sign of Jonah (Luke 11:29–32), which also alludes to the Old Testament to support the resurrection of Jesus. In Luke 11:30 Jesus states that as Jonah became (*egeneto*) a sign to the Ninevites, so will Jesus be a sign in "this" wicked generation (*genea ponēra*). If we ask how *Jonah* was a sign to his generation, then the answer must be in the way he was delivered from death and was thus able personally to preach to the Ninevites. The deliverance of Jonah was a sign to a hard-hearted people, warning them of the need to repent (which they did).[14] Jesus speaks of himself as one greater than Jonah (v. 32), one whose coming entails a greater deliverance, a greater message, and a greater need for repentance (cf. 10:13–15). This coheres with the close connection between the resurrection of Christ and the preaching of

---

14. In Matthew's account the focus is more on the preaching of Jonah (Matt. 12:41); in Luke it is more on the personal presence of Jonah (Luke 11:30).

repentance in Luke's writings (e.g., Luke 24:46–47; Acts 2:33–38; 13:36–39), which also has precedent in the preaching of repentance in Jonah-delivered-from-death. It is thus fitting that Jesus relates the sign of Jonah to judgment, since to repent is to be delivered from judgment and since Jesus as resurrected Lord is judge of all (cf. Acts 17:30–31).

It is also suggestive, given the relation between judgment and resurrection, that the queen of the South will rise up (*egerthēsetai*, Luke 11:31) in judgment on "this" generation, and the Ninevites will likewise rise up (*anastēsontai*) in judgment (v. 32).[15] For the one greater than Jonah is the one who was resurrected in a deliverance greater than Jonah's. We should also consider the possibility, as noted in chapter 3, that Jonah's death-and-resurrection experience—after he was thrown overboard from a ship—is echoed in the account of Paul's deliverance from death at sea in Acts 27.

It is thus not necessary for Luke to elaborate on the *means* of Jonah's deliverance for his account of the sign of Jonah to refer to the resurrection. (Cf., e.g., Matt. 12:40, which relates Jonah's three days and three nights in the belly [*koilia*] of the fish to Jesus's three days and three nights in the heart [*kardia*] of the earth [cf. Jon. 1:17].)[16] We can safely assume that the story of Jonah would have been familiar to Luke's audience since the sign of Jonah was a common component of the transmitted Jesus traditions. Further, in the early church the sign of Jonah was commonly understood to refer to the resurrection of Christ.[17] Luke's choice of wording that differs from Matthew's does not entail significant difference from Matthew's fuller account. This also means—though this point is less certain—that Matthew's emphasis on *three days* may also be implicit in Luke's account of the sign of Jonah.[18] It is not, however, necessary to press this particular "three days" correspondence, since elsewhere Luke makes it clear that the resurrection was on the third day (Luke 9:22; 18:33; 24:7, 46; Acts 10:40; cf. Luke 13:32; 24:21). As I argue in the next section, this "three days" finds Old Testament precedent as well.

Other Lukan texts that mention resurrection could also be mentioned, such as Luke 14:14; 15:32. Indeed, it is striking that resurrection language is used for the prodigal son: his journey to a far country was as though he died, but his return indicates new life (cf. 15:18, 24, 32). We have sufficient

15. These are Luke's two preferred verbs for resurrection.

16. Though phrasing similar to Luke's is found in D and some Latin manuscripts, demonstrating early reception history of Luke along the same lines as Matthew.

17. See, e.g., Justin, *Dial.* 107; Athanasius, *C. Ar.* 3.25.23; Cyril of Jerusalem, *Cat.* 4.12; cf. Irenaeus, *Haer.* 4.9.2; 4.33.4; 5.5.2.

18. Cf. Acts 27:19.

evidence in the Gospel of Luke to conclude that Luke views the resurrection as a scriptural message; Acts strengthens this observation.

The Old Testament and the Resurrection in Acts

Though we cannot say for certain what passages the Lukan Jesus would have expounded on the road to Emmaus, I have tried to sketch Luke's christological approach to the Old Testament in order to tease our exegetical imaginations into active thought.[19] Luke provides enough examples that we can begin to see the way he reads the Old Testament with respect to the resurrection. In what follows I will suggest how Luke's explicit statements about the resurrection in his Gospel and Acts 1–15 provide helpful context for considering Luke's more universal appeals to the Old Testament in the second half of Acts (cf., e.g., Acts 17:11; 23:6; 24:14–15; 25:8; 26:6–8, 22–23, 27; 28:17–20). Though such appeals on their own may lack specificity, by the second half of Acts, Luke has made it sufficiently clear not only *that* the Old Testament supports the resurrection but *how*. Utilizing in broad strokes a threefold division of the Old Testament (taking a cue from Luke 24:44, even if these do not refer to three divisions of Scripture), in what follows I consider some other possibilities for Old Testament resurrection texts that may be entailed in Luke's hermeneutical approach.[20]

THE LAW OF MOSES

We have already covered several texts from the Pentateuch that Luke uses to refer to the resurrection of Jesus. These include Exodus 3:6 (Luke 20:37) and Deuteronomy 18:15 (Acts 3:22, 26; cf. Luke 9:35). Yet if Luke takes a maximal christological approach to the resurrection in the Old Testament, we should consider other possibilities as well.[21] Genesis 22 appears to be an important passage in this regard. For example, elsewhere in the New Testament

19. Here I am channeling the definition of parables from C. H. Dodd, *The Parables of the Kingdom*, 4th ed. (London: Nisbet, 1938), 16.

20. For a helpful discussion on the OT foundations of resurrection, see Richard Bauckham, "The God Who Raises the Dead: The Resurrection of Jesus and Early Christian Faith in God," in *The Resurrection of Jesus Christ*, ed. Paul Avis (London: Darton, Longman and Todd, 1993), 136–54.

21. Cf. N. T. Wright, *The Resurrection of the Son of God*, COQG 3 (Minneapolis: Fortress, 2003), 197—commenting on Jewish debates: "The key question which the Sadducees pressed on the Pharisees (and, it appears, on Jesus) was: can you find the resurrection in the Torah itself, in the narrower sense of the Five Books of Moses? The answer was an emphatic 'Yes—once you know what you are looking for.'" Wright's survey includes texts not listed here. See also Jon D. Levenson, *Resurrection and the Restoration of Israel: The Ultimate Victory of the God of Life* (New Haven: Yale University Press, 2006), esp. 23–34.

Abraham's offering of Isaac in Genesis 22 is related to the hope of the resurrection (Heb. 11:17–19), and Romans 8:32 likely understands the Father's giving of the Son to be greater than Abraham's giving of Isaac.[22] In addition, Luke quotes Genesis 22:18 in Acts 3:25 to speak of the blessing of Abraham's offspring, and this blessing is realized through the resurrection of Jesus (cf. 3:26).[23] The fatherly pleasure expressed toward Jesus at his baptism (Luke 3:22, *ho huios mou ho agapētos*) may also recall Abraham's love for Isaac (Gen. 22:2). This divine voice from the baptism is echoed again on the Mount of Transfiguration (Luke 9:35, *ho eklelegmenos*),[24] and I have argued that the transfiguration anticipates Christ's glory in his resurrected state.[25] Indeed, the resurrection demonstrates divine approbation of Jesus's perfect obedience. Moreover, in Genesis 22 Abraham told his servants that he and Isaac(!) would return (v. 5), and it may be significant that this comes after his sight of Moriah on the third day (v. 4).

Other texts from the Pentateuch speak of new life after three days (e.g., the cupbearer in prison with Joseph [Gen. 40:12–13],[26] the prison experience of Joseph's brothers [42:17–18, 20]), or the experience of glory after three days (Israel at Sinai [Exod. 19:1, 11, 15–16; cf. 3:18; 5:3; 8:27; 10:22–23]). Though not all these may be compelling, given Luke's emphasis on the resurrection on the third day (Luke 9:22; 18:33; 24:7, 46; Acts 10:40; cf. Luke 13:32; 24:21), such "third day" precedents in Genesis may anticipate the resurrection of Christ.[27] Another relevant passage from Genesis is the renewal of the world after the flood in the days of Noah (cf. 2 Pet. 3:5–7), which may form part of the conceptual background for the *apokatastasis* in Acts 3:21.[28] These possibilities from Genesis would be in addition to Exodus 3, which Jesus invokes to rebuke the Sadducees' lack of belief in the resurrection in the Old Testament (Luke 20:37).

Another way Luke may have read the resurrection in the Old Testament concerns the renewal of the nation of Israel after exile. This can also be found

---

22. Cf. also the likely reference to Gen. 22:17 in Rom. 4:13, and more obviously to Gen. 22:16–17 in Heb. 6:13–14. See also *Pirqe R. El.* 31, noted in Levenson, *Resurrection and the Restoration*, 228.

23. See the marginal note in NA²⁸.

24. *Eklelegmenos* is the preferred reading, over *agapētos* or *eklektos*.

25. Luke's account of the baptism of Jesus, and perhaps the transfiguration, allude to Ps. 2:7—an OT text used in Acts 13:33 to speak of resurrection.

26. Contrast the negative result after three days for the baker (Gen. 40:18–19).

27. Cf. Arthur Darby Nock, "A Note on the Resurrection," in *Essays on the Trinity and the Incarnation*, ed. A. E. J. Rawlinson (London: Longmans, Green and Co., 1928), 50, which notes how common the "third day" is in the OT (referencing Johan Jakob Wettstein on Matt. 12:40).

28. Interestingly, the verbal form of the term (*apokathistēmi*) is used for the restoration of the cupbearer's office (and life) (Gen. 40:13, 21; 41:13).

in the Pentateuch, especially in the latter chapters of Deuteronomy (e.g., chs. 27–32). In Deuteronomy Moses speaks of blessings for covenantal obedience and cursings for covenantal disobedience. Though the apparent inevitability of the exile edges its way forward in these chapters, yet hope on the other side of exile remains (30:1–10; 32:43; cf. 33:29). This hope, as we have seen in Luke's appropriation of Ezekiel 36–37 in Acts 2, is often presented in terms of renewal of life. From this context in Deuteronomy also comes a fundamental tenet of Israel's belief: that the Lord is the one who kills and makes alive (Deut. 32:39; cf. 1 Sam. 2:6).[29]

All the Prophets

Luke often refers to the Old Testament using the shorthand *prophets* (cf. Luke 18:31; 24:25; Acts 3:18; 10:43; 13:40; 15:15; 26:27). In such cases "prophets" could serve as synecdoche for the Old Testament in general (since Luke considers both David and Moses to be prophets; cf. Acts 2:30; 3:22), or could refer to a division of the Old Testament (cf. Luke 24:44). For sake of organization, in this section I cover the (former and latter) prophets of the Hebrew canon, though I also include Daniel here. Since Luke's view is that "all the prophets" speak of the resurrection of Christ (cf. Luke 24:25, 27; Acts 3:21, 24–25; 10:43), there is much that I could say. I therefore must limit the following discussion to four categories of prophetic texts that Luke likely sees to be about the resurrection of Christ.

1. Davidic covenant. First are prophetic texts that speak about the Davidic covenant and the everlasting Davidic kingdom. In particular, the promises of 2 Samuel 7 (cf. 1 Chron. 17) provide much of the logical substructure for the resurrection preaching in Acts, not least with respect to the promise that the kingdom of the Son of David would abide forever (2 Sam. 7:13). This Davidic covenant also provides much of the background for other prophetic texts from the Old Testament that expound upon the Davidic covenant, such as Isaiah 9:6–7 [9:5–6 MT/LXX]—another Old Testament precedent for an everlasting, Davidic kingdom.[30] Similar texts are found throughout the Old Testament (e.g., Gen. 49:10; Ps. 89:4; Dan. 2:44; 4:34). As the speeches of Acts make clear, it is only by means of the resurrection that the Son of David

29. See Richard Bauckham, "Life, Death, and the Afterlife in Second Temple Judaism," in *Life in the Face of Death: The Resurrection Message of the New Testament*, ed. Richard N. Longenecker, MNTS (Grand Rapids: Eerdmans, 1998), 84; Levenson, *Resurrection and the Restoration*, 171–74; more skeptical is Robert Martin-Achard, *From Death to Life: A Study of the Development of the Doctrine of the Resurrection in the Old Testament*, trans. John Penney Smith (Edinburgh: Oliver and Boyd, 1960), 52–55.

30. Cf. the discussion in ch. 3 (under section "Paul's Pisidian Antioch Speech, Part 2").

could reign over an everlasting kingdom (Acts 2:29–32; 13:16–41; cf. Luke 1:33), and thus the resurrection is the means by which these Old Testament texts are realized.

2. *Narrative anticipations.* Second, several narratives in the prophets anticipate the resurrection of Christ. These include episodes in the ministries of Elijah and Elisha, the deliverance of Jonah, and Hezekiah's deliverance from death. Perhaps most important are the accounts of the powerful prophets Elijah and Elisha, which feature prominently in the Gospel of Luke and may even serve as a pattern for the work of Christ himself (see, e.g., Luke 4:25–27; 9:19, 30).[31] It is uniquely in Luke that we read of Jesus as a prophet, mighty in deed and word (24:19). Moreover, the Elijah and Elisha narratives provide precedents for raising the dead, such as the raising of the widow's only son at Nain (7:11–17). This recalls Elijah's raising of the widow's son at Zarephath (1 Kings 17:17–24) and Elisha's raising of the Shunammite woman's only son (2 Kings 4:32–37).[32] In addition, Elijah's ascent into heaven made him a figure ripe for eschatological anticipations (cf. Luke 9:8, 19, 30),[33] and therefore anticipates the greater ascension of the resurrected Christ. Indeed, Elijah is present in glory (along with Moses) on the Mount of Transfiguration, discussing Jesus's own *exodus* (9:31)—which must in some sense refer to Jesus's fuller experience of glory commencing with the resurrection.

Additionally, Hezekiah's deliverance from death anticipates the resurrection of Christ.[34] During the days of Sennacherib's threat,[35] Hezekiah became sick unto death. In response Hezekiah prayed for God's mercy and was granted another fifteen years of life (2 Kings 20:1–6; cf. Isa. 38:9–20). Interestingly, this new life was granted on the third day when Hezekiah went up to the Lord's temple (2 Kings 20:5). Here is an example of God's anointed being delivered from death to further the Davidic kingdom (v. 6). As we have seen with Acts, the full establishment of the Davidic kingdom comes through the resurrection

---

31. See, e.g., Thomas L. Brodie, "Luke the Literary Interpreter: Luke-Acts as a Systematic Rewriting and Updating of the Elijah-Elisha Narrative in 1 and 2 Kings" (ThD diss., Pontifical University of St. Thomas Aquinas [Vatican], 1981); Mark S. Giacobbe, "Luke the Chronicler: The Narrative Arc of Samuel-Kings and Chronicles in Luke-Acts" (PhD diss., Westminster Theological Seminary, 2018), 17–19, 150–51.

32. Levenson (*Resurrection and the Restoration*, 125–28) relates the resurrection episode of Elisha at Shunem with the account of Isaac's deliverance in Gen. 22. See also *Lev. Rab.* 27:4 (quoted in Levenson, *Resurrection and the Restoration*, 123); 2 Kings 13:21.

33. Recall also the translation of Enoch, by which he escaped death (Gen. 5:22–24). So Martin-Achard, *From Death to Life*, 65–69.

34. On the importance of Samuel, Kings, and Chronicles for Luke-Acts, see Giacobbe, "Luke the Chronicler."

35. Cf. T. R. Hobbs, *2 Kings*, WBC 13 (Waco: Word, 1985), 288–89.

of Christ. Though Hezekiah was a godly king (cf. 18:5–8),[36] Jesus's resurrection proves he is greater than Hezekiah.

Other stories of deliverance in the Old Testament that anticipate the resurrection of Jesus include the deliverance of Jonah (Luke 11:29–32), which I addressed above. One might also consider Daniel and the lion's den (Dan. 6:1–24) as another example where a righteous man is cast unjustly into the place of death, only to emerge alive in the morning. It is also possible the deliverance of Shadrach, Meshach, and Abednego (Hananiah, Mishael, Azariah) from the fire of death (3:1–30) would have been seen by Luke as an anticipation of the resurrection of Christ—especially in light of the supernatural presence with the three men. This is even more explicit in Daniel 3:88 LXX [OG/Theod.], where they confess that God has delivered them from Hades and saved them from the hand of death.[37] This language is similar to Luke's explanation of Jesus being delivered from the cords of death and Hades (Acts 2:24, 27, 31; cf. Ps. 18:6 [17:6 LXX]; 116:3 [114:3 LXX]).

3. Restoration as resurrection. A third category of prophetic texts speaks of Israel's restoration in terms of resurrection.[38] Ezekiel 37 is one of the key texts in this regard.[39] Ezekiel 37 speaks of a valley of dead bones coming to life by the Spirit of God, denoting the new life of Israel's restoration from exile (cf. 37:11–14). This immediately precedes Ezekiel's prophecy about the unification of the people under one king (vv. 15–28), which is realized in Acts by means of the resurrected Christ's universal lordship. Further, though Ezekiel 37 is indeed concerned with national restoration, it also speaks of the power of God to bring new life in a way that goes beyond restoration—God really can cause dead bones to live. This is assumed in Ezekiel's vision.[40]

Resurrection language is also found in Isaiah. Restoration is spoken of in resurrection terms in Isaiah 26:19 (cf. Luke 7:22). In Isaiah 25:6–8 Mount Zion will be home to a rich feast for all nations, and death will be swallowed up forever (v. 8).[41] Similarly, in Isaiah 28 God will overcome the covenant made

36. Though see 2 Chron. 32:25–26.

37. This text is also noted by Bauckham, "God Who Raises the Dead," 141 (though not in relation to Luke-Acts).

38. See here also Klaus Haacker, "Das Bekenntnis des Paulus zur Hoffnung Israels nach der Apostelgeschichte des Lukas," *NTS* 31 (1985): 443–45, which includes many of these texts and refers to such texts as "*metaphorische.*" Cf. Wright, *Resurrection of the Son of God*, 121–27; Levenson, *Resurrection and the Restoration*, 156–65.

39. See the discussion in ch. 2 (under section "The Spirit, the Resurrection, and the Latter Days").

40. See especially Calvin, *Inst.* 2.10.21; cf. Cohen-Matlofsky, "Resurrection," 111.

41. This text may be part of the background for Jesus's feeding the multitudes (Luke 9:10–17). Cf. David W. Pao and Eckhard J. Schnabel, "Luke," in *Commentary on the New Testament*

with death (vv. 15, 18), which finds its answer in the precious cornerstone of Zion (v. 16). This lines up with Luke's view of Jesus as the resurrected cornerstone of Psalm 118:22 [117:22 LXX] (Luke 20:17; Acts 4:11). For Luke the covenant with death is annulled through the resurrection of Jesus.

Resurrection language is also employed in Hosea. Hosea 6:2 speaks of the Lord reviving and raising up his people after three days.[42] The combination of *new life* on the *third day* seems also to accord with Luke's resurrection expositions. Hosea 13:14 is similar to Isaiah 28 in promising deliverance and redemption from death (cf. 1 Cor. 15:55).[43]

The prophets often employ resurrection language to speak of renewal and hope, which may also include the restoration of kingship. If this category of texts is granted, then the possibilities for Luke mining the Old Testament prophets for resurrection precedents could be quite extensive.[44] Many other texts would then come into focus, such as the raising up of the Davidic king in conjunction with the restoration of God's people (Jer. 30, esp. 30:9) or the springing up of a righteous branch of David (33:15). One might also consider the exaltation or vindication of the servant in Isaiah 52:13; 53:10–12,[45] which some see used in Acts 8 to emphasize the resurrection of Jesus.[46] It may even be that a comparatively minor character like Jehoiachin encapsulates the hope for Davidic, and therefore national, "resurrection."[47]

4. Physical resurrection. Fourth, the prophets also speak of physical resurrection.[48] The locus classicus is Daniel 12:1–3.[49] Though this text is perhaps exceptional in the clarity with which it speaks of physical resurrection, the

---

Use of the Old Testament, ed. G. K. Beale and D. A. Carson (Grand Rapids: Baker Academic, 2007), 310.

42. On the "third day" of Hos. 6:2 and resurrection in rabbinic tradition, see Harvey K. MacArthur, "On the Third Day," *NTS* 18 (1971/1972): 81–86; cf. Lee Tankersly, "'Thus It Is Written': Redemptive History and Christ's Resurrection on the Third Day," *SBJT* 16.3 (2012): 50–60; see also Levenson, *Resurrection and the Restoration*, 202–7.

43. On the prominence of Hosea (including chs. 6 and 13) in the early church, see C. H. Dodd, *According to the Scriptures: The Substructure of New Testament Theology* (London: Nisbet, 1952), 75–78. Dodd argues that Hosea was especially important for demonstrating resurrection (on the third day).

44. Cf., e.g., Donald E. Gowan, *Theology of the Prophetic Books: The Death and Resurrection of Israel* (Louisville: Westminster John Knox, 1998); Levenson, *Resurrection and the Restoration*.

45. See Martin-Achard, *From Death from Life*, 103–23.

46. See the discussion in ch. 4 (under section "Philip and the Resurrection").

47. See Matthew H. Patton, *Hope for a Tender Sprig: Jehoiachin in Biblical Theology*, BBR-Sup 16 (Winona Lake, IN: Eisenbrauns, 2017).

48. Haacker ("Das Bekenntnis des Paulus," 445) says such references reveal "*die Erwartung realer Totenauferweckung*" ("the expectation of a real resurrection of the dead").

49. See, e.g., Levenson, *Resurrection and the Restoration*, 201–2; Wright, *Resurrection of the Son of God*, 109.

concept of physical resurrection is clear enough throughout the prophets, given the frequent use of the image for the restoration of the people of God. Ideas similar to those found in Daniel 12 may be found in those texts that speak rather starkly of the restoration (or judgment) of dead bodies (cf. Isa. 66:24).[50] Frequent use of resurrection imagery also underscores God's activity and authority as Creator, since resurrection is a work of re-creation. This coheres with a worldview affirming the goodness and nobility of the created order, which will be a point seized consistently by early, orthodox Christians.[51]

THE PSALMS AND WISDOM LITERATURE

Though sometimes Luke speaks simply of the Law and Prophets (Luke 24:27), in Luke 24:44 Jesus adds the Psalms to this combination of texts, highlighting the importance of David for Luke's theology. In what follows I will focus on the Psalms, since these are explicitly mentioned by Jesus in 24:44, but will also consider other poetic and wisdom texts. Since we have seen specific texts from the Psalms that are employed in Acts in support of the resurrection, here I wish to highlight a few features of Luke's hermeneutical approach to the Psalms.

First, Luke understands David to be a prophet (Acts 2:30). This almost certainly means that Luke understood David to be the author of the psalms ascribed to him, as well as of some others that are not (e.g., Ps. 2:1–2 in Acts 4:25).[52] This prophetic character also corresponds to the predictive nature of the psalms quoted in support of the resurrection; David prophesies about the coming Christ (e.g., Acts 2:25).

Second, Luke finds in the Psalms promises of the Davidic covenant (e.g., Pss. 2:1–2, 7; 89:4; 132:11; cf. Acts 2:30–31; 4:25; 13:33), consistent with the promises of 2 Samuel 7. David as the anointed king of Israel is promised a son to sit on his throne (e.g., Psalm 110:1 [109:1 LXX] in Luke 20:41–44; Acts 2:34). Psalms about David and his kingdom (e.g., Ps. 61:6–7 [61:7–8 MT/60:7–8 LXX]) thus anticipate the consummate establishment of God's kingdom through the Son of David. For Luke, this kingdom is realized through the resurrection of Christ.

Third, the Son of David is the greater David whose deliverance is also greater (cf., e.g., Ps. 16:8–11 [15:8–11 LXX] in Acts 2:25–28; cf. 13:35; Ps. 118:22 [117:22 LXX] in Acts 4:11). Despite no known exceptions to the prin-

---

50. See, e.g., Elledge, *Resurrection of the Dead*, 68–71; John E. Goldingay, *Daniel*, WBC 30 (Nashville: Nelson, 1996), 308.

51. I discuss this briefly in ch. 8.

52. See also Rusam, *Das Alte Testament*, 267.

ciple that no one returns from Sheol,[53] the psalmist was confident that God would deliver him from Sheol (cf. Ps. 49:15 [49:16 MT/48:16 LXX]). David seems to have shared this hope. Yet David's sure hope of deliverance from death anticipated an even greater deliverance for the greater Son of David to come.

Looking beyond the Psalms, other poetic and wisdom texts may provide additional resurrection fodder for Luke. For example, whereas the righteous Christ was delivered from the birth-pains of death (Acts 2:24)—alluding to Psalm 18:6 (MT; 18:5 EVV); 116:3 (MT), which speak of the cords of death in Hebrew—Proverbs pictures sin as cords that entangle the unrighteous (5:22–23). This parallel, however, is not certain for Luke, since it relies on the verbal parallel of *ḥbl* in Hebrew (Ps. 18:6; 116:3; Prov. 5:22). Proverbs does, however, clearly contrast the way of the righteous unto life (e.g., 12:28; 15:24; 19:16, 23) with the way of the wicked unto the despair of death (e.g., 11:7; 19:16). Since Luke understands Christ as the fully righteous one (Luke 23:47; Acts 3:14; 7:52; 22:14) who is raised from death to life, he would plausibly see Jesus as the ultimate realization of righteousness-unto-life. Proverbs also assumes a future reckoning when injustice will be punished and the righteous rewarded.[54] In this light, it is significant that Luke speaks of the resurrected Christ as the final judge (Acts 17:30–31). A similar perspective is apparent in Qoheleth (cf. Eccles. 12:13–14). Finally, despite hesitations of many (and despite the difficulties of the Masoretic Text),[55] it seems evident that Job 19:25–27 was understood by some early Christians to speak of the hope of resurrection (*anastēsai to derma mou* [19:26 LXX]; cf. *1 Clem.* 26:3: *kai anastēseis tēn sarka mou tautēn*).[56] This has certainly been a prominent view in the history of Christian interpretation.[57]

53. See Richard Bauckham, *The Fate of the Dead: Studies on the Jewish and Christian Apocalypses*, NovTSup 93 (Leiden: Brill, 1998), 16, noted in Justin W. Bass, *The Battle for the Keys: Revelation 1:18 and Christ's Descent into the Underworld*, PBM (repr., Eugene, OR: Wipf & Stock, 2014), 22.

54. Following Bruce K. Waltke, *The Book of Proverbs: Chapters 1–15*, NICOT (Grand Rapids: Eerdmans, 2004), 104–7; cf. 73–76.

55. See, e.g., Martin-Achard, *From Death to Life*, 166–80; Wright, *Resurrection of the Son of God*, 98; K&D, 4:439–41; for the view that Job may be speaking of resurrection, see Bruce K. Waltke with Charles Yu, *An Old Testament Theology: An Exegetical, Canonical, and Thematic Approach* (Grand Rapids: Zondervan, 2007), 935–36, 968.

56. Following the Greek text of Michael W. Holmes, ed., *The Apostolic Fathers: Greek Texts and English Translations*, 3rd ed. (Grand Rapids: Baker Academic, 2007).

57. E.g., Calvin, *Inst.* 2.10.19; Francis Turretin, *Inst.* 12.5.19; 20.1.9; Herman Bavinck, *Reformed Dogmatics*, ed. John Bolt, trans. John Vriend, 4 vols. (Grand Rapids: Baker Academic, 2003–8), 4:602, 693; William Henry Green, *Conflict and Triumph: The Argument of the Book of Job Unfolded* (repr., Edinburgh: Banner of Truth, 1999), 95–105.

NONCANONICAL TEXTS

Though Luke does not explicitly quote any noncanonical texts in his exposition of the resurrection of Christ, it is clear that resurrection features prominently in many other texts shaped by scriptural traditions. To pursue this trajectory at any length would take us too far afield from the present task. But in brief, a number of noncanonical, early Jewish sources in the intertestamental period (and perhaps just after) indicate a rather widespread (though not to say uniform) belief in resurrection.[58] This insight corroborates Paul's statements in Acts that his belief in the resurrection accords with the traditions of his fathers (e.g., Acts 26:6–8). Some texts that seem particularly to reveal the Jewish resurrection ethos of the first century (and thus corroborate Paul's claims in Acts) include the resurrection assurances of the account of the martyrs in 2 Maccabees 7:9, 11, 22–23 (cf. *4 Macc.* 18:17) and texts from *1 Enoch* (e.g., esp. 22:13; 25:6; 90:33). Some texts seem rather explicitly to be drawing on scriptural language in support of the resurrection. We find this among Dead Sea scrolls such as the Messianic Apocalypse (4Q521 2 II, 12; cf. 7 + 5 II, 6), which Elledge has argued builds on Psalm 146:5–9; Isaiah 51:14; 61:1.[59] Also from Qumran are fragments of *Pseudo-Ezekiel* (4Q385, 4Q386, 4Q388), which refer to Ezekiel's vision of dry bones (Ezek. 37:1–14). Elledge has argued—following the DJD edition of Devorah Dimant—that these texts have in view physical resurrection, building on Genesis 1 and Isaiah 26:19.[60] Similarly, it is possible that the Hodayot (Thanksgiving Hymns) (1QH^a XIV, 32–37) include a resurrection message built on Daniel 12:1–3 and Isaiah 26:19.[61] Other texts could be considered as well (e.g., *2 Bar.* 50:1–3; *Sib. Or.* 4:181–82; *Liv. Pro.* 3:12; *L.A.B.* 3:10; *Pss. Sol.* 3:12; *T. Jud.* 25:1; *T. Benj.* 10:6–11[62]). An-

---

58. Surveys and discussions include Elledge, *Resurrection of the Dead*; Bauckham, "Life, Death, and the Afterlife," 80–95. I glean significantly from their discussions in what follows. See also Wright, *Resurrection of the Son of God*, 146–206; George W. E. Nickelsburg, *Resurrection, Immortality, and Eternal Life in Intertestamental Judaism and Early Christianity*, rev. ed., HTS 56 (Cambridge, MA: Harvard University Press, 2006), 23–218; Lidija Novakovic, *Raised from the Dead according to Scripture: The Role of Israel's Scripture in the Early Christian Interpretations of Jesus' Resurrection*, JCT 12 (London: Bloomsbury T&T Clark, 2012), 82–113; Kevin L. Anderson, *"But God Raised Him from the Dead": The Theology of Jesus's Resurrection in Luke-Acts*, PBM (repr., Eugene, OR: Wipf & Stock, 2006), 48–91; Alexey Somov, *Representations of the Afterlife in Luke-Acts*, LNTS 556 (London: Bloomsbury T&T Clark, 2017), 115–25, 133–34.

59. Elledge, *Resurrection of the Dead*, 160–64.

60. See Elledge, *Resurrection of the Dead*, 164–69, following Devorah Dimant, *Qumran Cave 4:XXI*, DJD 30 (Oxford: Clarendon, 2001), 35–37 (see also pp. 27, 34). Dimant's edition also includes transcriptions and translations. For 4Q521, see Émile Puech, ed., *Qumrân Grotte 4:XVIII*. DJD 25 (Oxford: Clarendon, 1998), 10–11, 23–24.

61. See Elledge, *Resurrection of the Dead*, 153–57.

62. The references to *T. Jud.* and *T. Benj.* come esp. from Haacker, "Das Bekenntnis des Paulus," 446. Regardless of the provenance one chooses for each of these writings, my point

other recent argument suggests that the practice of *ossilegium* (i.e., gathering bones in an ossuary) reflects a common Jewish belief in resurrection.[63] Less explicit, though perhaps in the tradition of Old Testament wisdom literature, Wisdom speaks of the immortality of righteousness (*dikaiosynē gar athanatos estin*, 1:15; cf. 1:12–16; 2:21–24), and eternal life for the righteous (*dikaioi de eis ton aiōna zōsin*, 5:15).[64]

Despite a diversity of views, noncanonical traditions such as these underscore the prominence of the scriptural framework for the resurrection message in a first-century Jewish-Christian context. As Elledge has rightly concluded, "Expressions of resurrection are deeply rooted in the language of earlier prophetic hopes."[65] This is also consistent with what we find in later rabbinic wrings, which find the resurrection in the Scriptures (e.g., *m. Sanh.* 10:1; *b. Sanh.* 90b; *Sifre* Deut. 32; *Mek. R. Ishmael*, Shirata 1; *Tg. Ps.-J.* Genesis 3:19).[66]

The upshot of this survey is that Paul's assertions that the resurrection accords with the traditions of his fathers is supported not only by biblical texts but also by a number of other texts (including later texts) from a similar religious background. Such texts corroborate the feasibility of Paul's claim.

Conclusion: The Resurrection and the Old Testament in Luke-Acts

This survey on the resurrection in the Old Testament is not designed to provide a full biblical theology of resurrection in the Old Testament.[67] My aims have been more modest—to illustrate some plausible ways that Luke may have found the resurrection in the Old Testament. For Luke the Old Testament clearly speaks of the resurrection of Christ,[68] and this explains the frequent appeal made to the Old Testament in support of the resurrection in Acts. It is no surprise that (as we saw in ch. 1) Daniel Marguerat concludes that Luke sees the resurrection to be the lever that opens the Scriptures.[69] Similarly,

---

is simply that such statements reveal the ethos of a worldview plausible for the Lukan Paul's in the first century. I make no argument either way whether Luke was Jew or gentile; the point stands regardless.

63. Cohen-Matlofsky, "Resurrection," 101–27.

64. See also Wis. 16:13–14.

65. Elledge, *Resurrection of the Dead*, 201.

66. Following Wright, *Resurrection of the Son of God*, 197–98; Elledge, *Resurrection of the Dead*, 202–4; Levenson, *Resurrection and the Restoration*, 23–32.

67. For more-systematic discussions of resurrection belief in the OT, see, e.g., Calvin, *Inst.* 2.10.19, 21–23; Turretin, *Inst.* 20.1.9–11; Geerhardus Vos, *Reformed Dogmatics*, trans. and ed. Richard B. Gaffin Jr., 5 vols. (Bellingham, WA: Lexham, 2012–16), 5:269–70.

68. Cf. Turretin, *Inst.* 12.7.45.

69. Marguerat, "Quand la résurrection se fait clef de lecture de l'histoire (Luc-Actes)," in *Resurrection of the Dead: Biblical Traditions in Dialogue*, ed. Geert Van Oyen and Tom

David Peterson has observed that for Luke, to understand the Scriptures is to understand the resurrection.[70] Luke's explicit statements are important for understanding his approach to the resurrection in the Old Testament, which is surely not limited to his explicit quotations.

Wrestling with this wide-ranging approach to the resurrection in the Old Testament is important for understanding Luke's more general appeals to Scripture. These often come at key junctures in Acts, when the apostles are forced to give a defense of their belief in the resurrected Christ. This is particularly the case with Paul's defenses in the second half of Acts, where we find very few explicit citations to the Old Testament.[71] Paul's consistent defense is that he has said nothing out of accord with the Scriptures or his ancestral traditions. An appreciation of this point helps us grasp an important, but often overlooked, aspect of Luke's purpose in Acts.

The Resurrection and the Purpose(s) of Acts

Thus far I have argued that Luke derives his resurrection message from the Old Testament, and that the resurrection of Christ fulfills the Scriptures. In this section I will build on this insight to discuss how Luke uses the manifest scriptural grounding of the resurrection as an *apologia pro scriptura* ("defense of Scripture") in Acts. To appreciate this is to appreciate one of the key purposes of Acts.

The Purpose(s) of Acts

There is no shortage of possibilities for the purpose of Acts.[72] A number of options have gained prominence.[73] A traditional, and still popular, position is

Shepherd, BETL 249 (Leuven: Peters, 2012), 189; cf. Marguerat, *Les Actes des Apôtres*, 2 vols., CNT 5a–b (Geneva: Labor et Fides, 2007–15), 1:97.

70. Peterson, "Resurrection Apologetics and the Theology of Luke-Acts," in *Proclaiming the Resurrection: Papers from the First Oak Hill College Annual School of Theology*, ed. Peter M. Head (Carlisle: Paternoster, 1998), 31; see also Howard Clark Kee, *Good News to the Ends of the Earth: The Theology of Acts* (London: SCM; Philadelphia: Trinity Press International, 1990), 7.

71. Though note the climactic force of Isa. 6:9–10 in Acts 28:25–27.

72. A related issue is the genre of Acts. For surveys of genre, see Sean A. Adams, "The Genre of Luke and Acts: The State of the Question," in *Issues in Luke-Acts: Selected Essays*, ed. Sean A. Adams and Michael W. Pahl, GH 26 (Piscataway, NJ: Gorgias, 2012), 97–120; Osvaldo Padilla, *The Acts of the Apostles: Interpretation, History and Theology* (Downers Grove, IL: IVP Academic, 2016), 52–72; Alan J. Bale, *Genre and Narrative Coherence in the Acts of the Apostles*, LNTS 514 (London: Bloomsbury T&T Clark, 2015), 48–66.

73. On the purpose of Acts see the surveys, which I have used in what follows, in Craig S. Keener, *Acts: An Exegetical Commentary*, 4 vols. (Grand Rapids: Baker Academic, 2012–15), 1:435–58; Robert Maddox, *The Purpose of Luke-Acts*, FRLANT 126 (Göttingen: Vandenhoeck & Ruprecht, 1982), 19–23; C. K. Barrett, *A Critical and Exegetical Commentary on the Acts of*

that Acts is an apologetic for Christianity (or, perhaps, an *apologia pro ecclesia*).[74] Others have swung the pendulum the other way and suggest that Acts is an apologetic for the Roman Empire.[75] Additional possibilities are an apologetic for Paul,[76] an apologetic for the gentile mission,[77] the confirmation of the gospel message,[78] a pattern for Christian discipleship,[79] or "the story of God's apocalypse in the mission of the church."[80] Broadly speaking, it is virtually certain Luke writes with an apologetic intent. However, it would be an oversimplification to think that Luke had only *one* purpose in mind; he almost certainly had several reasons for writing,[81] and likely more than one *apologetic* purpose.

Additionally, if Acts is to be understood as a form of historical monograph, which is quite likely, Luke's brand of historiography is much influenced by Old Testament historiography. It may even be that Luke is positioning himself as a writer of *biblical* history.[82] All told, it is likely best to conclude that

---

the Apostles, 2 vols., ICC (Edinburgh: T&T Clark, 1994–98), 2:xlix–liii; Abraham J. Malherbe, "'Not in a Corner': Early Christian Apologetic in Acts 26:26," *SecCent* 5 (1985–86): 193–94; Alexandru Neagoe, *The Trial of the Gospel: An Apologetic Reading of Luke's Trial Narratives*, SNTSMS 116 (Cambridge: Cambridge University Press, 2002), 4–22.

74. E.g., Burton Scott Easton, *Early Christianity: The Purpose of Acts, and Other Papers*, ed. Frederick C. Grant (London: SPCK, 1955), 41–57. Easton relates his argument that Luke desires to present Christianity as a *religio licita* ("permitted religion") to its relationship to Judaism— the early Christians were simply another Jewish party (46); see similarly Ernst Haenchen, *The Acts of the Apostles: A Commentary*, trans. R. McL. Wilson (Westminster: Philadelphia, 1971), 630, 693–94 (noted in Malherbe, "'Not in a Corner,'" 194n4). Haenchen relates this argument specifically to the resurrection (*Acts of the Apostles*, 693–94).

75. See Keener, *Acts*, 1:443–44; Barrett, *Commentary on the Acts*, 2:l.

76. E.g., A. J. Mattill Jr., "The Purpose of Acts: Schneckenburger Reconsidered," in *Apostolic History and the Gospel: Biblical and Historical Essays Presented to F. F. Bruce on His 60th Birthday*, ed. W. Ward Gasque and Ralph P. Martin (Grand Rapids: Eerdmans, 1970), 108–22.

77. See Keener, *Acts*, 1:436–41.

78. W. C. van Unnik, "The 'Book of Acts' the Confirmation of the Gospel," *NovT* 4 (1960): 26–59; cf. Neagoe, *Trial of the Gospel*, 14–16.

79. H. Douglas Buckwalter, *The Character and Purpose of Luke's Christology*, SNTSMS 89 (Cambridge: Cambridge University Press, 1996), 265.

80. C. Kavin Rowe, *World Upside Down: Reading Acts in the Graeco-Roman Age* (Oxford: Oxford University Press, 2009), 10.

81. This point echoes Keener, *Acts*, 1:435–58.

82. See especially Brian S. Rosner, "Acts and Biblical History," in *The Book of Acts in Its Ancient Literary Setting*, ed. Bruce W. Winter and Andrew D. Clarke, vol. 1 of *The Book of Acts in Its First Century Setting*, ed. Bruce W. Winter (Grand Rapids: Eerdmans, 1993), 65–82. Also note the argument that Acts is salvation history. James D. G. Dunn, "The Book of Acts as Salvation History," in *Heil und Geschichte: Die Geschichtsbezogenheit des Heils und das Problem der Heilsgeschichte in der biblischen Tradition und in der theologischen Deutung*, ed. Jörg Frey, Stefan Krauter, and Hermann Lichtenberger, WUNT 1/248 (Tübingen: Mohr Siebeck, 2009), 385–401, following Jacob Jervell, "The Future and the Past: Luke's Vision of Salvation History and Its Bearing on His Writing of Salvation History," in *History, Literature, and Society in the Book of Acts*, ed. Ben Witherington III (Cambridge: Cambridge University Press, 1996), 110.

Acts is a form of historical monograph written for a variety of apologetic purposes.[83]

If Acts is to be viewed as a work of apologetic historiography, which is strongly influenced by biblical historiography, I propose that Acts may also serve as an apologetic for Scripture. More specifically, in Acts Luke points to the resurrection not simply as a key to salvation or salvation history but also as a key indication of the truthfulness of Scripture.[84] By implication, this also serves as a defense for Paul and the Christian faith. An *apologia pro scriptura* is, in other words, at the same time an *apologia pro ecclesia* and an *apologia pro evangelio*.[85] This conclusion is built on several interconnected points.

First, Luke emphasizes throughout Luke and Acts that the resurrection is a scriptural message. Therefore, for one to understand the resurrection one must understand the Scriptures; likewise, to understand the Scriptures one must believe in the resurrection.[86]

Second, it therefore follows that those with knowledge of the Scriptures *should* believe in the resurrection (cf. Acts 26:27), and specifically in the resurrection of Jesus.[87] This assumption is manifested in Jesus's critique of the Sadducees' lack of understanding the scriptural basis for the resurrection (Luke 20:37), in the scribes' approval of Jesus's scriptural defense of the resurrection (v. 39), in the many Old Testament citations used in support of the resurrection (e.g., Ps. 16:8–11 [15:8–11 LXX] in Acts 2:25–28), and in the universal references to the Scriptures with respect to the resurrection (e.g., Luke 24:25–27, 44–47; Acts 24:14–15; 26:22–23, 27). Far from being a rejection of the scriptural heritage, the resurrection is the consummate fulfillment of the hopes of the Scriptures.[88] The early Christian belief in the resurrection is presented by Luke as the proper interpretation of the Scriptures. It is therefore fitting that Luke contrasts the Sadducees' disbelief in

83. This stands close to Keener, *Acts*, 1:114–15, 161–64, 435–58.

84. Cf. Dupont, "L'utilisation apologétique," 245–82, esp. 274–80, which focuses on "la passion et la résurrection de Jésus" (245); Dupont's argument is noted in Rusam, *Das Alte Testament*, 20n125. On resurrection and apologetic, see also Padilla, *Acts of the Apostles*, 227–36.

85. The phrase *apologia pro evangelio* is used by Neagoe, *Trial of the Gospel*, e.g., 22–24.

86. See also the perspective of Daniel Marguerat, "Luc-Actes: La résurrection à l'oeuvre dans l'histoire," in *Résurrection: L'après-mort dans le monde ancien et le Nouveau Testament*, ed. Odette Mainville and Daniel Marguerat, MdB 45 (Geneva: Labor et Fides, 2001), 213–14.

87. On the use of Scripture as "proof" in Acts, see Stephen S. Liggins, *Many Convincing Proofs: Persuasive Phenomena Associated with Gospel Proclamation in Acts*, BZNW 221 (Berlin: de Gruyter, 2016).

88. See, e.g., Keener, *Acts*, 1:449–50, 459–91; Barrett, *Commentary on the Acts*, 2:xlix–l; Herman N. Ridderbos, *The Speeches of Peter in the Acts of the Apostles* (London: Tyndale, 1962), 25–26; Jervell, *Theology of the Acts*, 90–91; cf. Martin Dibelius, *Studies in the Acts of the Apostles*, ed. Heinrich Greeven, trans. Mary Ling and Paul Schubert (London: SCM, 1956), 173–74.

the resurrection with the Pharisees' belief in the resurrection (Acts 23:8). What is more, we have seen in Acts some of the Pharisees among the early followers of Jesus (15:5)—including Paul himself (23:6; 26:5)—which must mean they were persuaded of the resurrection of Jesus. Gamaliel even defends on theoretical grounds allowing the apostolic preaching of the resurrection (5:34–39), which may also reflect the Pharisaic belief in the resurrection. For Luke the resurrection underscores not simply the truthfulness of Scripture but the Lord's faithfulness to his covenant promises.

Third, if the resurrection is properly understood as the true fulfillment of the covenant promises of God, then this consequently legitimizes Christianity. In this way, Luke's *apologia pro scriptura* also provides an *apologia pro ecclesia* and an *apologia pro evangelio*.

The Resurrection, the Scriptures, and Paul's Defenses

If the resurrection serves as an *apologia pro scriptura* in Acts, then one would expect to find both the resurrection and the Scriptures emphasized in legal contexts in Acts. This is indeed what we find, especially with respect to Paul's defenses (Acts 21–26).

I return now to Paul's defenses (see further in ch. 3) to illustrate how Luke's resurrection emphasis provides not only a defense of Paul and the church but also a defense of Scripture.

RESURRECTION DEFENSE IN JERUSALEM

Paul's appeal to the scriptural foundation of the resurrection is clear in his appearance before the Sanhedrin after he was seized at the temple in Jerusalem (22:30–23:10). Just before he is brought before the council, Paul's encounter with the resurrected Christ features prominently in his speech at the temple (22:1–21). It is when Paul is brought before the Sanhedrin that he makes his calculated move to focus on the resurrection (23:6), though we have seen sufficient indication throughout Acts that this was not simply an insincere rhetorical ploy. Instead, Paul truly was on trial for the resurrection, and this message is not out of accord with Scripture. Paul's fidelity to the law is contrasted with the conduct of the high priest, who strikes Paul in violation of the law (vv. 2–3; cf. Lev. 19:15).[89] Moreover, when Paul realizes he has spoken sharply to the high priest, he backtracks, since he knows the Scripture

---

89. See Eckhard J. Schnabel, *Acts*, ZECNT (Grand Rapids: Zondervan, 2012), 926; Joseph A. Fitzmyer, *The Acts of the Apostles: A New Translation with Introduction and Commentary*, AB 31 (New York: Doubleday, 1998), 717.

instructs God's people to respect their appointed leaders (v. 5; cf. Exod. 22:28 [22:27 MT/LXX]). Even in this Paul is demonstrated to be faithful to the law, which is consistent with his appeal to the antiquity of the resurrection hope (v. 6). Again Paul—who believes in the resurrection—is more faithful to the Scriptures than even the teachers of Israel.[90]

Resurrection Defense in Caesarea

We find much more detail in Paul's defenses in Caesarea. Before Paul arrives in Caesarea, the tribune Claudius Lysias writes a letter about the arriving prisoner. In his assessment the cause of the uproar was a matter of dispute about the Jewish law (23:29). Claudius Lysias particularly relates this to Paul's appearance before the council (Claudius Lysias himself was present; cf. vv. 10, 28), where the resurrection was key (v. 6).[91] The letter from Claudius Lysias again emphasizes the scriptural dimensions of the resurrection. If the debate before the council concerned the Jewish law, and if Paul's discussion before the council centered on the resurrection, then the crux of the debate must have been the relationship of the Jewish law to the resurrection.[92]

In Paul's defense before Felix he speaks of both his belief in Scripture and his belief in the resurrection. Paul worships the God of his fathers, and he believes everything in the Law and the Prophets, which includes the hope of the resurrection (Acts 24:14–15; cf. Luke 24:25–27, 44–47). Paul presses this point further when he echoes in 24:21 his statement before the council in 23:6: Paul was on trial because of the resurrection of the dead. By this point it is clear, especially in light of Paul's explicit invoking of Scripture before Felix, that it is not only Paul who is on trial. For if Paul is on trial for the resurrection of the dead (23:6; 24:21), and if the resurrection is the fulfillment of Scripture, then Scripture itself is also on trial. For Paul to defend the legitimacy of the resurrection is at the same time for him to defend the truthfulness of Scripture.

Paul sounds a similar note before Festus, where he again insists that he has done nothing contrary to the law of the Jews (25:8). This is echoed in Festus's explanation to Herod Agrippa II, that Paul's case revolves around the resurrection and its relationship to the Jewish religion (v. 19). If we desire more confirmation at this point, Luke does not disappoint. At the opening of his defense, Paul speaks of his life in Judaism and of his knowledge of God's promises to his fathers (26:4–8)—which must include the Scriptures. What is more, Paul's

---

90. Cf. Jervell, *Theology of the Acts*, 90–91; Jervell, *Luke and the People of God: A New Look at Luke-Acts* (Minneapolis: Augsburg, 1972), 170.

91. The debate may also have involved the role of the gentile mission (cf. 22:21).

92. See the engaging discussion in Rowe, *World Upside Down*, 62–71.

mention of the hope in God's promises (vv. 6–7) refers to the resurrection, since Paul summarizes the matter in 26:8: it should not be incredible to believe that God raises the dead. At stake in the debate on the resurrection is God's faithfulness to his covenantal promises. Paul's encounter with the risen Christ is again recounted (vv. 12–18), illustrating again the centrality of the resurrection.

After this Paul returns to the Scriptures in the final words of his defense: his message of salvation in the resurrected Christ is simply the fulfillment of the Law and the Prophets; for it was necessary for the Christ to die and rise from the dead and for the message of salvation to go forth to the gentiles (26:22–23). This is consistent with the three ways in which Scripture had to be fulfilled in Luke 24:44–47. Though Paul does not invoke any specific texts to support his claim,[93] by this point in Acts Paul has made the scriptural foundation for the resurrection sufficiently clear (e.g., Acts 13:16–41). Additionally, Luke has included a number of other scriptural defenses of the resurrection throughout Luke and Acts, so that by the time readers arrive at Acts 26, the scriptural contours of the resurrection are abundantly clear. In response to Paul's defense, Festus interjects that Paul is crazy (26:24); Paul responds by again appealing to the scriptural basis for the resurrection. If Agrippa believes in the prophets, then he ought to believe in the resurrection (v. 27). Neither here nor elsewhere (cf. 18:12–17) can Paul's resurrection message be shown to be out of accord with Scripture.

Resurrection Defense in Rome

Though Luke's account of Paul's stay in Rome does not include an appearance before Caesar, we nevertheless find Paul again defending his resurrection message from Scripture to the local Jewish leaders (28:17–20). Again Paul emphasizes that he has not transgressed the traditions of their fathers (v. 17), and he points to his belief in the hope of Israel as the reason for his chains (v. 20).

As we have seen throughout this study, the hope of Israel is a frequent, metonymic way for Paul to speak of the resurrection, which comes by means of the resurrection of Christ (cf. 23:6; 24:15; 26:6–7). It is therefore fitting to conclude this discussion of Paul's defenses with the summary insight that the resurrection of Christ marks the realization of the hope of Israel (28:20).

Conclusion

Luke's emphasis on the resurrection is at the same time an emphasis on the truthfulness of Scripture and on God's faithfulness to his covenant promises.

---

93. See, e.g., Barrett, *Commentary on the Acts*, 2:1166.

The resurrection demonstrates definitively that the Scriptures are true. To believe in the resurrection is to believe in the message of the Scriptures; to resist the resurrection message is to resist the scriptural message. The Scriptures are on trial in Acts, and it is the resurrection that preeminently provides Luke with his *apologia pro scriptura*.

If the resurrection is indeed so central to Luke's theology, then we need to consider the voice of Acts in concert with other New Testament voices in the context of the canon. To what degree is Luke distinctive? To what degree is he consistent with other New Testament witnesses? And what traces of this do we find in early Christian theology more broadly? These questions will be addressed in the final chapter of this study.

8

The Resurrection and Acts
in Early Christianity

In this final chapter I will consider the role of Acts in the emergence of the New Testament canon and the possibility that Acts plays an indispensable role contributing to the coherence of the canon. I will also consider how the centrality of the resurrection in Acts aids in that coherence.

Second, and closely related, I consider the role of the resurrection in the emergence of orthodox Christian theology. What did the resurrection say about early Christian belief? And what insights do we continue to gain from the centrality of the resurrection both in Acts and in early Christian theology more broadly?

Acts, the Resurrection, and the Canon of the New Testament

What is the role of Acts in the context of the emerging New Testament canon in the first few centuries of the common era? On the one hand, it seems that Acts did not fit neatly into or alongside any *one* corpus of books. Yet what might from one angle be viewed as awkwardness—does Acts fit anywhere?[1]—may better be seen as the *flexibility* of Acts. In other words, it is not so much that Acts struggles to find a home alongside other New Testament writings,

1. See C. K. Barrett, *A Critical and Exegetical Commentary on the Acts of the Apostles*, 2 vols., ICC (Edinburgh: T&T Clark, 1994–98), 2:lxix–lxx.

but Acts actually coheres remarkably well with several corpora of New Testament writings.

To be sure, to raise issues of canon is to wade into a number of debated waters. My argument does not necessitate a particular position for the date of the canon. Instead, my focus is on the place of Acts in collections of early Christian sacred texts; I consider the role of Acts in the context of the *emerging* canon. My aim here is twofold. First, I seek to demonstrate that Acts was remarkably flexible in its relation to other New Testament books in its early reception—it was read alongside the Gospels, the Pauline Epistles, and the Catholic Epistles. Second, I propose that this versatility of Acts is significantly attributable to the *content* of Acts, with the theological shadow of the resurrection looming large.

The Flexibility of Acts in the Canon

First to be considered is the flexibility of Acts in relation to other collections of New Testament books. Acts does not only appear in one, set place in early canonical lists, but is found in various positions.[2] It has often been argued that Acts plays an important, unifying role in the New Testament canon. According to David Trobisch, "No other writing connects the collection of units of the New Testament as well as Acts."[3] Similarly, David E. Smith writes that Acts is a literary unifier in the New Testament, which goes a long way to explaining its canonicity.[4] For Smith, the pneumatology of Acts is particularly important.[5] Smith recognizes the important precedent played by Adolf von Harnack in this regard.[6] Harnack argued that Acts provided a bridge between the emerging collection of the Gospels and Pauline Epistles.[7] Harnack goes

2. See Edmon L. Gallagher and John D. Meade, *The Biblical Canon Lists from Early Christianity: Texts and Analysis* (Oxford: Oxford University Press, 2017), 48–49.

3. Trobisch, *The First Edition of the New Testament* (Oxford: Oxford University Press, 2000), 84.

4. Smith, *The Canonical Function of Acts: A Comparative Approach* (Collegeville, MN: Liturgical Press, 2002), 9, 17. See also Smith, "Acts and the Structure of the Christian Bible," in *Contemporary Studies in Acts*, ed. Thomas E. Phillips (Macon, GA: Mercer University Press, 2009), 93–102.

5. See Smith, *Canonical Function of Acts*, 40. Smith also presents a diagram in which he presents Acts' functions as the focal point for the entire biblical canon (102). Smith's approach is echoed approvingly by David P. Moessner, "The Role of Acts in Interpreting the New Testament," *SacScript* 15 (2017): 260–71.

6. Smith, *Canonical Function of Acts*, 15, noting Adolf von Harnack, *The Origin of the New Testament and the Most Important Consequences of the New Creation*, trans. J. R. Wilkinson (New York: Macmillan, 1925), 104.

7. Harnack, *Origin of the New Testament*, 63–68; cf. 104; cf. Harnack, *History of Dogma*, trans. Neil Buchanan, 3rd ed., 4 vols. (New York: Dover, 1961), 1:162.

further: "Acts is in a certain way the key to the understanding of the idea of the New Testament of the Church, and has given it the organic structure in which it stands before us."[8] Though not agreeing entirely with Harnack, Jens Schröter believes that this view of Acts as a unifying factor in the canon is justified.[9] A similar note on the role of Acts in the canon as we know it today is sounded by Gregory Goswell, who echoes Smith's view that Acts is a sort of "glue" that secures the theological unity of the New Testament.[10]

I don't intend to follow every claim of the authors surveyed above. Instead, I will argue that we can appreciate this importance and flexibility of Acts in the way that Acts serves as the sequel to Luke and the other three Gospels, provides a fuller portrait of Paul than we encounter in the Pauline Epistles, and is a fitting introduction to the Catholic Epistles.

ACTS AND THE GOSPELS

It scarcely needs to be argued that Acts is in some sense a sequel to the Gospel of Luke. It is readily acknowledged that the two books share a common author, that Acts rounds out the narrative of Luke by picking up where the Gospel ends (i.e., the ascension of Jesus), and that Acts opens by addressing (the same) Theophilus. The prologue of Luke (1:1–4) most likely serves as a prologue to Acts as well.[11] Beyond this, many events in Acts are either parallel events to what one finds in Luke[12] or the fulfillment of things spoken in Luke that awaited a fuller realization. Three examples will suffice. First, the healings enacted by the hands of Peter and Paul recall the healings of Jesus, in whose name Peter and Paul minister (cf., e.g., Acts 3:6, 16; 4:10; 16:18; 19:13, 17). Second, promises such as that Christ will be a light to the gentiles, which is introduced in Luke (cf. Luke 2:32), find fuller realization in Acts (e.g., Acts 1:8; 9:15; 10:45; 11:1, 18; 13:47–48; 15:12, 14, 17, 19). Third,

---

8. Harnack, *Origin of the New Testament*, 67.

9. Schröter, *From Jesus to the New Testament: Early Christian Theology and the Origin of the New Testament Canon*, trans. Wayne Coppins, BMSEC (Waco: Baylor University Press, 2013), 294.

10. Goswell, "The Place of the Book of Acts in Reading the NT," *JETS* 59 (2016): 80–82, following Smith, "Acts and the Structure of the Christian Bible," 93 (cf. 95). See also the concise summary in Darian R. Lockett, *Letters from the Pillar Apostles: The Formation of the Catholic Epistles as a Canonical Collection* (Eugene, OR: Pickwick, 2017), 123–35.

11. So, e.g., Craig S. Keener, *Acts: An Exegetical Commentary*, 4 vols. (Grand Rapids: Baker Academic, 2012–15), 1:90, 93, 104, 173.

12. See, e.g., Michael D. Goulder, *Type and History in Acts* (London: SPCK, 1964); Charles H. Talbert, *Literary Patterns, Theological Themes and the Genre of Luke-Acts*, SBLMS 20 (Missoula, MT: Scholars Press and SBL, 1974); James R. Edwards, "Parallels and Patterns between Luke and Acts," *BBR* 27 (2017): 485–501.

the scriptural rationale for Jesus's statements in Luke 24:25–27, 44–47 finds much fuller exposition in Acts.

Acts is a sequel to more than just the Gospel of Luke. Inasmuch as Acts provides the apostolic exposition of the resurrection, it is the necessary sequel to *all four* canonical Gospels.[13] The resurrection is just as necessary for salvation as is the death of Jesus. Yet after his resurrection, the disciples' experiences with Jesus were different. Jesus came and went in a more mysterious manner. Jesus did not engage in an extensive teaching ministry after his resurrection. This explains the need for the apostles—if the resurrection is necessary for salvation, and if Jesus himself did not teach openly after his resurrection, then we may expect to find that later teaching focuses not just on the life and death of Jesus but on his resurrection (and ascension).[14] And indeed, this is consistent with the choice of and role of the disciples as *witnesses* to the resurrection. Acts helps us see just how central the resurrection was in early Christianity. Acts—along with the Epistles and Revelation—fills out the details for what the resurrection of Christ means, details that we encounter with comparative brevity in the Gospels.

It is also worth noting that in the manuscript tradition Acts is found bound with the Gospels most likely in $\mathfrak{P}^{45}$,[15] and possibly also in $\mathfrak{P}^{53}$.[16] Given that Acts follows the Gospels in some early canonical lists,[17] it may be surprising that $\mathfrak{P}^{45}$ and $\mathfrak{P}^{53}$ are the only two clear examples of Acts being physically bound with the Gospels among the earliest strata of manuscript evidence. Yet, significantly, these may be the earliest manuscripts of Acts we have.[18]

13. See also the discussions in C. Kavin Rowe, "History, Hermeneutics, and the Unity of Luke-Acts," in *Rethinking the Unity and Reception of Luke and Acts*, ed. Andrew F. Gregory and C. Kavin Rowe (Columbia: University of South Carolina Press, 2010), 43–48; Moessner, "Role of Acts," 267.

14. Cf. Brandon D. Crowe, *The Last Adam: A Theology of the Obedient Life of Jesus in the Gospels* (Grand Rapids: Baker Academic, 2017), 192–97.

15. On this point, the hesitation of Schröter, *From Jesus to the New Testament*, 285, 289, 293—especially regarding the fragmentary nature of $\mathfrak{P}^{45}$—seems unnecessary.

16. See Goswell, "Place of the Book of Acts," 70. $\mathfrak{P}^{53}$ is fragmentary; only portions of Matthew and Acts are extant. Cf. Larry W. Hurtado, *The Earliest Christian Artifacts: Manuscripts and Christian Origins* (Grand Rapids: Eerdmans, 2006), 37n90; Philip Wesley Comfort, *A Commentary on the Manuscripts and Text of the New Testament* (Grand Rapids: Kregel Academic, 2015), 66. Majuscule 0189, which contains Acts 5:3–21, is also likely early (third or fourth c.). See Christopher M. Tuckett, "The Early Text of Acts," in *The Early Text of the New Testament*, ed. Charles E. Hill and Michael J. Kruger (Oxford: Oxford University Press, 2012), 172–74; Kurt Aland and Barbara Aland, *The Text of the New Testament*, trans. Erroll F. Rhodes, 2nd ed. (Grand Rapids: Eerdmans, 1989), 104–5.

17. E.g., Muratorian Fragment, Eusebius of Caesarea, Amphilochius of Iconium, Third Synod of Carthage, and possibly Gregory Nazianzen. See table 8.1 below and sources noted there.

18. Thanks to Charles Hill for this observation.

Despite the relative dearth of manuscript evidence, few would debate the close thematic connections between Acts and the Gospels.

ACTS AND THE PAULINE EPISTLES

Despite the likelihood of the hyphen in Luke-Acts, this should not be taken to imply that Acts was read *only* alongside Luke. Acts is also closely correlated to the Pauline Epistles in the early church. The reasons are several. Acts provides much more historical context for Paul's travels, and for Paul's biography, than do his letters.[19] Moreover, Paul—who wrote more canonical letters than any other New Testament author—dominates the final half (or more) of Acts.[20] In this vein, it has also been argued that Acts provides the necessary apostolic credentials for Paul.[21] As we saw in the previous chapter, Acts has even been understood as an apologetic for Paul.[22]

The early manuscript evidence, however, provides little physical evidence of Acts being bound physically with the Pauline Epistles. Though the evidence is fragmentary, I am not aware of any early manuscript (i.e., second to third centuries, before the great majuscules) in which the Pauline Epistles are bound with Acts.[23] Historically some have suggested that the New Testament canon first appeared as Gospel + Apostle, with Acts joining the two together[24]—thus serving as what Henry Cadbury called the "arch, lintel, or keystone between the two old columns of the canon."[25] This is an intriguing possibility and would underscore the important role of Acts in the early church, but it also seems to require that the emergence of Acts as authoritative came later than the Fourfold Gospel and Pauline Epistles.[26]

---

19. On correlations between Acts and Paul's letters, see, e.g., Keener, *Acts*, 1:197, 221–57; Joseph A. Fitzmyer, *The Acts of the Apostles: A New Translation with Introduction and Commentary*, AB 31 (New York: Doubleday, 1998), 134–35. For one example see 2 Tim. 3:11 (cf. Acts 13:45–14:23).

20. Although, indeed, Acts should be considered the ongoing work of the risen and ascended Lord Jesus, still, Paul looms larger than any other earthly character in Acts.

21. Harnack, *Origin of the New Testament*, 52–53, 64–65; Henry J. Cadbury, *The Book of Acts in History* (London: Adam and Charles Black, 1955), 143.

22. See discussion in Keener, *Acts*, 1:223–24.

23. See the helpful chart in Hurtado, *Earliest Christian Artifacts*, appendix 1; see also Schröter, *From Jesus to the New Testament*, 293. Hebrews was typically included among the Pauline Letters. On the role of Hebrews in the NT canon, see Gregory Goswell, "Finding a Home for the Letter to the Hebrews," *JETS* 59 (2016): 747–60.

24. See, e.g., Harnack, *Origin of the New Testament*, 42–68; Cadbury, *Book of Acts in History*, 142–43.

25. Cadbury, *Book of Acts in History*, 143.

26. For the argument that the Fourfold Gospel and Paul were in place by the mid-second century, see Charles E. Hill, *Who Chose the Gospels? Probing the Great Gospel Conspiracy* (Oxford: Oxford University Press, 2010); Hill, "A Four-Gospel Canon in the Second Century?

Despite the apparent dearth of manuscript evidence for binding Acts with the Pauline Epistles, there is no doubt that Acts was often read in close conjunction with the Pauline Letters from an early date. Already in Irenaeus Acts is linked closely with Paul, which is not surprising given that Irenaeus was convinced Acts was penned by Luke, the traveling companion of Paul.[27] The same is true for Tertullian.[28] For example, Irenaeus argues that "Luke was inseparable from Paul, and his fellow-labourer in the Gospel."[29] He continues, building on the "we" passages in Acts, that "as Luke was present at all these occurrences, he carefully noted them down in writing," and his presence with Paul is again confirmed in 2 Timothy 4:10–11 and Colossians 4:14.[30]

Additionally, Acts comes just before Paul's Letters (and just after the Gospels) in the Muratorian Fragment, in Eusebius's discussion of *homologoumena*, in Amphilochius of Iconium, at the Third Synod of Carthage, possibly in Gregory Nazianzen, and in the Vulgate.[31] There is, in other words, much precedent for reading Acts alongside Paul—especially in the West[32]—and for reading Acts as a bridge between the Gospels and Paul. This understanding corresponds to the position of Acts that will be familiar to readers of Western Bibles today. Yet this was apparently not the most common correlation made in the earliest manuscript traditions, particularly in the East. Instead, Acts is more closely associated with the Catholic Epistles.

ACTS AND THE CATHOLIC EPISTLES

According to much of the early manuscript evidence, especially in the East, the most frequent collocation is made with Acts and the Catholic Epistles.[33]

Artifact and Arti-fiction," *EC* 4 (2013): 310–34; Graham N. Stanton, "The Fourfold Gospel," *NTS* 43 (1997): 317–46; Harry Y. Gamble, *Books and Readers in the Early Church: A History of Early Christian Texts* (New Haven: Yale University Press, 1995), 58–64; cf. Hurtado, *Earliest Christian Artifacts*, 35–40, 73–80.

27. Irenaeus, *Haer.* 3.1.1; 3.14.1.

28. See esp. *Marc.* 4.2.

29. Irenaeus, *Haer.* 3.14.1 (*ANF* 1:437).

30. Irenaeus, *Haer.* 3.14.1 (*ANF* 1:437).

31. See Gallagher and Meade, *Biblical Canon Lists*, 99–183; Goswell, "Place of the Book of Acts," 75, which notes the helpful lists in Samuel Berger, *Histoire de la Vulgate: Pendant les premiers siècle du moyen age* (Paris: Éditions Berger-Levrault, 1893), 339–41. See also table 8.1 below.

32. Cf. David R. Nienhuis, *Not by Paul Alone: The Formation of the Catholic Epistle Collection and the Christian Canon* (Waco: Baylor University Press, 2007), 86–87.

33. See, e.g., Goswell, "Place of the Book of Acts," 77–80; Nienhuis, *Not by Paul Alone*, 77; Trobisch, *First Edition of the New Testament*, 25–28; cf. Wolfgang Grünstäudl, "Was lange währt. . . : Die Katholischen Briefe und die Formung des neutestamentlichen Kanons," *EC* 7 (2016): 87–93.

Even where Acts follows the Gospels, it is most closely related to the Catholic Epistles, forming the so-called *Praxapostolos*. Among the manuscripts, $\mathfrak{P}^{74}$ manifests the order of Acts + Catholic Epistles.[34] Beyond this, Trobisch has argued that $\mathfrak{P}^{45}$—which is most often taken to contain the Fourfold Gospel and Acts—may instead be an example of the Fourfold Gospel plus the Praxapostolos.[35] However, this view has not thus far turned the tide of scholarly opinion on the contents of $\mathfrak{P}^{45}$.[36] More extensive evidence for the Praxapostolos may be found among the great Greek majuscules containing the New Testament, including Sinaiticus, Vaticanus, and Alexandrinus.[37] One also encounters the Praxapostolos in Cyril of Jerusalem, the thirty-ninth Festal Letter of Athanasius (367), Canon 59[/60] from the Synod of Laodicea (ca. 363),[38] and Epiphanius of Salamis.[39] In light of the clear and consistent proclivity of this combination of texts in the manuscript tradition, Trobisch has argued that the Praxapostolos was part of a "master copy" for how the New Testament ought to be constructed.[40] In a similar vein, Robert Wall has argued that Acts explains the final shape of the Catholic Epistles collection, which features James as the first book.[41]

Wall and Trobisch agree in several respects and have mounted interesting arguments for the role and the prominence of the Praxapostolos in the early church.[42] However, it is unclear that we find one *authoritative* or *normative order* of books in the New Testament (or even of subcollections therein).[43]

---

34. See Trobisch, *First Edition of the New Testament*, 28. Also noted in Larry W. Hurtado, "P45 as an Early Christian Artefact: What It Reflects about Early Christianity," *Teologisk Tidsskrift* 4 (2016): 305n26. Meade and Gallagher (*Biblical Canon Lists*, 44) observe that $\mathfrak{P}^{74}$ is comparatively late (seventh c.).

35. Trobisch, *First Edition of the New Testament*, 32–39.

36. See recently Hurtado, "P45 as an Early Christian Artefact," 291–307, esp. 293, 305n31.

37. See Trobisch, *First Edition of the New Testament*, 24–25. Trobisch also adds that we are uncertain about Ephraemi Rescriptus because of its fragmentary nature (25). See also the helpful survey of F. F. Bruce, *The Canon of Scripture* (Downers Grove, IL: IVP Academic, 1988), 205–6.

38. On the textual question regarding Canon 59, see Gallagher and Meade, *Biblical Canon Lists*, 131. Some identify this as Canon 60; cf. Bruce M. Metzger, *The Canon of the New Testament: Its Origin, Development, and Significance* (Oxford: Clarendon, 1987), 210, 312; Nienhuis, *Not by Paul Alone*, 76; Bruce, *Canon of Scripture*, 80.

39. For information on these sources and their contents, see Gallagher and Meade, *Biblical Canon Lists*, 70–173; Nienhuis, *Not by Paul Alone*, 76–79; Bruce, *Canon of Scripture*, 208–15; Metzger, *Canon of the New Testament*, appendix 4; Goswell, "Place of the Book of Acts," 77–80.

40. Trobisch, *First Edition of the New Testament*, 24–44.

41. Wall, "A Unifying Theology of the Catholic Epistles: A Canonical Approach," in *The Catholic Epistles and Apostolic Tradition*, ed. Karl-Wilhelm Niebuhr and Robert W. Wall (Waco: Baylor University Press, 2009), 22.

42. See also Schröter, *From Jesus to the New Testament*, 289–90.

43. Cf. also Richard Bauckham, *James*, NTR (London: Routledge, 1999), 116.

As we have seen, the Praxapostolos was not the only order of books in the ancient church, whether in the East or in the West.[44] Early Christian manuscripts exhibit a variety of orders,[45] even if the Catholic Epistles typically come after Acts and before the Pauline Epistles in most Greek manuscripts.[46] It is the *books* of the New Testament that are authoritative, and not a particular *order* of the books. Thus, though I have no doubt that we find helpful wisdom in the ancient and contemporary structures of the canon (along with the happy encouragement not to overlook any portion of the canon), this feature of reception history is more suggestive than determinative.[47] Nevertheless, one need not hesitate to acknowledge how frequently Acts is tied to the Catholic Epistles, which is replicated in many modern editions of the New Testament, such as those from Tregelles, Westcott and Hort, and more recently the Tyndale House Greek New Testament.

When we probe the reasons for the relative prominence of the Praxapostolos, several can be suggested. Perhaps most obviously, the characters one encounters in Acts correspond to the traditional authors of the Catholic Epistles (James, Peter, John, Jude).[48] Moreover, these characters, by and large (who have already been introduced to readers of the Gospels), dominate the opening chapters of Acts, and it is only after they appear in Acts that readers encounter Paul.[49] Along similar lines, it could be that the order of mission in Acts—to the Jew first, then to the gentile—corresponds to the Jewish character of early Christianity epitomized in the Jerusalem/pillar apostles of the Catholic Epistles (i.e., James the brother of Jesus, Peter, and John; cf. Gal. 2:9). It is thus only after we meet the Jerusalem apostles and read about the message coming to Israel that we meet Paul, who represents the mission to the gentiles.

It is also possible that the prominence of the Praxapostolos manifests the early emergence of both a Fourfold Gospel collection and a Pauline Letters

44. Cf. Nienhuis, *Not by Paul Alone*, esp. 85–90; Grünstäudl, "Was lange währt," 92.

45. A point noted, in conversation with Trobisch's thesis, by Hurtado, "P45 as an Early Christian Artefact," 293.

46. Metzger, *Canon of the New Testament*, 295–96, noted in Nienhuis, *Not by Paul Alone*, 77.

47. For a more positive assessment on the shape of the canon as a hermeneutical guide, see Matthew Y. Emerson, *Christ and the New Creation: A Canonical Approach to the Theology of the New Testament* (Eugene, OR: Wipf & Stock, 2013); cf. also Lockett, *Letters from the Pillar Apostles*.

48. Jude is most likely among the brothers of Jesus mentioned in Acts 1:14; cf. Cadbury, *Book of Acts in History*, 144.

49. See also Trobisch, *First Edition of the New Testament*, 84–85; Nienhuis, *Not by Paul Alone*, 79, 88; cf. Robert W. Wall, "The Acts of the Apostles: Introduction, Commentary, and Reflections," in vol. 10 of *NIB* (Nashville: Abingdon, 2002), 31.

collection. If these two collections were already in circulation by the mid-second century, then grouping Acts with the Catholic Epistles may have emerged out of necessity as well, since adding Acts to either a Fourfold Gospel collection or a Pauline Epistles collection would likely have been too large for a single codex.[50]

Table 8.1
Place of Acts in Select Manuscripts and Canon Lists

Manuscript / Canon List	Date	Position of Acts
$\mathfrak{P}^{45}$	3rd c.	Bound with Gospels; fragmentary (Praxapostolos less likely)
$\mathfrak{P}^{53}$	3rd c.	Bound with Matthew; fragmentary
$\mathfrak{P}^{74}$	7th c.	Praxapostolos; fragmentary
Codex Sinaiticus	4th c.	Praxapostolos, follows Pauline Epistles
Codex Vaticanus	4th c.	Praxapostolos, follows Gospels, precedes Pauline Epistles
Codex Alexandrinus	5th c.	Praxapostolos, follows Gospels, precedes Pauline Epistles
Codex Amiatinus (Vulgate)	8th c.	Follows Gospels, precedes Pauline Epistles
Muratorian Fragment	2nd c. [?]	Follows Gospels, precedes Pauline Epistles
Origen of Alexandria, Hom. Jos.	3rd c.	Follows Catholic Epistles (which follow the Gospels), precedes Pauline Epistles
Eusebius of Caesarea, Hist. eccl.	4th c.	Follows Gospels, precedes Pauline Epistles
Gregory Nazianzen, Carm.	4th c.	Follows Gospels (or Gospels + Revelation),[†] precedes Pauline Epistles
Amphilochius of Iconium, Iambi	4th c.	Follows Gospels, precedes Pauline Epistles
Vulgate	4th c.	Follows Gospels, precedes Pauline Epistles
Cyril of Jerusalem, Cat.	4th c.	Praxapostolos, follows Gospels, precedes Pauline Epistles
Athanasius of Alexandria, Ep. fest. 39	4th c.	Praxapostolos, follows Gospels, precedes Pauline Epistles
Cheltenham List (Mommsen Catalogue)	4th c.	Follows Pauline Epistles; separate from Catholic Epistles and from Gospels
Clermont List (insert in Codex Claromontanus)	4th c.	Follows Revelation; precedes Shepherd of Hermas

50. Thanks to Charles Hill who first suggested this to me. Cf. Cadbury, *Acts in History*, 144; Schröter, *From Jesus to the New Testament*, 293; Trobisch, *First Edition of the New Testament*, 26. On sizes of ancient codices, see Eric G. Turner, *The Typology of the Early Codex* (Philadelphia: University of Pennsylvania Press, 1977), 82–84; Gamble, *Books and Readers*, 67–69.

Manuscript / Canon List	Date	Position of Acts
Synod of Laodicea, Canon 59[/60]	4th c.	Praxapostolos, follows Gospels, precedes Pauline Epistles
Third Synod of Carthage*	4th c.	Follows Gospels, precedes Pauline Epistles
Epiphanius of Salamis, *Pan*.	4th c.	Praxapostolos, follows Pauline Epistles
Apostolic Canons	4th c.	Final book listed; separated from Catholic Epistles by two letters of Clement (*1–2 Clement?*) and eight books of the Constitutions
Jerome, *Epist*.	4th c.	Praxapostolos, follows Pauline Epistles

Source: For the information in this chart I have relied primarily on Gallagher and Meade, *Biblical Canon Lists*. See also Metzger, *Canon of the New Testament*, appendix 4; Bruce, *Canon of Scripture*; Moessner, "Role of Acts," 261–63. Information on papyri and majuscules can be found in NA[28].

† See Gallagher and Meade, *Biblical Canon Lists*, 146n377.

* In 397 this council approved the *Breviarium Hipponense*, which was a summary of the 393 Synod of Hippo. See the discussion in Gallagher and Meade, *Biblical Canon Lists*, 222–23.

Acts, the Resurrection, and the Unity of the New Testament

I have argued that Acts is flexible in its role in the canon. At this juncture I shall consider the way that the resurrection of Jesus in Acts is one important, though often overlooked, factor that unites Acts theologically to the other corpora of the New Testament.[51] To this end, I will trace out how I believe the flexibility of Acts in the canon is corroborated by the thematic unity of Acts with the various corpora, particularly in relation to the resurrection.

RESURRECTION IN THE GOSPELS AND ACTS

The resurrection is narrated toward the end of all four Gospels. (Though the end of Mark is more complicated, the resurrection is not in doubt.)[52] Yet it receives scant exposition. Much fuller explanations of the resurrection's scriptural rationale and implications are found in Acts. The resurrection is the vindication of the perfect obedience of Jesus and is proof that he was not bested by his enemies.[53] Without the resurrection, those who put Jesus to death would seem to have silenced him. However, the resurrection narratives

51. Cf. Floyd V. Filson, *Jesus Christ the Risen Lord: A Biblical Theology Based on the Resurrection* (Nashville: Abingdon, 1956), esp. 29, 48–49; John Webster, "Resurrection and Scripture," in *Christology and Scripture: Interdisciplinary Perspectives*, ed. Andrew T. Lincoln and Angus Paddison, LNTS 348 (London: T&T Clark, 2007), 138–55.

52. Even if one takes the ending of Mark to be at 16:8 (which I do), Jesus has predicted his resurrection three times (Mark 8:31; 9:31; 10:34), he has promised to meet the disciples in Galilee after he is raised up (14:28), the tomb is empty, and the angel tells the women that Jesus has risen, just as he said he would (16:6–7).

53. On this point, see Crowe, *Last Adam*, 193–95.

bespeak the righteousness of Jesus and his message. The focus on the resurrection of Jesus in Acts, therefore, is not unexpected in light of the endings of the Gospels. In this sense, the resurrection message of Acts serves as a fitting sequel to the Gospels and binds together the apostolic message in Acts with Jesus's victory over death in the Gospels. Acts gives us "the rest of the story."

Resurrection in Paul and Acts

The resurrection is also immensely important for the Pauline Epistles. I agree with the seminal work of Richard Gaffin that Paul's exposition of the resurrection of Jesus in 1 Corinthians 15 is of central significance for Paul's christological-soteriological outlook.[54] We also encounter the resurrection at the beginning of Romans, where Jesus is said to be "set apart as the Son of God in power according to the Spirit of holiness by his resurrection from the dead" (1:4). Here, as I have argued, Jesus's glorification is related to his status as both Christ and Lord. What Paul sets forth in epistolary form in Romans 1:3–4 is expounded in narrative fashion in Acts.[55] The role of the Holy Spirit is also instructive: in Acts the Holy Spirit is the Spirit of the resurrected and exalted Christ (cf. Acts 2:33), and the Spirit is consistently associated with the resurrected and exalted Christ in the Pauline corpus (Rom. 1:4; 8:9–11; 1 Cor. 15:45; 2 Cor. 3:17; 1 Tim. 3:16).

Additionally, the message of the gospel—which is closely related to the resurrection of Jesus in Romans 1:4—is rooted in the Old Testament Scriptures (v. 2), as I argued in chapter 7. The prominence of the resurrection in Paul's preaching in Acts accords with the Pauline corpus.[56] If we include Hebrews in the discussion of the Pauline letter collection (since Hebrews was often grouped with the Pauline Letters), then it would also fit this paradigm. Hebrews also assumes the importance of Jesus's resurrection (e.g., Heb. 1:3; 6:2; 7:16; 8:1–2; 11:35). Indeed, as David Moffitt has argued in his study of the resurrection in Hebrews, it would indeed be strange—in light of the broader teaching of the New Testament and Paul's Letters in particular—if the resurrection were *not* important in Hebrews.[57]

---

54. See Gaffin, *The Centrality of the Resurrection: A Study in Paul's Soteriology* (Grand Rapids: Baker, 1978).

55. See also 1 Tim. 3:16; 2 Tim. 1:10; 2:8, 11–12; 4:1.

56. Cf. Stanley E. Porter, *The Paul of Acts: Essays in Literary Criticism, Rhetoric, and Theology*, WUNT 1/115 (Tübingen: Mohr Siebeck, 1999), 167; Keener, *Acts*, 1:256.

57. Moffitt, *Atonement and the Logic of Resurrection in the Epistle to the Hebrews*, NovTSup 141 (Leiden: Brill, 2011), 1–2; cf. William L. Lane, "Living a Life in the Face of Death: The Witness of Hebrews," in *Life in the Face of Death: The Resurrection Message of the New Testament*, ed. Richard N. Longenecker, MNTS (Grand Rapids: Eerdmans, 1998), 264–68.

Resurrection in the Catholic Epistles and Acts

The resurrection serves as a close thematic link between Acts and both the Gospels and the Pauline corpus. The Catholic Epistles include much less direct exposition of the resurrection. And yet, on a careful reading, the resurrection is an important part of the theological topography of these letters as well. The resurrection of Jesus is explicitly mentioned in 1 Peter (1:3, 21; 3:21),[58] but it is presupposed in various other ways throughout the Catholic Epistles.

One of the shared features among the Catholic Epistles is the view that Jesus will return.[59] And if Jesus is going to return, he must presently be alive— resurrected after his suffering. For example, in James we read that Christ is the Lord whose return is imminent (James 5:7–8; cf. 1:12; 2:1). The "salvation ready to be revealed in the end time" (1 Pet. 1:5) also refers to the return of Christ, as a comparison with 1 Peter 1:7, 13 makes clear ("the revelation of Jesus Christ"). First Peter also motivates its readers by holding out the hope of the crown of glory that will appear when the chief Shepherd is revealed (5:4; cf. James 1:12). In 2 Peter the return of Christ is even more apparent, as the entire letter promotes godly ethics in light of eschatology (see esp. 2 Pet. 3). Additionally, the role of the transfiguration in 1:16–18 serves, as it does in the Gospels, as proof of the glory of Jesus that was revealed after his resurrection. In 2 Peter, the transfiguration also clearly anticipates the glorious return of Christ (cf. 1:19).

The Johannine epistles likewise include the promise that Jesus, who is eternal life (1 John 1:2), will return (2:28; 3:2; 4:17). Moreover, Wall has pointed out that the things that John has seen and heard (1 John 1:1–3) recall the similar statement of Peter and John in Acts 4:19–20.[60] If this is indeed a valid parallel, then it is significant that what was seen and heard in Acts is the resurrected Jesus. Additionally, the language of touching with hands in 1 John 1:1 may well recall the tactile experience of Thomas with the resurrected Lord in John 20:26–28, and the "seeing" recalls 20:29.[61]

In Jude 14 the coming of the Lord with thousands of his holy ones refers to the return of Christ.[62] Similarly, the exhortation in Jude 21 to wait for

---

58. Cf. Robert W. Wall, "Acts and James," in *The Catholic Epistles and Apostolic Tradition*, ed. Karl-Wilhelm Niebuhr and Robert W. Wall (Waco: Baylor University Press, 2009), 144.

59. For more exposition on the themes from the Catholic Epistles covered here, see Brandon D. Crowe, *The Message of the General Epistles in the History of Redemption: Wisdom from James, Peter, John, and Jude* (Phillipsburg, NJ: P&R, 2015).

60. Wall, "Unifying Theology of the Catholic Epistles," 25; cf. Wall, "Acts and James," 129–30.

61. I am indebted to Charles Hill for this latter observation, along with the possibility that the perfect tense in 1 John 4:2 bespeaks a continuing, fleshly existence of the resurrected Christ.

62. See Richard J. Bauckham, *Jude, 2 Peter*, WBC 50 (Nashville: Nelson, 1983), 96.

the mercy of the Lord Jesus Christ, yielding eternal life, also has in view the return of Christ. In Acts the return of Christ is implied in many passages but is expressly stated in Acts 1:11. And as I argued in chapter 5, the resurrection and return of Christ are both part of one movement of glory.

In addition to the focus on Christ's return, Jesus is associated with glory and identified as Lord in the Catholic Epistles. One of the clearest texts in this regard is James 2:1, where Jesus is identified as the Lord of glory.[63] Glory is frequently associated with Jesus in his resurrected state in the New Testament, as is the term Lord. Thus, it is fitting that Jesus is identified as *Lord* of *glory* in James 2:1.[64] A similar collocation of imagery is found in 2 Peter 3:18 (cf. 1:17). Jude speaks of the glory of the presence of the Lord, and the Spirit of glory and of God in 1 Peter 4:14 recalls the glory of Christ in his estate of suffering, which will in turn yield glory (v. 13). More extensively, Lord is one of the most frequent identifiers for Jesus in the Catholic Epistles, and the exposition of this title in Acts (in relation to the resurrection) is determinative for how readers of the Catholic Epistles are to understand Jesus's lordship.

These parallels between Acts and the Catholic Epistles pertaining to the resurrection raise the possibility that Acts provides the necessary framework for understanding the Lord whom we encounter in the Catholic Epistles.[65] The Catholic Epistles are brief and thus can only briefly invoke the broader context of the work of Jesus. It could be that one reason the Praxapostolos was a common collection in the early church is that the proper context for understanding the glorious, returning lordship of Jesus Christ in the Catholic Epistles is found in the expositions of the resurrection in Acts, which gives the rationale for Jesus as the returning judge (cf. Acts 1:11; 10:42; 17:31).

Resurrection in Acts and Revelation

More briefly, the thematic unity of Acts and the book of Revelation through the lens of the resurrection is also strong. From the outset of Revelation, Jesus is identified as the glorious one who has conquered death (1:5, 12–18). It is the risen Christ who reigns and guides his church in Revelation, and it is the risen Christ who reigns and guides his church in Acts.

---

63. On the Greek construction (*tou kyriou hēmōn Iēsou Christou tēs doxēs*), see Ralph P. Martin, *James*, WBC 48 (Waco: Word, 1988), 59–60. *Pace* Dale C. Allison Jr., *A Critical and Exegetical Commentary on the Epistle of James*, ICC (New York: Bloomsbury T&T Clark, 2013), 382–84, which argues for omitting *hēmōn Iēsou Christou*.

64. *Pace* Markus Vinzent, *Christ's Resurrection in Early Christianity and the Making of the New Testament* (Farnham, Surrey: Ashgate, 2011), 74–75; Allison, *Commentary on the Epistle of James*, 35.

65. Cf. Wall, "Acts and James," 129.

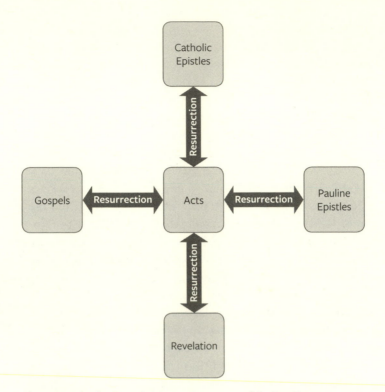

Figure 8.1 Role of Acts in relation to major corpora of the New Testament, noting the resurrection as a key ligament

Conclusion: Acts and the Resurrection in the Canon

I have argued two main points in this section on Acts in the context of the canon. First, Acts serves a unifying function in the New Testament canon, manifested in the various places it occupies in the manuscript traditions. Acts relates equally well to the Gospels, Pauline Epistles, and Catholic Epistles.

Second, thematically the resurrection is one specific, important link between Acts and these various subcollections within the New Testament canon. Acts serves as the conclusion to the Gospels and contextualizes the epistles (whether Pauline or Catholic) and their authors.[66]

In sum, the resurrection is central to the apostolic doctrine in Acts. And if Acts provides the proper context for reading the epistles, then it follows

66. See also David Trobisch, "The Book of Acts as a Narrative Commentary on the Letters of the New Testament," in *Rethinking the Unity and Reception of Luke and Acts*, ed. Andrew F. Gregory and C. Kavin Rowe (Columbia: University of South Carolina Press, 2010), 119–27 (esp. 121).

that the resurrection of Christ provides part of the necessary framework for interpreting all the New Testament epistles.

Acts, the Resurrection, and Early Christian Theology

As we conclude, I would like to consider briefly some ways that the physical resurrection of Jesus underscores the distinctiveness of the early Christian message. Acts itself is a witness to the centrality of belief in the physical resurrection in early Christianity, and we find evidence for this belief in the New Testament canon. Theologian Herman Bavinck put it well: "From the beginning the resurrection of Christ was an enormously important constituent of the faith of the church: without that faith it would never have started."[67] Indeed, in many ways the bodily resurrection encapsulates the distinctiveness of the Christian message in the ancient world and manifests a key point of unity among early orthodox Christians. The vine of early Christianity rose on the trellis of shared theological convictions; the physical resurrection was one of those key convictions.[68] Several implications are entailed in this doctrine.

First, the resurrection underscores the nature of orthodox Christology. In distinction from docetic and gnostic tendencies, the resurrection states that Jesus is true man, with a real body, who physically suffered and was physically raised from the dead.[69] This corresponds to the importance of the words and actions of Jesus in history, which are a concern of Acts (cf. 10:36–38) and

---

67. Bavinck, *Reformed Dogmatics*, ed. John Bolt, trans. John Vriend, 4 vols. (Grand Rapids: Baker Academic, 2003–8), 3:438.

68. See also Adolf Schlatter, "The Theology of the New Testament and Dogmatics," in *The Nature of New Testament Theology: The Contribution of William Wrede and Adolf Schlatter*, ed. and trans. Robert Morgan, SBT 2/25 (Naperville, IL: Alec R. Allenson, 1973), 140; Simon Gathercole, "*E Pluribus Unum*? Apostolic Unity and Early Christian Literature," in *The Enduring Authority of the Christian Scriptures*, ed. D. A. Carson (Grand Rapids: Eerdmans, 2016), 407–55. This is not, of course, to deny the presence of divergent views in the early church; it is simply to affirm that orthodox Christianity held to certain beliefs—including the bodily resurrection of Jesus—as constitutive of its identity; see esp. on the *regula fidei* below.

69. Cf. Charles H. Talbert, *Luke and the Gnostics: An Examination of the Lucan Purpose* (Nashville: Abingdon, 1966), which succeeds in showing the relevance for Luke-Acts in refuting Gnosticism, though it is unlikely that Gnosticism (however one defines it) had crystallized by the end of the first century; cf. Michael J. Kruger, *Christianity at the Crossroads: How the Second Century Shaped the Future of the Church* (Downers Grove, IL: IVP Academic, 2018), 7, 121–29. See also Richard Glöckner, OP, *Die Verkündigung des Heils beim Evangelisten Lukas*, WSAMA.T 9 (Mainz: Matthias-Grünewald-Verlag, 1975), 206. Irenaeus affirmed the bodily resurrection of Jesus (e.g., *Haer.* 3.16.6), in contrast to several nonorthodox teachings that denied the resurrection, including, e.g., those of Simon, Menander, Carpocrates (*Haer.* 1.23.5; 2.31.2); cf. Francis Turretin, *Inst.* 20.1.6–7.

early Christian theologians.[70] Paraenesis is tethered to the work of Christ in history.

Second, the resurrection affirms the goodness of creation. As one who is truly human, Jesus is raised and exalted in a human body. There is no need to escape from creation or from the physical body. As the second and last Adam, Jesus's abiding presence as the resurrected one affirms God's created order.[71] This further has implications for Christian ethics—what is done in and with the body is important in light of the resurrection.[72] Cyril of Jerusalem stated the matter starkly: "The root of all good works is the hope of the Resurrection."[73]

Third, the resurrection underscores the abiding normativity of the Old Testament and the continuity of God—the same God who created the world according to the Old Testament is the God of the New Testament. Neither the Old Testament nor the God of the Old Testament is to be avoided, dismissed, or rejected;[74] creation and indeed the Old Testament itself (which speaks of the goodness of creation) are confirmed to be good in Christ's resurrection. Though many hermeneutical questions must be addressed, we have seen in Acts that failure to believe the resurrection is failure to believe the Scriptures rightly. It is thus not surprising that many in the early days of the church who rejected the physical resurrection of Christ rejected the Old Testament (or its proper interpretation) as well; the two go hand in hand.

Fourth, the resurrection of Christ points to the public nature of Christianity. The resurrection of Christ was not something relegated to a corner (cf. Acts 26:26); it was public.[75] In contrast, many gnostic writings have more of a secretive or private character to them.[76] The resurrection of Christ as

---

70. E.g., Ign., *Eph.* 7:2; 18:2; 19:2; *Magn.* 9:1; *Rom.* 7:3; *Trall.* 9:1–10:1; cf. 2:1; *Phld.* (salutation); *Smyrn.* 1:1–3:3; 12:2; Pol., *Phil.* 2:2; *2 Clem.* 1:1–8; 9:5; *Ep. Apost.* 1.

71. Cf., e.g., Athenagoras, *Res.* 3, 11, 13–14; Irenaeus, *Haer.* 1.10.1; 3.18.7; 3.22.4; 3.23.1, 7; 5.19.1; *Epid.* 6; Tertullian, *Res.* 6–11.

72. E.g., Acts 17:30–31; 24:15, 25; 2 Cor. 5:10; 1 Thess. 4:3–8; *1 Clem.* 26:1; 28:1 (cf. *1 Clem.* 25–26); *2 Clem.* 9:1–11; Pol., *Phil.* 2:1–2; 5:2–3; 6:2; *Barn.* 21:1; *Herm.* 60:1–2; Irenaeus, *Haer.* 2.29.2; Athenagoras, *Res.* 11, 18–23, 25; Tertullian, *Res.* 14–17; see also Larry W. Hurtado, *Destroyer of the gods: Early Christian Distinctiveness in the Roman World* (Waco: Baylor University Press, 2016), 161–63 (cf. 31). Cf. C. Kavin Rowe, *World Upside Down: Reading Acts in the Graeco-Roman Age* (Oxford: Oxford University Press, 2009), 121, 153.

73. Cyril of Jerusalem, *Cat.* 18.1 (*NPNF*[2] 7:134), noted in Turretin, *Inst.* 20.1.6; cf. 20.1.18.

74. See Tertullian, *Marc.* 4–5; *Res.* 39; cf. Irenaeus, *Haer.* 3.12.2–4, 11; Athanasius, *Inc.* 1.4; 8.4–10.

75. E.g., 1 Cor. 15:3–8; Irenaeus, *Haer.* 3.1.1; cf. 1.1.3; 1.3.1; 3.15.1; 5.15.2; Athanasius, *Inc.* 23; Rowe, *World Upside Down*, 86.

76. E.g., Gos. Thom. *incipit*; Gos. Jud. 33; Acts Thom. 39. See the discussions in Bart D. Ehrman and Zlatko Pleše, *The Apocryphal Gospels: Texts and Translations* (Oxford: Oxford University Press, 2011), 306–7, 391; Günther Bornkamm, "The Acts of Thomas," trans. R.

a public event distinguishes early, orthodox Christian belief from many un-orthodox views.

Fifth, the resurrection of Christ is the firstfruits of the general, bodily resurrection (1 Cor. 15:20). Though one certainly encounters a variety of eschatological particulars in the early church—such as chiliasts and nonchiliasts[77]—the orthodox agreed on a future, bodily resurrection.[78] This resurrection emphasis of early Christianity proved to be a distinguishing tenet between the Christians and many of their neighbors.[79] Acts shows us that the resurrection of Christ anticipates and ensures the general resurrection, which has been a distinguishing mark of Christianity from the beginning. As Kavin Rowe has memorably stated, "The way the Christian story runs to its end is unintelligible without the bodily resurrection of Jesus."[80]

The importance of the resurrection—both christologically and more generally—is also evident in the rule of faith (*regula fidei*), which explicitly mentions Jesus's resurrection, and in some formulations specifically identifies the day of the resurrection as the third day (cf. 1 Cor. 15:4).[81] This *rule of faith* is exposited in Irenaeus's *Demonstration*[82] and is also foundational in *Against Heresies* (1.10.1; cf. 3.12.6). In both works Irenaeus emphasizes the resurrection's rootedness in the Old Testament, and he frequently refers to Acts in this regard (cf. *Epid.* 36–41, 62, 83–85, 96; *Haer.* 3.12).[83] This is consistent with Irenaeus's theology of Jesus as a second Adam (cf. *Haer.* 3.18). Irenaeus also speaks a great deal about Acts, the resurrection, and theological

McL. Wilson, in *New Testament Apocrypha*, by Edgar Hennecke, ed. Wilhelm Schneemelcher (Philadelphia: Westminster, 1965), 2:426–27.

77. See Charles E. Hill, *Regnum Caelorum: Patterns of Millennial Thought in Early Christianity*, 2nd ed. (Grand Rapids: Eerdmans, 2001).

78. See Hill, *Regnum Caelorum*, 4, 84, 99–100, 107, 172–73, 191, 250; J. N. D. Kelly, *Early Christian Doctrines*, 5th rev. ed. (Peabody, MA: Prince Press, 2007), 459–85.

79. See Tertullian, *Res.* 1, 3, 39; Arthur Darby Nock, *Conversion: The Old and the New in Religion from Alexander the Great to Augustine of Hippo* (Oxford: Clarendon, 1933), 247–49; N. T. Wright, *The Resurrection of the Son of God*, COQG 3 (Minneapolis: Fortress, 2003), 551; C. F. Evans, *Resurrection and the New Testament*, SBT 2/12 (Naperville, IL: Alec R. Allenson, 1970), 7–10; Robert Louis Wilken, *The Christians as the Romans Saw Them*, 2nd ed. (New Haven: Yale University Press, 2003), 104, 161.

80. Rowe, *One True Life: The Stoics and Early Christians as Rival Traditions* (New Haven: Yale University Press, 2016), 222.

81. For statements of the rule of faith, see Everett Ferguson, *The Rule of Faith: A Guide*, Cascade Companions (Eugene, OR: Cascade, 2015), esp. 1–15. References to the third day are found in Tertullian, *Praescr.* 13; *Virg.* 1.3–4; Hippolytus, *Noet.* 1.

82. See *Epid.* 3, 6; Stephen O. Presley, "The Rule of Faith and Irenaeus's *Demonstration* of the Order and Connection of the Scriptures," *ORA* (2010): 48–66.

83. Some of these are noted by Andrew Gregory, "Irenaeus and the Reception of Acts in the Second Century," in *Contemporary Studies in Acts*, ed. Thomas E. Phillips (Macon, GA: Mercer University Press, 2009), 48n3.

integrity of Scripture in *Against Heresies* 3.12. He is particularly concerned to emphasize that the apostles did not preach another God (3.12.2–14); the apostolic message is more ancient than the teachings of Marcion, Valentinus, or other heretical groups (3.12.5, 12).[84] Even before Irenaeus we appear to find references to Acts among the early fathers, many of which refer to the resurrection of Christ.[85] For example, a widely discussed allusion to Acts (and the resurrection) in Polycarp reads *hon ēgeiren ho theos, lysas tas ōdinas tou hadou* ("whom God raised, having loosed the birth-pains of Hades," *Phil.* 1:2), reflecting Acts 2:24 (*hon ho theos anestēsen, lysas tas ōdinas tou thanatou,* "whom God raised, having loosed the birth-pains of death").[86] Likewise, it is striking that this passage—even if it is an allusion to Acts—references an *Old Testament text* predicting the resurrection of Christ.[87]

It would be unnecessary and anachronistic to limit the centrality of the resurrection to the book of Acts or to trace early Christian belief in the resurrection solely back to the book of Acts. The resurrection was much more pervasive in early Christianity. Cyril of Alexandria saw the resurrection to be the key to understanding the whole Bible,[88] and Celsus ridiculed Christians in

---

84. Marcion's canon seems not to have included Acts (Tertullian, *Marc.* 5.2). So Judith M. Lieu, *Marcion and the Making of a Heretic: God and Scripture in the Second Century* (Cambridge: Cambridge University Press, 2015), 430n89; Schröter, *From Jesus to the New Testament*, 282–83, 293–94.

85. E.g., Pol., *Phil.* 1:2 (cf. Acts 2:24); Ign., *Smyrn.* 3:3 (cf. Acts 10:41); *1 Clem.* 18:1 (Acts 13:22); *2 Clem.* 20:5 (Acts 3:15); *Ep. Apost.* 15, 31, 34. One might also include the longer ending of Mark (16:9–20). For further discussion on early possible allusions to Acts, including some of the ones listed here, see Andrew Gregory, *The Reception of Luke and Acts in the Period before Irenaeus: Looking for Luke in the Second Century*, WUNT 2/169 (Tübingen: Mohr Siebeck, 2003), 299–351; Barrett, *Commentary on the Acts*, 1:33–48; cf. 2:lxiii–lxxi; Keener, *Acts*, 1:396–97; Ton H. C. van Eijk, *La résurrection des morts chez les Pères Apostoliques*, ThH 25 (Paris: Beauchesne, 1974), 77n74; Frank Dicken, "The Author and Date of Luke-Acts: Exploring the Options," in *Issues in Luke-Acts: Selected Essays*, ed. Sean A. Adams and Michael W. Pahl, GH 26 (Piscataway, NJ: Gorgias, 2012), 21–24. For additional early references to the resurrection, see Everett F. Harrison, "The Resurrection of Jesus Christ in the Book of Acts and in Early Christian Literature," in *Understanding the Sacred Text: Essays in Honor of Morton S. Enlin on the Hebrew Bible and Christian Beginnings*, ed. John Reumann (Valley Forge, PA: Judson, 1972), 217–31; Wright, *Resurrection of the Son of God*, 480–552.

86. Polycarp's wording *hadou* (Hades) in place of *thanatou* (death) could either be evidence of what we find in some (Western) witnesses to Acts 2:24, or it may reflect the Greek of Ps. 17:6 (18:5 EVV); or both. See also Gregory, *Reception of Luke and Acts*, 313–14. Polycarp mentions the resurrection in several other passages (*Phil.* 1:2; 2:1–3; 5:2; 6:2; 7:1; 12:2). In *Phil.* 7:1 we find the collocation of resurrection and judgment, which are both present in the resurrection context of Acts 17:31 (cf. 24:15, 25).

87. Cf. Tertullian, *Res.* 39: "The Acts of the Apostles, too, attest the resurrection. Now the apostles had nothing else to do, at least among the Jews, than to explain the Old Testament and confirm the New" (*ANF* 3:573).

88. See Robert Louis Wilken, "St. Cyril of Alexandria: The Mystery of Christ in the Bible," *ProEccl* 4 (1995): 459, 471, 473–74.

general for their belief in the resurrection.[89] Neither am I arguing that Acts and its resurrection message was written directly to combat Gnosticism. Instead, early Christian belief in the resurrection is seen with particular emphasis and clarity in Acts, which lends itself well to be used as a defense of the bodily resurrection. The resurrection is particularly important in the speeches of Acts.

The implications of these observations are far reaching, but I mention one in particular: if the resurrection is key to Acts (and the apostolic preaching therein), and if Acts is a key cog contributing to the coherence of the New Testament, then it follows that present-day articulations of the Christian message do well to feature the resurrection as a prominent emphasis as well.[90]

A Final Word

The stranger we encountered in the bookstore many years ago was right to draw attention to the centrality of Jesus's resurrection. In Acts, where we find the most extensive epitomes of apostolic speeches, the resurrection is on full display. The resurrection discussed at length in Acts also provides an entrée into New Testament and early Christian theology.[91] Indeed, it may be that a renewed appreciation for the resurrection in Acts will lead not just to a renewed appreciation of the place and message of Acts but to a renewed appreciation of the goodness of creation and the blessing of living in light of an integrated Christian theology.

The resurrection, after all, is consistently identified in Acts as a message of hope; it is a scriptural message of God's faithfulness to his promises. It is not just a message about what *has* been fulfilled but also a message about what *will* be fulfilled.

---

89. See Origen, *Cels.*, e.g., 1.7, 31, 50, 68, 70; 2.16, 58–59; 5.18, 22; 6.36; 7.16, 32, 35; 8.49–50; cf. Wilken, *Christians as the Romans Saw Them*, 104; Hurtado, *Destroyer of the gods*, 31.

90. See, e.g., Dennis E. Johnson, *The Message of Acts in the History of Redemption* (Phillipsburg, NJ: P&R, 1997), 154–61; Herman N. Ridderbos, *The Speeches of Peter in the Acts of the Apostles* (London: Tyndale, 1962), 18; Peter J. Scaer, "Resurrection as Justification in the Book of Acts," *CTQ* 70 (2006): 230. Cf. 1 Thess. 1:9–10, noted by Keener, *Acts*, 1:306.

91. Indeed, Acts makes a significant *christological* contribution, *pace* Barrett, *Commentary on the Acts*, 2:lxxxvii.

Bibliography

Abernethy, Andrew T. *The Book of Isaiah and God's Kingdom: A Thematic-Theological Approach*. NSBT 40. Downers Grove, IL: InterVarsity, 2016.

Adams, Sean A. *The Genre of Acts and Collected Biography*. SNTSMS 156. Cambridge: Cambridge University Press, 2013.

———. "The Genre of Luke and Acts: The State of the Question." In *Issues in Luke-Acts: Selected Essays*, edited by Sean A. Adams and Michael W. Pahl, 97–120. GH 26. Piscataway, NJ: Gorgias, 2012.

Aland, Kurt, and Barbara Aland. *The Text of the New Testament*. Translated by Erroll F. Rhodes. 2nd ed. Grand Rapids: Eerdmans, 1989.

Alford, Henry. *The Greek Testament*. Vol. 2, *Acts, Romans, Corinthians*. Revised by Everett F. Harrison. Chicago: Moody, 1958.

Alkier, Stefan. *The Reality of the Resurrection: The New Testament Witness*. Translated by Leroy A. Huizenga. Waco: Baylor University Press, 2013.

Allegro, John M., ed. *Qumrân Cave 4:I. 4Q158–4Q186*. DJD 5. Oxford: Clarendon, 1968.

Allison, Dale C., Jr. *A Critical and Exegetical Commentary on the Epistle of James*. ICC. London: Bloomsbury T&T Clark, 2013.

Anderson, Kevin L. *"But God Raised Him from the Dead": The Theology of Jesus's Resurrection in Luke-Acts*. PBM. Reprint, Eugene, OR: Wipf & Stock, 2006.

Bale, Alan J. *Genre and Narrative Coherence in the Acts of the Apostles*. LNTS 514. London: Bloomsbury T&T Clark, 2015.

Barrett, C. K. *A Critical and Exegetical Commentary on the Acts of the Apostles*. 2 vols. ICC. Edinburgh: T&T Clark, 1994–98.

Barrett, Kyle Scott. "Justification in Lukan Theology." PhD diss., Southern Baptist Theological Seminary, 2012.

Bass, Justin W. *The Battle for the Keys: Revelation 1:18 and Christ's Descent into the Underworld*. PBM. Reprint, Eugene, OR: Wipf & Stock, 2014.

Bates, Matthew W. *Salvation by Allegiance Alone: Rethinking Faith, Works, and the Gospel of Jesus the King*. Grand Rapids: Baker Academic, 2017.

Bauckham, Richard. *The Fate of the Dead: Studies on the Jewish and Christian Apocalypses*. NovTSup 93. Leiden: Brill, 1998.

———. *God Crucified: Monotheism and Christology in the New Testament*. Grand Rapids: Eerdmans, 1999.

———. "The God Who Raises the Dead: The Resurrection of Jesus and Early Christian Faith in God." In *The Resurrection of Jesus Christ*, edited by Paul Avis, 136–54. London: Darton, Longman and Todd, 1993.

———. *James*. NTR. London: Routledge, 1999.

———. "James and the Gentiles (Acts 15.13–21)." In *History, Literature, and Society in the Book of Acts*, edited by Ben Witherington III, 154–84. Cambridge: Cambridge University Press, 1996.

———. "James and the Jerusalem Church." In *The Book of Acts in Its Palestinian Setting*, edited by Richard Bauckham, 415–80. Vol. 4 of *The Book of Acts in Its First Century Setting*. Edited by Bruce W. Winter. Grand Rapids: Eerdmans; Carlisle: Paternoster, 1995.

———. *Jude, 2 Peter*. WBC 50. Nashville: Nelson, 1983.

———. "Life, Death, and the Afterlife in Second Temple Judaism." In *Life in the Face of Death: The Resurrection Message of the New Testament*, edited by Richard N. Longenecker, 80–95. MNTS. Grand Rapids: Eerdmans, 1998.

———. "Paul and Other Jews with Latin Names in the New Testament." In *The Jewish World around the New Testament: Collected Essays I*, 371–92. WUNT 1/233. Tübingen: Mohr Siebeck, 2008.

———. "The Restoration of Israel in Luke-Acts." In *The Jewish World around the New Testament: Collected Essays I*, 325–70. 1/WUNT 233. Tübingen: Mohr Siebeck, 2008.

———. *The Testimony of the Beloved Disciple: Narrative, History, and Theology in the Gospel of John*. Grand Rapids: Baker Academic, 2007.

Bauer, W., F. W. Danker, W. F. Arndt, and F. W. Gingrich. *Greek-English Lexicon of the New Testament and Other Early Christian Literature*. 3rd ed. Chicago: University of Chicago Press, 2000.

Bavinck, Herman. *Reformed Dogmatics*. Edited by John Bolt. Translated by John Vriend. 4 vols. Grand Rapids: Baker Academic, 2003–8.

Bayer, Hans F. "Christ-Centered Eschatology in Acts 3:17–26." In *Jesus of Nazareth—Lord and Christ: Essays on the Historical Jesus and New Testament Christology*, edited by Joel B. Green and Max Turner, 236–50. Grand Rapids: Eerdmans, 1994.

Beale, G. K. "The Descent of the Eschatological Temple in the Form of the Spirit at Pentecost, Part 1: The Clearest Evidence." *TynBul* 56.1 (2005): 73–102.

———. "The Descent of the Eschatological Temple in the Form of the Spirit at Pentecost, Part 2: Corroborating Evidence." *TynBul* 56.2 (2005): 63–90.

———. *A New Testament Biblical Theology: The Unfolding of the Old Testament in the New*. Grand Rapids: Baker Academic, 2011.

———. *The Temple and the Church's Mission: A Biblical Theology of the Dwelling Place of God*. NSBT 17. Downers Grove, IL: InterVarsity, 2004.

Beers, Holly. *The Followers of Jesus as the "Servant": Luke's Model from Isaiah for the Disciples in Luke-Acts*. LNTS 535. London: Bloomsbury T&T Clark, 2015.

Berger, Samuel. *Histoire de la Vulgate: Pendant les premiers siècle du moyen age*. Paris: Éditions Berger-Levrault, 1893.

Berkhof, Louis. *Systematic Theology*. 4th ed. Grand Rapids: Eerdmans, 1941.

Bird, Michael F. *Jesus the Eternal Son: Answering Adoptionist Christology*. Grand Rapids: Eerdmans, 2017.

———. "The Unity of Luke-Acts in Recent Discussion." *JSNT* 29 (2007): 425–48.

Blass, Friedrich, Albert Debrunner, and Robert W. Funk. *A Greek Grammar of the New Testament and Other Early Christian Literature*. Chicago: University of Chicago Press, 1961.

Blumhofer, C. M. "Luke's Alteration of Joel 3:1–5 in Acts 2:17–21." *NTS* 62 (2016): 499–516.

Bock, Darrell L. *Acts*. BECNT. Grand Rapids: Baker Academic, 2007.

———. *Luke*. 2 vols. BECNT. Grand Rapids: Baker Academic, 1994–96.

———. *Proclamation from Prophecy and Pattern: Lucan Old Testament Christology*. JSNTSup 12. Sheffield: JSOT Press, 1987.

Bornkamm, Günther. "The Acts of Thomas." Translated by R. McL. Wilson. In *New Testament Apocrypha*, by Edgar Hennecke, edited by Wilhelm Schneemelcher, 2:425–531. Philadelphia: Westminster, 1965.

Bovon, François. *Luc le théologien: Vingt-cinq ans de recherche (1950–1975)*. 2nd ed. MdB 5. Geneva: Labor et Fides, 1988

———. *Luke the Theologian: Fifty-Five Years of Research (1950–2005)*. 2nd rev. ed. Waco: Baylor University Press, 2006.

Brodie, Thomas L. "Luke the Literary Interpreter: Luke-Acts as a Systematic Rewriting and Updating of the Elijah-Elisha Narrative in 1 and 2 Kings." ThD diss., Pontifical University of St. Thomas Aquinas (Vatican), 1981.

Bruce, F. F. "The Acts of the Apostles: Historical Record or Theological Reconstruction?" *ANRW* 25.3:2569–603.

———. *The Acts of the Apostles: The Greek Text with Introduction and Commentary*. 2nd ed. Grand Rapids: Eerdmans, 1952.

———. *The Book of Acts*. NICNT. Grand Rapids: Eerdmans, 1988.

———. *The Canon of Scripture*. Downers Grove, IL: IVP Academic, 1988.

Bryan, Christopher. *The Resurrection of the Messiah*. Oxford: Oxford University Press, 2011.

Bryan, David K., and David W. Pao, eds. *Ascent into Heaven in Luke-Acts: New Explorations of Luke's Narrative Hinge*. Minneapolis: Fortress, 2016.

Buckwalter, H. Douglas. *The Character and Purpose of Luke's Christology*. SNTSMS 89. Cambridge: Cambridge University Press, 1996.

Buss, Matthäus Franz-Joseph. *Die Missionspredigt des Apostels Paulus im Pisidischen Antiochen: Analyse von Apg 13,16–41 im Hinblick auf die literarische und thematische Einheit der Paulusrede*. FB 38. Stuttgart: Katholisches Bibelwerk, 1980.

Cadbury, Henry J. *The Book of Acts in History*. London: Adam and Charles Black, 1955.

———. *The Making of Luke-Acts*. 2nd ed. London: SPCK, 1958.

Calvin, John. *Commentaries on the Epistle of Paul the Apostle to the Hebrews*. Trans. John Owen. Reprint, Grand Rapids: Baker, 2003.

———. *Commentary on the Prophet Isaiah*. Translated by William Pringle. Vol. 1. Reprint, Grand Rapids: Baker, 2003.

———. *Commentary upon the Acts of the Apostles*. Edited by Henry Beveridge. 2 vols. Reprint, Grand Rapids: Baker, 2003.

———. *A Harmony of the Evangelists*. Translated by William Pringle. 3 vols. Reprint, Grand Rapids: Baker, 2003.

———. *Institutes of the Christian Religion*. Edited by John T. McNeill. Translated by Ford Lewis Battles. 2 vols. LCC 20–21. Philadelphia: Westminster, 1960.

Carson, D. A. "John 5:26: *Crux Interpretum* for Eternal Generation." In *Retrieving Eternal Generation*, edited by Fred Sanders and Scott R. Swain, 79–97. Grand Rapids: Zondervan, 2017.

Charlesworth, James H., ed. *Old Testament Pseudepigrapha*. 2 vols. ABRL. Garden City, NY: Doubleday, 1983–85.

Cohen-Matlofsky, Claude. "Resurrection, from the Hebrew Bible to the Rock-Cut Tombs: An Inscribed Concept." *QC* 23 (2015): 101–27.

Comfort, Philip Wesley. *A Commentary on the Manuscripts and Text of the New Testament*. Grand Rapids: Kregel Academic, 2015.

Conzelmann, Hans. *Die Mitte der Zeit: Studien zur Theologie des Lukas*. 3rd ed. BHT 17. Tübingen: Mohr Siebeck, 1960.

———. *The Theology of Saint Luke*. Translated by Geoffrey Buswell. London: Faber and Faber, 1960.

Coxhead, Steven R. "The Cardionomographic Work of the Spirit in the Old Testament." *WTJ* 79 (2017): 77–95.

Crowe, Brandon D. *The Last Adam: A Theology of the Obedient Life of Jesus in the Gospels*. Grand Rapids: Baker Academic, 2017.

—. *The Message of the General Epistles in the History of Redemption: Wisdom from James, Peter, John, and Jude.* Phillipsburg, NJ: P&R, 2015.

—. *The Obedient Son: Deuteronomy and Christology in the Gospel of Matthew.* BZNW 188. Berlin: de Gruyter, 2012.

—. "The Passive *and* Active Obedience of Christ: Retrieving a Biblical Distinction." In *The Doctrine on Which the Church Stands or Falls: Justification in Biblical, Theological, Historical, and Pastoral Perspective*, edited by Matthew Barrett, 437–64. Wheaton: Crossway, 2019.

—. "The Sources for Luke and Acts: Where Did Luke Get His Material (and Why Does It Matter)?" In *Issues in Luke-Acts: Selected Essays*, edited by Sean A. Adams and Michael W. Pahl, 73–95. GH 26. Piscataway, NJ: Gorgias, 2012.

Croy, N. Clayton. "Hellenistic Philosophies and the Preaching of the Resurrection (Acts 17:18, 32)." *NovT* 39 (1997): 21–39.

Davies, W. D., and Dale C. Allison Jr. *A Critical and Exegetical Commentary on the Gospel according to St. Matthew.* 3 vols. ICC. Edinburgh: T&T Clark, 1988–97.

Deines, Roland. "Das Aposteldekret—Halacha für Heidenchristen oder christliche Rücksichtnahme auf jüdische Tabus?" In *Jewish Identity in the Greco-Roman World / Jüdische Identität in der griechisch-römischen Welt*, edited by Jörg Frey, Daniel R. Schwartz, and Stephanie Gripentrog, 323–98. AJEC 71. Leiden: Brill, 2007.

—. *Der Pharisäer: Ihr Verständnis im Spiegel der christlichen und jüdischen Forschung seit Wellhausen und Graetz.* WUNT 1/101. Tübingen: Mohr Siebeck, 1997.

Delling, Gerhard. "Die Jesusgeschichte in der Verkündigung nach Acta." *NTS* 19 (1972–73): 373–89.

deSilva, David A. "Paul's Speech in Antioch of Pisidia." *BibSac* 151 (1994): 32–49.

Dibelius, Martin. *Studies in the Acts of the Apostles.* Edited by Heinrich Greeven. Translated by Mary Ling and Paul Schubert. London: SCM, 1956.

Dicken, Frank. "The Author and Date of Luke-Acts: Exploring the Options." In *Issues in Luke-Acts: Selected Essays*, edited by Sean A. Adams and Michael W. Pahl, 7–26. GH 26. Piscataway, NJ: Gorgias, 2012.

Dimant, Devorah, ed. *Qumran Cave 4:XXI.* DJD 30. Oxford: Clarendon, 2001.

Dodd, C. H. *According to the Scriptures: The Substructure of New Testament Theology.* London: Nisbet, 1952.

—. *The Apostolic Preaching and Its Developments.* New York: Harper & Row, 1936.

—. *The Parables of the Kingdom.* 4th ed. London: Nisbet, 1938.

Doeve, J. R. *Jewish Hermeneutics in the Synoptic Gospels and Acts.* Assen: Van Gorcum, 1954.

Dunn, James D. G. *Beginning from Jerusalem.* Christianity in the Making 2. Grand Rapids: Eerdmans, 2009.

―――. "The Book of Acts as Salvation History." In *Heil und Geschichte: Die Geschichtsbezogenheit des Heils und das Problem der Heilsgeschichte in der biblischen Tradition und in der theologischen Deutung*, edited by Jörg Frey, Stefan Krauter, and Hermann Lichtenberger, 385–401. WUNT 1/248. Tübingen: Mohr Siebeck, 2009.

―――. "Works of the Law and the Curse of the Law (Galatians 3:10–14)." *NTS* 31 (1985): 523–42.

Dupont, Jacques. *Études sur les Actes des Apôtres*. LD 45. Paris: Cerf, 1967.

―――. *Nouvelles études sur les Actes des Apôtres*. LD 118. Paris: Cerf, 1984.

―――. "'ΤΑ 'ΟΣΙΑ ΔΑΥΙΔ ΤΑ ΠΙΣΤΑ' (Actes 13,34 = Isaïe 55,3)." In *Études sur les Actes des Apôtres*, 337–65. Paris: Cerf, 1967.

―――. "L'utilisation apologétique de l'Ancien Testament dans les discours des Actes." In *Études sur les Actes des Apôtres*, 245–82. Paris: Cerf, 1967.

Easton, Burton Scott. *Early Christianity: The Purpose of Acts, and Other Papers*. Edited by Frederick C. Grant. London: SPCK, 1955.

Edwards, James R. *The Gospel according to Luke*. PNTC. Grand Rapids: Eerdmans, 2015.

―――. "Parallels and Patterns between Luke and Acts." *BBR* 27 (2017): 485–501.

Ehrman, Bart D., and Zlatko Pleše. *The Apocryphal Gospels: Texts and Translations*. Oxford: Oxford University Press, 2011.

Eijk, Ton H. C. van. *La résurrection des morts chez les Pères Apostoliques*. ThH 25. Paris: Beauchesne, 1974.

Elledge, C. D. *Resurrection of the Dead in Early Judaism, 200 BCE–CE 200*. Oxford: Oxford University Press, 2017.

Ellingworth, Paul. *The Epistle to the Hebrews*. NIGTC. Grand Rapids: Eerdmans, 1993.

Emerson, Matthew Y. *Christ and the New Creation: A Canonical Approach to the Theology of the New Testament*. Eugene, OR: Wipf & Stock, 2013.

Epictetus. *The Discourses as Reported by Arrian*. Translated by W. A. Oldfather. 2 vols. LCL. Cambridge: Harvard University Press, 1925–28.

Eusebius. *Ecclesiastical History*. Translated by Kirsopp Lake and J. E. L. Oulton. 2 vols. LCL. Cambridge: Harvard University Press, 1926–32.

Evans, C. F. *Resurrection and the New Testament*. SBT 2/12. Naperville, IL: Alec R. Allenson, 1970.

Fee, Gordon D. *Pauline Christology: An Exegetical-Theological Study*. Peabody, MA: Hendrickson, 2007.

Ferguson, Everett. *The Rule of Faith: A Guide*. Cascade Companions. Eugene, OR: Cascade, 2015.

Ferguson, Sinclair B. *The Holy Spirit*. CCT. Downers Grove, IL: InterVarsity, 1996.

―――. "Ordo Salutis." In *New Dictionary of Theology*, edited by Sinclair B. Ferguson and David F. Wright, 480–81. Downers Grove, IL: InterVarsity, 1988.

———. *The Whole Christ: Legalism, Antinomianism, and Gospel Assurance—Why the Marrow Controversy Still Matters*. Wheaton: Crossway, 2016.

Ferguson, Sinclair B., and David F. Wright, eds. *New Dictionary of Theology*. Downers Grove, IL: InterVarsity, 1988.

Filson, Floyd V. *Jesus Christ the Risen Lord: A Biblical Theology Based on the Resurrection*. Nashville: Abingdon, 1956.

Fitzmyer, Joseph A. *The Acts of the Apostles: A New Translation with Introduction and Commentary*. AB 31. New York: Doubleday, 1998.

Franklin, Eric. *Christ the Lord: A Study in the Purpose and Theology of Luke-Acts*. London: SPCK, 1975.

Fuller, Michael E. *The Restoration of Israel: Israel's Re-gathering and the Fate of the Nations in Early Jewish Literature and Luke-Acts*. BZNW 138. Berlin: de Gruyter, 2006.

Gaffin, Richard B., Jr. *"By Faith, Not by Sight": Paul and the Order of Salvation*. Waynesboro, GA: Paternoster, 2006.

———. *The Centrality of the Resurrection: A Study in Paul's Soteriology*. Grand Rapids: Baker, 1978.

———. *"'For Our Sakes Also': Christ and the Old Testament in the New Testament."* In *The Hope Fulfilled: Essays in Honor of O. Palmer Robertson*, edited by Robert L. Penny, 61–81. Phillipsburg, NJ: P&R, 2008.

———. "The Holy Spirit." *WTJ* 43 (1980): 58–78.

———. "Justification in Luke-Acts." In *Right with God: Justification in the Bible and the World*, edited by D. A. Carson, 106–25. Grand Rapids: Baker, 1992.

———. "Pentecost: Before and After." *Kerux* 10.2 (1995): 3–24.

———. *Perspectives on Pentecost: New Testament Teaching on the Gifts of the Holy Spirit*. Phillipsburg, NJ: P&R, 1979.

———. *Resurrection and Redemption: A Study in Paul's Soteriology*. 2nd ed. Phillipsburg, NJ: P&R, 1987.

———. "The Work of Christ Applied." In *Christian Dogmatics: Reformed Theology for the Church Catholic*, edited by Michael Allen and Scott R. Swain, 268–90. Grand Rapids: Baker Academic, 2016.

Gallagher, Edmon L., and John D. Meade. *The Biblical Canon Lists from Early Christianity: Texts and Analysis*. Oxford: Oxford University Press, 2017.

Gamble, Harry Y. *Books and Readers in the Early Church: A History of Early Christian Texts*. New Haven: Yale University Press, 1995.

García Martínez, Florentino, and Eibert J. C. Tigchelaar, eds. *The Dead Sea Scrolls Study Edition*. 2 vols. Leiden: Brill, 1997–98.

Garland, David E. *Luke*. ZECNT. Grand Rapids: Zondervan, 2011.

Garner, David B. *Sons in the Son: The Riches and Reach of Adoption in Christ*. Phillipsburg, NJ: P&R, 2016.

Gasque, W. Ward. *A History of the Interpretation of the Acts of the Apostles*. Peabody, MA: Hendrickson, 1989.

Gathercole, Simon J. "*E Pluribus Unum*? Apostolic Unity and Early Christian Literature." In *The Enduring Authority of the Christian Scriptures*, edited by D. A. Carson, 407–55. Grand Rapids: Eerdmans, 2016.

———. *The Pre-existent Son: Recovering the Christologies of Matthew, Mark, and Luke*. Grand Rapids: Eerdmans, 2006.

Gaventa, Beverly Roberts. "Toward a Theology of Acts: Reading and Rereading." *Int* 42 (1988): 146–57.

Genz, Rouven. *Jesaja 53 als theologische Mitte der Apostelgeschichte: Studien zur ihrer Christologie und Ekklesiologie im Anschluss an Apg 8,26–40*. WUNT 2/398. Tübingen: Mohr Siebeck, 2015.

Giacobbe, Mark S. "Luke the Chronicler: The Narrative Arc of Samuel-Kings and Chronicles in Luke-Acts." PhD diss., Westminster Theological Seminary, 2018.

Gladd, Benjamin L. "The Last Adam as the 'Life-Giving Spirit' Revisited: A Possible Old Testament Background on One of Paul's Most Perplexing Phrases." *WTJ* 71 (2009): 297–309.

Glenny, W. Edward. "The Septuagint and Apostolic Hermeneutics: Amos 9 in Acts 15." *BBR* 22 (2012): 1–26.

Glöckner, Richard, OP. *Die Verkündigung des Heils beim Evangelisten Lukas*. WSAMA.T 9. Mainz: Matthias-Grünewald-Verlag, 1975.

Goldingay, John E. *Daniel*. WBC 30. Nashville: Nelson, 1996.

Gorman, Michael J. *Apostle of the Crucified Lord: A Theological Introduction to Paul and His Letters*. Grand Rapids: Eerdmans, 2004.

Goswell, Gregory. "Finding a Home for the Letter to the Hebrews." *JETS* 59 (2016): 747–60.

———. "The Place of the Book of Acts in Reading the NT." *JETS* 59 (2016): 67–82.

Goulder, Michael D. *Type and History in Acts*. London: SPCK, 1964.

Gowan, Donald E. *Theology of the Prophetic Books: The Death and Resurrection of Israel*. Louisville: Westminster John Knox, 1998.

Green, Joel B. *Conversion in Luke Acts: Divine Action, Human Cognition, and the People of God*. Grand Rapids: Baker Academic, 2015.

———. *The Gospel of Luke*. NICNT. Grand Rapids: Eerdmans, 1997.

———. "'Witnesses of His Resurrection': Resurrection, Salvation, Discipleship, and Mission in the Acts of the Apostles." In *Life in the Face of Death: The Resurrection Message of the New Testament*, edited by Richard N. Longenecker, 227–46. MNTS. Grand Rapids: Eerdmans, 1998.

Green, William Henry. *Conflict and Triumph: The Argument of the Book of Job Unfolded*. Reprint, Edinburgh: Banner of Truth, 1999.

Gregory, Andrew. "Irenaeus and the Reception of Acts in the Second Century." In *Contemporary Studies in Acts*, edited by Thomas E. Phillips, 47–65. Macon, GA: Mercer University Press, 2009.

———. *The Reception of Luke and Acts in the Period before Irenaeus: Looking for Luke in the Second Century*. WUNT 2/169. Tübingen: Mohr Siebeck, 2003.

Grindheim, Sigurd. "Luke, Paul, and the Law." *NovT* 56 (2014): 335–58.

Grünstäudl, Wolfgang. "Was lange währt . . . : Die Katholischen Briefe und die Formung des neutestamentlichen Kanons." *EC* 7 (2016): 71–94.

Haacker, Klaus. "Das Bekenntnis des Paulus zur Hoffnung Israels nach der Apostelgeschichte des Lukas." *NTS* 31 (1985): 437–51.

Haar, Stephen. *Simon Magus: The First Gnostic?* BZNW 119. Berlin: de Gruyter, 2003.

Haenchen, Ernst. *The Acts of the Apostles: A Commentary*. Translated by R. McL. Wilson. Philadelphia: Westminster, 1971.

Hamm, Dennis J., SJ. "Acts 3:12–26: Peter's Speech and the Healing of the Man Born Lame." *PRSt* 11 (1984): 199–217.

Hansen, G. Walter. "The Preaching and Defence of Paul." In *Witness to the Gospel: The Theology of Acts*, edited by I. Howard Marshall and David Peterson, 295–324. Grand Rapids: Eerdmans, 1998.

Harnack, Adolf von. *History of Dogma*. Translated by Neil Buchanan. 3rd ed. 4 vols. New York: Dover, 1961.

———. *The Origin of the New Testament and the Most Important Consequences of the New Creation*. Translated by J. R. Wilkinson. New York: Macmillan, 1925.

Harriman, K. R. "'For David Said concerning Him': Foundations of Hope in Psalm 16 and Acts 2." *JTI* 11 (2017): 239–57.

Harrison, Everett F. "The Resurrection of Jesus Christ in the Book of Acts and in Early Christian Literature." In *Understanding the Sacred Text: Essays in Honor of Morton S. Enlin on the Hebrew Bible and Christian Beginnings*, edited by John Reumann, 217–31. Valley Forge, PA: Judson, 1972.

Hays, Richard B. *Echoes of Scripture in the Gospels*. Waco: Baylor University Press, 2016.

Hengel, Martin. *Acts and the History of Earliest Christianity*. Translated by John Bowden. London: SCM, 1979.

———. *The Four Gospels and the One Gospel of Jesus Christ: An Investigation of the Collection and Origin of the Canonical Gospels*. Translated by John Bowden. Harrisburg, PA: Trinity Press International, 2000.

Hennecke, Edgar. *New Testament Apocrypha*. Edited by Wilhelm Schneemelcher. Translated by R. McL. Wilson. 2 vols. Philadelphia: Westminster, 1963–65.

Hickling, Colin. "John and Hebrews: The Background of Hebrews 2:10–18." *NTS* 29 (1983): 112–16.

Hill, Charles E. "A Four-Gospel Canon in the Second Century? Artifact and Artifiction." *EC* 4 (2013): 310–34.

———. *Regnum Caelorum: Patterns of Millennial Thought in Early Christianity.* 2nd ed. Grand Rapids: Eerdmans, 2001.

———. *Who Chose the Gospels? Probing the Great Gospel Conspiracy.* Oxford: Oxford University Press, 2010.

Hobbs, T. R. *2 Kings.* WBC 13. Waco: Word, 1985.

Holladay, Carl R. *Acts: A Commentary.* NTL. Louisville: Westminster John Knox, 2016.

———. "What David Saw: Messianic Exegesis in Acts 2." *SCJ* 19 (2016): 95–108.

Holmes, Michael W., ed. *The Apostolic Fathers: Greek Texts and English Translations.* 3rd ed. Grand Rapids: Baker Academic, 2007.

Horton, Dennis J. *Death and Resurrection: The Shape and Function of a Literary Motif in the Book of Acts.* Eugene, OR: Pickwick, 2009.

Hurtado, Larry W. *Destroyer of the gods: Early Christian Distinctiveness in the Roman World.* Waco: Baylor University Press, 2016.

———. *The Earliest Christian Artifacts: Manuscripts and Christian Origins.* Grand Rapids: Eerdmans, 2006.

———. *Lord Jesus Christ: Devotion to Jesus in Earliest Christianity.* Grand Rapids: Eerdmans, 2003.

———. "P45 as an Early Christian Artefact: What It Reflects about Early Christianity." *Teologisk Tidsskrift* 4 (2016): 291–307.

Irenaeus. *On the Apostolic Preaching.* Translated by John Behr. PPS. Crestwood, NY: St. Vladimir's Seminary Press, 1997.

Jantsch, Torsten. *Jesus, der Retter: Die Soteriologie des lukanischen Doppelwerks.* WUNT 1/381. Tübingen: Mohr Siebeck, 2017.

Jennings, Willie James. *Acts.* Belief. Louisville: Westminster John Knox, 2017.

Jervell, Jacob. *Die Apostelgeschichte: Übersetzt und erklärt.* KEK 3. Göttingen: Vandenhoeck & Ruprecht, 1998.

———. "The Future and the Past: Luke's Vision of Salvation History and Its Bearing on His Writing of Salvation History." In *History, Literature, and Society in the Book of Acts*, edited by Ben Witherington III, 104–26. Cambridge: Cambridge University Press, 1996.

———. *Luke and the People of God: A New Look at Luke-Acts.* Minneapolis: Augsburg, 1972.

———. *The Theology of the Acts of the Apostles.* Cambridge: Cambridge University Press, 1996.

Jipp, Joshua W. "The Beginnings of a Theology of Luke-Acts: Divine Activity and Human Response." *JTI* 8 (2014): 23–43.

———. "'For David Did Not Ascend into Heaven . . .' (Acts 2:34a): Reprogramming Royal Psalms to Proclaim the Enthroned-in-Heaven King." In *Ascent into Heaven in Luke-Acts: New Explorations of Luke's Narrative Hinge*, edited by David K. Bryan and David W. Pao, 41–59. Minneapolis: Fortress, 2016.

———. *Reading Acts*. Eugene, OR: Cascade, 2018.

Johnson, Dennis E. *The Message of Acts in the History of Redemption*. Phillipsburg, NJ: P&R, 1997.

Johnson, Luke Timothy. *The Acts of the Apostles*. SP 5. Collegeville, MN: Liturgical Press, 1992.

Johnston, George. "Christ as Archegos." *NTS* 27 (1981): 381–85.

Jones, Donald L. "The Title 'Author of Life (Leader)' in the Acts of the Apostles." *Society of Biblical Literature 1994 Seminar Papers*, 627–36. SBLSP 33. Atlanta: Society of Biblical Literature, 1994.

Josephus. Translated by Henry St. J. Thackeray et al. 10 vols. LCL. Cambridge: Harvard University Press, 1926–65.

Kee, Howard Clark. *Good News to the Ends of the Earth: The Theology of Acts*. London: SCM; Philadelphia: Trinity Press International, 1990.

Keener, Craig S. *Acts: An Exegetical Commentary*. 4 vols. Grand Rapids: Baker Academic, 2012–15.

———. *The Gospel of Matthew: A Socio-Rhetorical Commentary*. Grand Rapids: Eerdmans, 2009.

Keil, Carl Friedrich, and Franz Delitzsch. *Biblical Commentary on the Old Testament*. Translated by James Martin et al. 25 vols. Edinburgh, 1857–1978. Reprint, 10 vols., Peabody, MA: Hendrickson, 1996.

Kelly, J. N. D. *Early Christian Doctrines*. 5th rev. ed. Peabody, MA: Prince Press, 2007.

Kepple, Robert J. "The Hope of Israel, the Resurrection of the Dead, and Jesus: A Study of Their Relationship in Acts with Particular Regard to the Understanding of Paul's Trial Defense." *JETS* 20 (1977): 231–41.

Kilgallen, John J. "Acts 13,38–39: Culmination of Paul's Speech in Pisidia." *Bib* 69 (1988): 480–506.

Kim, Seyoon. *The Origin of Paul's Gospel*. WUNT 2/4. Tübingen: Mohr Siebeck, 1981. Reprint, Grand Rapids: Eerdmans, 1982.

Kirk, J. R. Daniel. *Unlocking Romans: Resurrection and the Justification of God*. Grand Rapids: Eerdmans, 2008.

Koester, Craig R. *Hebrews: A New Translation with Introduction and Commentary*. AB 36. New York: Doubleday, 2001.

Kruger, Michael J. *Christianity at the Crossroads: How the Second Century Shaped the Future of the Church*. Downers Grove, IL: IVP Academic, 2018.

Lane, William L. *Hebrews 1–8*. WBC 47A. Dallas: Word, 1991.

———. "Living a Life in the Face of Death: The Witness of Hebrews." In *Life in the Face of Death: The Resurrection Message of the New Testament*, edited by Richard N. Longenecker, 247–69. MNTS. Grand Rapids: Eerdmans, 1998.

Letham, Robert. *Union with Christ: In Scripture, History, and Theology*. Phillipsburg, NJ: P&R, 2011.

Levenson, Jon D. *Resurrection and the Restoration of Israel: The Ultimate Victory of the God of Life*. New Haven: Yale University Press, 2006.

Levine, Lee I. *The Ancient Synagogue: The First Thousand Years*. New Haven: Yale University Press, 2000.

Levison, John R. *Filled with the Spirit*. Grand Rapids: Eerdmans, 2009.

Lieu, Judith M. *Marcion and the Making of a Heretic: God and Scripture in the Second Century*. Cambridge: Cambridge University Press, 2015.

Liggins, Stephen S. *Many Convincing Proofs: Persuasive Phenomena Associated with Gospel Proclamation in Acts*. BZNW 221. Berlin: de Gruyter, 2016.

Lindars, Barnabas. *New Testament Apologetic: The Doctrinal Significance of the Old Testament Quotations*. London: SCM, 1961.

Lockett, Darian R. *Letters from the Pillar Apostles: The Formation of the Catholic Epistles as a Canonical Collection*. Eugene, OR: Pickwick, 2017.

Lövestam, Evald. *Son and Saviour: A Study of Acts 13, 32–37; With an Appendix: "Son of God" in the Synoptic Gospels*. ConBNT 18. Lund: Gleerup, 1961.

MacArthur, Harvey K. "On the Third Day." *NTS* 18 (1971/1972): 81–86.

Maddox, Robert. *The Purpose of Luke-Acts*. FRLANT 126. Göttingen: Vandenhoeck & Ruprecht, 1982.

Malherbe, Abraham J. "'Not in a Corner': Early Christian Apologetic in Acts 26:26." *SecCent* 5 (1985–86): 193–210.

Marguerat, Daniel. *Les Actes des Apôtres*. 2 vols. CNT 5a–b. Geneva: Labor et Fides, 2007–15.

———. "Luc-Actes: La résurrection à l'oeuvre dans l'histoire." In *Résurrection: L'après-mort dans le monde ancien et le Nouveau Testament*, edited by Odette Mainville and Daniel Marguerat, 195–214. MdB 45. Geneva: Labor et Fides, 2001.

———. *Paul in Acts and Paul in His Letters*. WUNT 1/310. Tübingen: Mohr Siebeck, 2013.

———. "Quand la résurrection se fait clef de lecture de l'histoire (Luc-Actes)." In *Resurrection of the Dead: Biblical Traditions in Dialogue*, edited by Geert Van Oyen and Tom Shepherd, 183–202. BETL 249. Leuven: Peters, 2012.

———. "The Resurrection and Its Witnesses in the Book of Acts." In *Reading Acts Today: Essays in Honour of Loveday C. A. Alexander*, edited by Steve Walton et al., 171–85. LNTS 427. London: T&T Clark, 2011.

———. *Résurrection: Une histoire de vie*. Poliez-le-Grand: Editions du Moulin, 2001.

Marshall, I. Howard. "Acts." In *Commentary on the New Testament Use of the Old Testament*, edited by G. K. Beale and D. A. Carson, 513–606. Grand Rapids: Baker Academic, 2007.

———. *Luke: Historian and Theologian*. Grand Rapids: Zondervan, 1970.

———. "The Resurrection in the Acts of the Apostles." In *Apostolic History and the Gospel: Biblical and Historical Essays Presented to F. F. Bruce on His 60th Birthday*, edited by W. Ward Gasque and Ralph P. Martin, 92–107. Grand Rapids: Eerdmans, 1970.

Marshall, I. Howard, and David Peterson. *Witness to the Gospel: The Theology of Acts*. Grand Rapids: Eerdmans, 1998.

Martin, Francis, ed. *Acts*. Volume 5 of *Ancient Commentary on Scripture: New Testament*. Downers Grove, IL: InterVarsity, 2006.

Martin, Ralph P. *James*. WBC 48. Waco: Word, 1988.

Martin-Achard, Robert. *From Death to Life: A Study of the Development of the Doctrine of the Resurrection in the Old Testament*. Translated by John Penney Smith. Edinburgh: Oliver and Boyd, 1960.

Mastricht, Petrus van. *Theoretical-Practical Theology*. Translated by Todd M. Rester. Edited by Joel R. Beeke. 7 vols. Grand Rapids: Reformation Heritage, 2018–.

Mattill, A. J., Jr. "The Purpose of Acts: Schneckenburger Reconsidered." In *Apostolic History and the Gospel: Biblical and Historical Essays Presented to F. F. Bruce on His 60th Birthday*, edited by W. Ward Gasque and Ralph P. Martin, 108–22. Grand Rapids: Eerdmans, 1970.

McDonough, Sean M. "Small Change: Saul to Paul, Again." *JBL* 125 (2006): 390–91.

Metzger, Bruce M. *The Canon of the New Testament: Its Origin, Development, and Significance*. Oxford: Clarendon, 1987.

———. *A Textual Commentary on the Greek New Testament*. 2nd ed. Stuttgart: Deutsche Bibelgesellschaft, 1994.

Moessner, David P. "Reading Luke's Gospel as Ancient Hellenistic Narrative." In *Reading Luke: Interpretation, Reflection, Formation*, edited by Craig G. Bartholomew, Joel B. Green, and Anthony B. Thiselton, 125–54. Scripture and Hermeneutics Series 6. Milton Keynes: Paternoster; Grand Rapids: Zondervan, 2005.

———. "The Role of Acts in Interpreting the New Testament." *SacScript* 15 (2017): 260–71.

Moffitt, David M. *Atonement and the Logic of Resurrection in the Epistle to the Hebrews*. NovTSup 141. Leiden: Brill, 2011.

Morgan-Wynne, John Eifion. *Paul's Pisidian Antioch Speech (Acts 13)*. Eugene, OR: Pickwick, 2014.

Moule, C. F. D. "The Christology of Acts." In *Studies in Luke-Acts: Essays Presented in Honor of Paul Schubert*, edited by Leander E. Keck and J. Louis Martyn, 159–85. Nashville: Abingdon, 1966.

Müller, Paul-Gerhard. *ΧΡΙΣΤΟΣ ΑΡΧΗΓΟΣ: Die religionsgeschichtliche und theologische Hintergrund einer neutestamentlichen Christusprädikation*. EHS.T 28. Bern: Herbert Lang; Frankfurt: Peter Lang, 1973.

Muller, Richard A. *Dictionary of Latin and Greek Theological Terms: Drawn Principally from Protestant Scholastic Theology*. Grand Rapids: Baker, 1985.

Murray, John. *The Epistle to the Romans*. 2 vols. NICNT. Grand Rapids: Eerdmans, 1959–65.

———. *Redemption Accomplished and Applied*. Grand Rapids: Eerdmans, 1955.

Nägele, Sabine. *Labhütte Davids und Wolkensohn: Eine auslegungsgeschichtliche Studie zum Amos 9,11 in der jüdischen und christlichen Exegese*. AGJU 24. Leiden: Brill, 1995.

Neagoe, Alexandru. *The Trial of the Gospel: An Apologetic Reading of Luke's Trial Narratives*. SNTSMS 116. Cambridge: Cambridge University Press, 2002.

Nickelsburg, George W. E. *Resurrection, Immortality, and Eternal Life in Intertestamental Judaism and Early Christianity*. Rev. ed. HTS 56. Cambridge, MA: Harvard University Press, 2006.

Nienhuis, David R. *Not by Paul Alone: The Formation of the Catholic Epistle Collection and the Christian Canon*. Waco: Baylor University Press, 2007.

Nock, Arthur Darby. *Conversion: The Old and the New in Religion from Alexander the Great to Augustine of Hippo*. Oxford: Clarendon, 1933.

———. "A Note on the Resurrection." In *Essays on the Trinity and the Incarnation*, edited by A. E. J. Rawlinson, 47–50. London: Longmans, Green and Co., 1928.

Novakovic, Lidija. *Raised from the Dead according to Scripture: The Role of Israel's Scripture in the Early Christian Interpretations of Jesus' Resurrection*. JCT 12. London: Bloomsbury T&T Clark, 2012.

Olinger, Danny E. *A Geerhardus Vos Anthology: Biblical and Theological Insights Alphabetically Arranged*. Phillipsburg, NJ: P&R, 2005.

Oliver, Isaac W. *Torah Praxis after 70 CE: Reading Matthew and Luke-Acts as Jewish Texts*. WUNT 2/355. Tübingen: Mohr Siebeck, 2013.

O'Toole, Robert F., SJ. "Activity of the Risen Jesus in Luke-Acts." *Bib* 62 (1981): 471–98.

———. "Acts 2:30 and the Davidic Covenant of Pentecost." *JBL* 102 (1983): 245–58.

———. *Acts 26: The Christological Climax of Paul's Defense (Ac 22:1–26:32)*. AnBib 78. Rome: Biblical Institute Press, 1978.

———. "Christ's Resurrection in Acts 13,13–52." *Bib* 60 (1979): 361–72.

———. *Luke's Presentation of Jesus: A Christology*. SubBi 25. Rome: Editrice Pontificio Istituto Biblico, 2004.

———. "Luke's Understanding of Jesus' Resurrection-Ascension-Exaltation." *BTB* 9 (1979): 106–14.

———. "Some Observations on *Anistēmi*, 'I Raise,' in Acts 3:22, 26." *ScEs* 31 (1979): 85–92.

Padilla, Osvaldo. *The Acts of the Apostles: Interpretation, History and Theology.* Downers Grove, IL: IVP Academic, 2016.

Pao, David W. *Acts and the Isaianic New Exodus.* Reprint, Grand Rapids: Baker Academic, 2002.

Pao, David W., and Eckhard J. Schnabel. "Luke." In *Commentary on the New Testament Use of the Old Testament*, edited by G. K. Beale and D. A. Carson, 251–414. Grand Rapids: Baker Academic, 2007.

Parsons, Mikeal C. *Acts*. Paideia. Grand Rapids: Baker Academic, 2008.

Parsons, Mikeal C., and Richard I. Pervo. *Rethinking the Unity of Luke and Acts.* Minneapolis: Fortress, 1993.

Patton, Matthew H. *Hope for a Tender Sprig: Jehoiachin in Biblical Theology.* BBR Sup 16. Winona Lake, IN: Eisenbrauns, 2017.

Penner, Todd. "Madness in the Method? The Acts of the Apostles in Current Study." *CBR* 2 (2004): 223–93.

Perkins, Pheme. "Resurrection and Christology: Are They Related?" In *Israel's God and Rebecca's Children: Christology and Community in Early Judaism and Christianity; Essays in Honor of Larry W. Hurtado and Alan F. Segal*, edited by David B. Capes, April D. DeConick, Helen K. Bond, and Troy Miller, 513–606. Waco: Baylor University Press, 2007.

Pervo, Richard I. *Acts: A Commentary.* Hermeneia. Minneapolis: Fortress, 2009.

———. *Luke's Story of Paul.* Minneapolis: Fortress, 1990.

Pesch, Rudolf. *Die Apostelgeschichte.* 2 vols. EKKNT. Zürich: Benzinger; Neukirchen-Vluyn: Neukirchener Verlag, 1986.

Peterson, David G. *The Acts of the Apostles.* PNTC. Grand Rapids: Eerdmans, 2009.

———. "Resurrection Apologetics and the Theology of Luke-Acts." In *Proclaiming the Resurrection: Papers from the First Oak Hill College Annual School of Theology*, edited by Peter M. Head, 29–57. Carlisle: Paternoster, 1998.

Pichler, Josef. *Paulusrezeption in der Apostelgeschichte: Untersuchungen zur Rede im pisidischen Antiochien.* IThS 50. Innsbruck: Tyrolia, 1997.

Pickup, Martin. "'On the Third Day': The Time Frame of Jesus' Death and Resurrection." *JETS* 56 (2013): 511–42.

Pietersma, Albert, and Benjamin G. Wright, eds. *A New English Translation of the Septuagint: And the Other Greek Translations Traditionally Included under That Title.* New York: Oxford University Press, 2007.

Pillai, C. A. Joachim. *Apostolic Interpretation of History: A Commentary on Acts 13:16–41.* Hicksville, NY: Exposition Press, 1980.

———. *Early Missionary Preaching: A Study of Luke's Report in Acts 13.* Hicksville, NY: Exposition Press, 1979.

Porter, Stanley E. *The Paul of Acts: Essays in Literary Criticism, Rhetoric, and Theology.* WUNT 1/115. Tübingen: Mohr Siebeck, 1999.

———. "The Unity of Luke-Acts and the Ascension Narratives." In *Ascent into Heaven in Luke-Acts: New Explorations of Luke's Narrative Hinge*, edited by David K. Bryan and David W. Pao, 111–36. Minneapolis: Fortress, 2016.

Presley, Stephen O. "The Rule of Faith and Irenaeus's *Demonstration* of the Order and Connection of the Scriptures." *ORA* (2010): 48–66.

Puech, Émile, ed. *Qumrân Grotte 4:XVIII.* DJD 25. Oxford: Clarendon, 1998.

Qimron, Elisha, and John Strugnell, eds. *Qumran Cave 4:V.* DJD 10. Oxford: Clarendon, 1994.

Rackham, Richard Belward. *The Acts of the Apostles: An Exposition.* 11th ed. WC. London: Methuen, 1930.

Reicke, Bo. "The Risen Lord and His Church: The Theology of Acts." *Int* 13 (1959): 157–69.

Rese, Martin. "Die Aussagen über Jesu Tod und Auferstehung in der Apostelgeschichte—ältestes Kerygma oder lukanische Theologoumena?" *NTS* 30 (1984): 335–53.

Ridderbos, Herman N. *Paul: An Outline of His Theology.* Translated by John Richard De Witt. Grand Rapids: Eerdmans, 1975.

———. "The Redemptive-Historical Character of Paul's Preaching." In *When the Time Had Fully Come: Studies in New Testament Theology*, 44–60. Grand Rapids: Eerdmans, 1957.

———. *The Speeches of Peter in the Acts of the Apostles.* London: Tyndale, 1962.

Rosner, Brian S. "Acts and Biblical History." In *The Book of Acts in Its Ancient Literary Setting*, edited by Bruce W. Winter and Andrew D. Clarke, 65–82. Vol. 1 of *The Book of Acts in Its First Century Setting*. Edited by Bruce W. Winter. Grand Rapids: Eerdmans, 1993.

Rothschild, Clare K. *Paul in Athens: The Popular Religious Context of Acts 17.* WUNT 1/341. Tübingen: Mohr Siebeck, 2014.

Rowe, C. Kavin. "Acts 2:36 and the Continuity of Lukan Christology." *NTS* 53 (2007): 37–56.

———. *Early Narrative Christology: The Lord in the Gospel of Luke.* BZNW 139. 2006. Reprint, Grand Rapids: Baker Academic, 2009.

———. "History, Hermeneutics, and the Unity of Luke-Acts." In *Rethinking the Unity and Reception of Luke and Acts*, edited by Andrew F. Gregory and C. Kavin Rowe, 43–65. Columbia: University of South Carolina Press, 2010.

———. *One True Life: The Stoics and Early Christians as Rival Traditions.* New Haven: Yale University Press, 2016.

———. *World Upside Down: Reading Acts in the Graeco-Roman Age.* Oxford: Oxford University Press, 2009.

Runesson, Anders. *The Origins of the Synagogue: A Socio-Historical Study.* ConBNT 37. Stockholm: Almqvist & Wiksell, 2001.

Rusam, Dietrich. *Das Alte Testament bei Lukas.* BZNW 112. Berlin: de Gruyter, 2003.

Saldarini, Anthony J. *Pharisees, Scribes and Sadducees in Palestinian Society: A Sociological Approach.* Wilmington, DE: Glazier, 1988.

Sanders, Fred, and Scott R. Swain, eds. *Retrieving Eternal Generation.* Grand Rapids: Zondervan, 2017.

Sargent, Benjamin. *David Being a Prophet: The Contingency of Scripture upon History in the New Testament.* BZNW 207. Berlin: de Gruyter, 2014.

Scacewater, Todd A. "The Divine Builder: Psalm 68 in Jewish and Pauline Tradition." PhD diss., Westminster Theological Seminary, 2017.

Scaer, Peter J. "Resurrection as Justification in the Book of Acts." *CTQ* 70 (2006): 219–31.

Schaefer, Christoph. *Die Zukunft Israels bei Lukas: Biblisch-frühjüdische Zukunftsvorstellungen im lukanischen Doppelwerk im Vergleich zu Röm 9–11.* BZNW 190. Berlin: de Gruyter, 2012.

Schlatter, Adolf. "The Theology of the New Testament and Dogmatics." In *The Nature of New Testament Theology: The Contribution of William Wrede and Adolf Schlatter,* edited and translated by Robert Morgan, 117–66. SBT 2/25. Naperville, IL: Alec R. Allenson, 1973.

Schnabel, Eckhard J. *Acts.* ZECNT. Grand Rapids: Zondervan, 2012.

———. "Fads and Common Sense: Reading Acts in the First Century and Reading Acts Today." *JETS* 54 (2011): 251–78.

Schreiner, Thomas R. *New Testament Theology: Magnifying God in Christ.* Grand Rapids: Baker Academic, 2008.

Schröter, Jens. *From Jesus to the New Testament: Early Christian Theology and the Origin of the New Testament Canon.* Translated by Wayne Coppins. BMSEC. Waco: Baylor University Press, 2013.

Schubert, Paul. "The Place of the Areopagus Speech in the Composition of Acts." In *Transitions in Biblical Scholarship,* edited by J. Coert Rylaarsdam, 235–61. Essays in Divinity 6. Chicago: University of Chicago Press, 1968.

Scott, J. Julius, Jr. "*Archēgos* in the Salvation History of the Epistle to the Hebrews." *JETS* 29 (1986): 47–54.

Sellner, Hans Jörg. *Das Heil Gottes: Studien zur Soteriologie des lukanischen Doppelwerks.* BZNW 152. Berlin: de Gruyter, 2007.

Sherwin-White, A. N. *Roman Society and Roman Law in the New Testament.* Oxford: Oxford University Press, 1963. Reprint, Eugene, OR: Wipf & Stock, 2004.

Sleeman, Matthew. *Geography and the Ascension Narrative in Acts.* SNTSMS 146. Cambridge: Cambridge University Press, 2009.

Smith, David E. "Acts and the Structure of the Christian Bible." In *Contemporary Studies in Acts*, edited by Thomas E. Phillips, 93–102. Macon, GA: Mercer University Press, 2009.

———. *The Canonical Function of Acts: A Comparative Approach*. Collegeville, MN: Liturgical Press, 2002.

Snodgrass, Klyne R. *Stories with Intent: A Comprehensive Guide to the Parables of Jesus*. Grand Rapids: Eerdmans, 2008.

Soards, Marion L. *The Speeches in Acts: Their Content, Context, and Concerns*. Louisville: Westminster John Knox, 1994.

Somov, Alexey. *Representations of the Afterlife in Luke-Acts*. LNTS 556. London: Bloomsbury T&T Clark, 2017.

Stanton, Graham N. "The Fourfold Gospel." *NTS* 43 (1997): 317–46.

Stendahl, Krister. "The Apostle Paul and the Introspective Conscience of the West." *HTR* 56 (1963): 199–215.

Stonehouse, Ned B. *The Areopagus Address*. London: Tyndale, 1949.

Strauss, Mark L. *The Davidic Messiah in Luke-Acts: The Promise and Its Fulfillment in Lukan Christology*. JSNTSup 110. Sheffield: Sheffield Academic, 1995.

Strutwolf, Holger, et al., eds. *Novum Testamentum Graece: ECM*. Part 3, *The Acts of the Apostles*. 3 vols. Stuttgart: Deutsche Bibelgesellschaft, 2017.

Stuart, Douglas. *Hosea–Jonah*. WBC 31. Nashville: Nelson, 1988.

Suetonius. *Lives of the Caesars*. Vol. 1. Translated by J. C. Rolfe. Introduction by K. R. Bradley. LCL. Cambridge: Harvard University Press, 1998.

Tajra, Harry W. *The Trial of St. Paul: A Juridical Exegesis of the Second Half of the Acts of the Apostles*. WUNT 2/35. Tübingen: Mohr Siebeck, 1989.

Talbert, Charles H. *Literary Patterns, Theological Themes and the Genre of Luke-Acts*. SBLMS 20. Missoula, MT: Scholars Press and SBL, 1974.

———. *Luke and the Gnostics: An Examination of the Lucan Purpose*. Nashville: Abingdon, 1966.

———. "The Place of the Resurrection in the Theology of Luke." *Int* 46 (1992): 19–30.

———. *Reading Acts: A Literary and Theological Commentary on the Acts of the Apostles*. New York: Crossroad, 1997.

Tankersly, Lee. "'Thus It Is Written': Redemptive History and Christ's Resurrection on the Third Day." *SBJT* 16.3 (2012): 50–60.

Tannehill, Robert C. "The Functions of Peter's Mission Speeches in the Narrative of Acts." *NTS* 37 (1991): 400–414.

———. *The Narrative Unity of Luke-Acts: A Literary Interpretation*. 2 vols. Philadelphia and Minneapolis: Fortress, 1986–90.

Tanner, J. Paul. "James's Quotation of Amos 9 to Settle the Jerusalem Council Debate in Acts 15." *JETS* 55 (2012): 65–85.

Thompson, Alan J. *The Acts of the Risen Lord Jesus: Luke's Account of God's Unfolding Plan.* NSBT 27. Downers Grove, IL: InterVarsity, 2011.

———. "The Trinity and Luke-Acts." In *The Essential Trinity: New Testament Foundations and Practical Relevance*, edited by Brandon D. Crowe and Carl R. Trueman, 62–82. London: Apollos, 2016.

Tipton, Lane G. "Union with Christ and Justification." In *Justified in Christ: God's Plan for Us in Justification*, edited by K. Scott Oliphint, 23–49. Fearn: Mentor, 2007.

Trobisch, David. "The Book of Acts as a Narrative Commentary on the Letters of the New Testament." In *Rethinking the Unity and Reception of Luke and Acts*, edited by Andrew F. Gregory and C. Kavin Rowe, 119–27. Columbia: University of South Carolina Press, 2010.

———. *The First Edition of the New Testament.* Oxford: Oxford University Press, 2000.

Tuckett, Christopher M. "The Early Text of Acts." In *The Early Text of the New Testament*, edited by Charles E. Hill and Michael J. Kruger, 157–74. Oxford: Oxford University Press, 2012.

Turner, Eric G. *The Typology of the Early Codex.* Philadelphia: University of Pennsylvania Press, 1977.

Turretin, Francis. *Institutes of Elenctic Theology.* Translated by George Musgrave Giger. Edited by James T. Dennison Jr. 3 vols. Phillipsburg, NJ: P&R, 1992–97.

Uytanlet, Samson. *Luke-Acts and Jewish Historiography: A Study on the Theology, Literature, and Ideology of Luke-Acts.* WUNT 2/366. Tübingen: Mohr Siebeck, 2014.

van Unnik, W. C. "The 'Book of Acts' the Confirmation of the Gospel." *NovT* 4 (1960): 26–59.

———. "Luke-Acts, a Storm Center in Contemporary Scholarship." In *Studies in Luke-Acts: Essays Presented in Honor of Paul Schubert*, edited by Leander E. Keck and J. Louis Martyn, 15–32. Nashville: Abingdon, 1966.

Verheyden, Joseph. "The Unity of Luke-Acts: One Work, One Author, One Purpose?" In *Issues in Luke-Acts: Selected Essays*, edited by Sean A. Adams and Michael W. Pahl, 27–50. GH 26. Piscataway, NJ: Gorgias, 2012.

Vermes, Geza. *The Complete Dead Sea Scrolls in English.* 4th ed. New York: Penguin, 1995.

Vielhauer, Philipp. "On the 'Paulinism' of Acts." In *Studies in Luke-Acts: Essays Presented in Honor of Paul Schubert*, edited by Leander E. Keck and J. Louis Martyn, 33–50. Nashville: Abingdon, 1966.

Vinzent, Markus. *Christ's Resurrection in Early Christianity and the Making of the New Testament.* Farnham, Surrey: Ashgate, 2011.

Vos, Geerhardus. *Biblical Theology: Old and New Testaments.* 1948. Reprint, Edinburgh: Banner of Truth, 1975.

———. "The Eschatological Aspect of the Pauline Conception of the Spirit." In *Redemptive History and Biblical Interpretation: The Shorter Writings of Geerhardus Vos*, edited by Richard B. Gaffin Jr., 92–125. Phillipsburg, NJ: P&R, 1980.

———. *The Pauline Eschatology*. Grand Rapids: Eerdmans, 1953.

———. "The Priesthood of Christ in the Epistle to the Hebrews." In *Redemptive History and Biblical Interpretation: The Shorter Writings of Geerhardus Vos*, edited by Richard B. Gaffin Jr., 126–60. Phillipsburg, NJ: P&R, 1980.

———. *Reformed Dogmatics*. Edited and translated by Richard B. Gaffin Jr. 5 vols. Bellingham, WA: Lexham, 2012–16.

———. *The Self-Disclosure of Jesus: The Modern Debate about the Messianic Consciousness*. Edited by J. G. Vos. 2nd ed. Grand Rapids: Eerdmans, 1953. Reprint, Phillipsburg, NJ: P&R, 2002.

Wall, Robert W. "Acts and James." In *The Catholic Epistles and Apostolic Tradition*, edited by Karl-Wilhelm Niebuhr and Robert W. Wall, 127–52. Waco: Baylor University Press, 2009.

———. "The Acts of the Apostles in Canonical Context." *BTB* 18 (1988): 15–24.

———. "The Acts of the Apostles: Introduction, Commentary, and Reflection." In vol. 10 of *NIB*, 3–368. Nashville: Abingdon, 2002.

———. "A Unifying Theology of the Catholic Epistles: A Canonical Approach." In *The Catholic Epistles and Apostolic Tradition*, edited by Karl-Wilhelm Niebuhr and Robert W. Wall, 13–40. Waco: Baylor University Press, 2009.

Wallace, Daniel B. *Greek Grammar beyond the Basics: An Exegetical Syntax of the New Testament*. Grand Rapids: Zondervan, 1996.

Waltke, Bruce K. *The Book of Proverbs: Chapters 1–15*. NICOT. Grand Rapids: Eerdmans, 2004.

Waltke, Bruce K., with Charles Yu. *An Old Testament Theology: An Exegetical, Canonical, and Thematic Approach*. Grand Rapids: Zondervan, 2007.

Walton, Steve. "The Acts—of God? What Is the 'Acts of the Apostles' All About?" *EvQ* 80 (2008): 291–306.

Warfield, Benjamin Breckenridge. "The Spirit of God in the Old Testament." In *Biblical and Theological Studies*, edited by Samuel G. Craig, 127–56. Philadelphia: P&R, 1968.

Waters, Guy Prentiss. *A Study Commentary on the Acts of the Apostles*. EP Study Commentary. Pistyll, Holywell, UK: Evangelical Press, 2015.

Webster, John. "Resurrection and Scripture." In *Christology and Scripture: Interdisciplinary Perspectives*, edited by Andrew T. Lincoln and Angus Paddison, 138–55. LNTS 348. London: T&T Clark, 2007.

Wénin, André. "Enracinement vétérotestamentaire du discours sur la résurrection de Jésus dans le Nouveau Testament." In *Resurrection of the Dead: Biblical Traditions in Dialogue*, edited by Geert Van Yen and Tom Shepherd, 3–23. BETL 249. Leuven: Peters, 2012.

Westerholm, Stephen. *Justification Reconsidered: Rethinking a Pauline Theme*. Grand Rapids: Eerdmans, 2013.

Whiston, William. *The Works of Josephus*. Rev. ed. Peabody, MA: Hendrickson, 1987.

Wilckens, Ulrich. *Die Missionsreden der Apostelgeschichte: Form- und traditions- geschichtliche Untersuchungen*. WMANT 15. Neukirchen-Vluyn: Neukirchener Verlag, 1961.

Wilken, Robert Louis. *The Christians as the Romans Saw Them*. 2nd ed. New Haven: Yale University Press, 2003.

———. *The First Thousand Years: A Global History of Christianity*. New Haven: Yale University Press, 2012.

———. "St. Cyril of Alexandria: The Mystery of Christ in the Bible." *ProEccl* 4 (1995): 454–78.

Wilson, Benjamin R. *The Saving Cross of the Suffering Christ: The Death of Jesus in Lukan Soteriology*. BZNW 223. Berlin: de Gruyter, 2016.

Wise, Michael O., Martin G. Abegg Jr., and Edward M. Cook. *The Dead Sea Scrolls: A New Translation*. New York: HarperOne, 2005.

Witherington, Ben, III. *The Acts of the Apostles: A Socio-Rhetorical Commentary*. Grand Rapids: Eerdmans, 1998.

Wolter, Michael. *The Gospel according to Luke*. Translated by Wayne Coppins and Christoph Heilig. 2 vols. BMSEC. Waco: Baylor University Press, 2016–17.

———. *Paul: An Outline of His Theology*. Translated by Robert L. Brawley. Waco: Baylor University Press, 2015.

Wright, N. T. *The New Testament and the People of God*. COQG 1. Minneapolis: Fortress, 1992.

———. *Paul: A Biography*. San Francisco: HarperOne, 2018.

———. *The Resurrection of the Son of God*. COQG 3. Minneapolis: Fortress, 2003.

Zehnle, Richard F. *Peter's Pentecost Discourse: Tradition and Lukan Reinterpretation in Peter's Speeches of Acts 2 and 3*. SBLMS 15. Nashville: Abingdon, 1971.

Zwiep, Arie W. "*Assumptus Est in Caelum*: Rapture and Heavenly Exaltation in Early Judaism and Luke-Acts." In *Christ, the Spirit and the Community of God: Essays on the Acts of the Apostles*, 38–67. WUNT 2/293. Tübingen: Mohr Siebeck, 2010.

Scripture and Ancient Writings Index

Author Index

Subject Index